ANSWERING
ISLAM

ANSWERING

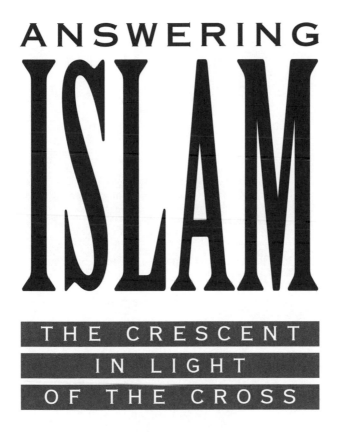

ISLAM

THE CRESCENT
IN LIGHT
OF THE CROSS

SECOND EDITION

Norman L. Geisler and Abdul Saleeb

Baker Books

A Division of Baker Book House Co
Grand Rapids, Michigan 49516

Published by Baker Books
a division of Baker Book House Company
P.O. Box 6287, Grand Rapids, Michigan 49516-6287

Third printing, May 2003

Printed in the United States of America

Library of Congress Cataloging-in-Publication Data

Geisler, Norman L.
    Answering Islam : the crescent in light of the cross / Norman L. Geisler and Abdul Saleeb.— 2nd ed.
      p.   cm.
    Includes bibliographical references and index.
    ISBN 0-8010-6430-9 (pbk.)
    1. Islam—Relations—Christianity. 2. Christianity and other religions—Islam. 3. Christianity—Apologetic works. 4. Islam—Controversial literature. I. Saleeb, Abdul. II. Title.
BP172 .G45   2002
239—dc21   2002002260

For information about all releases from Baker Book House, visit our web site:
http://www.bakerbooks.com

Contents

PREFACE TO SECOND EDITION

September 11, 2001, changed the world. For one thing, Christians can no longer ignore the worldwide challenge of Islam. It is this challenge that assures the future of books like *Answering Islam*. Never in our wildest imagination did we believe this book would hit the front page of *The Wall Street Journal* (Nov. 26, 2001) which declared:

> Religious publishing houses have produced a vast library of how-to books on recruiting Muslims. One of the best known is "Answering Islam," co-written by Norman Geisler, president of Southern Evangelical Seminary, in Charlotte, N.C., and Abdul Saleeb, a Muslim convert to Christianity. Published in 1993, the book had sold more than 42,000 copies.

What *The Journal* failed to say was that over half of these were sold in the first two months after September 11, a pace that remains unabated to date. Actually, the book was gradually dying before the towers fell. To put it mildly, the interest in the threat of Islam to Christianity was minimal before 9/11. That is understandable, since we had just survived the Communist threat, the Humanist threat, and were still undergoing the New Age threat. American Christians were simply not ready for another threat.

Today the tide has turned. Sales of the Qur'an are soaring. Not because Muslims are becoming more devout nor because converts to Islam increased dramatically as a result of the terrorists aerial bombing of the New York Trade Center. Rather, it is because non-Muslims suddenly realize that the religion of Islam, as embraced by millions of radical Muslims, has become a real threat, not only to Christianity but to freedom of religion in general and to our very way of life as Americans.

We have taken the occasion of these recent events to revise what has suddenly become a very popular book. Changes have been made throughout by updating, adding, and revising the entire manuscript. In addition, the section on Jihad has been amplified considerably by adding an entire Appendix on "Islam and Violence." We have also used the opportunity to add new material in crucial places to strengthen the Christian response to Islam.

Like many other battles in history, we believe that the pen is sharper than the sword. The real war will be won with words, not weapons. The success of Christianity over Islam as a world religion rises or falls on the battlefield of ideas.

Today, Islam is the second largest religion in the world, with over one billion adherents. That is one out of every five persons on earth. Indeed, Islam is now reputed to be the fastest growing religion in the world. This and recent events make it necessary for us to refocus our efforts to defend the Faith once for all delivered to the saints (Jude 3). As Thomas Aquinas is credited by history with answering Islam in the thirteenth century (in his *Summa contra Gentiles*), even so we must renew efforts to thwart the efforts of militant Muslims to destroy Christianity. This revised volume is offered as a humble beginning in this direction.

Acknowledgments

We wish to express our deep appreciation for those who have labored to make this manuscript better. This includes two Islamic experts, Dr. Kameel F. Kilada and Dr. Patrick Cate. In addition, David Johnson, Sharon Coomer, and our wives, Kenna and Barbara, spent endless hours typing, checking references, and doing appendixes. For all their help we are deeply grateful.

INTRODUCTION

Islam has rapidly grown to become the second largest religion in the world, with over one billion adherents—nearly one in every five persons on earth. In the United States there are presently more Muslims than Methodists. The most rapid growth is in the African American community.

What is more, Islam claims to be the true religion for humankind. It affirms that Muhammad is the "Seal of the Prophets," the last and the greatest of all prophets who superseded all prophets before him, including Jesus. The Qur'an is believed to be the verbally inspired Word of God, dictated to Muhammad by the angel Gabriel from the eternal original in heaven. It is said to contain the full and final revelation of God, surpassing and completing all previous revelations. By any measure these are outstanding claims that challenge all other religions and deserve careful scrutiny by any sincere seeker of truth.

In this book we propose to do three things. First, in Part One we will attempt to state, as clearly as we can, the fundamental beliefs of Islam concerning God, creation, prophets, Muhammad, the Qur'an, and salvation. This will be expressed primarily through Muslim sources such as the Qur'an, Muslim tradition (the *Hadith*), and Islamic commentators.

In Part Two we will attempt to respond to basic Muslim beliefs in God, Muhammad, and the Qur'an. Here we will analyze criticisms that have been offered and attempt to come to a conclusion as to whether there is support for the validity of the Islamic claims. Particular attention will be paid to the factual basis for and internal consistency of these claims.

Finally, in Part Three we will examine the evidence for the Christian counterclaim. Here arguments offered in support of Christian claims will be scrutinized in order to determine their veracity. The appendixes will deal with special topics such as Muslim sects, religious practices, the *Gospel of Barnabas,* Muslim use of modern biblical criticism, Islam and violence, and Black Islam.

My coauthor, using a pseudonym, was reared as a Muslim in an Islamic country. His familiarity with Arabic and Muslim beliefs and practices has added a very significant dimension to this book. Together with my background in Christian theology and philosophy, we have made an attempt not only to understand the Muslim and Christian views, but to examine them carefully in light of the evidence. We are in agreement with the Socratic dictum that "the unexamined life is not worth living." And we believe as well that the unexamined faith is not worth believing. Since both orthodox Islam and Christianity claim to be the true religion, it is incumbent upon thinking persons to examine carefully the evidence offered by both and to make their own decision in view of the evidence.

Norman L. Geisler

Part One

THE BASIC DOCTRINES
OF ORTHODOX ISLAM

This book is an attempt to understand and evaluate the claims of orthodox Islam from a Christian point of view. It is our belief that it is not possible to evaluate another viewpoint fairly without first understanding it. Since one of us is a Christian and the other was reared as a Muslim, we believe we have an advantage in understanding both points of view. Further, we appeal predominantly to the primary sources of each religion, especially to the Qur'an and the Bible. In order to enhance our understanding of each, we selected standard teachers and commentators from each religion. In this first part we try our best to set forth as objectively as possible the basic doctrines of orthodox Islam, steering away from differing opinions of rival sects and emphasizing what most Muslims believe.

1

Understanding Islamic Monotheism

Like most religions, there are several sects (see Appendix 1). Here we have tried to emphasize what most Muslims hold in common.

The strength of Islam is neither in its rituals nor in its ethics, but in its grasp of one great idea: monotheism. Among the religions of the world there is not one that has a shorter creed than Islam and not one whose creed is so well known and so often repeated. The whole system of Muslim theology, philosophy, and religious life is summed up in seven words: *La ilaha illa Allah, Muhammad rasul Allah,* "There is no god but Allah and Muhammad is Allah's Apostle." This is the motto of the Muslim's family life, the ritualistic formula that welcomes the infant as a believer, and the final message that is whispered in the ear of the dying. By repeating these words, the unbeliever is transformed into a Muslim and the backslider is welcomed back into a spiritual brotherhood. By this creed the faithful are called to prayer five times daily, and it is the platform on which all the warring sects of Islam unite. It is the very foundation of the Islamic religion.[1]

Since the idea of God is fundamental to Islam, this chapter will analyze the doctrine of God as presented in the Qur'an and orthodox Islamic theology. First, we will consider the significance of the very word for God, "Allah." Second, we will attempt to explain the nature and character of God as understood by orthodox Muslims. Third, we will focus our discussion on the relationship that exists between God and the rest of his creation, especially human beings.

1. Samuel M. Zwemer, *The Moslem Doctrine of God* (New York: American Tract Society, 1905).

MEANING OF THE TERM "ALLAH"

Allah is the personal name for God in Islam. We make no distinction in this book, as some do, between the word "Allah" and the English word "God." As one well-known Muslim author puts it, "*Al Lah* means 'the Divinity' in Arabic: it is a single God, implying that a correct transcription can only render the exact meaning of the word with the help of the expression 'God.' For the Muslims, *al lah* is none other than the God of Moses and Jesus."[2]

In agreement with this warning, Kenneth Cragg, the noted Christian scholar of Islam, also claims that "since both Christians and Muslim faiths believe in One supreme sovereign Creator-God, they are obviously refer-ring when they speak of Him, under whatever terms, to the same Being. To suppose otherwise would be confusing. It is important to keep in mind that though the apprehensions differ, their theme is the same. The differ-ences, which undoubtedly exist, between the Muslim and the Christian understanding of God are far-reaching and must be patiently studied. But it would be fatal to all our mutual tasks to doubt that One and the same God over all was the reality in both."[3] Arab Christians use the term "Allah" for God. Of course, their understanding of what this term means differs from that of Muslims, but both have the same referent in mind.

ETYMOLOGY OF THE WORD "ALLAH"

There has been much speculation and endless discussion among Mus-lim exegetes and lexicographers concerning the real significance of the Arabic word "Allah." A well-respected Muslim commentator, Beidhawi, suggests that Allah is derived "from an [invented] root *illaha* = to be in per-plexity, because the mind is perplexed when it tries to form the idea of the Infinite!"[4] Still, "according to the opinion of some Muslim theologians, it is infidelity (*kufr*) to hold that the word has any derivation whatever! . . . They say that God is not begotten, and so His name cannot be derived. He is the first, and had an Arabic name before the creation of the worlds."[5] The author of the *Muheet-el-Muheet* dictionary says: "Allah is the name of nec-essary Being. There are twenty different views as to the derivation of this name of the Supreme; the most probable is that its root is *illah*, the past participle form, or the measure *fi'al*, from the verb *ilaho* = to worship, to which the article was prefixed to indicate the supreme object of worship."[6]

2. Maurice Bucaille, *The Bible, the Qur'an and Science,* trans. Pannell and Bucaille (Par-is: Editions Seghers, 1988), 120–21.
3. Kenneth Cragg, *The Call of the Minaret* (New York: Oxford University Press, 1964), 36.
4. From the famous Muslim exegete Beidhawi (d. A.D. 1307), as cited by Zwemer, 24.
5. Related from Muhammad by Abu Huraira and cited by ibid., 24.
6. Ibid., 23.

Ajijola, a Muslim author and apologist, writes, "In the Arabic Language the word 'ilah' means 'one who is worshipped'. . . . The word 'Allah', on the other hand, is the essential personal name of God. 'La ilaha illa-Allah' would literally mean, 'There is no "ilah" other than the One Great Being known by the name Allah.'"[7]

Cragg, in his highly acclaimed work *The Call of the Minaret*, notes, "The Arabic form *ilahun* meaning 'a god' is similar to the Hebrew and Aramaic words for deity. When used with the definite article *Al-Ilahu* meaning 'The God' the *l* consonant of the article coalesces with the same letter in the first syllable of the word eliding the *i* sound to make *Al-lah*. If we take the word to be of genuine Arabic form this is the obvious origin. If, as some scholars believe, the word does not have this origin but is historically derived from a sister language, its significance is the same. Allah means 'God' which connotation English achieves by dismissing even the definite article and using the capital letter—a device which Arabic lacks."[8]

PRE-ISLAMIC USE OF THE WORD "ALLAH"

Even if the exact etymology of the word "Allah" cannot be determined with certainty,[9] one thing we can be sure about from historical records is that the Arabs of pre-Islamic days, despite all their idolatry, knew of and acknowledged Allah's existence as the supreme God. In proof of this point Cragg comments: "It is clear from the negative form of the Muslim creed, 'There is no god except God,' that the existence and lordship of Allah were known and recognized in pre-Islamic Arabia. The Prophet's mission was not to proclaim God's existence but to deny the existence of all lesser deities. The fact that Muhammad's own father bore the name Abd-Allah, slave of God, would indicate that God was known by that name prior to Islam."[10] Cragg goes on to say that "There can be no doubt then that the Prophet's contemporaries knew of a Supreme Being, but He did not dominate their minds. Rather they thought more directly and frequently of the lesser gods, the daughters, perhaps even the sons, of Allah who were far more intimately related to their daily lives, their wars, their harvests, and their fertility."[11]

Zwemer makes a similar point: "But history establishes beyond the shadow of a doubt that even the pagan Arabs, before Mohammed's time,

7. Alhaj A. D. Ajijola, *The Essence of Faith in Islam* (Lahore, Pakistan: Islamic Publications Ltd., 1978), 16.

8. Cragg, 37.

9. For disagreement with Cragg's explanation, see Arthur Jeffery, *Islam: Muhammad and His Religion* (New York: Bobbs-Merrill Company, Inc., 1958), 85.

10. Cragg, 37.

11. Ibid., 37–38.

knew their chief god by the name of Allah and even, in a sense, proclaimed His unity. In pre-Islamic literature, Christian or pagan, *ilah* is used for any god and *Al-ilah* (contracted to Allah), i.e., 'ο Θεός, the god, was the name of the Supreme. Among the pagan Arabs this term denoted the chief god of their pantheon, the Kaaba, with its three hundred and sixty idols. . . . As final evidence, we have the fact that centuries before Mohammed the Arabian Kaaba, or temple at Mecca, was called *Beit-Allah*, the house of God, and not *Beit-el-Alihet*, the house of idols or gods."[12]

MUHAMMAD'S ADAPTATION OF THE WORD "ALLAH"

Some Western scholars have speculated about Muhammad's adaptation of the word "Allah" for the one and only true God. Richard Bell writes, "Muhammad had, in fact, to meet the difficulty which . . . confronts all those who seek to introduce a high religion amongst a people of primitive ideas, whose language has no term for God quite free from polytheistic associations. He begins by using *rabb*, 'Lord', generally in some combination, such as 'my Lord', 'thy Lord', or as we have seen, 'Lord of this house'."[13] Bell adds, "He also uses Allah, but rather hesitatingly, [maybe] . . . because it was already combined with belief in subordinate deities. Then *ar-Rahman* appears alongside it. The use of too many names, however, had its disadvantages." This he believes "might lend colour to polytheistic ideas again. He seems to have solved the difficulty finally by adopting Allah as the name for Deity, retaining *rabb* in the sense of Lord, and associating with both words, descriptive epithets, and phrases." Apparently, "these set phrases were convenient as rhyming conclusions to verses. But they also had their use in dinning into the minds of his community his conception of God as all-powerful, all-knowing, as Judge and Ruler, as glorious, merciful, and compassionate."[14]

Of course we must understand that from the orthodox Muslim viewpoint any such Western speculations about Muhammad's adaptation and use of the term "Allah" in the Qur'an is unacceptable (see Chapter 5). Nevertheless, the important point on which all could agree is that Muhammad's great revolutionary achievement lies not in his mere use of the term "Allah," but in his conception of Allah and Allah's character.

---

12. Zwemer, 25–26. Also see W. Montgomery Watt, *Muhammad's Mecca* (Edinburgh: Edinburgh University Press, 1988), 31–36.

13. Richard Bell, *The Origin of Islam in Its Christian Environment* (London: Frank Cass and Company Ltd., 1968), 117.

14. Ibid.

THE NATURE OF ALLAH

ALLAH'S EXISTENCE AND ONENESS

Sura 112 is dedicated to the fundamental question "Who is God?" According to Islamic tradition, this chapter is Muhammad's definition of Allah. Classical commentator Zamakhshari (d. A.D. 1146) says, "Ibn Abbas related that the Koreish said, O Mohammed, describe to us your Lord whom you invite us to worship; then this Surah was revealed."[15] The sura reads: "In the name of God, Most Gracious, Most Merciful. Say: He is God, The One and Only; God, the Eternal, Absolute; He begetteth not, Nor is He begotten; And there is none Like unto Him." This sura "is held to be worth a third of the whole Qur'an and the seven heavens and the seven earths are founded upon it. To confess this verse, a tradition affirms, is to shed one's sins as a man might strip a tree in autumn of its leaves."[16]

The cornerstone of Muhammad's message was the absolute unity and sovereignty of God. In inviting his people to join him in the worship and service of the one true God he presents several arguments in defense of God's existence. The existence of God is not taken for granted in the Qur'an. Rather, it points out many ways in which reason leads to belief that God exists.

In over eighty passages the Qur'an draws attention to the wonders of visible nature in the heavens and on earth, as well as to the manifestations of life in plants and animals, especially in the realm of human life. Likewise, the physical, moral, and mental constitution of man, his origin and destiny, and the course of his history are appealed to as evidence of God's existence. Thus, there are two principal starting points for reflection about God's existence: the order of nature and the order of life. As the Qur'an puts it, "Verily in the heavens And the Earth are Signs For those who believe. And in the creation Of yourselves the fact That animals are scattered (through the earth), are signs For those of assured Faith" (45:3–4; cf. 51:20–21; 41:53). The Qur'an notes that there are signs (*ayat*) for those who use their reason (*ya'kilun*), who reflect (*yatafakkarun*) and understand (*yaf-kahun*); to those endowed with mental or reasoning faculties (*il-uli al-albab, li-uli al-nuha*), who hear (*yasma'un*), who have eyes (*uli al-absar*), who know (*ya'lamun*), believe (*yu'minun*), and are convinced (*yu-kinun*). Thus, all the basic sensible and intellectual capacities of human beings are appealed to as starting points in our knowledge of God.[17]

15. Cited by Zwemer, 31.
16. Cragg, 39. Also see Al-Bukhari, *The Translation of the Meanings of Sahih Al–Bukhari*, trans. Muhammad Muhsin Khan (Al-Medina: Islamic University), vol. 6, 493–95.
17. See Mohammed A. Abou Ridah, "Monotheism in Islam: Interpretations and Social Manifestations," in *The Concept of Monotheism in Islam and Christianity*, ed. Hans Kochler (Wien, Austria: Wilhelm Braumuller, 1982), 41.

Zwemer categorizes the Qur'anic arguments for God in the following way: "The passages of the Koran that teach the existence and unity of God (Allah) are either those that refer for proof of His unity to creation (6:96–100; 16:3–22; 27:60–65; etc.), or state that polytheism and atheism are contrary to reason (23:119), or that dualism is self-destructive (21:22), or bring in the witness of former prophets (30:29; 21:25; 39:65; 51:50–52)."[18]

In addition to arguments for God's existence, the Qur'an invites its audience to the worship of one God by using various graphic figures of speech and analogies. Those who call a god apart from Allah are like someone who stretches out his hands to water, that it may reach his mouth, but it will never reach it (13:14). Those who take for themselves protectors apart from Allah are like the spiders, who make for themselves houses that are the frailest of all (29:41). Whosoever associates anything with Allah is like someone who has fallen from the sky. Birds snatch him away or the wind sweeps him down into a bottomless pit.[19]

The Qur'an uses two words to describe the oneness of God, *ahad* and *wahid*. *Ahad* is used as an adjective. It is employed in two suras to deny that God has any partner or companion associated with him. In Arabic, this form means the negation of any other number. The second word, *wahid*, may mean the same thing as the first word, and is used this way many times in the Qur'an. However, it also has another usage: "the One, Same God for all." That is to say, there is only one God for Muslims, and he is the same God for all peoples. Thus, both God's unity and singularity are implied in the Muslim concept of God's oneness.[20]

This emphasis on the Oneness of God is such a fundamental aspect of Islam that one Muslim author writes, "In fact, Islam, like other religions before it in their original clarity and purity, is nothing other than the declaration of the Unity of God, and its message is a call to testify to this Unity."[21] Another Muslim writer expresses a similar point: "The Unity of Allah is the distinguishing characteristic of Islam. This is the purest form of monotheism, i.e., the worship of Allah Who was neither begotten nor beget nor had any associates with Him in His Godhead. Islam teaches this in the most unequivocal terms."[22]

It is due to this uncompromising emphasis on God's absolute unity that in Islam the greatest of all sins is the sin of *shirk*, or assigning partners to God. The Qur'an sternly declares "God forgiveth not [The sin of] joining other gods with Him; but He forgiveth Whom He pleaseth other

18. Zwemer, 28.
19. Abou Ridah, 49.
20. See Nassir El-Din El-Assad's inaugural lecture, in *The Concept of Monotheism in Islam and Christianity*, ed. Hans Kochler, 23.
21. Abdel Haleem Mahmud, *The Creed of Islam* (World of Islam Festival Trust, 1978), 20.
22. Ajijola, 55.

sins Than this: one who joins Other gods with God, Hath strayed far, far away [From the Right]" (4:116).

OTHER CHARACTERISTICS OF ALLAH

Besides the great truth of God's Oneness, or the doctrine of *tawhid*, which is an ever-present reminder on the pages of the Qur'an, what else are we to learn about God and his character? According to one Muslim authority, late professor of Islamic thought in the University of Chicago, Fazlur Rahman (d. 1988), "the Qur'an is no treatise about God and His nature: His existence, for the Qur'an, is strictly functional—He is the Creator and Sustainer of the universe and of man, and particularly the giver of guidance for man and He who judges man, individually and collectively, and metes out to him merciful justice."[23] The accuracy of Rahman's comment is substantiated when we consult a number of Muslim works on Islam and find very little on the subject of God's essence and character, except the sense in which the ninety-nine names for God are believed to reflect the character of God. For example, in *Introduction to Islam*,[24] written by Muhammad Hameedullah, we find chapters on the political system, judicial system, and economic system of Islam, but no chapter on the being and character of God! Some other contemporary books have devoted no more than a page or two to this topic. However, it must be pointed out that within the last 1,400 years, several Muslim schools of thought have formulated many doctrinal statements on theology proper.

One Muslim author writes: "God is the essence of existence. His Arabic name is Allah. He is The First and The Last. He is unique and nothing resembles Him in any respect. He is One and The One. He is self-sustained, does not need anything but everything needs Him."[25] This attribute is known as aseity, or self-existence. God is the Mighty and the Almighty. He is the Willer of existing things and the things that will exist, and nothing happens apart from his will. He is the Knower of all that can be known. His knowledge encompasses the whole universe that he has created and he alone sustains. God is completely sovereign over all his creation.

Further, "God comprehends everything, even suggestions of the mind, and the concealed secrets in the innermost part of breasts of men. God is Living. . . . He is The All Hearing of all audible things. He is The All Seeing." And "He speaks with an eternal Speech not resembling the speech

23. Fazlur Rahman, *Major Themes of the Qur'an* (Chicago: Bibliotheca Islamica, 1980), 3.

24. Muhammad Hameedullah, *Introduction to Islam* (Paris: Centre Culturel Islamique, 1969).

25. Muhammad Abdul Rauf, *Islam: Creed and Worship* (Washington, D.C.: The Islamic Center, 1974), 2–3.

of created things. God's Might, Will, Knowledge, Life, Hearing, Seeing and Speech are inherent attributes in Him, and not a thing or things apart from him."[26]

God is the Just, the Wise, the Merciful, the Compassionate, the Beneficent, the Eternal, the Creator, the Omnipresent, and the Lord of the universe. There is no god but God. In the words of the Qur'an, "God! There is no god But He—the Living, The Self-subsisting, Eternal. No slumber can seize Him Nor sleep. His are all things In the heavens and on earth. Who is there can intercede In His presence except As He permitteth? He knoweth What [appeareth to His creatures As] Before or After Or Behind them. Nor shall they compass Aught of His knowledge Except as He willeth. His Throne doth extend Over the heavens And the earth, and He feeleth No fatigue in guarding And preserving them For He is the Most High, The Supreme [in glory]" (2:255).

Muslims ascribe to God all the noble names and attributes that befit his holy character. However, traditionally they insist on learning and remembering the following thirteen attributes specifically: "Existence, Eternity, Perpetuity, Dissimilarity, Self-Sustenance, Unity, Might, Will, Knowledge, Life, Hearing, Sight and Speech."[27]

Another concise statement of orthodox Islam confesses: "The Originator of the world is God Most High, the One, the Eternal, the Decreeing, the Knowing, the Hearing, the Seeing, the Willing. He is not an attribute, nor a body, nor an essence, nor a thing formed, nor a thing bounded, nor a thing numbered, nor a thing divided, nor a thing compounded, nor a thing limited: He is not described by quiddity, *mahiyah*, nor by modality, *kaifiyyah*, and He does not exist in place or time. There is nothing that resembles Him and nothing that is beyond His Knowledge and Power. He has qualities from all eternity existing in His essence. They are not He, nor are they other than He. These include Knowledge and Power, and Life and Strength, and Hearing and Seeing and Doing and Creating and Sustaining and Speech."[28]

One contemporary Muslim writer concisely describes the Islamic view of God in this way: "In attempting to understand the nature and works of God, we learn that: God is only One without a partner or son. He is the Creator of the universe and everything that is to be found in the universe. He is the Compassionate and Merciful and His mercy is to all creatures." Further, "He is just. He is the Guide and Guardian of everything. He is pre-existent and eternal. He is all-knowing and all-wise. He is loving and provident, and His mercy for His creatures knows no boundary. He is all-

26. Ibid., 3.
27. Ibid., 4–5.
28. See Cragg, 60–61.

powerful and the Supreme Master of all the worlds. He is holy and cannot commit sins or do evil. He is independent and unique."[29]

THE NINETY-NINE NAMES OF ALLAH

Another typical Islamic answer to the question "Who is God?" is to point out Allah's "most beautiful names." The Qur'anic basis for this is found in 59:22–24:

> God is He, than Whom There is no other god; Who knows [all things] Both secret and open; He, Most Gracious, Most Merciful. God is He, than Whom There is no other god; The Sovereign, the Holy One, The Source of Peace [and Perfection], The Guardian of Faith, The Preserver of Safety, The Exalted in Might, The Irresistible, the Supreme: Glory to God! [High is He] Above the partners They attribute to Him. He is God, the Creator, The Evolver, The Bestower of Forms [Or Colours]. To Him belong The Most Beautiful Names: Whatever is in The heavens and on earth, Doth declare His Praise and Glory: And He is the Exalted In Might, the Wise.

Besides this Qur'anic admonition, the Islamic tradition relates that "Muhammad said, 'Verily, there are ninety-nine names of God and whoever recites them shall enter Paradise.'"[30] Regarding Allah's most beautiful names, Arthur Jeffery, the great European Islamicist, comments: "The lists of these names as found in the texts vary greatly. . . . Redhouse in his article in the *Journal of the Royal Asiatic Society* for 1880 collected from various lists no less than 552 different names for Allah."[31] Stanton, another well-known Islamicist, also comments that "these names are reckoned by the traditionalist Abu Hurairah as ninety-nine. . . . Taking this list as a basis, we find that twenty-six of the ninety-nine names are not found in the Qur'an in the form given, though they are based on passages which give something near it."[32] "Their variety is explained in part by the poetic style of the Qur'an, which tended to the use of rhyming endings, derived from a much smaller number of original roots with nuances or shades of adjectival meaning."[33]

Jeffery lists one sample of the ninety-nine names of God as found in the book *Tasbih Asma Allah al-Husna* written by Muhammad al-Madani:[34]

---

29. Badru D. Kateregga and David W. Shenk, *Islam and Christianity* (Grand Rapids: Eerdmans, 1981), 7.
30. See Zwemer, 34.
31. Jeffery, 93.
32. H. U. Weitbrecht Stanton, *The Teaching of the Qur'an* (New York: Biblo and Tannen, 1969), 33.
33. Cragg, 40.
34. See Jeffery, 93–98.

1. *Allah,* the Name that is above every name.
2. *al-Awwal,* the First, who was before the beginning (57:3).
3. *al-Akhir,* the Last, who will still be after all has ended (57:3).
4. *al-Badi,* the Contriver, who contrived the whole art of creation (2:117).
5. *al-Bari,* the Maker, from whose hand we all come (59:24).
6. *al-Barr,* the Beneficent, whose liberality appears in all his works (52:28).
7. *al-Basir,* the Observant, who sees and hears all things (57:3).
8. *al-Basit,* the Spreader, who extends his mercy to whom he wills (13:26).
9. *al-Batin,* the Inner, who is immanent within all things (57:3).
10. *al-Baith,* the Raiser, who will raise up a witness from each community (6:89, 91).
11. *al-Baqi,* the Enduring, who is better and more enduring (20:73, 75).
12. *at-Tawwab,* the Relenting, who relented toward Adam and relents to all his descendants (2:37).
13. *al-Jabbar,* the Mighty One, whose might and power are absolute (59:23).
14. *al-Jalil,* the Majestic, mighty and majestic is he.
15. *al-Jami,* the Gatherer, who gathers all men to an appointed Day (3:9).
16. *al-Hasib,* the Accounter, who is sufficient as a reckoner (4:6–7).
17. *al-Hafiz,* the Guardian, who keeps watch over everything (11:57, 60).
18. *al-Haqq,* the Truth (20:114).
19. *al-Hakem,* the Judge, who gives judgment among his servants (40:48, 51).
20. *al-Hakim,* the Wise, who is both wise and well informed (6:18).
21. *al-Halim,* the Kindly, who is both forgiving and kindly disposed (2:225).
22. *al-Hamid,* the Praiseworthy, to whom all praise is due (2:267, 270).
23. *al-Hayy,* the Living, who is the source of all life (20:111).
24. *al-Khabir,* the Well-Informed, who is both wise and well informed (6:18).
25. *al-Khafid,* the Humbler, who humbles some while he exalts others (cf. 56:3).
26. *al-Khaliq,* the Creator, who has created all things that are (13:16–17).
27. *Dhul-Jalal wal-Ikram,* Lord of Majesty and Honor (55:27).
28. *ar-Rauf,* the Gentle, who is compassionate toward his people (2:143).

29. *ar-Rahman*, the Merciful, the most merciful of those who show mercy (1:3; 12:64).
30. *ar-Rahim*, the Compassionate, who is gentle and full of compassion (1:3; 2:143).
31. *ar-Razzaq*, the Provider, who provides but asks no provision (51:57–58).
32. *ar-Rashid*, the Guide, who leads belicvers in the right-minded way (11:87, 89).
33. *ar-Rafi*, the Exalter, who exalts some while he humbles others (6:83).
34. *ar-Raqib*, the Watcher, who keeps watch over his creation (5:117).
35. *as-Salam*, the Peace-Maker, whose name is Peace (59:23).
36. *as-Sami*, the Hearer, who sees and hears all things (17:1).
37. *ash-Shakur*, the Grateful, who graciously accepts the service of his people (64:17).
38. *ash-Shahid*, the Witness, who is witness to all things (5:117).
39. *as-Sabur*, the Forebearing, who has great patience with his people.
40. *as-Samad*, the Eternal, who begets not and is not begotten (112:2).
41. *ad-Darr*, the Afflicter, who sends affliction as well as blessing (48:11).
42. *az-Zahir*, the Outer, who is without as well as within (47:3).
43. *al-Adl*, the Just, whose word is perfect in veracity and justice (6:115).
44. *al-Aziz*, the Sublime, mighty in his sublime sovereignty (59:23).
45. *al-Azim*, the Mighty, he who above all is high and mighty (2:255–56).
46. *al-Afuw*, the Pardoner, ever ready to forgive his servants (4:99–100).
47. *al-Alim*, the Knowing One, who is well aware of everything (2:29).
48. *al-Ali*, the High One, he who is high and mighty (2:255–56).
49. *al-Ghafur*, the Forgiving, who is both forgiving and well disposed (2:235).
50. *al-Ghaffar*, the Pardoning, ever ready to pardon and forgive (71:10).
51. *al-Ghani*, the Rich, since it is he who possesses all things (2:267, 270).
52. *al-Fattah*, the Opener, who clears and opens up the Way (34:26).
53. *al-Qabid*, the Seizer, who both holds tight and is open-handed (2:245–46).
54. *al-Qadir*, the Able, who has the power to do what he pleases (17:99, 101).
55. *al-Quddus*, the Most Holy One, to Whom all in heaven and on earth ascribe holiness (62:1).

56. *al-Qahhar*, the All-Victorious, who overcomes all (13:16–17).
57. *al-Qawi*, the Strong, sublime in his strength and his power (13:19).
58. *al-Qayyum*, the Self-Subsistent, eternally existing in and for himself alone (3:2).
59. *al-Kabir*, the Great One, who is both high and great (22:62).
60. *al-Karim*, the Munificent, who is not only rich but generous (27:40).
61. *al-Latif*, the Gracious, whose grace extends to all his servants (42:19).
62. *al-Mutaakhkhir*, the Defender, who when he wills defers punishment (14:42–43).
63. *al-Mumin*, the Faithful, who grants security to all (59:23).
64. *al-Mutaali*, the Self-Exalted, who has set himself high above all (13:9–10).
65. *al-Mutakabbir*, the Proud, whose pride is in his works (59:23).
66. *al-Matin*, the Firm, firm in his possession of strength (51:58).
67. *al-Mubdi*, the Originator, who both originates and restores (85:13).
68. *al-Mujib*, the Answerer, who responds when his servants call (11:61, 64).
69. *al-Majid*, the Glorious, praiseworthy and glorious is he (11:73, 76).
70. *al-Muhsi*, the Computer, who has counted and numbered all things (19:94).
71. *al-Muhyi*, the Quickener, who quickens and brings to life the dead (30:50).
72. *al-Mudhill*, the Abaser, who raises to honor or abases whom he will (3:26).
73. *al-Muzil*, the Separator, who will separate men from the false gods they vainly worship (10:28–29).
74. *al-Musawwir*, the Fashioner, who fashions his creatures how he pleases (59:24).
75. *al-Muid*, the Restorer, who both originates and restores (85:13).
76. *al-Muizz*, the Honorer, who honors or abases whom he will (3:26).
77. *al-Muti*, the Giver, from whose hand comes all good things (20:50, 52).
78. *al-Mughni*, the Enricher, who enriches men from his bounty (9:74–75).
79. *al-Muqit*, the Well-Furnished, provided with power over all things (4:85, 87).
80. *al-Muqtadir*, he who prevails, having evil men in his powerful grip (54:42).
81. *al-Muqaddim*, the Bringer-Forward, who sends his promises on ahead (50:28).

82. *al-Muqsit*, the Observer of Justice, who will set up the balances with justice (21:47–48).
83. *al-Malik*, the King, who is king of kings (59:23).
84. *Malik al-Mulk*, Possessor of the Kingdom, who grants sovereignty to whom he will (3:26).
85. *al-Mumit*, he who causes to die, just as he causes to live (15:23).
86. *al-Muntaqim*, the Avenger, who wreaks vengeance on sinners and succors the believers (30:47).
87. *al-Muhaimin*, the Preserver, whose watchful care is over all (59:23).
88. *an-Nasir*, the Helper, and sufficient as a helper is he (4:45, 47).
89. *an-Nur*, the Light, illuminating both earth and heaven (24:35).
90. *al-Hadi*, the Guide, who leads believers in the straight path (22:54).
91. *al-Wahed*, the One, unique in his Divine sovereignty (13:16–17).
92. *al-Wahid*, the Unique, who alone has created (74:11).
93. *al-Wadud*, the Loving, compassionate and loving to his servants (11:90, 92).
94. *al-Warith*, the Inheritor, unto whom all things will return (19:40–41).
95. *al-Wasi*, the Wide-Reaching, whose bounty reaches all (2:268, 271).
96. *al-Wakil*, the Administrator, who has charge of everything (6:102).
97. *al-Waliy*, the Patron, and a sufficient patron is he (4:45, 47).
98. *al-Wali*, the Safeguard, other than whom men have no sure guard (13:11–12).
99. *al-Wahhab*, the Liberal Giver, who gives freely of his bounty (3:8).

SIGNIFICANCE OF THESE NAMES

In considering these names, one Muslim writer boasts that "the Uniqueness of God is repeatedly affirmed in the Qur'an together with all the attributes of the true, perfect and sublime Creator, hence the *asma Allah alhosna* (the beautiful names of God). No similar attributes, in number or in meaning, are to be found in other sacred or non-sacred books." In fact, "Muslim theologians have divided the divine attributes in many ways: attributes of Majesty (*djalal*), Generosity (*ikram*) and Beauty (*djamal*), or: those of the essence (*al-dhat*), and those of actions (*af'al*), or: absolute and relative attributes."[35] Also "Some Muslim teachers divide these attributes into the natural sections of Power, Wisdom, and Goodness; others, more commonly, into Names of Terror (*asma'u'l jala-*

---

35. Abou Ridah, 46.

liyah), and names of Glory (*asma'u'l jamaliyah*), of which the former are the more numerous."[36]

It is important to note that "the actions appropriate to these names, most of which are participial or adjectival forms, are frequently noted in the events and situations of the Quranic story. . . . The Names are far, then, from being mere attributes to be listed in a theology: they are awesome realities of daily life. For God is Al-Haqq—'the Real,' 'the Veritable.'"[37] He is the Supreme Reality, the ground of all existence, whose nearness, judgment, and will are the great facts of human life.

The relative frequency with which the different names of God occur is a matter of deep interest. Their corresponding verbs—which have to do with strength, majesty, and greatness—are very prominent. Cragg observes that these names "are to be understood finally as characteristics of the Divine will rather than laws of His nature. Action, that is, arising from such descriptives may be expected, but not as a matter of necessity."[38] What gives unity to all God's actions is that he wills them all. As willer he may be recognized by the descriptions given him, but he does not essentially conform to any. The action of his will may be identified from its effects, but his will itself is inscrutable. From this it may be concluded that God is not necessarily loving, holy, and righteous in every situation. This explains the antithesis in certain names. There would be no antithesis if either element within it were essential to God's nature. The antithesis resides in the realm of the will, in that God wills both—hence, the tension remains.

For the Muslim, the seemingly contradictory actions of God are not problematic. The divine will is an ultimate beyond which neither reason nor revelation can go. "So God is the One Who leads astray, as well as the One Who guides. He is the One Who brings damage, as also does Satan. He is described also by terms like the Bringer-down, the Compeller, or Tyrant, the Haughty—all of which, when used of men, have an evil sense. In the Unity of the single will, however, these descriptions co-exist with those that relate to mercy, compassion, and glory."[39]

Allah's Relationship to His Creation

In regard to the Islamic view of God's relationship to the world, there is one constant emphasis in the Qur'an: God has transcendence, absolute uniqueness, and lordship. However, as Fazlur Rahman points out,

36. Stanton, 33–34.
37. Cragg, 41–42.
38. Ibid., 42.
39. Ibid., 42–43.

the verses of the Qur'an also "equally underline His infinite mercy. . . . God's lordship is *expressed through* His creation; His sustenance and provision of that creation, particularly and centrally of man; and finally, through re-creation in new forms."[40]

God's creation of nature *and* man, and of nature *for* man, is his most primordial mercy. His power, creation, and mercy are, therefore, not only completely coextensive but fully interpenetrating and fully identical: "He hath inscribed For Himself [the rule of] Mercy" (6:12); "My mercy extendeth To all things" (7:156). His very infinitude implies not a one-sided transcendence, but equally, his being "with" his creation. He is nearer to man than is man's jugular vein (50:16). Whenever a person lapses morally and then sincerely regrets it and "seeks God's pardon," God quickly returns to him. Indeed, among his often-mentioned attributes besides the "Merciful" and the "Compassionate" are the "Returner" (as the opposite of "forsaker": 2:37, 54, 160, 187; 5:39, 71; 9:117–18; 20:122; etc.), and the "Forgiver" (40:3; 2:173, 182, 192, 199, 218, 225–26, 235; and about 116 other occurrences), which are almost invariably followed by "Compassionate." For those who genuinely repent, God transforms their very lapses into goodness (25:70).[41]

Another prominent European Islamicist, Goldziher (d. 1921), comments, "In this God's absolute omnipotence, unlimited power to reward and punish, and severity toward obdurate malefactores join the attribute of compassion and clemency (*halim*). God is indulgent with sinners and forgiving to the repentant. 'He has made compassion (*al-rahma*) an inviolable law for Himself' (6:54)." The following tradition seems to be a kind of commentary on this Qur'an verse: "When God had completed creation, He wrote in the book that is kept by His side on the heavenly throne: 'My compassion overcomes my wrath.'" "Although He reaches with His punishment whom He will, His mercy encompasses all things" (7:156). Nor is love missing from the attributes of God in the Qur'an, as some suppose. Allah is *wadud*, "loving." "If you love God, follow me, and God will love you and forgive your sins." However, "God does not love the unbelievers" (3:32).[42]

Another important question is, "How does Islamic theology understand God's personal relationship to man?" In the language of the Qur'an this relationship is described in terms of master (*rabb*) and slave (*abd*). God is the Sovereign Monarch who requires man to submit to him as an obedient slave. And even though God is said to be closer to man than

40. Rahman, 6.
41. Ibid.
42. Ignaz Goldziher, *Introduction to Islamic Theology and Law*, trans. Andras and Ruth Hamori (Princeton: Princeton University Press, 1981), 24.

man's own jugular vein, the theme of an intimate relationship between God and man is not further developed either in the Qur'an or in orthodox Islamic theology (Islamic Sufism is an exception to this rule, as we shall see later). In an interesting comment, one Muslim author writes: "Beyond their speculations concerning God, the necessity of his existence, and his properties, Muslim theologians and philosophers have apparently felt no need to question the possibility and reality of a human experience of God." As a matter of fact, "it is even difficult to find an appropriate Arabic or Persian expression for 'experience of God' without running the risk of encroaching upon the absolute transcendence of the God of Islam, of anthropomorphizing him."[43]

This overpowering picture of God in the Qur'an has created its own tension in Islamic theology regarding God's absolute sovereignty and man's free will. "Orthodox Islam teaches the absolute predestination of both good and evil, that all our thoughts, words and deeds, whether good or evil, were foreseen, foreordained, determined and decreed from all eternity, and that everything that happens takes place according to what has been written for it. There was great discussion among the early Muslim theologians as to free will and predestination, but the free-will parties (*al-qadariyya*) were ultimately defeated."[44]

Consider these verses: "Say, Nothing will ever befall us save what Allah has written for us. He is our Patron, so let the believers put their trust in Allah" (9:51). "He whom Allah guides is he who is rightly guided, but whom He leads astray, those are the losers. Indeed, We have assuredly created for Gehenna many of both *jinn* and men. They have hearts with which they do not comprehend, they have eyes with which they do not see, they have ears with which they do not hear. Such are like cattle; nay, they are even further astray. Such are the heedless ones" (7:178–79). "Verily the sentence comes true on most of them, so they will not believe. We, indeed, have set shackles on their necks which reach to the chins so that they perforce hold up [their heads]. And We have set a barrier in front of them, and a barrier behind them, and We have covered them over so that they do not see. Thus it is alike to them whether thou warn them or dost not warn them; they will not believe" (36:7–10). "Had we so willed We should have brought every soul its guidance, but true is that saying of Mine: 'I shall assuredly fill up Gehenna with *jinn* and men together'" (32:13).[45]

43. Annemarie Schimmel and Abdoldjavad Falaturi, *We Believe In One God* (New York: Seabury Press, 1979), 85.
44. See Jeffery, 147–48.
45. We are here using Jeffery's more literal translation of the Qur'an.

In addition to these verses we can find an abundance of Muhammad's sayings and teachings in the *hadith* (Islamic tradition), that portray a similar view of God, as illustrated by the following:

> While we were sitting in company with the Apostle of Allah upon whom be Allah's blessing and peace—and a group of his Companions, Abu Bakr and Umar entered through one of the gates of the mosque. With them was quite a large body of people disputing with loud voices, the one contradicting the other, till they came to the Apostle of Allah. . . . Said he: "What is it you are disputing about that causes you to raise your voices so and make such a clamor?" "It is about the decree," they answered. "Abu Bakr asserts that Allah decrees good but does not decree evil, but Umar says that He decrees both alike."

Muhammad replied:

> "The decree necessarily determines all that is good and all that is sweet and all that is bitter, and that is my decision between you." Then he slapped Abu Bakr on the shoulder, and said: "O Abu Bakr, if Allah Most High had not willed that there be disobedience, He would not have created the Devil." Abu Bakr replied: "I seek pardon from Allah. I slipped and stumbled, O Apostle of Allah, but never again will I fall into error about this matter."[46]

In the *Sahih* of al-Muslim (d. A.D. 875), one of the most respected Muslim books on the traditions of Muhammad, we read:

> It may be that one of you will be performing the works of the people of Paradise, so that between him and Paradise there is the distance of only an arm's length, but then what is written (i.e., decreed) for him overtakes him, and he begins to perform the works of the people of Hell, into which he will go. Or maybe one of you will be performing the works of the people of Hell, so that between him and Hell there is the distance of only an arm's length, but then what is written for him will overtake him, and he will begin to perform the works of the people of Paradise, into which he will go.[47]

This attitude of God's absolute control over every aspect of his creation has obviously had a profound impact on Islamic theology and culture. One of the most respected Muslim theologians of all time, Al-Ghazali, writes:

> He willeth also the unbelief of the unbeliever and the irreligion of the wicked and, without that will, there would neither be unbelief nor irreli-

46. See Jeffery, 149–50.
47. Ibid., 150.

gion. All we do we do by His will: what He willeth not does not come to pass. If one should ask why God does not will that men should believe, we answer, "We have no right to enquire about what God wills or does. He is perfectly free to will and to do what He pleases." In creating unbelievers, in willing that they should remain in that state; . . . in willing, in short, all that is evil, God has wise ends in view which it is not necessary that we should know.[48]

In another Muslim theologian we read, "Not only can He (God) do anything, He actually is the only One Who does anything. When a man writes, it is Allah who has created in his mind the will to write. Allah at the same time gives power to write, then brings about the motion of the hand and the pen and the appearance upon paper. All other things are passive, Allah alone is active."[49]

One Islamic creedal statement reads, "And God Most High is the Creator of all actions of His creatures whether of unbelief or belief, of obedience or of rebellion: all of them are by the Will of God and His sentence and His conclusion and His decreeing."[50] Another confession states that "God's one possible quality is His power to create good or evil at any time He wishes, i.e. His decree. . . . Both good things and evil things are the result of God's decree. It is the duty of every Muslim to believe this. . . . When God rewards the pious, that is pure kindness and when He punishes the sinners, that is pure justice, since the piety of humans is not useful for God, nor does the sinner do Him any harm. It is He who causes harm and good. Rather the good works of some and the evil of others are signs that God wishes to punish some and to reward others." Thus, "if God wishes to draw someone close to Himself, then He will give him the grace which will make that person do good works. If He wishes to reject someone and put that person to shame, then He will create sin in him. God creates all things, good and evil. God creates people as well as their actions: He created you as well as what you do (Qur'an 37:94)."[51]

SUMMARY

We have touched on some of the most basic aspects of the Islamic view of God. God is absolutely one and in sovereign control of all things. He has no equals or partners. He possesses many names (traditionally

---

48. Abdiyah Akbar Abdul-Haqq, *Sharing Your Faith with a Muslim* (Minneapolis: Bethany Fellowship Inc., 1980), 152, taken from *Hughe's Dictionary*, 147.
49. Gerhard Nehls, *Christians Ask Muslims* (Bellville: SIM International Life Challenge, 1987), 21.
50. Taken from the Al-Nasafi's creed as cited by Cragg, 60–61.
51. Andrew Rippin and Jan Knappert, *Islam* (Manchester: University Press, 1986), 133.

ninety-nine) but none really describes his ineffable essence. Rather, they speak of "the sovereign free will of God." God is self-existent and totally independent from and transcendent over the whole universe. One of the most repeated moral descriptions of God is that he is merciful. Of course, it should be pointed out that such a vast topic, with all its interrelations with other points of Muslim theology, can certainly not be exhaustively treated in one short chapter. Having surveyed Islamic teachings on the character of God and his relationship to the world, we turn now to the Muslim conception of God and his activities in history.

2

THE ISLAMIC VIEW
OF CREATION AND MAN

One of the most prominent aspects of the Islamic view of God is the acknowledgment of him as the Creator. All that exists in the universe is created by God to declare his Oneness and glory. One Islamic scholar writes, "But what is the meaning of creation? The Koran answers: Everything is created to worship God and to serve Him in veneration. Adoration, service of God in the true sense of the word, is the meaning of creation and thus of history."[1]

THE CREATION OF HEAVEN AND EARTH

The rich natural theology of the Qur'an affirms, "The seven heavens and the earth, And all beings therein, Declare His glory: There is not a thing But celebrates His praise" (17:44). "Verily your Lord is God, Who created the heavens And the earth in six Days, And is firmly established On the Throne (of authority), Regulating and governing all things" (10:3). Further, "Blessed is He Who made Constellations in the skies, And placed therein a Lamp And a Moon giving light; And it is He Who made The Night and the Day To follow each other" (25:61). "He has created man: He has taught him speech (And Intelligence). The sun and the moon Follow courses (exactly) computed; And the herbs and the trees—Both (alike) bow in adoration. And the Firmament has He Raised high" (55:3–7). "It is He who hath created for you all things that are on earth; moreover His design comprehended the heavens, for He gave order and per-

1. Schimmel and Falaturi, 155.

fection to the seven firmaments; and of all things He hath perfect knowledge" (2:29).

According to the Qur'an, creation includes inanimate nature; the plant and animal kingdoms; spiritual beings such as angels and *jinn*; and finally human beings, who are the climax of God's creative activity.

Concerning the Islamic concept of universe and nature in general, the *Encyclopaedia Britannica* summarizes it well:

> In order to prove the unity of God, the Qur'an lays frequent stress on the design and order in the universe. There are no gaps or dislocations in nature. Order is explained by the fact that every created thing is endowed with a definite and defined nature whereby it falls into a pattern. This nature, though it allows every created thing to function in a whole, sets limits. . . . The universe is viewed, therefore, as autonomous, in the sense that everything has its own inherent laws of behaviour, but not as autocratic, because the patterns of behaviour have been endowed by God and are strictly limited.[2]

As one Muslim author writes, "everything in the world, or every phenomenon other than man is administered by God-made Laws. This makes the entire physical world necessarily obedient to God and submissive to His Laws, which, in turn, means that it is in a state of Islam [submission], or it is Muslim." Thus, "the physical world has no choice of its own. It has no voluntary course to follow on its own initiative but obeys the Law of the Creator, the Law of Islam or submission."[3]

Regarding God's creation of the natural order, the Qur'an teaches that "it is God who has Created the heavens And the earth, and all Between them, in six Days" (32:4). "We created the heavens And the earth and all Between them in Six Days, Nor did any sense Of weariness touch Us" (50:38). However, elsewhere the Qur'an declares that "He completed them As seven firmaments In two Days, and He Assigned to each heaven Its duty and command" (41:12). Again, "Say: Is it that ye Deny Him Who created The earth in two Days?" (41:9).

One Muslim writer summarizes the Qur'anic witness on creation in the following way:

> First, there were six periods for the creation in general. Second, there was an interlocking of the stages in the creation of the heavens and the earth. Third, the universe was initially a unique mass all in one block, which God by His power and will split up. Fourth, there is a plurality of heavens and

2. *The New Encyclopaedia Britannica*, 15th ed., 6–7.
3. Hammudah Abdalati, *Islam in Focus* (Indianapolis: American Trust Publications, 1975), 9.

earth, seven heavens being emphasized. Fifth, there is an intermediary world of planets and heavenly bodies between the heavens and the earth. Sixth, God alone is the Creator of nature and the universe, and neither of the two can be God or worshipped as such, for God is altogether transcendent over creation. Seventh, and finally, God created everything in an orderly and understandable manner.[4]

Because of the scarcity of details concerning the process of creation, later Muslim commentators added many legends to the story of creation to fill in the gaps in the Qur'anic passages.[5] Some modern Muslim scholars use these gaps to account for some sort of theistic evolutionary process.

THE CREATION OF ANGELS

Belief in angels plays an important part in the Islamic faith. The Qur'an and later Islamic theology have much to say about their existence and functions. In fact, belief in angels is one of the five main articles of the faith.

Ajijola points out that, "To be a Muslim, it is necessary to believe not only in God, in the life Hereafter, in the prophets and in the Books of God, but also in the angels of God."[6] This statement is based on the Qur'anic exhortation, "It is not righteousness That you turn your faces Towards East or West; But it is righteousness—To believe in God And the Last Day, And the Angels And the Book, And the Messengers" (2:177). According to a well-established tradition from Muhammad, "Belief in Angels is an essential part of faith. The Prophet was sitting once in the company of some people when Gabriel came to him and said, 'What is faith?' The Prophet replied, 'Faith is believing in God and His Angels.'"[7]

In his theological work *Al-Mufaredat,* one Islamic theologian, Imam Raghib Isfahani, writes:

> The angels are formed of light. They neither err nor commit sin. They are constituted so. Their sole occupation is to sing the hymns of Allah. They are free from baser appetites. Wrong beliefs about gods and goddesses have stemmed from the distorted notion of God's unshared authority. People believed that God had placed His domains under the authority of various angels who run the administration of their respective provinces under His command. The Quran has repeatedly contradicted this theory. It tells that the angels are not God's daughters nor are they benefactors in their own

4. Kateregga and Shenk, 10.
5. See Rippin and Knappert, *Islam,* 59–63.
6. Ajijola, 71.
7. Mahmud, 64.

right. They are the beings, who flinch not (from executing) the commands they receive from God. But do (precisely) what they are commanded to do.[8]

In reference to the activities and duties of angels, the great British scholar on Islam, H. A. R. Gibb, writes:

In the imagery of the Koran the angels are represented generally as God's messengers. They are . . . His creatures and servants and worship Him continually; they bear up His Throne, descend with His Decrees on the Night of Power, record men's actions, receive their souls when they die, and witness for or against them at the Last Judgment, and guard the gates of Hell. At the battle of Badr they assisted the Muslims against the vastly superior forces of the Meccans.[9]

Ajijola explains:

According to these *hadith* (traditional sayings of Muhammad): some angels question the dead in their graves. They are called *Munkir* and *Nakir*. Some angels just keep roaming about the world. They attend places where people pray to Allah, where religious lectures are being given or the Holy Qur'an is read. . . . These angels testify to Allah, the presence of those who attend such meetings. . . . The duties of the angels working in the world keep changing every morning and evening. The angels of night duty go back when morning prayers are said. The angels on day duty take over. These go back at the time of the *Asr* (evening) prayers and those having night duty return once again.[10]

In addition to the numberless multitudes of angelic beings, Muslims believe in four archangels: Gabriel (the angel of revelation, also recognized by many Muslims as the Holy Spirit, who is believed to have dictated the Qur'an word by word to the prophet Muhammad), Michael (the angel of providence, and also the guardian of the Jews), Israfil (the summoner to resurrection), and Izra'il (the angel of death). Among these archangels, Gabriel holds the most prominent place, due to his function as the bearer of divine revelation. "Say: Whoever is an enemy To Gabriel—for he brings down The [revelation] to thy heart. . . . Whoever is an enemy to God And His angels and apostles, To Gabriel and Michael—Lo! God is an enemy to those Who reject Faith" (2:97–98).

8. Kausar Niazi, *Creation of Man* (Karachi: Ferozoono, Ltd., 1975), 12.
9. H. A. R. Gibb, *Mohammedanism* (London: Oxford University Press, 1964), 56–57.
10. See Ajijola, 72.

JINN

In addition to angels God created other spiritual beings called *jinn.* The Qur'an declares, "We created man from sounding clay, From mud moulded into shape; and the *Jinn* race, We had Created before, from the fire Of a scorching wind" (15:26–27). Again we read, "I have only created *Jinn* and men, that They may serve Me" (51:56).

There has been much speculation concerning the identity and nature of *jinn*, but it is commonly believed that they are powerful, intelligent creatures who possess freedom of choice. Therefore, some are good and some are evil (cf. 72:11). They seem to be halfway between men and angels. According to Fazlur Rahman, the *jinn* "despite their fiery nature and much greater physical powers . . . are not fundamentally different from men, except for their greater proneness to evil and stupidity."[11] Occasionally they materialize in different forms and can be seen by human eyes, but most often they are invisible to the average individual.

There are several Qur'anic passages that describe their activities—such as *jinn* listening to the recitation of the Qur'an and being converted to Islam or being obedient servants to King Solomon (see 46:29ff.; 72:1–2). And in later Islamic theology and culture they play an even more prominent role. One contemporary Muslim author writes:

> Among the earlier scholars . . . nobody doubted their existence. But the later scholars swept by a wave of rationalism totally rejected the creation of *jinn.* Our submission is: How can we assume that the *jinn* cannot be seen when sufficient testimony is available to the fact that they have been seen by many. . . . In his famous work "*An-Nabuwwat,*" the Imam (Ibn Taimyya) writes that whosoever attains mastery over the *jinn*, is flown on their back to distant places. It was a common phenomenon, which he had himself witnessed. He says that many *jinn* who had succeeded in insinuating themselves into his disciples' company were given a severe beating by him. They took to their heels never to return.[12]

Several classical Muslim theologians have written on topics such as marriage relationships between human beings and *jinn*, the future destiny of *jinn*, whether prayer led by *jinn* is permissible, and cases of *jinn*-possessions. Formulas that protect individuals from the mischief of the *jinn* are offered by some.[13]

Unlike the majority of Muslim thinkers, the more Westernized Muslim theologian, Rahman, downplays the role of *jinn* in Qur'anic theology:

11. Rahman, 122.
12. See Niazi, 26.
13. Ibid., 25–28.

Could the *jinn* represent some earlier stage in the course of evolution? Be that as it may, mention of the *jinn* ceases in the Madinan period of the Qur'an, which continues to call itself "guidance for man" and, in fact, never addresses the *jinn* primarily, or even directly. (As we have said, even in the two passages where the *jinn* listened to the Qur'an, the Prophet himself did not experience them but the Qur'an reported to him about it.)[14]

SATAN

Concerning the Qur'anic names for Satan, Stanton writes, "The devil is called in the Qur'an indifferently by the Hebrew derivative Shaitan (Shatan) or the Greek *Iblis* (*diabolos*). The name Shaitan is generally used with the epithet *rajim* = stoned or accursed, sometimes *marid* or rebellious."[15]

There is a good deal of Islamic controversy regarding the identity of Satan. Some Qur'anic evidence seems to point to Satan as an angelic being. However, we are also told in the Qur'an that angels cannot disobey God and yet Satan obviously did. Therefore, many Muslim theologians have held the opinion that Satan belonged to the species of *jinn*.

Kateregga notes that "Muslim theology is of the view that *Iblis* (Satan) was not an angel but a *jinn* (spirit) and that he was a leader of a group of *jinn* who disobeyed Allah."[16] Yusuf Ali, the translator of the popular *The Holy Qur'an: Translation and Commentary*, commenting on 2:34, after acknowledging the possibility that Satan could be a fallen angel, goes on to say, "But the theory of fallen angels is not usually accepted in Muslim theology. In 18:50, Iblis is spoken of as a *Jinn*."[17]

Even though Satan was created before man, his rebellion against God according to the Qur'an was almost simultaneous with the creation of man. In 38:71–77 we read:

> Behold, thy Lord said To the angels: "I am About to create man From clay: When I have fashioned him (In due proportion) and breathed Into him of My spirit, Fall ye down in obeisance Unto him." So the angels prostrated themselves, All of them together: Not so Iblis: he Was haughty, and became One of those who reject Faith. (God) said: "O Iblis! What prevents thee from Prostrating thyself to one Whom I have created With My hands? Art thou haughty? Or art thou one Of the high (and mighty) ones?" (Iblis) said: "I am better Than he: Thou createdst Me from fire, and him Thou createdest from clay." (God) said: "Then get thee Out from here: for thou Art rejected, accursed. Any My curse shall be On thee till the Day Of Judgment.

14. See Rahman, 123. See also Abdullah Yusuf Ali, *The Holy Qur'an: Translation and Commentary* (Damascus: (Ouloom Al Qur'an, 1934), n. 929.

15. Stanton, 39.

16. See Kateregga and Shenk, 11.

17. Abdullah Yusuf Ali, *Meaning of the Glorious Qur'an*, 1:25.

Commenting on this scenario, Kateregga concludes: "It is our sincere belief as Muslims that Satan (*Iblis*) has been at the source and center of evil even before the creation of Adam, the first human being in history." So "Satan is the power and source of evil. Satan was the first creature to disobey and lead a rebellion against God."[18]

Since Satan's activities are particularly connected to his role as the chief deceiver of humankind (35:5; 4:120), and leading humankind astray from the straight path of God's will, it is necessary now to focus on the Muslim doctrine of human beings, who are the climax of God's creation.

THE CREATION OF HUMAN BEINGS

The creation of the human race is a fundamental Islamic belief. The origin and nature of human beings on earth are key to understanding their role in God's plan. The Qur'an affirms that Adam was the first human being whom God created. The first man is said to have been created in heaven and was expelled to the earth after his "fall." Some contemporary Muslim writers are hesitant to admit the historicity of Adam. Even the conservative writer, Ajijola, shys away from a dogmatic stand by suggesting that "[Adam] may *probably* be the first man and the progenitor of the human race."[19] However, most orthodox Muslims still hold to the traditional view that Adam was the first human being.[20]

God announces his plan of man's creation in this way: "Behold, thy Lord said to the angels: 'I will create A viceregent on earth.' They said: 'Wilt Thou place therein one who will make Mischief therein and shed blood?— Whilst we do celebrate Thy praises And glorify Thy holy (name)?' He said: 'I know what ye know not'" (2:30).

God created Adam from clay. "We created man from sounding clay, From mud moulded into shape" (15:26) and breathed into him his spirit. In 32:9 we read, "But He fashioned him In due proportion, and breathed Into him something of His spirit. And He gave You (the faculties of) hearing And sight and feeling."

Nowhere in the Qur'an are we told about the time and process of Eve's creation as the female companion for Adam. To fill in this gap, the most respected Muslim traditionalists, like Bukhari, cite the saying of the prophet that "Woman has been created from man's rib."[21] However, many students of the Qur'an place Eve's creation after the angelic prostration to Adam, since immediately after the above verses we read in

18. Kateregga and Shenk, 20.
19. Ajijola, 122, emphasis ours.
20. See Niazi, 6.
21. Ibid., 43.

2:35a, "We said, O Adam! dwell thou And thy wife in the Garden And eat of the bountiful things therein."

At the beginning, Adam and Eve were pure and sinless and enjoyed unbroken communion with their Creator. As Kateregga notes:

> At this time our first parents, Adam and Hauwa (Eve), were quite innocent in spiritual and material affairs. They had been placed in a spiritual Garden of innocence and bliss which was not on the earth but in the heavens. They did not know evil. However, as God's *khalifa* [viceregent or representative], they had been endowed, through the spirit of God, with the faculties of knowledge, will, and choice.[22]

HUMAN NATURE

Kateregga warns us that "some modern Muslim scholars believe that the Qur'anic evidence suggests that man has a certain Godlikeness. But the orthodox belief is that man has no Godlikeness." Thus, "God breathing into man His (God's) spirit is believed by some scholars to be the faculty of God—like knowledge and will, which if rightly used gives man superiority over all creation. However, this is not to make God into man, for God is absolutely transcendent over all creation."[23] It is this view that leads Kateregga to caution us even more about the Qur'anic expression that God breathed his spirit into man. He notes that:

> The Christian witness, that man is created in the "image and likeness of God," is not the same as the Muslim witness. Although God breathed into man His spirit . . . for Islam the only Divine quality that was entrusted to man as a result of God's breath was the faculty of knowledge, will, and power of action. If man uses these Divine qualities rightly in understanding God and following His law strictly, then he has nothing to fear in the present or the future, and no sorrow for the past.[24]

After the initial stage of Adam's creation, we encounter the peculiar Qur'anic account of the contest between Adam and the angels, and God's command to the angels to bow down and prostrate themselves before Adam:

> And He taught Adam the nature Of all things; then He placed them Before the angels, and said, "Tell Me The nature of these if ye are right." They said, "Glory to Thee: of knowledge We have none, save what Thou Hast taught us: in truth it is Thou Who art perfect in knowledge and wisdom." He said: "O Adam! tell them Their natures." When he had told them, God said: "Did

22. Kateregga and Shenk, 21.
23. Ibid., 15.
24. Ibid., 100–101.

I not tell you That I know the secrets of heaven And earth, and I know what ye reveal And what ye conceal?" And behold, We said to the angels: "Bow down to Adam" and they bowed down: Not so Iblis: he refused and was haughty: He was of those who reject Faith (2:31–34).

This divine command to the angels to prostrate themselves to Adam has occasioned much discussion among Muslim commentators, since in Islam such a worshipful gesture is due only to God. To avoid such an implication Niazi writes,

> Great commentators like Abdullah Ibn Abbas and Immam Razi regard *Sajda* (prostrating) as synonymous with humility, submission ... and meekness. . . . What God commanded the angels to do was not to throw themselves in prostration as we do in prayer. They were ordered only to bow before Adam. The physical touching of the ground with forehead and hands was not meant. Some scholars think that it was a physical prostration, no doubt, but was of a different character. It was differential prostration, which was permissible under earlier Shariahs ("dispensations"). . . . Some commentators hold that though the angels did bow before Adam, their obeisance in actuality was directed to an higher object. It was done to God Almighty Himself, from whom the command came: Adam only served as Qibla, precisely as the Kaaba does. Prayer is not addressed to that stony structure: it is addressed to the Master of the House.[25]

Niazi adds quickly, "Whichever argument be the weightiest of the three, there should be no hesitation in accepting that God Almighty directed the angels to co-operate with (rather follow) man in the discharge of his duties as the viceroy of God."[26] Whatever their differences, it is sufficient to say that most orthodox Muslims view this account as God's declaration of man's superiority to angels in regard to capacity for learning and growth.[27]

HUMAN SIN

Human beings were created innocent and free but chose to sin against God. Sin, however, is not an irradicable part of human nature. Muslims believe that God forbade Adam and Eve to approach and partake of a particular (though nameless) tree in the Garden. In continuation of the command to enter the Garden, 2:35b says, "but approach not this tree, Or ye turn into harm and transgression." Satan misled Adam and Eve into disobeying their Lord and tasting of the forbidden tree. A conversation had

25. Niazi, 21–23.
26. Ibid.
27. See Kateregga and Shenk, 11.

already taken place between God and Satan, after the latter refused to obey God's command to bow down to Adam (7:12–18):

> (God) said: "What prevented Thee from bowing down When I commanded thee?" He said: "I am better Than he: Thou didst create Me from fire, and him from clay." (God) said: "Get thee down From this: it is not For thee to be arrogant Here: get out, for thou Art of the meanest (of creatures)." He said: "Give me respite Till the day they are Raised up." (God) said: "Be thou Among those who have respite." He said: "Because thou Hast thrown me out Of the Way, lo! I will Lie in wait for them On Thy Straight Way: Then I will assault them From before them and behind them, From their right and their left: Nor wilt Thou find, In most of them, Gratitude (for Thy mercies)." (God) said: "Get out From this, disgraced And expelled. If any Of them follow thee,—Hell will I fill With you all."

Commenting on this event, Fazlur Rahman attempts to explain the situation as follows:

> Iblis or Satan thus appears more cunning and artful than strong, more deceitful and contriving than forthrightly challenging, more beguiling, treacherous, and "waylaying" than giving battle. This is why he shall say on the Day of Judgment to those who will accuse him of leading them astray, "God made you a true promise whereas I made you a false promise. I had no power over you but only invited you [to error] and you accepted my invitation. Do not blame me but [only] yourselves. I cannot help you, nor can you help me" (14:22).

Rahman adds, "His (Satan's) master-stratagem consists in 'embellishing' or 'causing to look attractive' the dross of the world as tinsel, or causing to look burdensome or frightening that which is really fruitful and consequential. . . . Satan made their [evil] deeds look attractive in their eyes" (8:48).[28]

Soon after the entrance of Adam and Eve into the Garden, Satan began his mission of leading humankind astray. Man's first parents were deceived by Satan and were eventually expelled from heaven (7:20–25):

> Then began Satan to whisper Suggestions to them, bringing Openly before their minds All their shame That was hidden from them (Before): he said: "Your Lord Only forbade you this tree, Lest ye should become angels Or such beings as live for ever." And he swore to them Both, that he was Their sincere adviser. So by deceit he brought about Their fall: when they Tasted of the tree, Their shame became manifest To them, and they began To sew together the leaves Of the Garden over their bodies. And their Lord called

28. Rahman, 125.

Unto them: "Did I not Forbid you that tree, And tell you that Satan Was an avowed Enemy unto you?" They said: "Our Lord! We have wronged our own souls: If Thou forgive us not And bestow not upon us Thy Mercy, we shall Certainly be lost." (God) said: "Get ye down, With enmity between yourselves. On earth will be your dwelling-place And your means of livelihood,—For a time." He said: "Therein shall ye Live, and therein shall ye Die; but from it shall ye Be taken out (at last)."[29]

Despite some general similarities to the biblical version of man's fall, there are radical differences between the Christian and the Islamic interpretations of Adam's transgression. Whereas in Christian theology man's disobedience is viewed as a fundamental turning point in his relationship to God, according to the Muslim perspective this was only a single slip on Adam and Eve's part that was completely forgiven after their repentance. It had no further effect on the nature of man and the rest of the creation. Neither does the fact that man was expelled from Paradise to earth (as a direct result of this transgression of divine command) play a significant role in the Islamic anthropology or soteriology. Kateregga writes, "Many Muslims think that Adam and Hauwa were first kept in the Heavenly Garden for a trial of their inclinations before they were to be sent to earth where they had been appointed as *khalifa*."[30] Niazi adds: "Adam's ejectment from the Garden has been interpreted by small-minded people as a sort of punishment." However, "the order 'get ye down' was repeated after pardon had been granted, in order to dispel the notion that the Fall resulted from a sinful act. . . . Adam was created as God's viceroy. . . . He had to have come down to this world to manage it."[31]

Concerning the significant gap between the Christian and Muslim understanding of the "fall," Kateregga writes:

The Christian witness that the rebellion by our first parents has tragically distorted man, and that sinfulness pervades us individually and collectively, is very much contrary to Islamic witness. Islam teaches that the first phase of life on earth did not begin in sin and rebellion against Allah. Although Adam disobeyed Allah, he repented and was forgiven and even given guidance for mankind. Man is not born a sinner and the doctrine of the sinfulness of man has no basis in Islam.[32]

29. It is difficult to understand why according to the Qur'an Satan should tempt man by promising him that he would become like angels or become immortal. Man was certainly created higher than all the angels as the Qur'an itself affirms. And why should man have feared death if he was pure and sinless?

30. Kateregga and Shenk, 17.

31. Niazi, 67–68.

32. Kateregga and Shenk, 101.

Another Muslim author, Faruqi, notes that "in the Islamic view, human beings are no more 'fallen' than they are 'saved.' Because they are not 'fallen,' they have no need of a savior. But because they are not 'saved' either, they need to do good works—and do them ethically— which alone will earn them the desired 'salvation.'" Indeed, "salvation is an improper term, since, to need 'salvation,' one must be in a predicament beyond the hope of ever escaping from it. But men and women are not in that predicament." So "Islam teaches that people are born innocent and remain so until each makes him or herself guilty by a guilty deed. Islam does not believe in 'original sin'; and its scripture interprets Adam's disobedience as his own personal misdeed—a misdeed for which he repented and which God forgave."[33]

Abdalati understands the fall as a "symbolic event," contending that "it tells that the human being is imperfect and ever wanting even if he were to live in paradise. But committing a sin or making a mistake, as Adam and Eve did, does not necessarily deaden the human heart, prevent spiritual reform or stop moral growth." The idea of original sin "has no room in the teachings of Islam. Man, according to the Qur'an (30:30) and to the Prophet, is born in a natural state of purity or *fitrah*." Whatever becomes of man after birth is the result of external influence and intruding factors.[34]

Ajijola claims that the story of man's fall is "highly allegorical." Its purpose is to show "that every man must carry on a struggle with his passions until he acquires the mastery over them." He then suggests that Adam disobeyed the divine commandment "through forgetfulness and not intentionally."[35] Based on the opinion of several Muslim exegetes, Niazi claims that "it is proved that the imperative mood employed in the Quran (referring to God's command of abstaining from the tree) does not necessarily mean that whosoever acts against it is a sinner. It is sometimes an advice which man is expected to follow to his own advantage. The directive given to Adam falls under this category."[36] He even concludes that "Adam had committed no sin" but only made "a mistake"![37] Another Muslim theologian claimed that "to call Adam a sinner or a wayward is unbelief"![38]

This reluctance on the part of Muslim scholars to denounce Adam's act of disobedience as a great evil in the sight of a holy and righteous God stands in sharp contrast to the Christian view of man's fall: that the death

33. Isma'il R. Al-Faruqi, *Islam* (Niles, Ill.: Argus Communications, 1984), 9.
34. Abdalati, 31–32.
35. Ajijola, 130–31.
36. Niazi, 53.
37. Ibid., 66.
38. Ibid., 63.

and condemnation of all human beings (except Christ) find their cause in the rebellion of Adam against the Creator (Rom. 5:12–19). However, once we consider other aspects of Islamic theology, such as the Muslim understanding of sin and prophethood, we begin to realize why Muslim theologians do not draw a great deal of attention to man's fall.[39]

Regarding the Qur'anic references to sin, the European Islamicist, Stanton, writes:

> *Sin*—The principal terms for this are *khati'ah* (Hebrew *khet'*), *ithm* (Hebrew *asham*) and *dhanb*. The last of these occurs thirty-eight times and refers chiefly to ceremonial offenses. *Ithm* occurs twenty-nine times and largely in the same sense. *Khati'ah* occurs only five times. It comes nearest to the idea of sin as a missing of the mark or standard set up by God. The teaching of the Qur'an about sin as such is very sparse. Certain sins, such as pride, covetousness, etc., are denounced on occasion, but the sin which comprehends all others is *shirk* = association, namely, of other deities with Allah. That is unpardonable.[40]

Because of the Qur'an's attitude toward sin, many orthodox Muslim theologians have traditionally adopted a nominalistic view of ethics.[41] An act is not intrinsically right or wrong. It is only right when God specifically declares it to be such according to his will. Since the Qur'an itself does not seem to put much emphasis on the gravity of Adam's transgression, many Muslim theologians have, understandably so, been unwilling to go beyond the Qur'anic pronouncements.

Another important issue involved here is that, according to most Muslims, the prophets of God are either totally sinless or at least protected from major sins or shortcomings (though this theological belief is not based on any explicit statements in the Qur'an). And since in Islam Adam is recognized as the first prophet to humankind, it follows that Adam must have been spared from committing a major sin. We read in 2:38–39, "Get ye down all from here; And if, as is sure, there comes to you Guidance from Me, whosoever Follows My guidance, on them Shall be no fear, nor shall they grieve." Based on this verse and other traditions from Muhammad, Niazi writes:

> Adam, at a number of places in the Quran and the Traditions, has clearly been mentioned not only as a prophet but as an Apostle also. We have added the word apostle because prophecy means to be a recipient of inspi-

39. See J. Dudley Woodberry, "Different Diagnoses of the Human Condition," in *Muslims and Christians on the Emmaus Road* (Monrovia: MARC, 1989), 149–60.

40. Stanton, 56.

41. See John Alden Williams, *Islam* (New York: George Braziller, 1962), 192–93.

ration only. An apostle, on the other hand is one who is the bearer of Shariah (Law). . . . Adam, as testified by the above verse, was a recipient of
inspiration . . . (also) it shows that Adam was an Apostle, who had also a
shariah of his own. . . . Ibn Al-Kathir also has quoted the following tradition
by Hazrat Abu Zar. "I asked the Messenger of Allah whether Adam was a
prophet. He said: 'Yes a prophet and a messenger. God also talked to him
face to face.'"[42]

Attempting to address this tension in Islamic theology, Kateregga
writes, "Adam having repented was made Allah's first messenger on
earth. He was to show guidance to his children. How could God entrust
such a high office to an evildoer?"[43]

HUMAN PURPOSE

Going beyond the accounts of creation and the origin of humankind,
what does Islam teach about human beings in general? What is man?
What is his purpose? And how does he achieve his highest good? The
Islamic answer is that human beings are finite, mortal creatures, who
have been honored by God to be his representatives and servants on
earth. Even though human beings are not sinful and have no fallen
nature, they are intrinsically weak, frail, imperfect, and constantly forgetful of God.

It should be noted that occasionally "some Muslim theologians have
held to a doctrine of Hereditary Sin. . . . Also, there is a famous tradition
that the Prophet of Islam said, 'No child is born but the devil hath
touched it, except Mary and her son Jesus.'"[44] Further, "Other passages
refer to humankind as sinful (or unjust—*zulum*—14:34/37; 33:72), foolish (33:72), ungrateful (14:34/37), weak (4:28/32), despairing or boastful
(11:9/12–10/13), quarrel-some (16:4), and rebellious (96:6)."[45] The
Qur'an even declares that "if God were to punish Men for their wrong-
doing, He would not leave, on the (earth), A single living creature"
(16:61). Ayatollah Khomeini even went so far as to say, "You should pay
attention and all of us should pay attention [to the fact] that man's calamity is his carnal desires, and this exists in everybody, and is rooted in the
nature of man. Amen!"[46] Nonetheless, the view that sin is inherited has
been rejected by the vast majority of Muslim scholars.

42. Niazi, 7–8.
43. Kateregga and Shenk, 23.
44. Michael Nazir-Ali, *Frontiers in Muslim-Christian Encounter* (Oxford: Regnum
Books, 1987), 165.
45. For an excellent discussion on this subject, see Woodberry, 155.
46. "Islamic Government Does Not Spend for Its Own Grandeur," *Kayhan International,* 4 Sept. 1985, cited by Woodberry, ibid., 159.

According to Kateregga and the majority view in Islam, the Qur'an teaches that "all people are born as true Muslims, innocent, pure, and free (30:30). There is no single act which has warped the human will."[47] This belief seems to be based on a well-known tradition from the prophet that says, "Every infant is born according to the 'Fitra' ('on God's plan'), then his parents make him a Jew or a Christian or a Magian."[48]

Fazlur Rahman comments:

> On the whole, despite the sad accounts of the human record in the Qur'an, its attitude is quite optimistic with regard to the sequel of human endeavor. It also advocates a healthy moral sense rather than the attitude of self-torment and moral frenzy represented, for example, by the teaching of Paul and many Sufis, which require some sort of *savior ex machina*. Given a merciful and just God and the solidarity of character called *taqwa*, human well-being is provided for: "If you avoid the major evils that have been prohibited to you, We shall obliterate [the effects of] occasional and smaller lapses" (4:31).[49]

As God's *khalifa* (trustee on earth), man has received the privilege of being in authority over the rest of the creation. "We made animals subject To you, that ye May be grateful" (22:36). Further, "We have honoured the sons of Adam; provided them with transport on land and sea; given them for sustenance things good and pure; and conferred on them special favours, Above a great part Of Our Creation" (17:70 [see also 7:10]). Commenting on the significance of man's position as *khalifa*, Kateregga writes:

> God has honoured man, His *khalifa*, with the authority over His countless creatures. He has been commissioned to use nature for his own welfare (Qur'an 33:72). As a *khalifa*, he is chosen to cultivate the land and enrich life with knowledge and meaning. Nature is subject to man. . . . Man alone enjoys the right to use nature for his own good in obedience to the Divine commands.[50]

However, it should be noted that this understanding of man as God's steward on earth is a fairly recent concept in Islamic theology.[51] As it was mentioned in the first chapter, by far the most prominent "Qur'anic conception of the relation of the human race to God is dominated by two

47. Kateregga and Shenk, 17–18.
48. Abdul-Haqq, 158.
49. Rahman, 30.
50. Kateregga and Shenk, 12.
51. W. Montgomery Watt, *Islam and Christianity Today* (London: Routledge and Kegan Paul, 1983), 127.

words, *abd* and *rabb*. In relation to God a human being is an *abd* or 'slave', while God is the *rabb*, usually translated 'lord' but perhaps connoting rather something more august such as 'sovereign.'"[52]

Closely related to this image of man as slave and God as the absolute sovereign, is the idea of the limitedness or, according to some orthodox schools, the nonexistence of human freedom. W. Montgomery Watt writes:

> In the Qur'an and in early Muslim thinkers no use was made of the conception of human freedom. A person was regarded as somehow responsible for his acts (or at least some of them), but there was also a deep awareness of the constraints upon human action. Any idea of human freedom, however, would necessarily have implied a rebellion against the status of *abd* or slave with regard to God. Thus freedom could be in no sense an ideal to be striven for, but only a disaster to be avoided.[53]

It is outside the scope of this chapter to explore any further this tension between the doctrine of divine sovereignty and human freedom in Islamic theology (see Chapter 1). The debates continue, but it is sufficient to point out that since almost the very beginning of Islam, the orthodox position has been that God creates human acts or creates the power in the individual to do a particular act, while the human agents only "acquire" or "appropriate" these actions (*kasb*). "The conception implied that an individual had a sufficient degree of responsibility for an act for it to be credited or debited to his account. In this way the justice of God's judgment was preserved."[54]

In regard to the Qur'anic view of man's purpose for existence, we can once again refer to 51:56: "I have only created . . . men that They may serve Me." In 49:13 we read, "O mankind! We created You from a single (pair) Of male and female, And made you into Nations and tribes, that Ye may know each other. . . . Verily The most honoured of you In the sight of God Is (he who is) the most Righteous of you." Another important verse in this context is 21:16: "Not for (idle) sport did We Create the heavens and the earth And all that is between!"

It is generally agreed that according to orthodox Islam, the purpose of man is not to know God and become more conformed to his character, but to understand his will and become more obedient to his commands. This, for example, is the view of the champion of orthodoxy, Ibn Taymia.[55] Of course, in Islam this is not looked on as a deficiency, since

52. Ibid., 125.
53. Ibid., 127.
54. Ibid., 126.
55. See Williams, 206.

the emphasis of the Qur'an is not on revealing who God is but on what he wills, as man's highest calling.

Abdalati writes:

> Man alone is singled out as being endowed with intelligence and the power of making choices. And because man possesses the qualities of intelligence and choice he is invited to submit to the good Will of God and obey His Law. . . . But if he chooses disobedience he will deviate from the Right Path and . . . will incur the displeasure and punishment of the Law-Giver.[56]

An important principle that should be mentioned at this point is the fact that in Islam, as in the Judeo-Christian tradition before it, this life and this world are not the end but a preparation, a testing ground for the hereafter. It is in this context that it becomes significant and purposeful for man to act good and ethically. Abdalati comments:

> Life may be likened to a journey starting from a certain point and ending at a certain destination. It is a transitory stage, an introduction to the Eternal Life in the Hereafter. In this journey man is a traveller and should be concerned with only what is of use to him in the Future Life. . . . He should do all the good he can and make himself fully prepared to move any minute to Eternity. . . . The best use of life, therefore, is to live it according to the teachings of God and to make it a safe passage to the Future Life of Eternity. Because life is so important as a means to an ultimate end, Islam has laid down a complete system of regulations and principles to show man how to live it, what to take and what to leave, what to do and what to shun, and so on.[57]

Human beings can achieve their ultimate good by obeying the regulations of divine commands as prescribed in the Qur'an (see Chapter 6).

It is appropriate to conclude this section with Kateregga's analysis of humankind's situation:

> Good as man may be, he still cannot measure up to the goodness and perfection of Allah, his Creator. History has shown that man is negligent, careless, and forgetful. He is good, but imperfect. Being imperfect, he needs constant reminding. That is why God sent His prophets and messengers to help man achieve perfection. Through the prophets, God has repeatedly reminded man of the Law of God. . . . Man has to be reminded constantly of the right path through prophets and revelation.[58]

56. Abdalati, 9.
57. Ibid., 29.
58. Kateregga and Shenk, 16–18.

SUMMARY

Creation is a fundamental teaching in Islamic monotheism. God is Creator of heaven and earth. He created not only the physical universe, but also spiritual beings such as angels and *jinn*. God created humankind innocent, but they have made choices to their own detriment. Nevertheless, human beings are not essentially evil, but basically good. They are finite, mortal creatures, who are honored by God to be his representatives and servants on earth. Even though human beings are not essentially sinful and have no fallen nature, they are intrinsically weak, frail, imperfect, and constantly forgetful of God. Consequently, God sends them prophets to call them to submit to his sovereign will.

3

PROPHETS

According to Islam, prophets are needed for two basic reasons: (1) humans are frail, and (2) God cares for his creatures. Hence God sends prophets to call people back to himself. Thus, the belief in God's sovereign care for his wayward creation gives rise to the belief in prophets as the bearers of his divine message. This is a natural deduction in Islamic theology. In fact, belief in the prophets and belief in their Scriptures are two of the five doctrinal pillars of Islam (along with belief in God, his angels, and the last day).

In this chapter we will discuss the Muslim understanding of the role and significance of prophets with special focus on Jesus. Since God gave prophets inspired Scripture, we will also look at the Muslim attitude toward various divine scriptures, including the Bible, and the people of other Scriptures such as Jews and Christians.

THE MEANING AND FUNCTION OF PROPHETS

In Islamic theology there are two particular Arabic words that are roughly equivalent to the English word "prophet." The Qur'anic term *rasul* signifies "one who is sent" (the Arabic rendering of the Greek *apostolos*), and the Arabic term *nabi* signifies "one who carries information and proclaims news from God" (this word is identical to the Hebrew *nabi*, prophet). Although these terms are sometimes used interchangeably, many Muslim theologians understand *rasul* to mean one who is sent with a divine Scripture, while *nabi* is one who orally proclaims God's message to a possibly smaller audience and adheres to the Scriptures previously sent.[1]

1. See Kateregga and Shenk, 34; Muhammad Abdul Rauf, *Islam: Creed and Worship* (Washington, D.C.: The Islamic Center, 1974), 5.

The fundamental emphasis in Islam regarding the identity of a prophet is on the fact that he must be a human being. Ajijola writes:

> The prophet, according to the Holy Qur'an, must be a human being, and hence it does not accept the doctrine of incarnation, or God in flesh. The reformation of man is entrusted to men to whom the Divine will is revealed, because only a man could serve as a model for men. . . . How could God in flesh serve as a model for frail human beings who have to meet hundreds of temptations, whereas for God there exists no possible temptation?[2]

Cragg adds a helpful insight when he notes that "it is the insistent requirement of the concept of prophethood in Islam that it must exclude and negate the concept of Incarnation, whereas, as Christians see it, prophethood deepens and climaxes into 'the Incarnate Word.'" Thus, "in Islam, spokesmanship comprehends all that may be done for God in this world."[3]

Besides being a human being, there are other important characteristics that serve as qualifications for being a prophet. Abdalati writes, "All the prophets of God were men of good character and high honor. . . . Their honesty and truthfulness, their intelligence and integrity are beyond doubt. They were infallible in that they did not commit sins or violate the Law of God."[4]

Muslim scholars are of the opinion that prophets are either completely sinless or at least free from all major sins or faults. Some orthodox Muslims claim that even the power of sinning does not exist in prophets. For example, Ibn Khaldun, the classical Muslim scholar (d. 1406), claims that "their characteristic mark is that before the coming of revelation to them they were all found to be naturally good and sagacious, such men as shun blameworthy actions and all things unclean." This, he believes "is the meaning of their impeccability (*isma*). Thus, they seem to have an instinctive inclination to rise above things that are blameworthy, and even shrink from them as though such things were repugnant to their inborn disposition."[5]

As to the purpose of the prophets, the Qur'an and Islamic theology are unequivocal: "To every people (was sent) An Apostle: when their Apostle Comes (before them), the matter Will be judged between them With justice, and they Will not be wronged" (10:47). "For We assuredly sent Amongst every People an apostle, (With the Command), 'Serve God, and eschew Evil'" (16:36). "Raised high above ranks. . . . (He is) the Lord Of the

---

2. Ajijola, 233.
3. Kenneth Cragg, *Jesus and the Muslim* (London: George Allen and Unwin, 1985), 287.
4. Abdalati, 27; see also Rauf, 5.
5. Jeffery, *Islam: Muhammad and His Religion*, 135–36.

Throne (of authority): By His Command doth He Send the spirit (of inspi-ration) To any of His servants He pleases, that it may Warn (men) of the Day Of Mutual Meeting" (40:15).

Two prominent aspects of prophethood are clearly expressed in the above verses. First is the belief that God has raised up an individual in each particular community to warn its people. Second is the Muslim con-viction that every prophet has proclaimed the same basic message, which consists of inviting the people to acknowledge the oneness of God, submit to his Laws, and do good works in view of the hereafter. Kateregga writes:

> Some of Adam's offspring who were righteous followed Allah's teaching, but others drifted into evil activities. They compromised the true guidance by associating Allah with other gods and objects. In order to provide man with firm and constructive guidance, God raised prophets among every people. The fundamental message proclaimed by all prophets was the same. They taught or reminded man of the unity of God, the reward of lead-ing a good, pious, and peaceful life, the day of judgment, and the terrible punishment for unbelievers. All prophets brought this same message (Islam) from Allah.[6]

Rahman confirms this, claiming that "all Messengers have preached essentially the same message, that there is one, unique God to Whom alone service and worship are due."[7] He goes on to note that "different prophets have come to different peoples and nations at different times, but their messages are universal and identical. All these messages ema-nate from a single source: 'The Mother of the Book' (43:4; 13:39)."[8]

In agreement with the above views, Abdalati argues that "because Islam means submission to the Good Will of God and obedience to His Beneficial Law, and because this is the essence of the message of all God-chosen messengers, a Muslim accepts all the prophets previous to Muhammad without discrimination." Thus, "he believes that all those prophets . . . were Muslims, and that their religion was Islam, the only true universal religion of God."[9]

Besides this particular mission that is shared by all prophets, classi-cal Islamic theology has assigned other functions to the coming of mes-sengers. This was summed up well by one medieval Muslim scholar who writes:

> The Apostle may come: 1) to impose a new Law and to abrogate what pre-ceded it; 2) to confirm a preceding Law in part and to abrogate it in part; 3)

---

6. Kateregga and Shenk, 36.
7. Rahman, 83.
8. Ibid., 163.
9. Abdalati, 9.

to summon men to observe the Law of his predecessor; 4) to impose the simple profession of God's unity and the acknowledgement of his own prophethood; 5) to impose that and also the observance of additional legal practices and positive ordinances; 6) to incite men to the observance of the Law of a Prophet who is his contemporary.[10]

WHO ARE THE PROPHETS?

Who are these individuals whom Muslims have acknowledged as God's prophets throughout history? The exact number of prophets is not stated in the Qur'an (40:78), but is based on the belief that every community has had a messenger. Muslim tradition has put the number at 124,000. Interestingly, most of the prophets mentioned in the Qur'an are biblical characters. For example, in 6:84–86, after recounting the story of Abraham, God declares: "We gave him Isaac And Jacob: all (three) We guided: And before him We guided Noah, And among his progeny, David, Solomon, Job, Joseph, Moses, and Aaron: Thus do We reward Those who do good: And Zakariya and John, And Jesus and Elias: All in the ranks Of the Righteous: And Ismail and Elisha, And Jonas, and Lot."

Another similar list in 4:163–65 reads:

> We have sent thee inspiration, as We sent it to Noah and the Messengers after him: We sent inspiration to Abraham, Ismail, Isaac, Jacob and the Tribes, to Jesus, Job, Jonah, Aaron, and Solomon, and to David We gave the Psalms. Of some apostles We have already told thee the story; of others we have not;—and to Moses God spoke direct;—Apostles who gave good news as well as warning, that mankind, after (the coming) of the Apostles, should have no plea against God.

Besides the above names, several other prophets are also mentioned by name in the Qur'an: Adam, Hud, Salih, Idris, Luqman, Dhul-qarnain, Shu'aib, Dhu'l-Kifl, Uzair, and finally Muhammad, the Seal of prophethood. Due to the ambiguity of some Qur'anic passages, some students of the Qur'an believe twenty-eight prophets are mentioned by name,[11] but others accept only twenty-five of these names as referring to prophets.[12]

Also with the exception of Adam and Uzair (Ezra), the rest of the names have no clear correspondence to biblical characters. Some scholars try to identify all these names with a biblical character,[13] but most

10. Al-Baqillani, *Miracle and Magic*, ed. Richard J. McCarthy (Place de l'Etoile: Librairie Orientale, n.d.), 17.

11. See Ajijola, 119.

12. See Rauf, 8; Kateregga and Shenk, 35.

13. Geoffrey Parrinder, *Jesus in the Qur'an* (New York: Oxford University Press, 1977), 40.

acknowledge that several of the names probably refer to Arabian prophets and reformers of the neighboring vicinities.

It is beyond the scope of this chapter to discuss in detail the many Qur'anic passages that retell several Old Testament stories, either based directly on Old Testament narratives or adopted from the Jewish apocrypha. However, no less than eight chapter headings in the Qur'an recall characters of the Old and New Testaments. The sura of Joseph (Jacob's son) is the longest narrative in the Qur'an. Moses is the most frequently mentioned prophet in the Qur'an. David and Solomon receive no less than thirty-three mentions, and the story of Noah appears some thirty times.[14]

Among the prophets, five are recognized to be in the highest rank and are given the title of *ulu'l-'Azm* (people of the determination or perseverance). They are: Muhammad (the apostle of God), Noah (the preacher of God), Abraham (the friend of God), Moses (the speaker with God), and Jesus (the word of God).[15] Some also include Adam (the chosen of God) as the sixth person in the list. Based on the evidence in the Qur'an alone it is safe to say that Abraham appears to occupy the highest position among the prophets. As Muhammad's relationship with Jews and Christians deteriorated, he went beyond the figures of Jesus and Moses back to Abraham. In this way he hoped to show the superiority of Islam by appealing directly to Abraham as the father of Muslims. As the Qur'an states, "Abraham was not a Jew Nor yet a Christian; But he was true in Faith, And bowed his will to God's, [Which is Islam]" (3:67). However, in Islamic theology, it is Muhammad who is the greatest and the last of all prophets. It is also believed that each one of these apostles brought a divine scripture, but Muslims believe the books revealed to Noah and Abraham are no longer in existence.

THE MESSAGE OF THE PROPHETS

Even though many of the details of the stories of prophets are quite different from their biblical version, the theme of most Qur'anic stories is almost identical. The underlying message is that throughout history God has raised from each people a prophet or messenger. The prophet invites his people to worship the One and true God (often vindicating the truthfulness of his mission by accomplishing many miraculous deeds). Usually, however, the majority refuse to listen to him and bring upon themselves the divine judgments of flood, fire, or earthquake, while the faithful few are spared and rewarded.

14. Charis Waddy, *The Muslim Mind* (London/New York: Longman, 1976), 17.
15. See Rauf, 8.

The unity of the prophets' mission and message plays an important role in Islamic theology. Beginning with Adam as the first prophet and ending with Muhammad as the last, all prophets form an unbreakable chain. Throughout all ages they have preached the same fundamental message from God: submission to the divine will, which is the very meaning of the word "Islam." For example, in 2:136 we read, "Say ye: 'We believe In God, and the revelation Given to us, and to Abraham, Isma'il, Isaac, Jacob, And the Tribes, and that given To Moses and Jesus, and that given To (all) Prophets from their Lord: We make no difference Between one and another of them: And we bow to God (in Islam)'" (also see 2:132; 5:114).

TENSION BETWEEN ISLAM AND OTHER RELIGIONS

Islamic belief in divine prophets has brought it in tension with other faiths since almost the very beginning of Muhammad's mission in Arabia. Theoretically, all revealed religions should be compatible since they all find their source in one God. But in reality it has always been apparent to many that there exist grave differences among the great world religions. Faruqi gives a typical analysis of this situation from an Islamic perspective:

> If all prophets have conveyed one and the same message, whence come all the religions of history? Assuming that they are genuine, Islam answers that there can be no difference in the messages of the prophets since their source is one, namely, God. . . . But Islam asserts that variations of space and time, acculturation by alien influences, and human whims and passions caused people to slip from the truth. The result was that the religions of history all erred more or less from the truth because none has preserved the original text of its revelation.[16]

Another scholar on Islam voices a similar analysis when he notes that "in the Muslim view there is one primordial religion which has existed from the beginnings of humanity. . . . The differences between religions are due not so much to difference in revelation as to specific historical factors and in particular to the different people's distortions of their prophets' fundamentally identical teachings."[17]

Because Islam eventually claimed messages from God that were contrary to other communities of faith, such as Jews and Christians, it was inevitable that there would be a conflict with them. This is not true of

16. Al-Faruqi, *Islam*, 10.
17. Jacques Waardenburg, "World Religions as Seen in the Light of Islam," in *Islam: Past Influence and Present Challenge*, ed. Alford T. Welch and Pierre Cachia (New York: State University of New York Press, 1979), 246.

Muhammad's earlier revelations. In the Meccan messages of Muhammad there are positive statements about Jews and Christians. Here the prophet expects a warm welcome from the Arabian Jews and Christians concerning his divine commission and proclamation of God's unity. However, as time went on and Muhammad was rejected by the majority of Jews and Christians as an imposter, Muhammad's attitude toward these people shifted dramatically. And the change in his disposition becomes clearly reflected not only in the later verses of the Qur'an and his treatment of the Jews, but also to a great extent in Islamic theology and culture. Indeed, it is from this that a Jihad (Holy War) emerges (see Chapter 8).

In the Meccan and even some early Medinan revelations, we can detect a very friendly attitude toward Jews and Christians: "Those who believe (in the Qur'an), And those who follow the Jewish (scriptures), And the Christians . . . Any who believe in God And the Last Day, And work righteousness, Shall have their reward With their Lord: on them Shall be no fear, nor shall they grieve" (2:62). Also in 29:46 we read, "And dispute ye not With the People of the Book, except with means better . . . But say, 'We believe In the Revelation which has Come down to us and in that Which came down to you.'"

After Muhammad was rejected by Jews and Christians, he took a different attitude toward people of the Book: "O ye who believe! Take not the Jews And the Christians For your friends and protectors: They are but friends and protectors To each other" (5:54). "If anyone desires A religion other than Islam (submission to God), Never will it be accepted Of him; and in the Hereafter He will be in the ranks Of those who have lost (All spiritual good)" (3:85). Of course, from one passage in the Qur'an it seems that Muhammad felt more fond of Christians than Jews: "Strongest among men in enmity To the Believers wilt thou Find the Jews and Pagans; And nearest among them in love To the Believers wilt thou Find those who say, 'We are Christians'" (5:85). But as Richard Bell points out, "The relationship with the Christians ended as that with the Jews had ended—in war."[18] Thus we read in 9:29, "Fight those who believe not In God . . . Nor acknowledge the Religion Of Truth, (even if they are) Of the People of the Book, Until they pay the *Jizya* With willing submission, And feel themselves subdued."

According to the Qur'an, the reason for such a change of tone toward the people of the book is that the Jews in particular, despite their many blessings from the Lord and the fact that they had received many prophets for their guidance, consistently broke their covenant with their Lord and repeatedly rejected his messengers (4:155–61). In a very graphic illustration we read, "The similitude of those Who were charged With the

18. Bell, 159.

(obligations Of the) Mosaic Law, But subsequently failed In those (obligations), is That of a donkey Which carries huge tomes (But understands them not)" (62:5). One peculiar charge against the Jews is that they called Uzair (Ezra) a son of God (9:30). The specific charge against Christians is that they had blasphemously raised Jesus to equality with God. Furthermore, they divided themselves into various sects, and each sect ignored the light of their own common Scripture. Finally, their rebellion reached its limit when they rejected God's final messenger, even though they secretly felt convicted of the truthfulness of his message (3:110; cf. 45:16–17; 5:14; 57:16).

Because of the Jewish and Christian breach of their covenants with God, the Qur'an claims that God has set aside the former communities of faith (*ummat*) and has now entrusted his commands to his new people, the Muslims. "Ye are the best Of Peoples, evolved For mankind, Enjoining what is right, Forbidding what is wrong, And believing in God" (3:110; cf. 6:89).

Along with this change of opinion regarding the former *ummat*s we can also detect a certain shift (even if not a total rejection) in the Qur'anic pronouncements concerning former Scriptures. For example, in many instances, particularly in the earlier Meccan suras, the Judeo-Christian Scriptures are given such noble titles as "the Book of God," "the Word of God," "a light and guidance to man," "a decision for all matters, and a guidance and mercy," "the lucid Book," "the illumination (*al-furqan*)," "the gospel with its guidance and light, confirming the preceding Law," and "a guidance and warning to those who fear God."[19] Christians are told to look into their own Scriptures to find God's revelation for them (5:50), and even Muhammad himself at one point is exhorted to test the truthfulness of his own message against the contents of the previous divine revelations to Jews and Christians (10:94).

However, on other occasions, especially in the later Medinan suras, the Qur'an gives a less favorable view of the previous Scriptures (especially the Old Testament), mainly due to the alleged distortions imposed on them by the teachers of the Law. The charges against people of the Book and their tampering with their Scriptures include concealing God's Word (2:42; 3:71), verbally distorting the message in their books (3:78; 4:46), not believing in all the parts of their Scriptures (2:85), and not knowing what their own Scriptures really teach (2:78). Even though in their historical contexts most of these charges were directed against the Jews, by implication Muslims have also included the Christians. It is due to these apparent conflicts in the Qur'anic accounts that we find in the history of Islam, and

19. John Takle, "Islam and Christianity," in *Studies in Islamic Law, Religion and Society*, ed. H. S. Bhatia (New Delhi: Deep and Deep Publications, 1989), 217.

even among contemporary Muslims, various contradictory views regarding the Bible, the Jews, and Christians. For instance, the well-known Egyptian reformer, Muhammad Abduh (d. 1905) writes: "The Bible, the New Testament and the Qur'an are three concordant books; religious men study all three and respect them equally. Thus the divine teaching is completed, and the true religion shines across the centuries."[20] Another Muslim author tries to harmonize the three great world religions in this way: "Judaism lays stress on Justice and Right: Christianity, on Love and Charity: Islam, on Brotherhood and Peace. But in the main, the fundamental similarities between the three faiths must not be lost sight of in a meticulous examination of details."[21]

On the other hand, by far the most typical Islamic approach to this subject is characterized by comments of the Muslim apologist, Ajijola. He writes:

> The first five books of the Old Testament do not constitute the original Torah, but parts of the Torah have been mingled up with other narratives written by human beings and the original guidance of the Lord is lost in that quagmire. Similarly the four Gospels of Christ are not the original Gospels as they came from Prophet Jesus ... the original and the fictitious, the Divine and the human are so intermingled that the grain cannot be separated from the chaff. The fact is that the original Word of God is preserved neither with the Jews nor with the Christians. Qur'an, on the other hand, is fully preserved and not a jot or tittle has been changed or left out in it.[22]

The Qur'anic commentator Yusuf Ali shares a similar viewpoint. Regarding the New Testament, he contends that "the *Injil* spoken of by the Qur'an is not the New Testament. It is not the four Gospels now received as canonical by Christians. It is the single Gospel which, Islam teaches, was revealed to Jesus, and which he taught. Fragments of it survive in the received canonical Gospels and in some others of which traces survive."[23]

THE CORRUPTION (*TAHRIF*) OF SCRIPTURE

These charges bring us to the Islamic doctrine of *tahrif,* or corruption of the Judeo-Christian Scriptures. Based on some of the above Qur'anic verses and, more important, exposure to the actual contents of other

20. Emile Dermenghem, *Muhammad and the Islamic Tradition* (Westport: Greenwood Press, Publishers, 1974), 138.
21. See Waddy, 116.
22. Ajijola, 79.
23. David Sox, *The Gospel of Barnabas* (London: George Allen & Unwin, 1984), 33.

Scriptures, Muslim theologians have generally formulated two different responses. According to Nazir-Ali, "the early Muslim commentators (e.g. Al-Tabari and Ar-Razi) comment that the alteration is *tahrif bi'al ma'ni*, a corruption of the meaning of the text without tampering with the text itself. Gradually, the dominant view changed to *tahrif bi'al-lafz*, corruption of the text itself."[24] The Spanish theologians Ibn Hazm and Al-Biruni, along with most Muslims, hold this view.

Another Qur'anic scholar claims that "the biblical Torah was apparently not identical with the pure *tawrat* given as a revelation to Moses, but there was considerable variation in opinion on the question to what extent the former scriptures were corrupted." On the one hand, "Ibn-Hazm, who was the first thinker to consider the problem of *tabdil* systematically, contended . . . that the text itself had been changed or forged (*taghyr*), and he drew attention to immoral stories which had found a place within the corpus." But on the other hand, "Ibn-Khaldun held that the text itself had not been forged but that Jews and Christians had misinterpreted their scripture, especially those texts which predicted or announced the mission of Muhammad and the coming of Islam. Now it depended very much on his particular interpretation of *tabdil* whether a Muslim scholar showed more or less respect for the Bible, and whether and how he could quote from it. Ibn-Hazm, for instance, rejects nearly the whole Old Testament as a forgery, but cheerfully quotes the *tawrat* when bad reports are given of the faith and behaviour of the *Banu Isra'il* as proofs against the Jews and their religion."[25]

In addition to the above charges against the Jews, there have also been several direct charges against Christians and their Scriptures. The accusations are: (1) There has been a change and forgery of textual divine revelation; (2) there have been doctrinal mistakes such as the belief in the incarnation of Christ, the trinity of the Godhead, and the doctrine of original sin; (3) there have been mistakes in religious practices such as the sacraments, use of images, and other church laws.[26]

Also based on the Islamic doctrine of progressive revelation, Muslims claim that the Qur'an fulfills, and even sets aside the previous, less complete revelations. One Muslim theologian echoes this conviction by stating that a Muslim needs to believe in the *tawrat*, the *Zabur* (the Psalms of David), and the *Injil* (Gospel). But he then claims that "according to the most eminent theologians" the books in their present state "have been tampered with," and goes on to say, "It is to be believed that the Qur'an is the noblest of the books. . . . It is the last of the God-given scriptures to

24. Nazir-Ali, 46.
25. Waardenburg, 257.
26. Ibid., 261-63.

come down, it abrogates all the books which preceded it. . . . It is impossible for it to suffer any change or alteration."[27]

Another important debate among Muslim theologians on this point is the question of the eternal destiny of people of the Book. Even though the majority of the average Muslim masses might consider anyone who has been a "good person" worthy of eternal salvation, accounting for all the Qur'anic evidences on this subject has created much uncertainty.

Among orthodox Muslim theologians, Jews and Christians were generally regarded as unbelievers (*kafar*) because of their rejection of Muhammad as a true prophet from God. For example, we notice that even though Tabari (d. 923), the most respected Muslim commentator of all time, distinguishes between the people of the Book and the polytheists (*mushrikun*), and expresses a higher opinion of the former, he clearly declares that the majority of Jews and Christians are in unbelief and transgression because of their refusal to acknowledge Muhammad's truthfulness.[28]

Adding to this complication is the charge against the Christian belief in the divinity of Christ, a belief that amounts to committing the unpardonable sin of *shirk*, and is condemned throughout the Qur'an. The Qur'anic condemnation of Christians is highlighted in 5:75, "They do blaspheme who say: 'God is Christ the son Of Mary. . . . Whoever Joins other gods with God—God will forbid him The Garden, and the Fire Will be his abode.'"

On the other hand, the contemporary Muslim theologian, Fazlur Rahman, goes against "the vast majority of Muslim commentators." He champions the opinion that salvation is not acquired by formally joining the Muslim faith, but as the Qur'an points out, by believing in God and the last day and by doing good deeds.[29] The debate continues and each individual Muslim can take a different side of this issue based on his own understanding of the Qur'anic evidence. Regarding the salvation of other groups such as the Hindus, Buddhists, and Zoroastrians, Muslim opinion varies. Some Muslims view these religions as being originally similar to Islam and from God but no longer true to their origin. Others reject them as false religions from the very beginning.

THE PROPHET JESUS IN ISLAM

No chapter on the Islamic view of prophets can be complete, especially for the Christian reader, without a brief mention of the Muslim

27. Jeffery, 126–28.
28. Peter Antes, "Relations with the Unbelievers in Islamic Theology," in Schimmel and Falaturi, 104–5; see also *Islamochritiana*, 1980, 6, 105-48.
29. See Rahman, 166–67.

understanding of Jesus Christ. Whereas there are some areas of general agreement between the Qur'anic and Old Testament views of prophets (with one major exception being the Islamic claim that they were sinless), there is little substantial correspondence between the Qur'anic and New Testament views of the person of Jesus Christ. According to the Qur'an Jesus was merely a human being who was chosen by God as a prophet and sent for the guidance of the people of Israel.

THE NATURE OF CHRIST

Interestingly, in spite of its emphasis on the humanity of Jesus, in many respects the Qur'an seems to portray Jesus as a unique prophet in history. Jesus is mentioned in ninety-three verses of fifteen suras, a total of ninety-seven times (although in most cases quite briefly and only as a name in the prophetic list). He is recognized as a great Hebrew prophet, and only his name along with Abraham's, appears in every list of prophets. The Qur'an gives Jesus such honorary titles as the "Messiah" (used eleven times), "the Word of God," and "the Spirit of God" (4:169–71), "the Speech of Truth" (19:34–35), a "Sign unto men," and "Mercy from (God)" (19:21).

We must note that even though the above titles and activities have much significance in Christian theology, as they relate to the divine character of Christ, "to the Muslim they lack entirely the content of deity."[30] Many Christian writers have tried to read too much into these passages in their attempts to prove certain biblical doctrines from the text of the Qur'an.[31] But if we are to do justice to the Qur'anic text, we ought to let Islamic theology speak for itself in determining the significance of the above titles.[32] As one scholar on Islam warns:

> It is primarily Christian missionaries, or certain Orientalists who are either themselves theologians, or who are well disposed to Christian theology, who overestimate the role of Jesus in the Koran. They are misled by the way of understanding Jesus which they retain from their Christian Tradition. It is no surprise that, under such circumstances, they arrive at false conclusions and evaluations.[33]

So what exactly is this Qur'anic picture of Jesus? And what role, if any, does Jesus play in the Muslim awareness? Despite the fact that the account of Jesus' life is filled with extraordinary miracles, and the titles for Jesus are very complimentary, the Qur'anic verdict concerning his

30. Takle, 218.
31. Abdul-Haqq, 67–68.
32. See Cragg, 32–33.
33. Smail Balic, "The Image of Jesus in Contemporary Islamic Theology," in Schimmel and Falaturi, 3.

identity is clearly summarized in 5:75, "Christ the son of Mary Was no more than An Apostle; many were The apostles that passed away Before him. His mother Was a woman of truth. They had both to eat Their (daily) food."

This attitude is also expressed by Kateregga. He writes, "Muslims do respect the Messiah, Jesus, profoundly, but they do not believe that he is, therefore, superior to all prophets. In fact, the Qur'an affirms that Jesus foretold the coming of the Seal of the Prophets [Muhammad]."[34]

Furthermore, both the Qur'an and the universal opinion of Muslims vehemently insist that Jesus is not the divine Son of God. The Qur'an is filled with verses that speak against the idea of God begetting a son. In 19:35 we read, "It is not befitting To (the majesty of) God That He should beget A son. Glory be to Him! When He determines A matter, He only says To it, 'Be,' and it is." And in 10:68 we read, "They say, 'God hath begotten A son'—Glory be to Him! He is self-sufficient. . . . No warrant Have ye for this! Say ye About God what ye know not?" In another instance we are specifically told that the creation of Jesus was similar to Adam, by the fact that both were created by God's command (3:59).

Besides the Qur'anic charge that the idea of God begetting a son is against the truth of God's majesty and glory, it seems that the Qur'an and Muslims have generally understood the idea of a begotten Son of God quite literally. In 72:3 we read, "And exalted is the Majesty Of our Lord: He has Taken neither a wife Nor a son." Commenting on this verse, Yusuf Ali observes that Islam denies "the doctrine of a son begotten by God, which would also imply a wife of whom he was begotten."[35] And reasoning from this physical understanding of sonship, the world-renowned Muslim apologist, Ahmad Deedat, argues, "If Jesus is God, and the very Son of God because He has no earthly father, then Adam is a greater God, because he had no father and no mother! Simple, basic common sense demands this deduction."[36]

The Qur'an affirms the virgin birth (19:16–21; 3:37–45) and Jesus' many miraculous acts recorded in the New Testament, such as his healings and raising people from the dead. It also refers to miracles of Jesus recorded in the New Testament apocryphal books, such as creating live birds from clay and speaking as a newborn infant in his cradle proclaiming his prophethood (19:29–31; 5:113). In addition the Qur'an affirms that God "raised him up" to heaven (4:158).[37]

---

34. Kateregga, 47.
35. Yusuf Ali, 1625.
36. Anis A. Shorrosh, *Islam Revealed* (Nashville: Thomas Nelson, 1988), 266.
37. For an excellent work on all the Qur'anic references to Jesus, see Parrinder.

In addition to these Qur'anic accounts, we also see a reverential treatment of Jesus in Islamic tradition. In one hadith from Bukhari we read that the prophet Muhammad said, "Whoever believes there is no god but God, alone without partner, that Muhammad is His messenger, that Jesus is the servant and messenger of God, His word breathed into Mary and a spirit emanating from Him . . . shall be received by God into Heaven."[38] And again according to Bukhari, we are told that on another occasion the prophet said, "I am nearest of men to the Son of Mary. Between Jesus and me there has been no prophet."[39] There is also a strong prophetic tradition that every child born in the world has been struck by the devil except Jesus (some accounts also add Mary).

However, it is a mistake to think that based on the above passages we can entertain the thought that Islam portrays Christ as someone more than a mere prophet. For example, regarding the Islamic understanding of the virgin birth, Cragg insightfully comments:

> The fascinating situation in Islam is that virgin birth stands alone, does not serve, or effectuate, Incarnation, indeed, quite excludes it. Mary is understood as the virgin mother of the prophet Isa. She gives birth to him without human intervention in order that he and she may be 'signs' and that his prophethood . . . may enter the world. [40]

CHRIST'S MISSION

Many Muslims believe that Jesus' ministry was limited to the nation of Israel, and his revelation was basically one of confirmation and revision of the Mosaic covenant (5:46–47). For example, Yusuf Ali, in his commentary to the Qur'an, states, "The mission of some of the apostles, like Jesus, was different—less wide in scope than that of Mustafa (Muhammad)."[41]

Of the actual content of Jesus' life and message we are given little information in the Qur'an. What we are told is that he was given the gospel by God as guidance for his people, invited people to worship one God (5:72), permitted the Jews to do certain things that were forbidden by the previous law, and performed many miracles for his disciples and the people around him. In agreement with this judgment, Cragg writes:

> The immediate impression on the general reader from what the Qur'an has to tell him about Jesus is that of its brevity. . . . It is further surprising that within the limits of some ninety verses in all no less than sixty-four belong

38. *Understanding Islam and the Muslims,* prepared by the Islamic Affairs Dept., The Embassy of Saudi Arabia, Washington, D.C., no date.
39. See Parrinder, 39.
40. See Cragg, 67.
41. Yusuf Ali, 96.

to the extended, and partly duplicate, nativity stories. . . . This leaves a bare twenty-six or so verses to present the rest and some reiteration here reduces the total still further. It has often been observed that the New Testament Gospels are really passion narratives with extended introduction. It could well be said that the Jesus cycle in the Qur'an is nativity narratives with attenuated sequel.[42]

Cragg goes on to say that the idea that "Jesus had a specific—some would say a limited—mission to Jewry is stressed in the Qur'an. Only Muhammad as the 'seal of the prophets' belongs to all times and places." Thus, "the 'universality' which Christianity is alleged to have 'read into' Jesus, violating this more explicitly Jewish vocation, is seen as part of that de-Semiticisation of Jesus' Gospel, which is . . . attributed to the early Gentile Church."[43]

CHRIST'S DEATH

Besides the fundamental Muslim and Christian disagreement concerning the person and mission of Jesus Christ, there is also the centuries-long debate about the Qur'anic denial of Jesus' crucifixion. In a context in which the Qur'an is strongly condemning the Jews for repeatedly breaching their covenant with their God, we come upon a highly controversial account in 4:157–59:

> That they said (in boast), 'We killed Christ Jesus The son of Mary, The Apostle of God';—But they killed him not, Nor crucified him, But so it was made To appear to them, And those who differ Therein are full of doubts, With no (certain) knowledge, But only conjecture to follow, For of a surety They killed him not:— Nay, God raised him up Unto Himself; and God Is Exalted in Power, Wise;—And there is none Of the People of the Book But must believe in him Before his death; And on the Day of Judgment He will be a witness against them.

Commenting on the above passage, Yusuf Ali writes: "The end of the life of Jesus on earth is as much involved in mystery as his birth. . . . The Orthodox Christian Churches make it a cardinal point of their doctrine that his life was taken on the Cross, that he died and was buried, that on the third day he rose in the body. . . . The Quranic teaching is that Christ was not crucified nor killed by the Jews, notwithstanding certain apparent circumstances which produced that illusion in the minds of some of his enemies; that disputations, doubts and conjectures on such matters are vain; and that he was taken up to God."[44]

42. Cragg, 25–26.
43. Ibid., 27.
44. Yusuf Ali, 230.

There are various speculations among Muslim commentators regarding the last hours of Jesus' life on earth. Based on the phrase that "it was made to appear to them," orthodox Muslims have traditionally interpreted this to mean that Jesus was not crucified on the cross, but that God made someone else look like Jesus and this person was mistakenly crucified as Christ. And the words "God raised him up unto Himself" have often been taken to mean that Jesus was taken up alive to heaven without dying.

As to the identity of this "substitute" and the question of how this substitute was changed into the likeness of Jesus, Muslim commentators are not in agreement. Candidates for this individual have ranged from Judas to Pilate to Simon of Cyrene or one of Jesus' close disciples. Some have claimed that one of the disciples volunteered to take upon himself the likeness of Jesus so his master could escape the Jews, but others have insisted that God cast Jesus' likeness on one of Jesus' enemies.[45] One example is the view of Baidawi, the learned thirteenth-century jurist and exegete whose commentary has been regarded by Sunni Muslims almost as a holy book:

> It is related that a group of Jews reviled Isa |Jesus| . . . then the Jews gathered to kill him. Whereupon Allah informed him that he would take him up to heaven. Then Isa said to his disciples, "Which one of you is willing to have my likeness cast upon him, and be killed and crucified and enter Paradise?" One of them accepted, and Allah cast the likeness of Isa upon him, and he was killed and crucified. It is said also that he was one who acted the hypocrite toward Isa, and went out to lead the Jews to him. But Allah cast the likeness of Isa upon him, and he was taken and crucified and killed.[46]

The view that Judas replaced Christ on the cross was again recently popularized in the Muslim world by *The Gospel of Barnabas* (see Appendix 3). Regarding the question of what then happened to Jesus himself, Muslims usually contend that Jesus escaped the cross by being taken up to heaven and that one day he will come back to earth and play a central role in the future events. Based on some of the alleged sayings of Muhammad it is believed that just before the end of time Jesus will come back to earth, kill the Antichrist (*al-Dajjal*), kill all pigs, break the cross, destroy the synagogues and churches, establish the religion of Islam, live for forty years, and then will be buried in the city of Medina beside the prophet Muhammad.[47]

Of course we need to point out that even though these views have been held by orthodox Islam throughout the centuries, some Muslim thinkers

45. See Sox, Chapter 6; Parrinder, 108–11.
46. See Sox, 96.
47. See ibid., 116–17. Also see our discussion of this point in Chapter 6.

today are beginning to distance themselves from such theological expressions (although this trend still does not apply to the traditionalist Muslim camps or the average masses). The well-respected Egyptian writer, Hussein Haykal, writes:

> The idea of a substitute for Christ is a very crude way of explaining the Quranic text. They had to explain a lot to the masses. No cultured Muslim believes in this nowadays. The text is taken to mean that the Jews thought they killed Christ but God raised him unto Him in a way we can leave unexplained among the several mysteries we have taken for granted on faith alone.[48]

Several Qur'anic verses speak or hint about the death of Christ (2:87; 3:55; 4:157–58; 19:33). Thus, several Muslim groups today believe that 4:157–59, if taken within the total Qur'anic context, must be understood to say that it was Jesus who was tortured on the cross, but that he did not die there. This is in contradistinction to the traditional view of the more ambiguous verses, which suggest that Jesus' death must be referring to his second coming. The explanation adopted by this view is usually a version of the swoon theory. The major adherents of this view are the Ahmadiyyas (originating in Pakistan), a highly active Islamic group in the West, who are often considered by orthodox Muslims to be a heretical sect (see Appendix 1). This particular group also believes that Jesus eventually died in India, and that his grave is still there today.

The great majority of Muslims believe that Jesus did not die on the cross but that he was taken up bodily into heaven. This they base on the Qur'anic passage that declares: "Behold! God said: 'O Jesus! I will take thee And raise thee to Myself'" (3:55).[49]

It might seem perplexing as to why the Qur'an should deny the death of Christ, an event that is considered by the great majority of humankind as an uncontested fact of history. Sir Norman Anderson explains the Qur'anic motivation for this denial:

> The rationale of this is that the Qur'an regularly reports that earlier prophets had at first encountered resistance, unbelief, antagonism and persecution; but finally the prophets had been vindicated and their opponents put to shame. God had intervened on their behalf. So Jesus, accepted in the Qur'an as one of the greatest of the prophets . . . could not have been left to

48. See Haykal's *City of Wrong*, 222, taken from Parrinder, 112.
49. Contrary to the majority view, the late rector of Al-Azhar University in Cairo in 1942 denied the bodily ascension of Christ by claiming that neither the Qur'an nor the sacred traditions of the Prophet in any way "authorize the correctness of the belief . . . that Jesus was taken up to the heaven with his body, and is alive there even now, and would descend therefrom in the latter days" (Parrinder, 124).

his enemies. Instead, God must have intervened and frustrated their evil purpose. Muhammad, as himself a prophet—even the 'seal' of prophets—had a personal interest in the certainty of divine succour. If Messiah ʿĪsā had been allowed to die in this cruel and shameful way, then God himself must have failed—which was an impossible thought.[50]

CONCLUSION

In the final section of this chapter we focused our attention on the Muslim view of Jesus, mainly because of its importance for the Christian reader. However, it is of utmost importance that when speaking of prophets, we should focus on the one whom Muslims believe is the last and greatest prophet, Muhammad. Belief in the prophethood of Muhammad is the second part of the Islamic *shahada*, "There is no god but Allah, and Muhammad is His prophet." Furthermore, according to the Muslim understanding of the prophets' roles in history, all the prophets prior to the advent of Muhammad were limited in their mission. Since their teachings have either been completely lost or severely corrupted, and because their revelations were partial and incomplete,[51] it becomes absolutely necessary for us to understand how, according to Islam, Muhammad fulfills and completes the office of prophet. Therefore, it is necessary to turn our attention to a historical study of the person of Muhammad and his significant role in Islamic theology.

50. Norman Anderson, *Islam in the Modern World* (Leicester: Apollos, 1990), 219.
51. See Ajijola, 117–18.

4

MUHAMMAD

Islam cannot be understood without considering the role of the prophet Muhammad. He is important both for the inception of Islam as a major world religion, and the shaping of Islamic theology and civilization for the past fourteen centuries. It is because of his great significance that we devote this chapter to a study of Muhammad. First, we will look at the life and career of Muhammad in seventh-century Arabia. Then we will focus on his impact and place in Islamic culture and theology.

MUHAMMAD'S LIFE

BIRTH AND YOUTH

We have very little reliable historical information about Muhammad's birth and formative years as a Meccan youth. However, this much we know: He was born into the Hashim family of the powerful tribe of Quraysh around A.D. 570 in Mecca, a great city of commerce in the Arabian peninsula. Muhammad's father, Abdullah, passed away before his son's birth, and his mother, Amina, died when he was only six years old. At the age of eight Muhammad lost his influential grandfather, Abd al-Muttalib, who had been taking care of him since his birth. He was then put under the care of his loving uncle, Abu Talib.

According to legend, a host of angels joyously attended his birth.[1] As soon as the infant was born, he fell to the ground, took a handful of dust and gazed toward heaven, proclaiming, "God is Great." He was born

---

1. Annemarie Schimmel, *And Muhammad Is His Messenger: The Veneration of the Prophet in Islamic Piety* (Chapel Hill: The University of North Carolina Press, 1985), 150–51.

clean, circumcised, with his navel cord already cut.[2] Many other global signs are said to have followed this event, such as the appearance of a light that illuminated the palaces of Bostra in Syria,[3] and the flooding of a lake that "caused the palace of Khosroes (the King of Persia) to crack, and the fire of Zoroastrians to die out."[4]

Even though Muhammad was part of a noble and prosperous family, it appears that at the time the household of Abu Talib was somewhat poverty-stricken; the young Muhammad had to earn his own livelihood by serving as a shepherd boy and trader. One important incident recounted in all his biographies relates to a business trip that the young child (around the age of twelve) took with his uncle's caravan to Syria. It is said that a Syrian monk by the name of Buhaira recognized the young Muhammad as the coming final prophet who had been prophesied about in all the previous Scriptures. He then advised Muhammad's uncle to "guard him carefully against the Jews, for by Allah! if they see him, and know about him what I know, they will do him evil."[5]

Overall, what we can gather from Islamic sources is that Muhammad, though orphaned, lived a relatively normal childhood. As Haykal comments, "Muhammad grew like any other child would in the city of Makkah."[6] Of course, according to Islamic tradition one major exception in the case of Muhammad is the fact that he was spared from participating in the pagan activities of Meccan life.[7] He was also known to be sincere and honest and his title even before his call to prophethood was Al-Amin, the faithful one.

MARRIAGE AND ADULT LIFE

At the age of twenty-five, after conducting a successful caravan trade to Syria for a wealthy widow by the name of Khadija, Muhammad accepted Khadija's offer to marry her. Despite the fact that she was fifteen years his senior, the marriage proved to be a happy one for both. The couple had two sons who died in infancy, and four daughters. Almost nothing is known about this stage of Muhammad's adult life except that it seems his good reputation and respect constantly grew among his people.

2. Tor Andrae, *Mohammed, the Man and his Faith,* trans. Theophil Menzel (New York: Harper & Row, Publishers, 1955), 35; Ali Dashti, *Twenty Three Years* (London: George Allen & Unwin, 1985), 2.

3. See Schimmel, 150–51.

4. Mahmud, 39.

5. Ibn Ishaq, *Sirat Rasul Allah* [*The Life of Muhammad*], trans. A. Guillaume (New York: Oxford University Press, 1980), 81.

6. Muhammad Husayn Haykal, *The Life of Muhammad* (North American Trust Publications, 1976), 55.

7. Ibid., 59.

It is during this time period that many have speculated Muhammad grew more and more discontent with the paganism and idolatry of his society. This was not unique since several other prominent citizens of Mecca at that time had already denounced the paganism of their homeland and declared their faith in the one true God, including Jews and Christians.[8] In accordance with the custom of the pious souls, Muhammad began the practice of devoting "a period of each year to a retreat of worship, asceticism, and prayer."[9] Some say he would spend the whole month of Ramadan in a cave on Mount Hira two miles north of the city of Mecca, living on meager rations and meditating in peace and solitude.[10]

PROPHETIC CALL

After years of meditation in solitude, finally in the year A.D. 610, when Muhammad was forty years of age, he believed that he received his prophetic call from God through the angel Gabriel. Ibn Ishaq, the earliest biographer of Muhammad, relates the story in the following way:

> When it was the night on which God honoured him with his mission and showed mercy on His servants thereby, Gabriel brought him the command of God. 'He came to me,' said the apostle of God, 'while I was asleep, with a coverlet of brocade whereon was some writing, and said, "Read!" I said, "What shall I read?" He pressed me with it so tightly that I thought it was death; then he let me go and said, "Read!" I said, "What shall I read?" He pressed me with it again so that I thought it was death; then he let me go and said "Read!" I said, "What shall I read?" He pressed me with it the third time so that I thought it was death and said "Read!" I said, "What then shall I read?"—and this I said only to deliver myself from him, lest he should do the same to me again. He said: "Read in the name of thy Lord who created, Who created man of blood coagulated. Read! Thy Lord is the most beneficent, Who taught by the pen, Taught that which they knew not unto men"[96:1–5]. So I read it, and he departed from me. And I awoke from my sleep, and it was as though these words were written on my heart.'[11]

There are conflicting opinions among Muslim historians about several of the details of the above account.[12] However, this appears to be the most accepted version of the beginning of Muhammad's prophetic career.

---

8. Three of these individuals later became Christians. See Haykal, 67–68.

9. See Haykal, 70.

10. Many Western historians of Islam see this practice as a result of the influence of the Syrian Christian monks.

11. Ibn Ishaq, 106.

12. See Andrae, 44–47; and Jeffery, *Islam, Muhammad and His Religion*, 15–21.

At first Muhammad was deathly afraid of the source of his newly found revelation, believing that he was possessed by a *jinn* or evil spirit. But he found in Khadija a great source of comfort and encouragement. Khadija is also said to have relayed this incident to her Christian cousin Waraqah, who upon hearing her descriptions reassured her that Muhammad's source of revelation was the same as that of Moses, and that he too would be a prophet of his nation. Ibn Ishaq relays the following account:

> And I came to Khadija and sat by her thigh and drew close to her. She said, "O Abu'l-Qasim [Muhammad], where has thou been?" . . . I said to her, "Woe is me poet or possessed." She said, "I take refuge in God from that. . . . God would not treat you thus. . . . This cannot be, my dear. Perhaps you did see something." "Yes, I did," I said. Then I told her of what I had seen; and she said, "Rejoice, O son of my uncle, and be of good heart. Verily, by Him in whose hand is Khadija's soul, I have hope that thou wilt be the prophet of this people." Then she rose and gathered her garments about her and set forth to her cousin Waraqa B. Naufal . . . who had become a Christian and read the scriptures and learned from those that follow the Torah and the Gospel. And when she related to him what the apostle of God told her he had seen and heard, Waraqa cried, "Holy! Holy! Verily by Him in whose hand is Waraqa's soul, if thou has spoken to me the truth . . . he is the prophet of this people."[13]

After the advent of the first revelation came a long interval of silence that, according to some accounts, lasted about three years. Once again Muhammad sank into the depths of despair, feeling forsaken by God and even entertaining thoughts of suicide. But this interlude also passed and the prophet resumed receiving the messages from the angel.

Muhammad began his ministry by preaching his mission—first among his friends and relatives secretly, and thereafter publicly in the city. He called this new faith Islam (submission) and claimed that he was merely a warner to his people. His basic message consisted of belief in the one sovereign God, resurrection and the last judgment, and the practicing of charity to the poor and the orphans. Among his first converts were his loyal wife Khadija, his cousin Ali, his adopted son Zaid, and his lifelong faithful companion Abu Bakr.

THE PEOPLE'S RESPONSE

Even though Muhammad was gradually attracting a small group of followers, most of whom were young and of no great social standing, the great majority of the powerful and influential Meccans opposed this new

13. See Ibn Ishaq, 106–7. For the account of Muhammad's original revelation and his subsequent doubt and reassurance, also see Al-Bukhari, vol. 1., 2–4.

self-proclaimed prophet. The opposition grew from indifference to hostility against the new faith. Several factors were involved in the dynamics of this antagonistic relationship.

On a religious level the powerful Meccans resisted Muhammad's doctrine of God's oneness, since it went against their belief in the power of idols, gods, and goddesses. Some modern historians believe that the Meccans of Muhammad's time no longer had an active faith in their own religious institutions but were interested in preserving the central sanctuary of Mecca as a lucrative destination for pilgrimages. They also showed a great dislike for Muhammad's constant warning of the hereafter, the last judgment. On the social or cultural level, the Meccans rejected Muhammad because of their fear that their inherited way of life was being attacked and destroyed. The old was threatened by the new, a scenario not uncommon in the history of humankind (34:43).

Another interesting insight gathered from evidence in the Qur'an is that an important cause for "the indignation of the leading circles, then, was that a common man . . . who possessed no natural claim to authority and prestige, should set himself up as a prophet and claim to have authority over others."[14]

These elements gave rise to a new wave of persecution against Muhammad and his followers. We are not certain about the extent of the persecution of Muslims in Mecca. There was some direct physical violence, especially toward the less affluent individuals in the society. However, Muhammad's life was well protected by virtue of his close ties to Abu Talib, but he was not immune from verbal abuse by his mocking opponents (such as accusations that he was a soothsayer, a madman, or even demon-possessed), or occasional annoyances such as having filth thrown at his house. The continual harassment of his followers is said to have led to the flight of a considerable number of Muslims, who sought refuge under the Christian king of Abyssinia.

The earliest biographers of the prophet mention an interesting incident that occurred during this mid-Meccan period. It is related that in one of his sermons in front of the leaders of Meccan antagonists, Muhammad, in order to win the support of his opponents, proclaimed that the favorite deities al-Lat, al-Uzza, and Manat could be considered divine beings whose intercession was effectual with God. But soon the prophet believed these words to be interpolations of Satan and substituted the words that we now have in 53:19–23 (see also 22:51). These have become known as the "Satanic verses." Some modern biographers of Muhammad, like Haykal, try to discredit this story. But to many, it seems inconceivable that later generations of Muslims should have invented

14. Andrae, 122.

this about their own prophet. Other contemporary Muslims, like Rahman, view this incident as perfectly intelligible. As Watt points out,

> The first thing to be said about the story is that it cannot be a sheer invention. Muhammad must at some point have recited as part of the Qur'an the verses which were later rejected as satanic in origin. No Muslim could possibly have invented such a story about Muhammad, and no reputable Muslim scholar would have accepted it from a non-Muslim unless fully convinced of its truth. The Muslims of today tend to reject the story since it contradicts their idealized picture of Muhammad; but, on the other hand it could be taken as evidence that Muhammad was 'a human being like themselves' (41:6; etc.).[15]

As the tension between the believers and the Meccan aristocrats increased, it became obvious to Muhammad that his mission was not succeeding in Mecca; he needed to seek a new base of operation. Furthermore, in the year 619, he also lost his faithful wife, Khadija, and his staunch, but unbelieving protector, Abu Talib. After the passing of Abu Talib, Muhammad's safety was no longer guaranteed.[16]

Another often repeated story about this latter part of the Meccan period is Muhammad's journey into heaven. According to Islamic tradition, one night the prophet was taken by the angel Gabriel from Mecca to Jerusalem (hence the importance of Jerusalem in Islam), and then through the seven heavens where he visited with all the previous prophets (Jesus was found in the second heaven, Moses in the sixth, and Abraham in the seventh). Finally he was taken into the presence of God where he received the specific procedures for the Islamic worship of daily prayers.[17] Many contemporary Muslim authors consider this story a purely spiritual event.[18]

The news of this fantastic mystical experience led to an increase in the hostility of the Meccan opposition, and even many of the faithful began to doubt their prophet's truthfulness. Muhammad's situation was getting more bleak, especially after several attempts to find a basis for support among some of the neighboring Arab towns and tribes failed. However, Muhammad soon found a refreshing relief from the representatives of the city of Yathrib, later called Medina. In the summer of A.D. 621, a dozen men from Medina who were participating in the annual pilgrimage to Ka'bah in Mecca, at the time a pagan shrine, secretly confessed

15. W. Montgomery Watt, *Muhammad's Mecca*, 86.

16. For the Arab customs of family protection, see ibid., 15–20.

17. Andrew Rippin and Jan Knappert, eds. and trans., *Textual Sources for the Study of Islam* (Manchester: University Press, 1986), 68–72; Jeffery, 35–46; and Williams, 66–69.

18. See Haykal, 139–47.

Islam before Muhammad. At the pilgrimage in the following year, a representative party of seventy-five people from Medina not only accepted the faith of Islam, but also invited Muhammad to their city and pledged an allegiance to defend their prophet as they would their own kin.[19]

THE HIJRA (FLIGHT)

Shortly after this welcoming invitation Muhammad ordered his followers to make their way to Medina, a city about two hundred miles north of Mecca. The Muslims slipped away in small groups and about 150 of them emigrated. When the Meccan leaders were informed about the Muslim migration they plotted to kill Muhammad before he could leave the city to join his followers in Medina. But on the night of the planned assassination, the prophet and his close companion, Abu Bakr, successfully escaped from the city by taking the unfrequented routes to Medina and reached that city safely on September 24, A.D. 622.

This journey was a monumental turning point in the development of Islam. As the *Shorter Encyclopedia of Islam* points out, "The migration of the Prophet . . . has been with justice taken by the Muslims as the starting-point of their chronology, for it forms the first stage in a movement which in a short time became of significance in the history of the world."[20]

Quite unlike the Meccans, Muhammad was well received in Medina. Medina was different from Mecca on several accounts. From a religious perspective the residents of Medina were more inclined toward monotheism, due to the strong cultural influence of several well-established Jewish tribes in the area. It is also reported in Islamic tradition that the natives of Medina had heard from the Jews that a prophet was soon to appear in the region. The Medinans, therefore, were eager to accept Muhammad as the prophet who was to come and claim him for their own.

Social factors also played an important role in Muhammad's acceptance in Medina. It was a prosperous agricultural city; however, it was being dragged into a series of bloody feuds among its leading tribes. Therefore, "in inviting Muhammad to Medina, many of the Arabs there probably hoped that he would act as an arbiter among the opposing parties,"[21] and so bring back a period of peace and stability to the city.

Muhammad's ingenuity is clearly evident in this rapid progression of circumstances. Whereas in Mecca he was for the most part a purely religious figure, in Medina he immediately became an able diplomat and

19. These are known as the two pledges of Al-Aqaba.
20. H. A. R. Gibb and J. H. Kramers, eds., *Shorter Encyclopedia of Islam,* (Ithaca: Cornell University Press, 1953), 397.
21. *The New Encyclopaedia Britannica,* 15th ed., 22:3.

politician. Now he could not only exhort his audience by Qur'anic revelations, but also enforce his ideals through his newly gained political powers.

Muhammad's primary task consisted of consolidating the various Arab clans, the two Muslim parties of Muhajirun (the Meccan Muslims who emigrated with Muhammad), Ansar (the native Medinans who had embraced Islam), and even the influential Jewish tribes into one unified front. He was remarkably successful in unifying the various factions by drawing a new constitution for the city of Medina, by which every group was obligated to coexist peacefully and support each other against foreign attacks. Also in this legal document Muhammad was acknowledged as the prophet, with the final authority to settle civil disputes.

Muhammad's success was somewhat offset by his failure to win the support of the three Jewish clans. At first it seems that the prophet made some important concessions in order to find favor with the Jews. For example, in conformity with Jewish custom, he prescribed that his disciples turn in the direction of Jerusalem when praying, and adopted *Ashura*, the Jewish day of atonement, as a festival. Also, the introduction of the midday prayer at this time probably had its basis in Judaism. However, the Jews rejected Muhammad's message and his claim to prophethood, mainly due to the discrepancies between the Qur'anic revelations and their own sacred Scriptures.

Eventually Muhammad changed his policy toward the Jews. He altered the prayer direction from Jerusalem to the shrine of Mecca with the support of a Qur'anic revelation (2:142) and changed the time of fasting from the feast of *Ashura* to the whole month of Ramadan (the ninth lunar month in the Arabic calendar). The Qur'anic pronouncements also became more severe in their criticisms of the Jews (cf. 9:29; 98:6). It was at this time that the Qur'anic emphasis on Abraham as a central figure in the history of Islam became noticeable (cf. 4:125; 3:89; 6:89). This stands in contradistinction to Judaism's focus on Moses and Christianity's emphasis on Jesus. It also manifests a shift in Islamic theology toward a more Arabian character.[22]

In addition to the important task of tribal unification, another serious challenge that Muhammad faced was finding some means of livelihood for the Meccan believers who had sacrificially left their city and belongings to follow their prophet to Medina. A few of the emigrants were able to carry on trade in the markets and some performed common labor. But the majority of them soon became involved, with Muhammad's sanction, in raiding the commercial Meccan caravans. The prophet himself led three such raids in the first year. Doubtless the purpose of these

22. See Andrae, 137–39.

attacks was not only to obtain financial reward, but also to impress the Meccans with the growing power of the Muslim force.

The Qur'an also endorsed Muhammad's new policy by granting permission "[to fight], because They are wronged. . . . [They are] those who have Been expelled from their homes In defiance of right,—(For no cause) except That they say, 'Our Lord Is God'" (22:39–40). A later revelation commands, "Then fight in the cause Of God, and know that God Heareth and knoweth all things" (2:244). And it seems that because of the unwillingness of some believers to fight, the Qur'an introduced some new incentives to those who do (as opposed to "those who sit at home and receive no hurt") such as "special rewards" and entrance to Paradise (cf. 4:95–96; 3:194–95).[23]

For various reasons all the Muslim raids that happened within the first eighteen months failed to procure any booty, and there was hardly any contact between the two parties. The first actual fighting between the Muslims and the pagan Quraysh occurred in January 624 when a small band of Muslims ambushed a Meccan caravan, killed one of its attendants, captured two, and safely brought back the plunder to Medina. This action caused a great uproar since it was believed that the Muslims, by Muhammad's instructions, had shed blood during the sacred month of Rajab. The pagan Arabs believed that four of the months of the year were sacred—an idea that is also sanctioned by the Qur'an (9:36).

Muhammad was at first hesitant to divide up the booty among his followers, but eventually a Qur'anic revelation ended the prophet's doubt:

> Fighting is prescribed For you, and ye dislike it. But it is possible That ye dislike a thing Which is good for you . . . But God knoweth, And ye know not. They ask thee Concerning fighting In the Prohibited Month. Say: "Fighting therein Is a grave (offence); But graver is it In the sight of God To prevent access To the path of God, To deny Him, To prevent access To the Sacred Mosque, And drive out its members." Tumult and oppression Are worse than slaughter (2:216–17).

THE BATTLE OF BADR

The prospect of gaining more booty from the enemy boosted the Muslim morale so that "for his next expedition Muhammad was able to collect 300 men, at least a hundred more than on any previous occasion."[24] Muhammad himself led this campaign after receiving a report that a large caravan, which had all the Meccan merchants concerned for its safe

---

23. For further discussion of Jihad (Holy War) see Chapter 8 and Appendix 5.
24. W. Montgomery Watt, *Muhammad at Medina* (Oxford: Clarendon Press, 1956), 10.

return and was later said to be worth fifty thousand dinars, was heading back to Mecca.

The man in charge of the caravan was the great Meccan leader, Abu Sufyan. Having realized the danger that lay ahead for his merchandise, he sent a timely request to Mecca for backup troops. The Meccans responded immediately and sent an army of about 950 fighting men to confront the Muslim attack. From the size of the force we can assume that the Meccans were thinking of so intimidating Muhammad that he would put an end to his raiding of caravans in the future.

In March 624, in a place called Badr, the two forces met. The Muslims were outnumbered three to one. Because of Muhammad's superior military strategy and his followers' zeal in fighting for the cause of Islam, however, he overpowered the overconfident Meccan leadership; the Muslim army dealt a serious blow to their enemies. Over the course of the battle about forty-five men were killed, including some of the leading men of Mecca and seventy were taken prisoner; the Muslims lost only fourteen people.

Muhammad interpreted the victory at Badr as a definite sign of God's vindication of his prophethood (just as God had marvelously delivered prophets before him in vindication of their message). The prophet was informed that his triumph was "a day of decision" and that it was God himself and his angels who had fought on the Muslims' side. "It is not ye who Slew them; it was God" (8:17). And the believers were inspired by the verse, "O Apostle! rouse the Believers To the fight. If there are Twenty amongst you . . . They will vanquish two hundred: if a hundred, They will vanquish a thousand Of the unbelievers" (8:65).

Immediately following Badr, Muhammad's prestige greatly increased. Relying on his newly elevated status, Muhammad launched the systematic elimination of his opponents in Medina, which in Muhammad's mind had always posed a real threat to the stability of the Islamic community. This extermination involved the assassination of some poets who had satirized the prophet in verse, and also the expulsion of one of the three Jewish tribes from Medina.[25] During this period Muhammad began the long series of multiple marriages that further strengthened his position as the head of the community.[26]

THE BATTLE OF UHUD

The Meccans were well aware of their humiliating defeat, and once again under the leadership of Abu Sufyan, prepared themselves for another confrontation with the Muslim forces. Exactly one year after Badr, the two armies met again in the vicinity of Medina, near the mountain of

25. See Watt, *Muhammad at Medina*, 14–16; and Haykal, 243–44.
26. For a list of Muhammad's wives, see Watt, *Muhammad at Medina*, 393–99.

Uhud. Muhammad's supporters were outnumbered three to one, with the Meccans having three thousand men against one thousand Muslims.

Despite the numerical superiority of the Meccans, at first the battle went in favor of the Muslims and the Quraysh began to flee. However, the tides were quickly turned when the Muslim archers abandoned their positions, against Muhammad's expressed orders, and rushed forward to share in the plunder. The Meccan cavalry took advantage of this opportunity to attack the Muslims from the rear. Muslims started to run in all directions. Further confusion was created when the false rumor spread in the camp that the enemy had killed the prophet. But Muhammad and the bulk of his force eventually withdrew to a secure position, and the Meccans, rejoicing in their victory, set out for home.

Muhammad's defeat struck a psychological blow to his prestige in the region. The "hypocrites" (*munafeqoon*), Muhammad's opponents in Medina, along with the Jewish antagonists made no secret of their delight at Muhammad's misfortunes. Several Muslim parties were ambushed and killed by Muhammad's enemies, and in one case a bedouin tribe even dared to defy the prophet's authority by massacring forty Muslim missionaries.

Despite these setbacks Muhammad continued his efforts to strengthen his position. He led or authorized more attacks on the neighboring tribes "which seems to have aimed at extending his own alliances and at preventing others from joining the Meccans."[27] Also, barely one year after defeat at Uhud, Muhammad expelled the second Jewish tribe from Medina and confiscated all their properties. The plunder left for the Muslims was so much that Haykal, in his biography of Muhammad, writes, "this prize was greater than anything the Muslims had so far seized."[28]

THE SIEGE OF MEDINA

After their victory in Uhud, the Meccans realized that they needed to crush Muhammad's growing power once and for all. In the spring of A.D. 627 Abu Sufyan led a great Arab confederacy of ten thousand men against the Muslims of Medina. This time Muhammad decided to harvest the crop and remain within the city, and—as a tradition states—based upon the advice of a Persian disciple, the Muslims dug a ditch in front of the unprotected parts of their city. The Meccans surrounded Medina for about two weeks. But after several failures to cross the trench, the break up of their coalition by Muhammad's secret negotiations with various tribes, and unfavorable weather conditions, the besiegers lost their determination and began to withdraw.

27. *The New Encyclopaedia Britannica*, 15th ed., 22:4.
28. See Haykal, 278.

Muhammad's position was greatly strengthened after this silent victory. Shortly after the siege, Muhammad attacked the last Jewish tribe of Medina based on the suspicion that they had plotted with the Meccan enemies against Muslims. Unlike the previous two Jewish tribes that had been simply expelled from the city, this time all the men of the tribe were put to death and the women and children were sold into slavery. Regarding this merciless verdict, Tor Andrae writes:

> One must see Mohammad's cruelty toward the Jews against the background of the fact that their scorn and rejection was the greatest disappointment of his life, and for a time they threatened completely to destroy his prophetic authority. For him, therefore, it was a fixed axiom that the Jews were the sworn enemies of Allah and His revelation. Any mercy toward them was out of the question.[29]

THE CONQUEST OF MECCA

Muhammad's power for the next two years was quickly on the rise. The prophet led many more successful campaigns that brought about greater financial benefits to his community. Consequently, more people were steadily joining the fold of Islam.[30]

Meanwhile the military and economic strength of Mecca was in rapid decline. Furthermore, several of their leading men had defected and joined Muhammad's ranks. In March 628 the Meccans made a peace treaty (the treaty of Hudaybiah) with Muhammad that clearly indicated they could no longer think of Muhammad as a rebellious fugitive but as an opponent of equal rank.

Over a year after the peace treaty, an attack of Meccan allies on Muhammad's allies caused the treaty to be nullified. Taking full advantage of this breach of the covenant, in January 630 Muhammad with an army of ten thousand men invaded his beloved city of Mecca with virtually no resistance. He immediately cleansed the Kaabah of its idols and, with only a few exceptions, promised a general pardon to all the leaders of Mecca and even gave each one of the prominent Meccans, including Abu Sufyan, generous gifts and rewards for their surrender. Thus he not only conquered his long-time enemies but also won their respect and admiration. As Andrae claims, "it is rarely that a victor has exploited his victory with greater self-restraint and forbearance than did Mohammed."[31]

29. See Andrae, 155–56.
30. Some critics say that this was because "the religious attraction of Islam was apparently supplemented by material motives." See *The New Encyclopaedia Britannica*, 4.
31. See Andrae, 166.

MUHAMMAD'S FINAL YEARS

After Mecca surrendered to Muhammad, a large number of tribes in the Arabian peninsula followed suit and professed their allegiance to the prophet; others submitted after being defeated by the Muslim armies. As a general rule, the heathen tribes were obligated to denounce paganism and profess Islam, whereas Christians and Jews could practice their own faith but had to pay tributes and taxes. It is certainly one of Muhammad's greatest accomplishments that he was able to incorporate all the many Arab tribes into one unified and powerful nation under the banner of Islam.

In March 632 Muhammad personally led the Islamic pilgrimage to Mecca and delivered his farewell address to tens of thousands of his followers. Three months later in June 632, at the age of sixty-three, the prophet of Islam died a sudden but natural death.

MUHAMMAD'S PLACE IN ISLAM

So far we have looked at Muhammad from a purely historical perspective. However, like all other religious personalities, there is another significant aspect to the prophet of Islam: the crucial place he holds in the lives and faith of millions of his dedicated followers worldwide. We will devote the latter part of this chapter to examining Muhammad's great impact in shaping Islamic culture and theology.

MUHAMMAD'S IMPACT ON ISLAMIC CULTURE

"Muslims will allow attacks on Allah: there are atheists and atheistic publications, and rationalistic societies; but to disparage Muhammad will provoke from even the most 'liberal' sections of the community a fanaticism of blazing vehemence."[32] Wilfred Cantwell Smith's insightful analysis of the deep and widespread veneration that exists in Muslim society for their prophet is as true today as when he wrote it in 1946.

From the judgment of Ibn Taymiyya (the fourteenth-century Muslim theologian claiming that anyone defaming the prophet must be executed without any possibility for repentance)[33] to Ayatollah Khomeini's *fatwa* (a religious/legal judgment) for the extermination of the British author Salmon Rushdie, we see a vivid illustration of the Muslim world's fanatical love for Muhammad. In two powerful images, Iqbal, the greatest twentieth-century Muslim thinker of India (d. 1938), summed up the

32. Wilfred Cantwell Smith cited by Annemarie Schimmel, "The Prophet Muhammad as a Centre of Muslim Life and Thought," in Schimmel and Falaturi, 35.
33. Ibn Taymiyya, *A Muslim Theologian's Response to Christianity*, ed. and trans. Thomas F. Michel (Delmar, N.Y.: Caravan Books, 1984), 70. It is ironic that Ibn Taymiyya himself received heavy punishment for his alleged lack of veneration for the prophet when he spoke against certain popular un-Qur'anic exaggerations.

feeling of millions of Muslims in this way: "Love of the Prophet runs like blood in the veins of his community." And "You can deny God, but you cannot deny the Prophet!"[34]

The adoration for the prophet became a fundamental factor not only in Islamic art and literature, but also in shaping the many details of Muslim life and civilization soon after Muhammad's death. Encouraged by the Qur'anic injunction found in 33:21, "Ye have indeed In the Apostle of God A beautiful pattern (of conduct) For any one whose hope is In God and the Final Day" (also 4:80; 7:157; 14:44). The reports of Muhammad's sayings (*hadith*) and actions (*sunnah*) were tirelessly collected by subsequent generations. Even though these hadiths were never regarded as equal to the Qur'an, they were viewed as an uninspired record of inspired words and actions. Eventually Muslim theologians of the second and third centuries of the Islamic era, after much examination of the texts (*matn*) of these hadiths and their chains of narrators (*isnads*), put it in the book forms that we have today.[35]

While among all Muslims the Qur'an is the only sacred and inspired book, nevertheless, the hadiths of the prophet are also foundational because of all the minute details that they provide regarding almost every aspect of Muslim life and practice. Ajijola writes, "(Muhammad's) life became a source of inspiration to his followers. Even minute acts and deeds of him have been recorded by his companions and contemporaries for the benefit of mankind."[36] The Muslim author, Kateregga, writes:

> The *Hadith* is not a Holy Book (revelation) as the Qur'an and the previous Scriptures. However, to the Muslims the importance of *Hadith* ranks only second to the Holy Qur'an. The *Hadith* is complementary to the Qur'an. It helps to explain and clarify the Holy Qur'an and to present the Qur'an in a more practical form. . . . As Muslims, our knowledge of Islam would be incomplete and shaky if we did not study and follow the *Hadith*. Similarly an outsider cannot understand Islam if he ignores the *Hadith*.[37]

The greatest Muslim theologian of all time, Al-Ghazali (d. A.D. 1111), in his classical *Ihya ulum ad-din* (Revival of Religious Sciences), explained the importance of observing the prophet's tradition in this way:

34. See Schimmel, 239, 256.
35. In Sunni Islam, there are six canonical collections of *hadith* with the two most revered ones being that of *Sahih* of al-Bukhari, and *Sahih* of al-Muslim. For a brief and concise discussion on *hadith* literature, see *Encyclopaedia Britannica*, 10–12.
36. Ajijola, 217.
37. See Kateregga and Shenk, 31.

Know that the key to happiness is to follow the *sunna* [Muhammad's actions] and to imitate the Messenger of God in all his coming and going, his movement and rest, in his way of eating, his attitude, his sleep and his talk. . . . God has said: "What the messenger has brought—accept it, and what he has prohibited—refrain from it!" (59:7). That means, you have to sit while putting on trousers, and to stand when winding a turban, and to begin with the right foot when putting on shoes.[38]

An interesting example of Muslim piety in following the prophetic tradition is found in Sayyid Ahmad Khan, the nineteenth-century Indian reformer, who emphatically believed that it was better not to eat mangoes since the prophet had never touched this favorite fruit of India. Also it is said that the great mystic Bayezid Bistami did not eat watermelons for sixty years because he could not establish how Muhammad would have cut melons![39]

Of course these are radical examples of emulating the prophet's lifestyle. Even though the majority of pious Muslims do not go to such extremes, they do try their best to follow Muhammad's example in many details of their daily living. Schimmel, a prominent scholar on Islam at Harvard University, observes the influence of prophetic tradition on unifying the Islamic culture:

It is this ideal of the *imitatio Muhammadi* [imitation of Muhammad] that has provided Muslims from Morocco to Indonesia with such a uniformity of action: wherever one may be, one knows how to behave when entering a house, which formulas of greeting to employ, what to avoid in good company, how to eat, and how to travel. For centuries Muslim children have been brought up in these ways.[40]

The prophetic tradition has not only greatly influenced every detail of the life of the individual believer, but it has also been the foundation of Islamic law and social government. Islamic law, or *shari'a,* is based on the Qur'an, the *hadith, ijma'* (the consensus of the community), and *qiyas,* the application of analogical reasoning to the other three sources for the deduction of new rules. There are four established systematized schools of law in Sunni Islam, "so that today most Sunni Muslims will be found following the *madhab* (system) of one of these four, ordering their religious and community life according to the prescriptions worked out by the jurists of one of these schools."[41]

---

38. See Schimmel, 31.
39. Ibid., 44.
40. Ibid., 55.
41. See Jeffery, xiii. See also Goldziher, "Development of Law" in *Introduction to Islamic Theology and Law.*

In order to avoid stereotyping the Muslim world, it is necessary to note here that even though Islamic *sunna* and *shari'a* (Islamic civil law) play a fundamental role in the cultures of Muslim countries, much of the traditional and religious mores have been broken down in the past century due to the massive influence of Western culture on these lands. For example, in many instances reformist groups within Islam are rejecting a strict reliance on prophetic *hadith*. Also, one can find a great deal of nominal Muslims in Islamic countries whose lifestyles are not in accordance with guidelines set by the Qur'an and the prophet. The same can be said of governmental laws that in many ways follow the more democratic and Western patterns of government as opposed to the strict obedience of Islamic *shari'a*.[42]

MUHAMMAD'S PLACE IN ISLAMIC THEOLOGY

Muslims' great respect for Muhammad notwithstanding, it is very important to point out that standard Islamic theology in no way considers him divine. As Schimmel accurately warns, "Neither in theological nor in phenomenological terms can Muhammad be likened to the Christ of Christianity—hence the Muslims' aversion to the term 'Muhammadans,' which seems to them to imply a false parallel to the concept of 'Christians.'"[43] As the second part of Islamic confession makes clear, Muhammad is only the prophet of God.

However, having said this we need to point out that there are diverse, and sometimes contradictory, attitudes held by various Muslim groups regarding the importance of the person of Muhammad. These attitudes range from considering him as merely an upright human being who became the recipient of divine revelation, to a semidivine and almost eternal being.

According to the Qur'anic evidence and orthodox Islam, Muhammad was only a human being whom God chose to be the final messenger to humankind, and who was used as a means to introduce the purest and the most perfect religion of Islam to the world. "Every previous prophet of God was sent to a particular people, but Muhammad was sent to all human beings of the world until Doomsday."[44] In 6:50 we read, "Say: 'I tell you not That with me Are the Treasures of God, Nor do I know What is hidden, Nor do I tell you I am An angel. I but follow What is revealed to

42. Schimmel's analysis of the current situation in the Middle East is that "awareness of the danger that now confronts Islamic tradition has certainly contributed to the sudden growth of Muslim fundamentalism that came as such a surprise to the unprepared Western world" (55).

43. Ibid., 24.

44. Muhammad Abul Quasem, *Salvation of the Soul and Islamic Devotions* (London: Kegan Paul International, 1983), 32.

me!'" Muhammad was told that "if it were Our Will, We could take away That which We have Sent thee by inspiration: Then wouldst thou find None to plead thy affair In that matter as against Us" (17:86). And in 29:50 we read Muhammad's clear admission that "I am Indeed a clear Warner." In accordance with the above Qur'anic statements, Abdalati, an orthodox Muslim author, writes:

> The Muslims worship God alone. Muhammad was only a mortal being commissioned by God to teach the word of God and lead an exemplary life. He stands in history as the best model for man in piety and perfection. He is a living proof of what man can be and of what he can accomplish in the realm of excellence and virtue. Moreover, the Muslims do not believe that Islam was founded by Muhammad, although it was restored by him in the last stage of religious evolution.[45]

Admitting Muhammad is only human is no embarrassment for orthodox Islam because of its strict monotheism (see Chapters 1 and 2). But as we mentioned earlier, according to orthodox Islam, prophethood is the height of God's activity in the world, and since with Muhammad God closed the office of prophethood this was the greatest honor that God could bestow on a human being. For Muslims, therefore, Muhammad is the last and the greatest of all prophets (*khatam al-anbiya*). In a well-known *hadith* Muhammad's greatness is stated this way:

> I have been granted excellence over the other prophets in six things: the earth has been made a mosque for me, with its soil declared pure; booty has been made lawful for me; I have been given victory through the inspiring of awe at the distance of a month's journey; I have been given permission to intercede; I have been sent to all mankind; and the prophets have been sealed with me.[46]

A popular Muslim classic by Kamal ud Din ad Damiri gives us the following description of the beloved prophet:

> Mohammed is the most favored of mankind, the most honored of all apostles, the prophet of mercy, the head or Imam of the faithful, the bearer of banner of praise, the intercessor, the holder of high position, the possessor of the River of Paradise, under whose banner the sons of Adam will be on the Day of Judgment. He is the best of prophets, and his nation is the best of nations . . . and his creed is the noblest of all creeds. He performed manifest miracles, and possessed great qualities. He was perfect in intellect, and was of noble origin. He had an absolutely graceful form, complete gen-

45. Abdalati, 8.
46. See Schimmel, 62.

erosity, perfect bravery, excessive humility, useful knowledge ... perfect fear of God and sublime piety. He was the most eloquent and the most perfect of mankind in every variety of perfection.[47]

Traditionally Islamic apologetics have provided several lines of reasoning for proving the superiority of Muhammad over previous prophets. "The chief of these proofs," according to the book *Mizan'ul Haqq,* are:

(1) That the Old Testament and the New both contain clear prophecies about him.
(2) That the language and the teaching of the Qur'an are without parallel, and thus the Qur'an alone is a sufficient proof of the truth of Muhammad's claims.
(3) That Muhammad's miracle(s) is (are) a seal set by God Most High on his claims.
(4) That his life and character prove him to have been the last and the greatest of prophets.
(5) That the rapid spread of Islam shows that God Most High sent it as his final revelation to men.[48]

Contemporary defenders of Islam offer variations on the above classical themes, but generally speaking these are still the five major arguments in support of Muhammad. (For further discussion of this topic, see Chapter 8.)

Besides the orthodox understanding of Muhammad's role as merely a messenger, though the greatest of all prophets, popular Islam soon developed other beliefs about its prophet that went beyond the Qur'anic boundaries. One important deviation was the belief in Muhammad as an intercessor for his community before God.

The Qur'an rejects the possibility of intercession on the Day of Judgment (2:48, 254). But in 2:255, it is stated that no one can intercede with God "except As He (God) permitteth." Therefore, many Muslims understood that this special permission for intercession (*shafa'ah*) was certainly granted to Muhammad whom the Qur'an had called a mercy to humankind.

In addition to this possible interpretation of the Qur'an, many hadiths were also produced in early Islam in support of this doctrine. One popular tradition describes the last day in which all humankind goes from one

47. Joseph Gudel, *To Every Muslim An Answer* (Thesis, Simon Greenleaf School of Law, 1982), 72.
48. C. G. Pfander, *The Mizanu'l Haqq (Balance of Truth)* (Villach, Austria: Light of Life, 1986), 225–26.

prophet to the next to ask for intercession. All prophets from Adam to Jesus refuse to accept this role because of their unworthiness. But eventually Muhammad accepts the role as intercessor, for he can successfully lead his community into Paradise.

Thousands of beautiful Islamic poems and moving prayers speak of the Muslims' hope for Muhammad's intercession for their salvation. For example, Ibn Khaldun, the great North African philosopher, asked the prophet Muhammad, "Grant me by your intercession, for which I hope, a beautiful page instead of my ugly sins!" Another Muslim thinker exhorted his hearers by these words: "If a man brings on the Day of Resurrection as many good works as those of all the people in the world and does not bring with them the calling down of blessing on the Prophet, his good works are returned to him, unacceptable." The Muslim poet Tilimsani invoked Muhammad thus: "I have sins, abundant—but perhaps your intercession may save me from Hellfire." And the greatest lyrical poet of Urdu, Mir Taqi Mir, writes, "Why do you worry, O Mir, thinking of your black book? The person of the Seal of the Prophets is a guarantee for your salvation!"[49]

Closely related to the Muslims' hope for Muhammad's intercession and blessing is the universal Islamic formula of blessing the prophet, "God bless him and give him peace." (The Shi'ite version also asks for blessing on Muhammad's family.) This practice finds its basis in the Qur'an itself, which claims, "God and His Angels Send blessings on the Prophet: O ye that believe! Send ye blessings on him, And salute him With all respect" (33:56). Also, several hadiths explain the advantages of often repeating this blessing on Muhammad. One *hadith* promises that for every blessing called on the prophet, God will return that blessing ten times. Another *hadith* encourages believers to bless the prophet often on Fridays since the greetings are put before him on that day.[50]

Another popular tendency among some Muslims, which is of course condemned by orthodox Islam, is the veneration of Muhammad to the extent of almost deifying him. Once again there is an abundance of alleged hadiths that support this position. One *hadith* speaks of Muhammad's preexistence, and another states that he was the purpose of God's creation of the universe. "I was prophet when Adam was still between clay and water." "Had it not been for thee I (God) had not created the world."[51] One popular *hadith* among the Iranian Muslims has God saying, "I am an Ahmad without 'm'." Ahmad is another name for Muhammad. If the letter 'm' is omitted from the word it becomes *Ahad* (one),

49. See Schimmel, 88, 96.
50. Ibid., 92–93.
51. See Gudel, 73.

which is another name for God. This *hadith* is supposed to show the insignificant difference that exists between God and the person of Muhammad.

This process of Muhammad's dehumanization took an additional turn in the popular doctrine of *Nur-i-Muhammadi*, or the Light of Muhammad. According to many Islamic books of tradition God first created the light of Muhammad and from that light he later proceeded to make the rest of creation.[52] So Muhammad was not only the goal and reason for all creation but also the material cause of creation. It is also this light of Muhammad that each prophet was able to manifest to a certain degree.[53]

One further step in exalting the Prophet was to also find him ninety-nine most noble names. Nazir-Ali, a perceptive scholar on Islam, writes that a certain popular devotional book "contains a list of 201 names of Muhammad (as against ninety-nine for God!). Many of the names are identical to certain divine names. . . . Moreover names of God are given just before the names of the Prophet, almost to encourage comparison!"[54] Schimmel writes that quite early in Islam even the ninety-nine names for the prophet seemed insufficient; "soon two hundred names were enumerated, later even a thousand. Popular belief even holds that the Prophet is called a special name by each type of creature."[55]

Concerning Muhammad's position in popular Islam, Nazir-Ali observes:

> The extent of this veneration in modern Pakistani society is astonishing. The society nominally adheres to *Sunni* orthodoxy. But *Muhammad*-veneration is projected through the mass media, school books and cultural events all of which contribute to the deification of the Arabian Prophet. The following examples illustrate this point: "Though my link with the Divinity of God be severed, May my hand never let go of the hem of the Chosen One (i.e. Muhammad)."

This is a quotation from a poem being taught in some Muslim schools. Since Relationship with the transcendent God is seen to be distant, it is only through Muhammad that one even dares to approach his throne. In *Qawwalis* (a popular cultural event), Muhammad is praised in verse. This often takes the form of deification: "If *Muhammad* had not been, God himself would not have existed!" This is an allusion to the close relationship Muhammad is supposed to have with God. In the media,

52. Abdul-Haqq, 128–29.
53. See Dashti, 62–63.
54. Nazir-Ali, 133.
55. Schimmel, 111–12. For a list of the ninety-nine names, see Schimmel's appendix, 257–59.

Muhammad is often given titles like "Savior of the World" and "Lord of the Universe."[56]

CONCLUSION

In conclusion it is important to point out that despite the un-Qur'anic exalted position of Muhammad in popular Islamic piety, his position in Islamic theology is not comparable to the person of Christ in Christian theology. The ultimate foundation of Islam is not the person of Muhammad, but rather the Qur'an, the uncreated and eternal Word of God. As Schimmel reminds us:

> Even though Muhammad was elevated to luminous heights and reached a position comparable, in certain ways, to that of Logos in Christian theology, yet even as the Perfect Man he remained *abduhu,* God's servant and His creature—the most beloved of His creatures, to be sure . . . the idea of an incarnation in the Christian sense was and is absolutely impossible in the Islamic tradition. . . . The axis of Islam is not the person of the Prophet but rather the Word of God, as revealed through him and laid down in the Koran.[57]

So in order to properly understand Islam, it is necessary to turn our attention to the cornerstone of Islam, the Qur'an. This is the subject of the next chapter.

---

56. Nazir-Ali, 130–31.
57. See Schimmel, 142.

5

THE QUR'AN

The Qur'an is the foundation of Islam.[1] No adequate knowledge of Islam is possible without a basic understanding of the Qur'an. Although belief in all divine Scriptures is a major Islamic doctrine, for Muslims the Qur'an holds such an incomparable place among other revealed Scriptures that it demands separate treatment. First we will explore the historical background, literary style, and some of the major themes of the Qur'an. Then we will focus on the significance of the Qur'an as divine revelation.

A SURVEY OF THE QUR'AN

COMPILATION OF THE QUR'AN

Muhammad did not write down his revelations but gave them orally. Shortly after Muhammad's death, it became necessary to collect all the scattered pieces and chapters of his revelations into one book for use in the Muslim community. As long as the prophet was alive, he acted as God's mouthpiece within the community and no urgent need was felt to gather all his divine revelations into one collection. However, with the death of their prophet, Muslims were convinced that God's revelation to humankind was finalized. As 5:4 puts it, "This day have I Perfected your religion For you, completed My favour upon you, And have chosen for you Islam as your religion." So with the death of Muhammad, the demand for collecting and compiling this final revelation in written form became a pressing concern.

The process of compiling the Qur'an is reported by Muslim historians. According to Islamic tradition different fragments of the Qur'an were revealed to Muhammad verbatim by the angel Gabriel over a period of

---

1. For an excellent general introduction to the Qur'an, see W. Montgomery Watt, *Bell's Introduction to the Qur'an* (Edinburgh: Edinburgh University Press, 1970).

twenty-three years (25:32; 17:106). After each such occasion the prophet would recite the words of revelation to those present (thus the word "Qur'an," which means reading or reciting).[2] Many of the devout believers memorized these Qur'anic portions as they were revealed and used them for private meditation or public worship, especially the shorter Meccan suras.[3] Tradition also relates that Muhammad's scribes wrote the revelations on "pieces of paper, stones, palm-leaves, shoulder-blades, ribs, and bits of leather."

About a year after Muhammad's death, especially in the battle of Yamamah (A.D. 633),[4] a great number of those who could recite the Qur'an by memory (*hafiz*) were killed. Some of the companions of Muhammad, mainly due to the promptings of Umar, who later became the second Caliph of Islam, ordered the collection of the Qur'an because of the fear that the knowledge of it might fade away. Zayd ibn Thabit, one of Muhammad's most trusted secretaries, was appointed to this task. According to Zayd's testimony, "during the lifetime of the prophet the Qur'an had all been written down, but it was not yet united in one place nor arranged in successive order."[5] Zayd's own account is preserved for us in *Sahih* of Al-Bukhari:

> Narrated Zid bin Thabit: Abu Bakr As-Siddiq sent for me when the people of Yama-ma had been killed (i.e., a number of the Prophet's Companions who fought against Musailama). (I went to him) and found 'Umar bin Al-Khattab sitting with him. Abu Bakr then said (to me), 'Umar has come to me and said, "Casualties were heavy among the Qurra of the Qur'an (i.e., those who knew the Qur'an by heart) on the day of the Battle of Yamama, and I am afraid that more heavy casualties may take place among the Qurra on other battlefields, whereby a large part of the Qur'an may be lost. Therefore I suggest you (Abu Bakr) order that the Qur'an be collected." I said to 'Umar, "How can you do something which Allah's Apostle did not do?" 'Umar said, "By Allah, that is a good project." 'Umar kept on urging me to accept his proposal till Allah opened my chest for it and I began to realise the good in the idea which 'Umar had realised. Then Abu Bakr said (to me), 'You are a wise young man and we do not have any suspicion about you, and you used to write the Divine Inspiration for Allah's Apostle. So you should search for (the fragmentary scripts of) the Qur'an and collect it (in one book).' By Allah! If they had ordered me to shift one of the mountains, it would not have been heavier for me than this ordering me to collect the

2. Nazir-Ali, 124.
3. Cf. Sura 73:1–7; and also see Yusuf Ali's *Holy Qur'an*, Intro. C.41.
4. This was a major battle between the Muslim forces and the followers of a new self-proclaimed Arabian prophet.
5. This is related by Jalalu'd Din a's Suyuti, taken from Stanton, 10–11. See also Mohammed Pickthall's intro to his English trans. of the Qur'an.

Qur'an. . . . So I started looking for the Qur'an and collecting it from (what was written on) palm-leaf stalks, thin white stones and also from the men who knew it by heart.[6]

Despite the above account from the most trusted traditionalist in Islam, Al Bukhari (d. 870), popular orthodox Muslim theory holds that the Qur'an was arranged in the same form that we have today under Muhammad's and Gabriel's direct supervision.[7]

Some time later during the reign of Uthman, the third Muslim Caliph, Muslims were faced with another crisis regarding the Qur'an. It was reported to Uthman that several Muslim communities were using different versions of the Qur'an and it was feared that this uncertainty as to which Qur'anic reading was the correct one might subsequently lead to great doctrinal confusion. According to the report of Bukhari this news reached Uthman from Hudhaifa, general of the Muslim army in the campaign of Armenia, who had noticed such debates among his own troops.

Once again Zayd was called to head the new project of editing an official revised version of the Qur'an. After the production of the revised version, which followed the dialect of the Quraish, several copies of this new authoritative Qur'an were sent to each major center of the Islamic empire and all the other copies of the Qur'an were recalled and burned by the expressed order of the Caliph Uthman.

> Narrated Anas bin Malik: Hudhaifa bin Al-Yaman came to Uthman at the time when the people of Sham and the people of Iraq were waging war to conquer Arminya and Adharbijan. Hudhaifa was afraid of their [the people of Sham and Iraq] differences in the recitation of the Qur'an, so he said to 'Uthman, "O the chief of the Believers! Save this nation before they differ about the Book [Qur'an] as Jews and the Christians did before." So 'Uthman sent a message to Hafsa saying, "Send us the manuscripts of the Qur'an so that we may compile the Qur'anic materials in perfect copies and return the manuscripts to you." Hafsa sent it to 'Uthman. 'Uthman then ordered Zaid bin Thabit, 'Abdullah bin Az-Zubair, Sa'id bin Al-As, and 'Abdur-Rahman bin Harith bin Hisham to rewrite the manuscripts in perfect copies. 'Uthman said to the three Quraishi men, "In case you disagree with Zaid bin Thabit on any point in the Qur'an, then write it in the dialect of Quraish as the Qur'an was revealed in their tongue." They did so, and when they had written many copies, 'Uthman returned the original manuscript to Hafsa. 'Uthman sent to every Muslim province one copy of what they had copied, and ordered that all the other Qur'anic materials, whether written in fragmentary manuscripts or whole copies, be burnt.[8]

6. Al-Bukhari, vol. 6, 477–78.
7. Kateregga and Shenk, 29–30; and Bucaille, 134.
8. See Al-Bukhari, 478–79.

All Qur'anic scholars agree that the Uthmanic version of the Qur'an has practically remained intact to the present day.

ARRANGEMENT OF THE QUR'AN

The Qur'an is slightly shorter than the New Testament. It is divided into 114 chapters, called suras, of unequal length. Eighty-six of the chapters were revealed during the Meccan period and twenty-eight at Medina. Each chapter is divided into verses (*ayat*). The three shortest suras have three verses each (103, 108, 110), while the second sura, which is the longest, is divided into 286 verses. Each sura (with one exception) begins with a *bismillah* that is translated into English as "In the name of God, Most Gracious, Most Merciful." Each sura also contains a title that is often derived from a word or a phrase within the chapter (such as, "The Cow," "Jonah," "The Fig," and "He Frowned"). However, in most cases these titles do not indicate the theme of the whole chapter.

A somewhat unusual feature of the Qur'an is that its suras are not placed in any chronological or logical order. Generally speaking the chapters are arranged according to length from larger to smaller—with the exception of the first one, which functions as a short introductory prayer. This has "resulted . . . in an inversion of the chronological order, as the longest Suras, which are mainly the latest, come first, while the shortest and earliest are placed last."[9] Most of the longer chapters have verses that come from the most varied periods of Muhammad's ministry, thus making the composite suras or sections of them even harder to date accurately. One critical Muslim scholar, Ali Dashti, claims that "Unfortunately the Qur'an was badly edited and its contents are very obtusely arranged."[10] However, most conservative Muslims defend this arrangement.[11]

THE LITERARY STYLE OF THE QUR'AN

The Qur'an is written in the form of Arabic poetry and prose. The *Shorter Encyclopedia of Islam* contains the following description of the literary form of the Qur'an:

> The style is quite different in the earlier and later parts of the Kur'an, although it bears everywhere undeniably the stamp of the same individual.

9. Stanton, 15.
10. Dashti, 28. Also see *The New Encyclopaeida Britannica*; and the footnote in Goldziher, 28–30. Concerning this issue Arthur Jeffery makes the following insightful comment: "None of the longer Suras save Sura XII deals with any one subject consistently . . . the arrangement is clearly haphazard, though some modern Muslim writers make fantastic attempts to show a purposeful arrangement of the material in the Suras." Jeffery, 47.
11. See Mahmud Ahmad, 368–71; *Muslim World League Journal*, Aug. 82, 13; and Kateregga and Shenk, 29.

... In the earlier revelations one is carried away by the wild fancy and rhapsodic presentation, sometimes also by a warmer feeling. . . . In the later sections also higher flights are not lacking . . . but as a rule his imagination soon . . . gave place to passages of prose. . . . The Prophet now often indulges in repetitions of long stories or psychological explanations, or polemics.[12]

Another authority describes the Qur'anic style this way: "The shortest verses generally occur in the earliest *surahs*, in which the style of Muhammad's revelation comes very close to the rhymed prose (*saj*) used by the *Kahins*, or soothsayers, of his time." Furthermore, "as the verses get progressively longer and more circumstantial, the rhymes come farther and farther apart. There is also a change of linguistic style: the earlier *surahs* are characterized by short sentences, vivid expressions, and poetic force; and the later ones become more and more detailed, complicated and, at times, rather prosaic in outlook and language."[13]

Of course, for orthodox Muslims "the absolute perfection of the language of the Kur'an is an impregnable dogma."[14] So any contrast between the literary quality of the earlier and later suras is a moot point for a Muslim who considers the Qur'an to be the ultimate proof of its own inspiration by reason of its unapproachable beauty in style from beginning to end (see Chapter 9).

Another important point regarding style is that "the Qur'an generally appears as the speech of God, who mostly speaks in the first person plural ("We")."[15] And even "when the prophet Muhammad is speaking to his compatriots, his words are introduced by the command, 'Say,' thus emphasizing that he is speaking on divine injunction only. At times the form is also dramatic, bringing in objections by Muhammad's opponents and answering them by counter arguments."[16] Predicated on this style of direct divine address, Muslims believe that the New Testament and much of the Old Testament are thereby disqualified from being God's Word.

MAJOR QUR'ANIC THEMES

We have already discussed some of the major themes of the Qur'an, such as God, man, sin, prophets, and divine Scriptures. We will touch on the Islamic view of salvation in the next chapter. In this section, we will briefly survey some of the major teachings of the Qur'an in chronological

12. Gibb and Kramers, 276; also see Goldziher, 11–12.
13. *The New Encyclopaedia Britannica*, 6; also see Stanton, 13–14.
14. See Gibb and Kramers, 276.
15. Like the Bible (cf. Gen. 1:26), the use of "we" is regal, being reserved for royalty and deity but is not a sign of plurality in God.
16. *The New Encyclopaedia Britannica*, 6.

order, covering the twenty-three-year period during which the Qur'an was revealed to Muhammad.

Western scholars have commonly classified the Qur'an according to four stages: early, mid-, and late Meccan, and the Medinan period. This construction has been popular with Western scholars since the time of Noldeke's *History of the Qur'an* (1860).[17] Here we will avoid the somewhat technical differentiation between the mid- and late Meccan stage and will only touch on the prominent features of the earlier and later Meccan and the Medinan periods.

THE MECCAN PERIOD

During the first period of Muhammad's ministry there is a "marked simplicity of concept" in the earliest suras of the Qur'an.[18] Muhammad is primarily a "warner" (87:9). The initial revelations mainly consisted of calling men to moral reform in response to the fact that they are accountable before the Creator. They foretell the imminent day of judgment and graphically describe the destiny of the lost in hell and the future of the saved in Paradise.

Shortly after this, the oneness and transcendence of the true God and Creator become the prevailing theme, in the form of a "series of short addresses full of excited passion, glowing imagination and no little poetic power."[19] According to an early Muslim tradition, Muhammad did not explicitly attack the pagan gods of Mecca at the beginning of his ministry. An early authority, Al-Zuhri (d. A.D. 713), gives us the following account:[20]

> Secretly and publicly Allah's Apostle called men to Islam, and those who were willing among the young men and the common people accepted the call of Allah. . . . The unbelievers of Quraish tribe did not oppose what he said. . . . This they continued to do until Allah began to attack their gods whom they served beside Him, and until He proclaimed that their fathers who died in unbelief were lost. Then they began to hate the Prophet and show their enmity to him.

Muhammad faced strong rejection by the majority of the unbelieving Meccans that resulted in a new emphasis in the Qur'anic revelations. Gradually the suras get longer and more argumentative in tone. In ever-increasing detail the revelations expound on the proofs and evidences in nature and human life for the existence and power of God.

17. See Gibb and Kramers; and Goldziher, 12 and footnote.
18. Sir Norman Anderson, *The World's Religions* (Grand Rapids: Eerdmans, 1987), 94.
19. See Gibb and Kramers, 284.
20. Andrae, 116; see also Gibb and Kramers, 284.

It is also at this time that we are introduced to the long and repetitious biblical narratives of the Old and New Testament prophets. Since, according to the Qur'an, many Old Testament personalities functioned as God's prophets, Islamic scholars see in these prophetic stories a significant psychological (and even doctrinal) element. Commenting on the nature of Muhammad's revelations, Schimmel writes:

> In the middle period, during the times of crises and persecutions, they often spoke of the suffering and afflictions that were showed upon earlier prophets who, like Muhammad, did not meet with any understanding among their compatriots and were tried hard until God gave them victory over their enemies. These revelations certainly helped Muhammad to continue on his chosen path despite the growing hostility of the Meccans.[21]

THE MEDINAN PERIOD

This chronological division of the Qur'an is the only one that is accepted by all Muslims and in fact has been so since almost the very beginning of Islam. In the Medinan suras not only the literary style but also the content stands in great contrast to the Meccan period. In the person of Muhammad there is a striking transition from a preacher to a prince. This causes no concern for the Muslim, who sees in this transformation the case for Muhammad's greatness in effectively adapting to different circumstances.

In Medina, Muhammad becomes the "beautiful model." He is to be obeyed along with God; he is sent as "a Mercy for all creatures," and God and angelic beings call blessings on the prophet (33:21; 4:80; 21:107; 33:56). With this change in Muhammad's role also came a change in the Qur'anic revelation. The problems of Mecca were now past, and the newly found Islamic community needed new direction. Once again Schimmel writes: "In Medina, Islam became institutionalized, and the contents of the Prophet's later revelations, correspondingly, often concern civic problems and treat politically and socially relevant questions such as emerged from Muhammad's activity as a leader of political community."[22]

The whole structure of Islamic ethics, law, and jurisprudence finds its foundation largely in the revelations of this period.[23] An important feature of the Medinan revelations is the final break with the Jewish and Christian faiths of his time.[24] The revelations gradually become more forceful in their denouncements of Jews and Christians, and there is an obvious attempt to bring Islam more in line with its Arabian character. As an example we can note the difference in Muhammad's treatment of

21. Schimmel, 16.
22. Ibid.
23. For a brief discussion of the Qur'anic law, see Stanton, 63–71.
24. See Chapters 3 and 4 for further discussion on this point.

Abraham in the Meccan and Medinan revelations. In Mecca it was often claimed that no prophet had been sent to Arabs before Muhammad. Abraham holds a prominent position among the prophets and he is called a *hanif* (an original monotheist) in contrast to the polytheists. However, later in Medina we are to understand that Abraham lived in Mecca and founded the sanctuary of Mecca with the help of his son Ishmael (the ancestor of the Arabs). Now when Muhammad refers to Abraham as *hanif* it is in order to contrast him to the Jews and Christians. The religion of Abraham (which predates Judaism and Christianity) is the pure and original religion that Muhammad is sent to restore and complete.[25]

It is in this connection that the important Qur'anic doctrine of abrogation (*nasikh*), which is closely connected to the Islamic concept of progressive revelation, arises. As the Qur'an itself puts it: "None of Our revelations Do We abrogate Or cause to be forgotten, But We substitute Something better or similar" (2:106; also see 16:101; 13:39). The Qur'anic scholar, Arthur Jeffery, explains this doctrine in the following way:

> The Qur'an is unique among sacred scriptures in teaching a doctrine of abrogation according to which later pronouncements of the Prophet abrogate, i.e., declare null and void, his earlier pronouncements. The importance of knowing which verses abrogate others has given rise to the Qur'anic science known as *Nasikh wa Mansukh,* i.e., "the Abrogators and the Abrogated."[26]

The implications of this doctrine can be profound when we consider the transition between the Meccan and the Medinan suras. The Muslim theologian, Ibn Salam, in his book *Kitab an-Nasikh wa'l Mansukh,* writes, "Abrogation in Allah's Book is of three kinds. One kind is where both text and prescription have been abrogated. Another is where the text has been abrogated but the prescription remains. Yet another is where the prescription has been abrogated but the text remains."[27]

Under the first category the author cites several instances taken from the traditions in which a Qur'anic text and its principle have been removed from the present-day Qur'an. In the second category we are told about the verse about "stoning" as a punishment for adultery. It is claimed that the text has been abrogated, but the prescription (against adultery) stands. About the third category he writes, "Examples of where the prescription has been abrogated but the text remains are to be found in sixty-three Suras. Instances are the saying of prayers facing toward the Jerusalem shrine, the former fastings, letting the polytheists be, and

25. See Gibb and Kramers, 285.
26. See Jeffery, 66.
27. Ibid., 67.

turning from the ignorant."[28] As an explanation to these references Jeffery notes, "The earlier practice of facing toward Jerusalem in prayer, mentioned in II, 143/138, was abrogated by the command in II, 144/139 ff. to turn toward the sacred mosque in Mecca; the earlier practice of fasting like the Jews in Muharram ten days of Ashura was abrogated by the command to fast the whole thirty days of Ramadan (II, 183, 179 ff.); XLIII, 89, which orders that the polytheists be let alone, and VII, 199/198, which bids the Prophet turn away from the ignorant, are both said to be *abrogated by the Verse of the Sword (II, 191/187), which orders their slaughter.*"[29]

The doctrine of abrogation has also worked the other way around, especially among the Sufis (see Appendix 1) and in some small progressive Islamic circles of modern times. Some have argued that it is in the message of the Meccan period that "the primarily 'religious' quality of Islam, the 'essence' which prior to the political/military order at Medina, is enshrined."[30] However, this view has not won any general acceptance among orthodox Muslims.

THE QUR'AN AS ISLAMIC SCRIPTURE

All that has been said so far serves simply as an introduction to the most important fact about the Qur'an: its unique position in Islam. No significant insight about the Qur'an is possible without an appreciation of the profound admiration that millions of faithful Muslims (beginning from the time of Muhammad himself) have had and continue to have for their holy book. Therefore, the remainder of this chapter is devoted to an exploration of the status of the Qur'an in Islam.

In an article entitled, "The Muslim Lives by the Qur'an," professor Yusuf K. Ibish writes with penetrating insight about the status of the Qur'an in Islam:

> I have not yet come across a western man who understands what the Qur'an is. It is not a book in the ordinary sense, nor is it comparable to the Bible, either the Old or New Testaments. It is an expression of Divine Will. If you want to compare it with anything in Christianity, you must compare it with Christ Himself. Christ was the expression of the Divine among men, the revelation of the Divine Will. That is what the Qur'an is. If you want a

28. Ibid., 68.
29. Ibid., emphasis ours.
30. Kenneth Cragg, "Contemporary Trends in Islam," in Woodberry, 33–35. Cragg goes on to say that such dichotomies between the Meccan and the Medinan messages "do not commend themselves to the generality of Muslims anywhere." Such views are nothing "more than marginal, with little chance of practical expression in the given temper of today" (35).

comparison for the role of Muhammad, the better one in that particular respect would be Mary. Muhammad was the vehicle of the Divine, as she was the vehicle. . . . There are western orientalists who have devoted their life to the study of the Qur'an, its text, the analysis of its words, discovering that this word is Abyssinian, that word is Greek by origin. . . . But all this is immaterial. The Qur'an was divinely inspired, then it was compiled, and what we have now is the expression of God's Will among men. That is the important point.[31]

Another Muslim scholar, highly conversant with Western scholarship, agrees with the above point. In his *Ideals and Realities of Islam*, Seyyed Hossein Nasr writes,

The Word of God in Islam is the Quran; in Christianity it is Christ. . . . To carry this analogy further one can point to the fact that the Quran, being the Word of God, therefore corresponds to Christ in Christianity and the form of this book, which like the content is determined by the dictum of heaven, corresponds in a sense to the body of Christ. The form of the Quran is the Arabic language which religiously speaking is as inseparable from the Quran as the body of Christ is from Christ Himself. Arabic is sacred in the sense that it is an integral part of the Quranic revelation whose very sounds and utterances play a role in the ritual acts of Islam.[32]

These comments provide a feeling for the majestic and incomparable place of the Qur'an in Islam. Whereas in Christianity in the beginning was the Word and the Word became flesh, in Islam in the beginning was the Word and the Word became a Book! It is therefore very important for us to know something of the relationship of this Book to Islamic theology.

Throughout the Qur'an we are constantly reminded that the Qur'an is not a human (or even angelic) product, but is wholly from God himself who is revealing it to the prophet Muhammad: "Praise be to God, Who hath sent to His Servant The Book, and hath allowed Therein no Crookedness" (18:1); "The revelation Of this Book Is from God, The Exalted in Power, Full of Wisdom. Verily it is We Who have Revealed the Book to thee In Truth" (39:1–2); "(God) Most Gracious! It is He Who has Taught the Qur'an" (55:1–2; see also 3:7; 41:2–3; 12:1–2; 20:113; 25:6; 2:2–4; 43:43–44; 6:19; 39:41. For responses to the charge that the Qur'an has been produced by a source other than God, see 26:210–11; 10:37).

We are also told that the Qur'an is not simply a revelation from God but a book that finds its origin in a heavenly "Mother of the Book": "Nay,

---

31. Waddy, 14.

32. Seyyed Hossein Nasr, *Ideals and Realities of Islam* (London: George Allen & Unwin, 1975), 43–44.

this is A Glorious Qur'an, (Inscribed) in A Tablet Preserved!" (85:21–22); "We have made it A Qur'an in Arabic, That ye may be able To understand (and learn wisdom). And verily, it is In the Mother of the Book, In Our Presence, high (In dignity), full of wisdom" (43:3–4; cf. 13:39).

Therefore, from the very beginning of Islam the Qur'an was considered by all Muslims as the Word of God par excellence. The absolute admiration that Muhammad and his companions displayed for this book is documented in many Islamic traditions. This reverence for the Qur'an continued to grow after Muhammad's death, reaching a point that "after a hundred years a fierce controversy arose among the religious scholars on the question whether it (the Qur'an) was created or is, like God himself, uncreated, i.e. not preceded by non-existence. This controversy went on for centuries."[33]

Eventually, the orthodox schools defeated the position of the Mu'tazilites ("the Seceders"), a group of Muslim theologians who sought to combine Greek rationalism with Islamic thought, and strongly denied the eternality of the Qur'an. (This group, which was widely popular at one point, is no longer in existence; however, some of their influence—such as the doctrine of the Qur'an's createdness—can be seen in the theology of Shi'ite Islam). Three Muslim Caliphs even attempted to declare it a heresy for anyone to teach the idea that the Qur'an was created, and the Caliph Al-Mutawakkil (d. A.D. 850), went so far as to "decree the death penalty for anyone who taught that the Word of God is created."[34]

Goldziher, one of the greatest European authorities on Islam, succinctly explains this great Islamic controversy: "One of the weightiest subjects of dogmatic debate was the concept of the divine word. How is one to understand the attribution of speech to God? How is one to explain the operation of this attribute in the act of revelation embodied in the holy scriptures?"[35]

Although Muslim scholars realize that these kinds of questions belong in the context of the theory of God's attributes, they were treated as separate subjects of theological discussion. Orthodox Islam answers these questions by noting that speech is an eternal attribute of God, which is without beginning or intermission, exactly like his knowledge, might, and other characteristics of his infinite being. Consequently, revelation, which is the acknowledged manifestation of God's speaking, did not originate in time by a specific act of God's creative will, but has existed from all eter-

33. Dashti, 147. Some scholars of Islam see in this controversy a direct influence of the Christian doctrine of Logos. See Abdul-Haqq, 62–63.

34. Williams, 179.

35. See Goldziher, 97.

nity. So, according to orthodox Muslim doctrine, the Qur'an is the uncreated speech of God that has existed in the mind of God from eternity.[36]

The great Sunni authority, Abu Hanifa, expressed the orthodox viewpoint as follows:

> The Qur'an is the word of God, and is His inspired word and revelation. It is a necessary attribute of God. It is not God, but still is inseparable from God. It is written in a volume, it is read in a language, it is remembered in the heart, and its letters and its vowel points, and its writing are all created, for they are the works of men, but God's word is uncreated. Its words, its writing, its letters, and its verses are for the necessities of man, for its meaning is arrived at by their use, but the word of God is fixed in the essence of God, and he who says that the word of God is created is an infidel.[37]

So for Muslims the Qur'an is not simply regarded as *their* holy book, one among many other divine revelations. The Qur'an is the eternal Word of God that descended (*tanzil*) to Muhammad in order to be the final light and guidance for humankind. Even though some Muslims have made certain pluralistic claims about the relationship of the Qur'an with other Scriptures (see Chapter 3), according to orthodox Islam the Qur'an by its very nature supersedes all previous revelations.

A DIVINE GUIDE FOR HUMANKIND

On many occasions the Qur'an refers to itself as a "Clear Argument" (*al-Burhan*), or "Light" (*an-Nur*), or "The Explanation" (*al-Bayan*).[38] In fact, after the first chapter of the Qur'an, which functions as an introductory prayer, the second chapter starts with the verse, "This is the Book: In it is guidance sure, without doubt, To those who fear God" (2:2).

Similar to the position of Christ in the Christian faith as the climax and finality of God's revelation to man, the Qur'an holds a similar role in the Islamic faith. As Abdul Ahad Dawud writes, "For after the Revelation of the Will and Word of Allah in the Holy Qur'an there is the end of the prophecy and of revelation."[39] However, before going any further we need to mention one fundamental difference. Whereas in Christianity Christ is believed to be the self-disclosure of God, in Islam the emphasis

36. Ibid.
37. See Abdul-Haqq, 62. Also see Al-Maturidi's defense of the orthodox position against the Mutazilites in Williams, 182. For a modern and somewhat mystical explanation of the eternality of the Qur'an, see Nasr, 53.
38. Ajijola, 104.
39. Gudel, 35–36; and Abdu'l-Ahad Dawud, *Muhammad in the Bible* (Kuala Lumpur: Pustaka Antara, 1969).

of the Qur'an is not on revealing God per se, but more important, on disclosing the commands of God. As Kenneth Cragg observes,

> The revelation communicated God's Law. It does not reveal God Himself
> . . . the genius of Islam is finally law and not theology. In the last analysis the
> sense of God is a sense of Divine command. In the will of God there is none
> of the mystery that surrounds His being. His demands are known and the
> believer's task is not so much exploratory, still less fellowship, but rather
> obedience and allegiance.[40]

It is due to this Qur'anic emphasis, on revealing the will and commands of God regarding the many details of life, that the Muslims view the Qur'an as the ultimate and most suitable divine guidance for man. Ajijola writes, "The Qur'an is a comprehensive code of life covering every aspect and phase of human life. This Book of God lays down the best rules relating to social life, commerce and economics, marriage and inheritance, penal laws and international conduct, etc." [41]

In addition to the many mundane laws of the Qur'an that serve as evidence for the practicality and ultimacy of divine guidance,[42] the Qur'an is also considered the final revelation from God because of the belief that it perfects and fulfills previous divine revelations. In 10:37, we read, "This Qur'an . . . is A confirmation of (revelations) That went before it, And a fuller explanation Of the Book—wherein There is no doubt—From the Lord of the Worlds." Kateregga expresses a basic Muslim conviction when he writes,

> Therefore, the Qur'an, as the final revelation, is the perfection and culmi-
> nation of all the truth contained in the earlier Scriptures (revelation).
> Though sent in Arabic, it is the Book for all times and for all mankind. The
> purpose of the Qur'an is to guard the previous revelations by restoring the
> eternal truth of Allah. The Qur'an is the torch-light by which humanity can
> be rightly guided onto the straight path.[43]

Another contemporary Muslim writer, Abdalati, adds: "These Muslims have good reasons to believe that their Book, the Glorious Qur'an, is the Master Book of Revelation and the Standard of Religious Truth." Thus, "they also believe that Islam has come to reaffirm the Eternal Divine Mes-

---

40. Cragg, *The Call of the Minaret,* 55, 57. See Chapter 1 for further discussion of Islamic theology.
41. Ajijola, 90.
42. Abdalati, 196–97.
43. Kateregga and Shenk, 27.

sage and settle the past religious disputes so that man may embark upon creative constructive activities in all walks of life."[44]

This same Muslim attitude can be seen in somewhat harsher tones in the writings of the classical orthodox theologian, Ibn Taymiyya:

> The guidance and true religion which is in the *shari'a* brought by Muhammad is more perfect than what was in the two previous religious laws. . . . The law of the Torah, unlike that of the Qur'an, is lacking in completeness. . . . In the Torah, the Gospel, and the books of the prophets there are no useful forms of knowledge or upright deeds which are not found in the Qur'an, or else there is found that which is better. In the Qur'an there is found guidance and true religion in beneficial knowledge and upright deeds which are not in the other two books.[45]

Since for Islam the Qur'an is the divine revelation par excellence, it follows logically that in the present age we must abandon all previous Scriptures and submit ourselves to the guidance of the Qur'an. "It is on account of these special features of the Qur'an that all the people of the world have been directed to have faith in it, to give up all other books and to follow it alone, because it contains all that is essential for living in accordance with God's pleasure."[46]

In all these doctrinal discussions we should not lose sight of one fact: the belief that the Qur'an provides divine guidance for life is accepted not only as an intellectual dogma, but as a daily and lifelong reality for faithful Muslims. Once again, Yusuf Ibish perceptively points out, "the Muslims live by the Qur'an. From the first rituals of birth to the principal events of life and death, marriage, inheritance, business contracts: all are based on the Qur'an."[47] In a similar style, Hossein Nasr writes, "not only do the teachings of the Qur'an direct the life of a Muslim, but what is more the soul of a Muslim is like a mosaic made up of formulae of the Qur'an in which he breathes and lives."[48]

Concerning the place of the Qur'an in the life of a faithful Muslim, Anis Shorrosh contends that

> The Quran is held in the greatest esteem and reverence among Muslims as their holy scripture. They dare not touch it without first being washed and purified. They read it with the greatest care and respect, never holding it below their waist. They swear by it and consult it on all occasions.

44. See Abdalati, xiii. Of course, some claim that this statement is not corroborated by historical facts, since Islam has not really settled past religious disputes.

45. Ibn Taymiyya, 350–69.

46. Ajijola, 96; cf. 94–96.

47. See Waddy, 14.

48. Nasr, 61.

They carry it with them to war, write sentences of it on their banners, suspend it from their necks as charm, and always place it on the highest shelf or in some place of honor in their houses. It is said that the devil runs away from the house in which a portion of the Quran . . . (the second sura), is read.[49]

A DIVINE MIRACLE

Not only is the Qur'an the ultimate divine revelation, but for Muslims (including Muhammad himself), it is also the ultimate divine miracle. The "miracle of the Qur'an" is certainly the most fundamental and popular doctrine about the Qur'an for the majority of Muslims, even more than the doctrine of the eternality of the Qur'an.

It is an interesting fact that from almost the very beginning of his ministry Muhammad claimed that the Qur'an was his only miracle. In 2:23, the prophet is commanded to say, "And if ye are in doubt As to what We have revealed From time to time to Our servant, Then produce a Sura Like thereunto; And call your witnesses or helpers (If there are any) besides God, If your (doubts) are true" (cf. 10:38). In 17:88, there is another bold challenge of the prophet to the unbelievers: "Say: 'If the whole Of mankind and *Jinn* Were to gather together To produce the like Of this Qur'an, they Could not produce The like thereof, even if They backed up each other With help and support.'"

This absolute confidence in the miraculousness of the Qur'an has remained unshaken among Muslims to this day. In a sense this is the foundation of Islam and the most essential evidence for the prophethood of Muhammad. Al-Baqillani, a classical theologian, in his book *Ijaz al-Qur'an* (The Miracle of the Qur'an), writes: "What makes it necessary to pay quite particular attention to that [branch of Qur'anic] science [known as] *Ijaz al-Qur'an* is that the prophetic office of the Prophet—upon whom be peace—is built upon this miracle."[50] A contemporary Muslim author, Faruqi, observes that "Muslims do not claim any miracles for Muhammad. In their view, what proves Muhammad's prophethood is the sublime beauty and greatness of the revelation itself, the Holy Qur'an, not any inexplicable breaches of natural law which confound human reason."[51]

---

49. Shorrosh, 21. Also see Jeffery, 58–66.

50. See Jeffery, 54.

51. Al-Faruqi, 20. Some scholars qualify Faruqi's statement, noting that many Muslims believe (though without Qur'anic evidence) that Muhammad performed a multitude of fantastic miracles involving inexplicable breaches of natural law. Haykal, the modern biographer of Muhammad, also voices the same opinion: "Muhammad . . . had only one irresistible miracle—the Qur'an," xxvi.

THE MIRACULOUS NATURE OF THE QUR'AN

Muslim apologists have offered many evidences for the divine origin of the Qur'an. Most of them fit under one or more of the following arguments. (The arguments will be elaborated more fully later in Chapter 9. Here we will give only the general outline of each point.) The weight of these arguments varies from scholar to scholar. Generally speaking, however, more weight is given to the first few, and the first one seems to be given the most weight by the majority of Muslim apologists.

THE ARGUMENT FROM UNIQUE LITERARY STYLE

According to this argument the Qur'an "is wonderfully arranged, and marvelously composed, and so exalted in its literary elegance as to be beyond what any mere creature could attain."[52] By revelation Muhammad claimed that "this Qur'an is not such As can be produced By other than God" (10:37). He boasts that "if the whole Of mankind and *Jinn* Were to gather together To produce the like Of this Qur'an, they Could not produce The like thereof, even if They backed up each other With help and support" (17:88).

It is the belief of all Muslims that "The Qur'an is the greatest wonder among the wonders of the world. It repeatedly challenged the people of the world to bring a chapter like it, but they failed and the challenge remains unanswered up to this day." They believe that the Qur'an "is second to none in the world according to the unanimous decision of the learned men in points of diction, style, rhetoric, thoughts and soundness of laws and regulations to shape the destinies of mankind."[53] This, they contend, is proof positive that the Qur'an is the very Word of God.

THE ARGUMENT FROM MUHAMMAD'S ILLITERACY

This argument supports the former one. In fact, they form a unit. For if it is a marvel in itself that such a literary masterpiece as the Qur'an was produced at all, then it is even more amazing that it was written by someone who was illiterate (7:157).

THE ARGUMENT FROM THE PERFECT PRESERVATION OF THE QUR'AN

The fact that the Qur'an has been kept from any textual corruption is another evidence often given by Muslims for the miraculous nature of the Qur'an's marvelous preservation. Suzanne Haneef, for example, proudly notes that "the Holy Qur'an is the only divinely revealed scripture in the history of mankind which has been preserved to the present

52. Al-Baqillani, *Ijaz al-Qur'an*, 38, as cited by Jeffery, 57.
53. Nehls, 38.

time in its exact original form."[54] Since this is true of no other holy book, who but God could be the cause?

THE ARGUMENT FROM PROPHECIES IN THE QUR'AN

Muslims also use fulfilled prophecy to defend the miraculous nature of the Qur'an. How else, they say, could Muhammad have accurately predicted events in advance, such as the Roman victory over the Persians (30:2–4)?

THE ARGUMENT FROM THE UNITY OF THE QUR'AN

Islamic scholars sometimes appeal to the fact that the Qur'an has no contradictions as evidence of its divine origin: "Do they [unbelievers] not consider The Qur'an (with care)? Had it been from other Than God, they would surely Have found therein Much discrepancy" (4:82). Yusuf Ali claims that "the unity of the Qur'an is admittedly greater than that of any other sacred book. And yet how can we account for it except through the unity of God's purpose and design?"[55]

THE ARGUMENT FROM THE SCIENTIFIC ACCURACY OF THE QUR'AN

More recently it has been popular to argue that the Qur'an's scientific accuracy is proof of its divine authority. Bucaille insists that the scientific evidence "will lead to the conclusion that it is inconceivable for a human being living in the Seventh century A.D. to have expressed assertions in the Qur'an on highly varied subjects that do not belong to his period and for them to be in keeping with what was to be revealed only centuries later. For me, there can be no human explanation of the Qur'an."[56]

THE ARGUMENT FROM THE AMAZING MATHEMATICAL STRUCTURE OF THE QUR'AN

One recent popular proof for the Qur'an's divine origin is a mathematical miracle based on the number nineteen. Rashad Khalifa contends that "the Quranic initials and their mathematical distribution prove two things beyond a shadow of doubt: The Quran is the word of God and the Quran has been perfectly preserved."[57]

THE ARGUMENT FROM CHANGED LIVES

Finally, Muslim scholars sometimes argue that the changed lives and cultures effected by the Qur'an are evidence of its divine origin. Ajijola

---

54. Suzanne Haneef, *What Everyone Should Know About Islam and Muslims* (Chicago: Kazi Publications, 1979), 18–19.

55. Ali, 205.

56. Bucaille, 130.

57. Rashad Khalifa, *Quran: A Visual Presentation of the Miracle* (Karachi: Haider Ali Muljee, 1983), 200.

claims that "the transformation wrought by the Holy Qur'an is unparalleled in the history of the world and thus its claim to being unique stands as unchallenged today as it did thirteen centuries ago. . . . No faith ever imparted such a new life to its votaries on such a wide scale."[58]

CONCLUSION

By now we can see the exalted place of the Qur'an in Islam. However, like other monotheistic faiths, understanding divine scripture is not in itself the final goal. The Qur'an is a guide and this life is a preparation for the eternal life hereafter. It is of utmost importance that the believer be and remain on the straight path and in the end be saved from the eternal wrath of God and received into God's blessing in heaven. Therefore, it is only appropriate that we should also understand the Muslim views of salvation and afterlife in order to grasp the totality of the Islamic message to man. The next chapter will be devoted to a discussion of these important topics.

58. Ajijola, 100–101.

6

ENDTIMES AND SALVATION

So far we have covered some of the most fundamental doctrines of Islam: God, humans, sin, prophethood, and the Qur'an. However, like all monotheistic faiths, Islam is not concerned simply with the relationship of God and man in this world. The ultimate goal is the salvation of people in the world to come. This life is only a preparation for either a life of eternal bliss in heaven or damnation in hell (3:185b).

The beginning messages of the Qur'an consist mainly of warnings about the horrors of the coming day of judgment. People are challenged to live righteously in view of the fact that one day they will be held accountable for their actions. Indeed, in a very real sense the doctrines of eternal salvation or damnation constitute "the central theme" of the Qur'an.[1] As a book written by two Islamic scholars points out:

> So intense is the Qur'anic concern for and insistence on the day to come when all will be held accountable for their faith and their actions, that the ethical teachings contained in the Book must be understood in the light of this reality. Faith in the day of resurrection for the Muslim is his specific affirmation of God's omnipotence, the recognition of human accountability as a commitment to the divine unicity.[2]

Furthermore, Islam, along with the Judeo-Christian tradition, affirms the purposeful direction and significance of a linear view of history. Time has a beginning and an end, and it is within this framework of history, moving from the creation to the end (eschaton) "which God makes manifest [by] His signs and His commands, and at the same time it is the arena in which humanity exhibits its acceptance or rejection of those signs."[3]

1. Quasem, 19.
2. Jane Smith and Y. Haddad, *The Islamic Understanding of Death and Resurrection* (Albany: State University of New York Press, 1981), 2.
3. Ibid., 4.

Thus, it is appropriate that we conclude our exposition of Islam with a brief examination of Islamic eschatology (last things) and soteriology (salvation). In the first part of this chapter we will consider the Islamic views on death and afterlife, endtimes, the final judgment, and heaven and hell. In the second part we will deal more specifically with the question of salvation in Islam. What are the conditions of salvation? And in the final analysis who will be saved and who will be lost?

ISLAMIC ESCHATOLOGY[4]

DEATH OF THE INDIVIDUAL

Generally, Islamic eschatological manuals start with a discussion of the individual's death, especially since the Qur'an itself places great emphasis on the fact of human mortality. For example, in 3:185 we read, "Every soul shall have A taste of death: And only on the Day Of Judgment shall you Be paid your full recompense." The idea of human death and final judgment is also closely related in 23:15–16: "After that, at length Ye will die. Again, on the Day Of Judgment, will ye be Raised up."

Although the fact of human death is a Qur'anic certainty, the Qur'an says very little about the process of death and the condition of the deceased before the final resurrection. As is often the case, Islamic tradition goes into great detail in order to fill in these gaps.

The process of death is described in 56:83 where it claims that the soul of the dying man comes up to his throat. And in 6:93 it declares that at the time of death, "the angels Stretch forth their hands, [Saying], 'Yield up your souls.'" As for the process of death for unbelievers, 8:50 says, "If thou couldst see, When the angels take the souls Of the Unbelievers [at death], [How] they smite their faces And their backs, [saying]: 'Taste the Penalty of the blazing Fire'" (cf. 79:1–2).

Exactly what happens after this stage the Qur'an does not say. It is at this point that we notice a heavy reliance on the hadith material in order to explain the events that follow death.[5] According to a famous tradition,

---

4. These stages are based on the divisions of the Muslim author Muhammad Khouj, *The End of the Journey: An Islamic Perspective on Death and the Afterlife* (Washington, D.C.: The Islamic Center, 1988).

5. Two points need to be mentioned here. First, in classical theological manuals there is also a heavy reliance on tradition to describe in full and fanciful detail the painful struggle of death itself. Since many in contemporary Islam have rejected such fanciful descriptions of death, we will not consider this point any further (see Smith and Haddad, 34–38, and their Chapter 4). Second, in the discussion that follows, Smith and Haddad correctly warn us that "to isolate specific events or references or to attempt to find in these a natural progression is in one sense a misdirected effort, for the events function primarily to support from a variety of perspectives the basic fact of human responsibility" (77).

the soul of the faithful person, which is easily removed from the body, is clothed in a heavenly and sweet smelling garment by radiant and smiling angels. The soul is taken through the seven heavens, entering the presence of God who then orders the angels to return the soul to its earthly body until the day of judgment. On the other hand, the soul of the unbelieving person is removed from its body with a great deal of struggle. The angel of death clothes the soul with a foul smelling garment. The angel responsible for the wicked soul also tries to take the soul through the various levels of heaven but the gates of heaven are not opened to them (7:40), and the soul is then also returned to its body.[6] It should be added that "all of these events . . . happen so quickly that when the soul is returned to the body, the washers are still busy taking care of the corpse."[7]

LIFE IN THE GRAVE

According to orthodox (and also popular) Islam, the abode of death—"life in the grave" or *barzakh*—is a very active place. Most Muslims believe that there are two angels, usually called *Munkar* and *Nakir*, who visit the dead person to ask him a series of questions about his faith. The accounts do not agree on exactly what questions will be asked of the deceased. However, most versions indicate that after entering the grave, the angels ask the dead person to sit up; they ask him who is his Lord, what is his religion, and who is his prophet. "The correct answers, which the virtuous know immediately, are God, Islam, and Muhammad."[8]

For the believers who pass the test successfully the angels make their graves more spacious, and open a window through which they can gaze at the Garden and receive the winds and odor of Paradise. For unbelievers who fail the test, the angels "open a door to hell fire for him. Thus the deceased feels the heat and hot winds from hell and his grave narrows until his ribs merge into one another."[9]

The idea of torment after death is also a widely held belief among orthodox Muslims. According to a hadith related by Aisha, the prophet claimed that "the torment of the grave is a fact." Aisha continued, "Never did I see henceforth Allah's Messenger (*pbuh* [peace be upon him]) observe his prayer and not seek refuge with Allah from the torment of the grave."[10] In another hadith, Muhammad explained the torture of the grave in this way:

6. See Khouj, 19–23.
7. See Smith and Haddad, 40.
8. Ibid., 42.
9. Khouj, 22.
10. Ibid., 31.

Anas said that he heard Allah's Messenger (*pbuh*) saying: "When the servant is placed in a grave and his friends abandon him, he hears the noise of their shoes." Two angels come and make him sit and then say: "What do you have to say about this person—Muhammad (*pbuh*)." The believer would say: "I bear witness to the fact that he is the servant of Allah and His Messenger." It would be said to him: "Look to your seat in hell fire. Verily Allah has changed it for your seat in paradise," and he sees them both and it would be said to the hypocrite and unbeliever: "What did you say about this person (Allah's Apostle)" and he would say: "I do not know. I used to say what other people used to say." It would be said: "You neither knew nor followed those who have been saved from hell fire (believers)." He would be beaten with iron hammers and utter a shout which would be heard by all near him, except man and *jinn*.[11]

Of course, the above hadith only touches on the torment of the grave in reference to unbelievers. There are also other reports that talk about a general torment for almost every one. Many prominent Muslim theologians, including Al-Ghazali, thought "it is too simple merely to conclude that there will be a black and white division into those who are punished in this intermediate period in the grave and those who are not." Therefore, they argued "that with few exceptions each individual will undergo some kind of torment, slight or heavy, dependent upon the particular configuration of his or her *deen* (religion or faith) while on earth."[12] Thus, "orthodoxy came to accept as a fact, that the faithful and faithless alike will suffer the pressure [*daght*] of the tomb, although only the *kafir* [unbelievers] also must undergo the *adhab* or more strenuous forms of punishment."[13] It is often suggested that the difference between the torment of the believer and the unbeliever, besides its intensity, is that whereas the torment for the unbeliever is a prefiguring of the final destiny of the wicked, the believer's torment is mostly designed to have a purging effect on the soul.[14]

Many assumed that after the period of the punishment most individ-

11. Ibid., 31–32. Khouj does not address the contradiction between these two hadiths. According to the hadith related by Aisha, Muhammad himself sought refuge from the torment of the grave. While the hadith from Anas indicates that the sole criterion for the torture in the grave is based on not having a correct attitude toward the prophethood of Muhammad. He does not explain how the prophet himself could fear failing such a test.

12. Smith and Haddad, 45.

13. Ibid., 46.

14. In the history of Islam some groups, such as the Mu'tazilites, the majority of philosophers, and many among the Shi'ites, have denied the possibility of the events just described and have found the idea of punishment or rewards while in the grave unacceptable. "For the majority of Muslims, however, the punishment of the grave has been a reality, affirmed in the creeds . . . and specified in the *hadiths* of strong and not-so-strong chains of transmission" (Smith and Haddad, 47).

uals fall into a "sleep state." Yet a great majority seem to adhere to a belief that the spirits of the deceased will continue to be fully conscious and active in this period of *barzakh*. Even though the Qur'an seems clear that the dead cannot hear the living (27:80), many traditions and reports indicate that the dead hear quite well. According to one hadith the prophet affirmed that the dead speak and even visit each other.[15] According to another hadith, Muhammad said, "Any man who visits the grave of his brother and sits near it will make his brother feel happy and less lonely. The deceased will respond to his brother, although the latter will not be able to hear or respond."[16]

There is certainly no uniform Islamic opinion about the activities of departed souls at this stage. According to a report from Abu Hurayra, when a believer dies his spirit circles around his house for about a month, observing how his belongings are handled. Then for a year his spirit circles around his grave, observing those who have prayed and mourned for him. After a year his spirit reaches the place "where the spirits are gathered together for the day of resurrection."[17] According to Al-Ghazali, there are four categories of spirits. Some wander around the earth. Some "God allows to slumber." Others, like the spirits of martyrs, remain in their graves for two or three months and then are flown up to the Garden. The spirits in the fourth category, which includes those of the prophets and saints, are given free choice to do what they please, so that some have gone to heaven and some have chosen to remain on earth.[18]

Of course, we ought to point out that many contemporary Muslims reject these vivid accounts of classical theology and have decided not to speculate about the details of postmortem experience. "The great majority of contemporary Muslim writers, in fact, choose not to discuss the afterlife. They are satisfied with simply affirming the reality of the day of judgment and human accountability without providing any details or interpretive discussion."[19]

According to Smith and Haddad, most modern Muslim thinkers who treat questions of the afterlife can be divided into three basic categories. In one category we find the *traditionalists*, who affirm the classical teachings as continually valid and see their task mainly in "presenting the material in modern Arabic, which makes it accessible to the average reader."[20] A second group, which the authors identify as the *modernists*, are mainly "interested in discussing the nature of human responsi-

15. Ibid., 51.
16. See Khouj, 34.
17. See Smith and Haddad, 50.
18. Ibid., 52–53.
19. Ibid., 100.
20. Ibid.

bility and accountability ... [and] their approach to the material is homiletic rather didactic."[21] Many writers in this category acknowledge that even though human language must be used to describe the condition of life after death, this language must not be conceived in a literal sense, but in a spiritual or metaphorical sense.[22] In an interesting comment, an influential Muslim author writes, "The Messenger of God warned that sinners, after death, will be tormented by so many snakes; some simple-minded men have examined the graves of the sinners and wondered at failing to see these snakes. They do not understand that the tormenting snakes have their abode within the unbeliever's spirit, and they exist in him even before he died, for they were but his own evil qualities symbolized."[23]

The last group is classified as the *spiritualists*. This group is for the most part a direct result of Western research in the field of spiritism and communicating with the spirit world.[24] It is obvious therefore that there is no widespread Islamic consensus on the exact nature and details of the afterlife.

THE FINAL HOUR

As mentioned earlier, in Islam there is not only an emphasis on the fact of individual death, but also a parallel emphasis on the consummation of history as we know it prior to the day of judgment. Like other monotheistic faiths, Islamic theology has developed a doctrine of last things dealing with the specific topic of the "endtimes."

The Qur'an affirms that although "the Hour is coming," God has purposefully designed to "keep it hidden" (20:15). In 33:63, we read, "Men ask thee concerning The Hour: say, 'The knowledge Thereof is with God (alone)': And what will make thee Understand?—perchance The Hour is nigh!" Even though the exact hour is unknown to all except God, the Qur'an gives certain other "hints" about the coming of the last hour. Based on these suggestions and many prophetic hadiths, Islamic doctrine has attempted to systematize the series of events that are to precede the final judgment.

High on the list of Qur'anic "signs" of the last days are the cataclysmic events that are so dramatically described throughout the Qur'an. For example in 82:1–5, we read, "When the Sky Is cleft asunder; When the Stars Are scattered; When the Oceans Are suffered to burst forth; And when the Graves Are turned upside down;— (Then) shall each soul know What it hath sent forward And (what it hath) kept back." In sura 81 a sim-

21. Ibid., 106.
22. Ibid., 104–13.
23. Ibid., 110.
24. Ibid., 113–26.

ilar description is given: "When the sun (With its spacious light) Is folded up; When the stars Fall, losing their lustre; When the mountains vanish; ... When the oceans Boil over with a swell; ... (Then) shall each soul know What it has put forward" (vv. 1–3, 6, 14).

According to the majority of Muslims (though not based on the Qur'an but on prophetic tradition), this universal disintegration of nature is preceded by a widespread moral decadence. Based on numerous hadiths, it is believed that godly wisdom will "suffer complete extinction"; there will be an increase in the usage of wine, and "committing adultery and rape will be common activities."[25] Truth, honesty, and piety will decrease, while there will be a great rise in injustice and moral corruption of all kinds. An interesting hadith from Bukhari reports that "the number of males would decrease whereas females would increase till there will be only one male to look after fifty women."[26]

While these are the more "general signs" of the approaching last hour, many theological manuals also give a list of more specific signs. According to a tradition from Al-Muslim, the prophet gave the following comment about the last hour:

> Thereupon he [Muhammad] said: "It will not come until you see ten signs." And (in this connection) he made a mention of the smoke; the *Dajjal* [often called Anti-Christ]; the beast; the rising of the sun from the west; the descent of Jesus, son of Mary; the Gog and Magog; and land-slidings in three places, one in the east, one in the west, and one in Arabia at the end of which fire would burn forth from the Yemen, and would drive people to place of their assembly.[27]

It is outside the scope of this chapter to discuss every item in the above list of apocalyptic occurrences. As can be expected, there is an abundance of traditions describing each sign in colorful detail.[28] However, it is very interesting that according to many Muslim commentators, the most important sign of the closeness of the hour is the coming of Christ, his destruction of the false Messiah, and establishment of peace and righteousness on earth.

The popular Islamic picture of the Antichrist, or *Dajjal*, graphically portrays him as blind in one eye, with the word *kafir*—unbeliever—written on his forehead; his primary function is to mislead the unbelieving masses by claiming divinehood and the power to perform miracles. He

25. Khouj, 39.
26. Ibid., 38–39.
27. Ibid., 42–43.
28. Ibid., 42–60. Of course Muhammad Khouj, like many other Muslim writers, makes no attempt to put these events in any chronological order.

will "spread mischief" over the world, and all people except true believers will be fascinated by him.[29]

At the height of *Dajjal*'s activity the Messiah will descend to the earth and will destroy the Antichrist and then establish the true religion of Islam. According to a very popular tradition, Muhammad said, "By Him in whose hands my soul is; surely Jesus, the son of Mary, will soon descend amongst you as a just ruler: he will break the cross and kill the pigs and there will be no *jizya* (taxation taken from non-Muslims)."[30] It is then claimed that after a certain period Jesus himself will die and be buried near Muhammad and the first two Muslim Caliphs in the city of Medina.[31] However, even though the majority of Sunni Muslims believe in Jesus' second coming and his central role as the savior of the world during the end time, the majority of Shi'ite Muslims identify this savior figure not as Jesus but as the *Mahdi* ("divinely-guided one"). According to Shi'ite tradition *Mahdi* was the twelfth Imam (successor and descendant of Muhammad) who miraculously disappeared and will one day reappear to establish righteousness on the earth.[32]

Another often-mentioned end time sign that has its basis in the Qur'an (though the passages are somewhat obscure) is the appearance of Gog and Magog (18:92–98; 21:96–97). According to Muhammad Khouj, "On Allah's command, the Gog and Magog will come out of their dam at the time of Jesus' descent."[33] The exact nature of Gog and Magog and their relationship to the Antichrist is difficult to determine. But many believe that Gog and Magog are two nations of powerful human beings who will be greatly multiplied during the end times and will bring destruction to the earth. A prophetic hadith claims that at the appointed time God will destroy them by a plague of worms.[34]

From the signs discussed so far it seems clear that not much effort has been made on the part of Muslim theologians to make a coherent chronological order of the above listed events. But it is safe to say that after all the signs have come to pass, this third stage ends with the final devastation of the cosmic structure as a preparation for the general resurrection of all humankind.

29. See Khouj, 44–47.

30. Ibid., 54.

31. For a fascinating description of the grave that is already provided for Jesus, see Zwemer, *The Muslim Christ* (London: Oliphant, Anderson and Ferrier, 1912), 107–9.

32. Some Muslims, like the classical theologian Ibn Khaldun, affirmed the distinct roles of both Jesus and *Mahdi* and proposed a theory whereby both these characters will be cooperating with each other in bringing world peace (see Smith and Haddad, 69–70).

33. Khouj, 55.

34. Ibid., 58.

The Resurrection of all Humankind

As Smith and Haddad remark, "perhaps no single point in the entire sequence of eschatological events can match this period of the trumpet soundings for drama and excitement."[35] Concerning this event the Qur'an says (69:13–16) that "when one Blast is sounded On the Trumpet, And the earth is moved, And its mountains, And they are crushed to powder At one stroke,—on that Day Shall the (Great) Event Come to pass, And the sky will be Rent asunder, for it will That Day be flimsy." Also in 39:68, we read, "The Trumpet will (just) Be sounded, when all That are in the heavens And on earth will swoon, Except such as it will Please God (to exempt). Then will a second one Be sounded, when, behold, They will be standing And looking on!"

Islamic tradition identifies the angel of Death or Israfil as the one who with God's permission will blow the final trumpet calls. Commenting on the above Qur'an verses, Muhammad Khouj writes, "with the first blow, every living creature, whether on earth or in the sky, that Allah wants to die will die. With the second blow, Allah will resurrect everyone who died from the beginning of creation until the last moment of life."[36] Some classical writers, based on several Qur'anic texts that proclaim everything will perish except God's face (28:88; 55:26–27), go so far as to say that all the angels—including the angel of death himself—will die in order that God's unity (*tawhid*) might be exalted.[37] After an unknown period of "time" God will resurrect all the dead,[38] starting with Israfil who will blow the trumpet call of resurrection.

The fact of bodily resurrection is a cornerstone of Muhammad's early preaching. On numerous occasions the prophet was mocked for his belief in the corporeal resurrection, but he stood steadfast in his affirmation of it. "See they not that God, Who created the heavens And the earth ... Is able to give life To the dead? Yea, verily He has power over all things" (46:33). Rebuking man's unbelief in God's power, the Qur'an says, "And he makes comparisons For Us, and forgets his own (Origin and) Creation: He says, 'Who can give Life to (dry) bones And decomposed ones (at that)?' Say, 'He will give them Life Who created them For the first time! For He is well-versed In every kind of creation!'" (36:78-79).

According to orthodox Muslim belief, God will recreate each individual's body in its original shape from every person's imperishable seed (*ajub al-dhanab*), and will then rejoin every soul to its body. It is believed

35. Smith and Haddad, 71.
36. Khouj, 61.
37. See Smith and Haddad, 71–73.
38. Al-Bukhari states in a tradition that the resurrection comes about by God sending rain on the earth (Khouj, 64).

that everyone will feel that it has been a short time since his or her death.[39]

After all humankind is resurrected they will then be gathered before the throne of God. Some traditions say that all "will be assembled bare-foot, naked and uncircumcised," absolutely powerless before their cre-ator.[40] After the resurrection "the individual is said to be given ample opportunity to contemplate the imminent recompense for his past faults. The whole process culminates in what is called the terror of the place of assembly [*al-mahshar*], or the time of standing before God [*al-mauquf*]."[41]

There are many references throughout the Qur'an to this awesome meeting between human beings and their Creator. Concerning the fate of the unbelievers we read, "Say thou: 'Yea, and ye shall Then be humili-ated (On account of your evil).' Then it will be a single (Compelling) cry: And behold, they will Begin to see! They will say, 'Ah! Woe to us! this is The Day of Judgment!' (A voice will say,) 'This is the Day Of Sorting Out, whose Truth ye (once) denied'" (37:18–21). However, for the believers, "The Great Terror will Bring them no grief: But the angels will meet them (With mutual greetings): 'This is your Day—(The Day) that ye were prom-ised'" (21:103). Another comparison between the two groups is found in 80:33–42:

> At length, when there Comes the Deafening Noise—That Day shall a man Flee from his own brother, And from his mother And his father, And from his wife And his children. Each one of them, That Day, will have Enough concern (of his own) To make him indifferent To the others. Some Faces that Day Will be beaming, Laughing, rejoicing. And other faces that Day Will be dust-stained; Blackness will cover them: Such will be The Rejecters of God, The Doers of Iniquity (also see 74:9–10; 75:35–39; 78:40).

Finally, after a certain amount of time (based on 70:4) which some speculate will last fifty thousand years, and others (based on 32:5) a thou-sand, the command will be given that all should "bow in adoration" (68:42). And while the Qur'an says that the unbelievers will be unable to fall in prostration, tradition affirms that the believers will gladly do so, and the stage will be set for the moment of reckoning.

THE DAY OF ACCOUNTING

"When Allah assembles people in His presence, He will begin to judge them on the scale of absolute justice. Everything a person does . . .

39. Ibid., 64–67.
40. See Smith and Haddad, 74.
41. Ibid., 75.

including intentions and desires, will be accounted for on this day. At that moment, nobody can help anyone else because a person's deeds and intention will speak for him."[42] So writes a contemporary and orthodox Muslim author, Muhammad Khouj. He adds, "each individual has two angels—one on his right who records his good deeds and one on his left who records the bad deeds. By Allah's orders, these angels registered every single act and intention of every human being."[43] Khouj's comments are based on the many Qur'anic passages that assure us of the absolute justice of God in his judgment of humankind, and the fact that each individual is judged based on his own record in his earthly life.

For example, 18:49 declares that "the Book (of Deeds) Will be placed (before you); And thou wilt see The sinful in great terror Because of what is (recorded) Therein; they will say, 'Ah! woe to us! What a book is this! It leaves out nothing Small or great, but Takes account thereof!' They will find all that they Did, placed before them: And not one will thy Lord Treat with injustice." And 17:13–14 affirms that "every man's fate We have fastened On his own neck: On the Day of Judgment We shall bring out For him a scroll, Which he will see Spread open. (It will be said to him:) 'Read thine (own) record: Sufficient is thy soul This day to make out An account against thee.'"

In addition to the Book of Deeds as a witness to the individual's faith and action, the Qur'an also mentions the witness of the prophets against the unbelievers and for the believers of their community (16:89). A further testimony regarding the individual's past actions will be parts of the person's own body. "That Day shall We set A seal on their mouths. But their hands will speak To Us, and their feet Bear witness, to all That they did" (36:65).

According to the Qur'anic imagery, the divine judicial process is carried out by the means of a scale (*mizan*), which is used for balancing the individual's good deeds against the bad deeds. "Then those whose balance (Of good deeds) is heavy—They will attain salvation: But those whose balance Is light, will be those Who have lost their souls; In Hell will they abide" (23:102–3). The outcome of the divine decision is handed to the individual; it is described in 69:18–31:

> That Day shall ye be Brought to Judgment: Not an act of yours That ye hide will be hidden. Then he that will be Given his Record In his right hand Will say: 'Ah here! Read ye my record! I did really understand That my Account would (One Day) reach me!' And he will be In a life of Bliss. . . . And he that will Be given his Record In his left hand, Will say: 'Ah! would That my record

42. Khouj, 70.
43. Ibid., 72.

had not Been given me! And that I had never Realised how My account (stood)! . . .' (The stern command will say): 'Seize ye him, And bind ye him, And burn ye him In the Blazing Fire.'

The last phase of the process of judgment is the crossing of the *sirat* (or *seerat*), the bridge over hell. The references in the Qur'an to this bridge are quite obscure (36:66; 37:23–24), but as usual tradition has supplied all the details about this final process. Muhammad Khouj claims that "after Allah judges the people and divides them into categories, He will set a *seerat*. The edge of the *seerat* is like a sword as fine as a hair and more hot than fiery charcoal. Then people will be asked to go through the *seerat*." Of course, "the more dedicated and committed a person is to his beliefs, the easier he will go through this *seerat*. Some will go through it like lightning. Some will go through it like wind, others like pouring rain, and still others as fast as horses. The last of these will be crawling."[44]

Unlike the faithful, those condemned at the judgment will not be able to cross successfully, but will fall into the abyss of hell. Commenting on the significance of the bridge, Smith and Haddad remark that "The symbolic imagery of this term (*sirat*) is especially rich: it is completely appropriate that the term used repeatedly in the Qur'an to represent the proper and prescribed mode of action for all the faithful, the straight path, should be in a much more specific sense the last modality in the process that assesses the degree to which every individual has followed that path." And "the *sirat* in Islamic thought seems to be yet another means of verifying rather than testing the relative merit of any given individual."[45]

Before we consider the Islamic view of eternal existence in heaven or hell, it is important at this point that we should also briefly discuss the popular Islamic understanding of intercession and its role in obtaining salvation. As we mentioned in Chapter 4, in much of popular Islam Muhammad's prophetic role as an apostle is closely tied to his salvific role as an intercessor.[46]

The exact time of Muhammad's intercession in the order of final events is a disputed point. Some reports mention it before the crossing of the bridge and some after. One of the most popular stories of the prophet's intercession, as related by Al-Ghazali, places this event much earlier, after the sounding of the trumpets:

44. Ibid., 79.
45. Smith and Haddad, 78–79.
46. This popular belief goes against the general Qur'anic testimony regarding the possibility of intercession (2:48; 6:51), and is also rejected by many orthodox Muslims. It is interesting that Khouj, for example, in his sequence of eschatological events, makes no mention of Muhammad's intercession for his community.

According to this account Muslims waiting for the judgment for a thousand years seek restlessly for one of the prophets to intercede for them with God. They go from one to the next, but each has to refuse because of some particular problem or sin he has committed: Adam for eating the fruit of the tree, Noah for being too concerned for himself while his people were drowning, Abraham for disputing with his community about the din of God, Moses for killing a man, and Jesus because he and his mother are worshipped as gods. Finally they go to Muhammad, and the Prophet says, "I am the right one! I am the right one [to intercede] insofar as God allows it for whomever He wills and chooses." Moving towards the pavilions of God, the Prophet asks for and is granted permission to intercede. The veils are raised, he falls in prostration for a thousand years, praising God, and the Throne itself trembles in tribute to him.[47]

Not only is Muhammad given the permission to intercede, but his intercession is so effective that many of those who had been originally condemned to hell are released from hell and taken to heaven due to the mercy of the prophet.[48] Thus popular belief is that the most sinful will be saved by Muhammad's intercession and God's mercy at the final time. The prevailing opinion is that all but the *mushrikun*, those who have committed the worst sin of impugning the *tawhid* [unity] of God, have the possibility of being saved. Of course, despite the emphasis put on Muhammad as the agent of intercession, only by the mercy of God can anyone be saved from the fire: "God will take out of the Fire everyone who has said the testimony [*shahada*]," says al-Subki, "and none will remain save the *kafirun* [unbelievers]."[49]

HEAVEN AND HELL

The Qur'an is consistent in its emphasis that "the alternative for each individual at the day of judgment are two: the bliss of the garden or the torment of the fire."[50] Those who cross the *sirat* successfully enter heaven and those who fall off of it are thrown into the abyss of hell. In addition to the Qur'anic emphasis on the reality of these two destinies, the Qur'an (and of course Islamic tradition) provides an elaborate depiction of heaven and hell. Concerning the torments of hell, the Qur'an declares: "For it is a tree That springs out Of the bottom of Hell-fire: The shoots of its fruit-stalks Are like the heads Of devils." It continues: "then on the top of that They will be given A mixture of Boiling water. Then shall their return Be to the (Blazing) Fire" (37:62–68). Fur-

47. See Smith and Haddad, 80.
48. Ibid., 82.
49. Ibid., 81.
50. Ibid., 84.

ther, when unbelievers see hell "from a place far off, They will hear its fury and its raging sigh." And "when they are cast, Bound together, into a Constricted place therein, they will plead for destruction There and then!" (25:12–13). Furthermore, it has fierce "boiling hot water" (55:44), with "a fierce Blast of Fire and Boiling Water, And in the shades Of Black Smoke" (56:42–43). "When they are cast therein, They will hear The (terrible) drawing in Of its breath Even as it blazes forth, Almost bursting with fury" (67:7–8). The people of the Fire are sighing, wailing, and wretched (11:106). Their scorched skins are constantly exchanged for new ones so that they can taste the torment anew (4:45). They drink festering water and though death appears on all sides, they are not able to die (14:16–17). People are linked together in chains of seventy cubits (69:30–32), wearing pitch for clothing and fire on their faces (14:50). Boiling water will be poured over their heads, melting their insides as well as their skins, and hooks of iron will drag them back should they try to escape (22:19–21).[51]

On the other hand, heaven, which is usually referred to in the Qur'an as "Gardens of Felicity" (37:43), "is a place where believers find whatever their hearts desire."[52] In heaven people will be "facing each other On Thrones (of dignity)," and they will drink "from a clear-flowing fountain, Crystal-white, of taste Delicious to those Who drink (thereof)." The faithful are promised the companionship of young and beautiful women. For "beside them will be Chaste women, restraining Their glances, with big eyes (Of wonder and beauty)" (37:48). "They will recline (with ease) On Thrones (of dignity) Arranged in ranks; And We [God] shall join them To Companions, with beautiful Big and lustrous eyes" (52:20; cf. also 56:22; 55:72; 44:54). They are content, peaceful, and secure. They do not engage in idle talk and experience only peace. None will ever taste death. "Rather, they will enjoy gentle speech, pleasant shade, and ever available fruit, as well as all the cool drink and meat they desire. They will drink from a shining stream of delicious wine, from which they will suffer no intoxicating aftereffects" (37:45–47). The faithful will wear armlets of gold and pearls as well as green and gold embroidered robes of the finest silk, and will be waited on by menservants (cf. 52:24; 56:17; 74:19).[53]

However, not all heavenly pleasures are described in this fashion. There are also references to a spiritual joy that is far greater than the pleasures of the above descriptions. For example, in 9:72, we read, "God hath promised to Believers, Men and women, Gardens Under which rivers

51. Ibid., 85–86.
52. Khouj, 82.
53. See Smith and Haddad, 88–89.

flow, To dwell therein, And beautiful mansions In Gardens of everlasting bliss. But the greatest bliss Is the Good Pleasure of God: That is the supreme felicity."

In discussing the Qur'an's portrait of heaven and hell it is important to point out how Muslims themselves have generally understood these accounts. Concerning this point Smith and Haddad write,

> The Islamic community has expressed a variety of interpretations as to whether or not the rewards and punishments of the life to come are to be understood in their most literal sense. While the predominant understanding has been of the corporeal nature of the ultimate recompense, the positive affirmation of the reality of physical torment and pleasure, this view has generally not insisted that the realities of the next world will be identical with those of this world. While definitely physical, recompense in the ultimate sense is generally understood to have a reality beyond what we are now able to comprehend. It is, in effect, another application of the Ash'ari principle of *bila kayf* (without being able to understand precisely how).[54]

In support of the above statement Muhammad Khouj is a typical example. Even though he is a contemporary orthodox Muslim who seems quite literal in his understanding of the traditional Islamic approach to afterlife, he writes: "When Allah mentions milk, honey, and wine, He uses them to evoke an image of immense beauty. He also portrays the believers' companions, who are beautiful ladies and handsome gentlemen, in language that we can easily understand. These descriptions actually signify the everlasting happiness for those in heaven."[55]

This is not to say that Muslim literalists do not believe there will be beautiful *hurs* (virgins) in heaven who will be in their constant service, but it is to show that they leave the possibility open that some of the Qur'anic descriptions are purely symbolic, and that their exact meaning will not be known until the believers enter heaven. Besides these traditionalists, there are a number of Muslims who deny all the physical descriptions of heaven and understand them in purely spiritual terms.[56]

As to the duration of heaven and hell, all Muslims agree that the state of bliss in heaven is eternal. The Qur'an itself assures believers of the eternality of heaven (3:198; 4:57; 50:34; 25:15). But there is no unanimous agreement as to the duration of the lost in hell. The Qur'an speaks

54. Ibid.
55. Khouj, 83. Also see Yusuf Ali, 1464–70.
56. See Nasr.

of the punishment and torment of eternity, and describes the fire and hell itself as eternal (10:52; 32:14; 41:28; 43:74). The majority of orthodox Muslims accept the eternality of hell based on this testimony. On the other hand, based on passages such as 78:23, 11:107, and 6:128, which indicate the damned will remain in fire for a long time or will be there as long as God wills, many contemporary Muslims believe that the Qur'an leaves open the possibility that the punishment of hell will not last forever.[57]

ISLAM'S DOCTRINE OF SALVATION

With its emphasis on the realities of heavenly bliss for believers and untold woe for unbelievers, it is only natural that the Qur'an should be explicit about the conditions for gaining heaven and avoiding hell. These are issues of eternal significance and call for discussion here.

THE NATURE OF SALVATION

As we already noted (in Chapter 2), the Islamic view of human beings acknowledges no fallenness or depravity. Man's fundamental problem is not usually viewed as rebellion against God, but as weakness and forgetfulness that are inherent in human nature. Therefore, the Islamic view of salvation takes a decisively different form from the Christian view of this doctrine. Kateregga writes, "Islam does not identify with the Christian conviction that man needs to be redeemed. The Christian belief in the redemptive sacrificial death of Christ does not fit the Islamic view that man has always been fundamentally good, and that God loves and forgives those who obey his will."[58] Another Muslim author, Hasan Askar, writes, "In Islam there is no such thing, in principle, as conversion, but restoration, a returning, and a remembering. . . . The greatest challenge upon this earth is not so much to explore God as to remember that there is one."[59] European Islamicist Stanton observes that "inasmuch as sin in the Qur'an does not include a taint of nature, but only a proneness to wrong actions due to the weakness of man, its [Islamic] conception of salvation does not include the element of regeneration."[60] Thus, salvation in Islam is for the most part a future state experienced only in the hereafter. It includes pardon from past sins and deliverance from hell, as well as gaining God's favor and acceptance to heaven.

---

57. See Smith and Haddad, 92–95, 143–44.
58. Kateregga and Shenk, 141. Also see Abdalati, 18.
59. Taken from Cragg, *Jesus and the Muslim,* 260.
60. Stanton, 57.

THE MEANS TO SALVATION

Muslim theologian, Muhammad Abul Quasem, in his book *Salvation of the Soul and Islamic Devotions*, writes, "The Qur'an teaches that the means to salvation in the Hereafter on the human side are belief or faith (*iman*) and action (*amal*): salvation cannot be achieved without these two means."[61] For support of this statement we can take 5:10 as a representative example: "To those who believe And do deeds of righteousness Hath God promised forgiveness And a great reward."

As to what exactly constitutes saving faith, Quasem claims that "the faith taught by the Qur'an and the Tradition is very simple to understand and to form within oneself; its understanding is much easier than that of the Christian faith which involves the Trinity, sin, atonement and so on." Rather, "It has three basic ingredients—so basic that absence of any one of them negates the presence of faith as a whole. . . . *All three elements are needed for salvation.*"[62] These elements are: "belief in the oneness of God, belief in the prophecy of Muhammad, and belief in life after death."[63] Concerning the prophethood of Muhammad the individual ought to believe that "He was the last prophet. Every previous prophet of God was sent to a particular people, but Muhammad was sent to all human beings of the world until Doomsday."[64] The first two parts of this faith form the well-known Islamic *shahada* or confession of faith. "The *shahada* is so essential a part of faith that it alone, without the remaining part, is generally known as faith or *iman*."[65] But belief in the future life is also essential. "The physical nature of future life is so strongly emphasized in the Qur'an and Tradition that its denial is considered as infidelity (*kufr*), which causes eternal damnation."[66]

Quasem correctly points out the fundamental ingredients of Islamic faith, but traditionally Muslim theologians have articulated the Islamic faith according to the following five or six categories. "*Iman*" writes Rauf, "embodies the belief in the following: God and his attributes, the prophets and their virtues, the angels, the sacred books, the day of resurrection, and *Qadar*, namely that God decrees everything that happens in the world." He continues: "Whosoever believes in these six parts of the Islamic faith is called *Mu'min*, i.e., believer; and whoever denies these

61. Quasem, 29. For Qur'anic references, see 2:25; 4:57, 122, 173; 5:10; 13:29; 14:23; 18:107; 22:14, 23.
62. Quasem, 31, emphasis ours.
63. Ibid., 31–33.
64. Ibid., 32.
65. Ibid., 33.
66. Ibid.

parts or any of them is called *kafir*, i.e., unbeliever."[67] Some Muslims do not consider *qadar* as an article of faith, and so acknowledge only five articles of faith.

Corresponding to the above categories are similar ones that have to do with good works, which the Muslim is required to do in order to obtain salvation. The five religious pillars of Islam consist of reciting the confession, prayer, fasting, almsgiving, and pilgrimage to Mecca (see Appendix 2). The pilgrimage should be performed at least once in a lifetime if the individual has an able body and can afford the trip. Some Muslims have also included *jihad*, an exertion in the cause of God or a holy war, as a sixth pillar of Islam (see Chapter 8 and Appendix 5).

Performance of these acts are extremely important for obtaining salvation, prayer being the most important.[68] Kateregga writes, "Belief alone is not enough. Man must practically perform all the duties required of him by the Islamic faith. He must do the *ibadat* (devotional worship). . . . Worship involves performing all the primary duties commanded by God and all other good deeds."[69] Quasem emphasizes that salvation is dependent upon proper and correct performance of these acts.[70] This is why almost all religious manuals go into meticulous detail about the correct way that each of the above religious duties should be performed.[71] Quasem's treatment of these religious duties is to the point:

> Islamic devotions are of two types, namely obligatory and supererogatory. Obligatory devotional acts are ritual prayer, fasting, divine tax, and pilgrimage to Mecca. Ritual prayer is obligatory five times a day; more than this is supererogatory. Fasting during one full lunar month of Ramadan is obligatory; to fast on other great days of the year is supererogatory. . . . The 'saving' merit of the four obligatory devotions accrues from their perfect performance which, of course, is impossible in the case of most people. . . . Imperfections in the obligatory devotions . . . can be made good by occasional performance of them as supererogatory devotions in the way just mentioned. In the case of gross imperfections, there is a severe need of their performance as supererogatory, otherwise salvation will be impossible. If

67. Rauf, 1.
68. See Khouj, 76–77.
69. Kateregga and Shenk, 57. See also Mahmud, 1.
70. See Quasem, 36, 49.
71. As opposed to an emphasis on the strict obedience of Islamic rituals early in Islam, a great number of hadiths began to circulate that made the obtaining of salvation much easier than the Qur'an itself stated. One hadith taught that a mere affirmation of the oneness of God was enough for entering heaven (Abdul-Haqq, 168). Another hadith indicated that a man was saved for giving water to a dog. And yet another one relayed the story of a woman who went to hell for being cruel to a cat (Dermenghem, 117–18. See also Mahmud, 82).

imperfections are little, as in the case of saints and ascetics, performance of obligatory acts as super-erogatory will effect the higher grade of salvation.[72]

Quasem goes on to categorize devotional acts as obligatory, required, emphasized, praiseworthy, a matter of etiquette, and permissible. On the negative side there are acts that are unlawful, forbidden, not allowed, or not permissible, slightly disliked, and gravely disliked.[73]

Therefore, in a very real sense, Islam teaches that heaven can be earned by the good works of the believer as long as he is careful to fulfill his religious obligations and makes up for his shortcomings by performing other favorable duties. As the Qur'an says, "Then those whose balance (Of good deeds) is heavy,—They will attain salvation: But those whose balance Is light, will be those Who have lost their souls; In Hell will they abide" (23:102–3) The Qur'an also talks about those who give their lives "to earn the pleasure of God" (2:207) and that "God will deliver those who fear Him, for they have earned Heaven" (39:61).[74]

On this point Kateregga writes,

> Abu Huraira reports in a Hadith, that an Arab came to the Prophet and said, "Guide me to a deed by doing which I shall enter paradise." The Prophet replied, "Worship God and do not associate anything with Him, observe the prescribed prayer, pay the obligatory *zakat* (alms), and fast during Ramadhan." The Arab responded, "By Him in whose hand is my soul, I shall not add anything to it nor fall short of it." When he had left the Prophet remarked, "If anyone wishes to look at a man who will be among the people of paradise, let him look at this man."

Based on this hadith, Kateregga concludes, "So if anyone performs all his essential obligations (*ibadah* [or *ibadat*]), without leaving out any one of them, his place is in paradise. It is through proper worship that man can hope for paradise."[75]

For Muslims this of course does not deny that God's mercy and forgiveness play a fundamental role in salvation. The Qur'an consistently testifies to the fact that God is merciful, compassionate, and forgiving. For example, in 39:53 we read, "Say: 'O my Servants who Have transgressed against their souls! Despair not of the Mercy Of God: for God forgives All sins: for He is Oft-Forgiving, Most Merciful.'" God's grace in saving the sinner on the day of judgment is seen in the fact that he multiplies the good deeds of the person. The reward for a good deed is ten times more than it should be while punishment for an evil deed is only in equal pro-

72. Quasem, 37–38.
73. Ibid, 40–43.
74. See Mahmud, 62.
75. Kateregga and Shenk, 64–65.

portion. The evil of the believer is even changed into good (4:40; 6:160; 25:70). According to one tradition, Muhammad insisted that "without the mercy of God no one can attain salvation by virtue of his action." His companions asked, "Not even you, O the messenger of God?" He replied, "Not even I. God will, however, cover me with mercy."[76] God's mercy is also shown in the belief that after a certain period of time God himself will bring out a large number of the damned from hell, not because of their own merit but to demonstrate his compassion on his creatures.

THE UNCERTAINTY OF SALVATION

There is no assurance of salvation in Islam. From the very beginning of Islam almost all Muslims have feared for their eternal destiny. Al-Ghazali informs us:

> Yet all the fathers used to refrain from giving a definite reply concerning belief, and were extremely careful not to commit themselves. In this connection Sufyan al-Thawri said, "He who says, 'I am a believer in the sight of God,' is a liar; and he who says 'I am really a believer,' is an innovator. . . ." Once upon a time Hassan (al-Basri) was asked, "Art thou a believer?" To which he replied, "If it be the will of God." Thereupon he was told, "O Abu Said, why do you qualify your belief?" He answered and said, "I fear saying 'yes,' and then God will say, 'Thou hast lied Hassan.' Then I shall rightly merit His punishment. . . ." Alqamah was once asked "Are you a believer?" To which he replied, "I do hope so. If it be the will of God."[77]

To many Muslims the lack of assurance of salvation is not considered a weakness but a reality that can motivate continued obedience. Faruqi insists that "great as it may be in the eyes of Islam for any person to make the decision to enter the faith, the entry constitutes no guarantee of personal justification in the eyes of God . . . there is nothing the new initiate can do which would assure him or her of salvation." Islam "denies that a human can attain religious felicity on the basis of faith alone. . . . only the works and deeds constitute justification in God's eyes. . . . On the scale of virtue and righteousness, people occupy varying positions." The scale of justice itself "is infinite, and there is no point at which Muslims may carry their titles to Paradise, as it were, in their pockets. Everyone strives and some strive more than others. . . . *Religious justification is thus the Muslims' eternal hope, never their complacent certainty, nor for even a fleeting moment.*"[78]

An exception to this is when one fights in a Jihad (Holy War). This gives the devotee direct access to heaven should he so serve in the cause of

---

76. See Quasem, 45.
77. See Abdul-Haqq, 166–67. Also see Bhatia, 224.
78. Faruqi, *Islam*, 5, emphasis ours.

Allah. The Qur'an declares: "Those who have left their homes, Or been driven out therefrom, Or suffered harm in My Cause, Or fought or been slain,—Verily, I will blot out From them their iniquities, And admit them into Gardens With rivers flowing beneath;—A reward from the presence Of God, and from His Presence Is the best of rewards" (Sura 3:195 cf. 2:25; 3:157–158; 4:57, 95–96; 22:58–59).

SALVATION IN OTHER RELIGIONS

Before concluding this chapter we will address the question of who will be saved. As mentioned before (in Chapter 3), many contemporary Muslims claim that anyone, regardless of his particular faith, can obtain salvation provided that he has been a "doer of good" in his life. In support of this claim Muslims often cite 2:111–12:

> And they say: "None Shall enter Paradise unless He be a Jew or a Christian." Those are their (vain) desires. Say: "Produce your proof If ye are truthful." Nay,—whoever submits His whole self to God And is a doer of good,—He will get his reward With his Lord; On such shall be no fear, Nor shall they grieve.

Also 2:62 declares that "Those who believe (in the Qur'an), And those who follow the Jewish (scriptures), And the Christians and the Sabians,—Any who believe in God And the Last Day, And work righteousness, Shall have their reward With their Lord: on them Shall be no fear, nor shall they grieve."

The Qur'an defines true believers as "those who believe in God and His Apostles" (4:152). The negative side of this is clearly given to us in 4:150–51, which proclaims that "those who deny God And His apostles, and (those Who) wish to separate God from His apostles, Saying: 'We believe in some But reject others;' And (those who) wish To take a course mid-way,—They are in truth (Equally) Unbelievers; And We have prepared For Unbelievers a humiliating Punishment."

According to the testimony of the above verses, anyone who rejects the prophethood of Muhammad is an unbeliever and is destined for "a humiliating punishment." This practically includes all the people of the world who are outside the fold of Islam. In addition to failing this criterion, Christians are also condemned to the "abode of Fire" due to their belief that "God is Christ the son Of Mary" (5:75). The only unpardonable sin in Islam is not acknowledging the Unity of God. Since Christians are guilty of this sin their condemnation is assured.[79]

79. According to earlier Meccan suras, Christians and Jews, as people of the Book (*ahl el kitab*) were viewed as going to heaven. Many Muslims might still believe this, even though it is difficult to reconcile with these later suras.

In agreement with this understanding of Islam, one Muslim scholar, Muhammad Muhsin Khan, attempts to prove in no uncertain terms that the Christians and Jews are guilty of committing the major unpardonable sin of *shirk* due to their disbelief in Islam. He concludes his argument with a hadith from Muhammad: "Prophet Muhammad said, 'Any Jew or Christian who heard about me and did not believe in me and what was revealed to me of the Holy Qur'an and any traditions, his ultimate destination is the Hell Fire.'"[80]

Other world religions such as Buddhism and Hinduism also fail other criteria, such as their lack of belief in one Supreme God and creator. Therefore, orthodox Islam is just as exclusive as any other major world religion. Even though Muslims believe that God at times had sent prophets to other nations, since the advent of Muhammad the path of salvation is only made available through the religion of Islam. As Abul Quasem points out, "Faith just outlined is, according to the Qur'an, the only wholly valid faith to be found on the surface of the earth since the advent of Islam until Doomsday. Faiths of previous revealed religions are not entirely free from corruption now and so cannot be a means to salvation. . . . The faith of Islam is the only completely valid faith."[81]

In agreement with the above opinion, Muhammad Hameedullah claims that "A Muslim venerates the Torah, the Psalter and the Gospel as the word of God, yet he abides by the latest and the most recent of the words of God, namely the Quran. Whoever remains attached to the preceding laws, cannot be considered, by the Legislator, as law-abiding and obedient."[82] We conclude this discussion with 3:85: "If anyone desires A religion other than Islam (submission to God), Never will it be accepted Of him; and in the Hereafter He will be in the ranks Of those who have lost (All spiritual good)."

CONCLUSION

We have now finished our survey of major Islamic doctrines. We began with a discussion of God and the central place that God has in Islamic theology. Then the Islamic teaching on creation was examined, especially man and the relationship that exists between him and his Creator. Following that we saw how God's relationship to man was linked by the chain of prophets, and how the prophets were used by God to communicate his will to man, to guide man in the straight path. More specifically the person and role of Muhammad as the final prophet and the

80. See Muhammad Muhsin Khan in his introduction to *The Translation of the Meanings of Sahih Al-Bukhari* vol. 1, 56–61.
81. Quasem, 34.
82. Hameedullah, 81. Also see Kateregga and Shenk, 79.

role of the Qur'an as the final revelation of God to humankind was considered. Finally, we examined what Islam teaches regarding the destiny of human beings and how they should behave in order to be saved in the life to come.

In subsequent sections we will deal more with the questions regarding the truthfulness and adequacy of Islamic teachings.

Part Two

A CHRISTIAN RESPONSE TO BASIC MUSLIM BELIEFS

In Part One we attempted to clear away Christian misunderstanding of Islamic teachings by appealing primarily to the only inspired source of Islamic teaching, the Qur'an. In order to enhance our understanding of Muslim doctrine we cited recognized Muslim traditions, teachers, and commentators. In Part Two we will attempt to respond to basic Muslim beliefs—such as God, Muhammad, and the Qur'an—from a Christian perspective. The basis for the evaluation will be largely internal and factual; we will point out misunderstandings, inconsistencies, and inaccuracies. The primary purpose here is to examine the logical and evidential grounds for the Islamic claim that Muhammad is the unique prophet of God who offers the full and final revelation of God in the Qur'an.

7

AN EVALUATION OF
ISLAMIC MONOTHEISM

No reasonable person rejects what he or she does not first attempt to understand. This is why we have made a sincere effort to set forth the Islamic view as clearly and correctly as possible (in Part One) before offering an evaluation of it. Too often other persons' views are rejected for the wrong reason—for holding a position they never espoused. Having attempted to set forth as clearly as we can what Islam teaches, we turn our attention now to an evaluation of it. Our discussion of Muslim monotheism will fall into two categories. First, we will review its characteristic features. Then, we will evaluate some of the problems critics have noted with the Islamic view of God.

A REVIEW OF SOME CENTRAL THEMES
IN ISLAMIC MONOTHEISM

Since we have already discussed in detail what Muslims believe about God (see Chapter 1), we will only briefly outline here some of the main emphases.

GOD AS THE ABSOLUTE ONE (HIS UNITY)

Fundamental to the Islamic view of God is his absolute and indivisible unity (*tawhid*). In sura 112 Muhammad defines God in these words: "Say: He is God, The One and Only; God, the Eternal, Absolute; He begetteth not, Nor is He begotten; And there is none Like unto Him." This sura "is held to be worth a third of the whole Qur'an and the seven heavens and the seven earths are founded upon it. To confess this verse, an Islamic tradition affirms, is to shed one's sins as a man might strip a tree in autumn of its leaves."[1]

---

1. Cragg, *The Call of the Minaret*, 39.

Two words are used in the Qur'an to describe the oneness of God: *ahad* and *wahid*. *Ahad* is used to deny that God has any partner or companion associated with him. In Arabic, this means the negation of any other number. The word *wahid* may mean the same as the first word or it may also mean "the One, Same God for all." That is to say, there is only one God for Muslims, and he is the same God for all peoples. Thus, both God's unity and singularity are implied.[2]

God's Oneness is such a fundamental aspect of Islam that, as one Muslim author put it, "Islam, like other religions before it in their original clarity and purity, is nothing other than the declaration of the Unity of God, and its message is a call to testify to this Unity."[3] Another Muslim writer adds, "The Unity of Allah is the distinguishing characteristic of Islam. This is the purest form of monotheism, i.e., the worship of Allah Who was neither begotten nor beget nor had any associates with Him in His Godhead. Islam teaches this in the most unequivocal terms."[4]

It is because of this uncompromising emphasis on God's absolute unity that the greatest of all sins in Islam is the sin of *shirk*, or assigning partners to God. The Qur'an sternly declares "God forgiveth not (The sin of) joining other gods With Him; but He forgiveth Whom He pleaseth other sins Than this: one who joins Other gods with God, Hath strayed far, far away (From the Right)" (4:116).

GOD AS ABSOLUTE RULER (HIS SOVEREIGNTY)

In the words of the Qur'an, "God—There is no god But He—the Living, The Self-subsisting, Eternal. No slumber can seize Him Nor sleep. His are all things In the heavens and on earth. Who is there can intercede In His presence except As He permitteth? He knoweth What (appeareth to His creatures As) Before or After Or Behind them. Nor shall they compass Aught of His knowledge Except as He willeth. His Throne doth extend Over the heavens And the earth, and He feeleth No fatigue in guarding And preserving them For He is Most High, The Supreme (in glory)" (2:255).

God is self-sustaining and does not need anything; rather, everything needs him. This attribute is known as aseity, or self-existence. God is the Mighty and the Almighty. He is the Willer of existing things and the things that will exist; and nothing happens apart from his will. He is also the Knower of all that can be known. His knowledge encompasses the whole universe that he has created and he alone sustains. God is completely sovereign over all his creation.

---

2. See Nassir El-Din El-Assad in Kochler, 23.
3. Mahmud, 20.
4. Ajijola, 55.

Many of God's ninety-nine names speak of his sovereignty. He is *Al-Badi*, the Contriver, who contrived the whole art of creation (2:117); *Al-Jabbar*, the Mighty One, whose might and power are absolute (59:23); *Al-Jalil*, the Majestic, mighty and majestic is he; *Al-Jami*, the Gatherer, who gathers all men to an appointed day (3:9); *Al-Hasib*, the Accounter, who is sufficient as a reckoner (4:6–7); *Al-Hakem*, the Judge, who gives judgment among his servants (40:48–51); *Al-Aziz*, the Sublime, mighty in his sublime sovereignty (59:23); *Al-Ali*, the High One, he who is high and mighty (2:225–26); *Al-Qadir*, the Able, who has the power to do what he pleases (17:99-101); *Al-Quddus*, the Most Holy One, to whom all in heaven and on earth ascribe holiness (62:1); *Al-Mutaali*, the Self-Exalted, who has set himself high above all (13:9–10); *Al-Muizz* , the Honorer, who honors or abases whom he will (3:26); *Al-Muqsit*, the Observer of Justice, who will set up the balances with justice (21:47-48); *Al-Malik*, the King, who is king of kings (59:23); *Malik al-Mulk*, Possessor of the Kingdom, who grants sovereignty to whom he will (3:26); *Al-Muntaqim*, the Avenger, who wreaks vengeance on sinners and succors the believers (30:47); *Al-Wahed*, the One, unique in his divine sovereignty (13:16); *Al-Wahid*, the Unique, who alone has created (74:11); *Al-Wakil*, the Administrator, who has charge of everything (6:102).

GOD AS ABSOLUTE JUSTICE (HIS EQUITY)

Several of God's names bespeak his absolute justice. *Al-Jalil*, the Majestic, mighty and majestic is he. *Al-Jami*, the Gatherer, who gathers all men to an appointed day (3:9); *Al-Hasib*, the Accounter, who is sufficient as a reckoner (4:6); *Al-Hakim*, the Judge, who gives judgment among his servants (40:48); *Al-Adl*, the Just, whose word is perfect in veracity and justice (6:115); *Al-Quddus*, the Most Holy One, to whom all in heaven and on earth ascribe holiness (62:1); *Al-Muqsit*, the Observer of Justice, who will set up the balances with justice (21:47–48); *Al-Muntaqim*, the Avenger, who wreaks vengeance on sinners and succors the believers (30:47).

GOD AS ABSOLUTE MERCY

Contrary to a popular misunderstanding, especially among Christians,[5] Allah is a God of mercy. Indeed, some of God's names depict this very characteristic. For example, God is *Ar-Rahman*, the Merciful, the most merciful of those who show mercy (1:3; 12:64). He is also *Al-Wadud*, the Loving, compassionate and loving to his servants (11:90, 92). He has

5. This misunderstanding may arise out of the fact that God is never named or called "Father." This is because for Muslims this would imply a son which, as absolutely one, he could not have.

imposed the law of mercy upon himself (6:12) and he says, "My Mercy extendeth to all things" (7:156). Muhammad said in the Qur'an, "If ye do love God, Follow me: God will love you And forgive you your sins. For God is Oft-Forgiving, Most Merciful" (3:31).

GOD AS ABSOLUTE WILL (HIS VOLITIONALITY)

There is a certain mystery about God's names. Cragg affirms that these names "are to be understood as characteristics of the Divine will rather than laws of His nature. Action, that is, arising from such descriptives may be expected, but not as a matter of necessity."[6] What gives unity to all God's actions is that he wills them all. As willer he may be recognized by the descriptions given him, but he does not conform to any. The action of his will may be identified from its effects, but his will of itself is inscrutable. This accounts for the antithesis in certain of God's names that will be discussed below. For example, God is "the One Who leads astray" as well as "the One Who guides."

GOD AS ABSOLUTELY UNKNOWABLE (HIS INSCRUTABILITY)

Since everything is based in God's will and since his effects are sometimes contradictory and do not reflect any absolute essence, God's nature is really unknowable. Indeed, "the Divine will is an ultimate beyond which neither reason nor revelation go. In the Unity of the single will, however, these descriptions co-exist with those that relate to mercy, compassion, and glory."[7] God is named from his effects, but he is not to be identified with any of them. The relation between the Ultimate Cause (God) and his creatures is extrinsic, not intrinsic. That is, God is called good because he causes good, but goodness is not part of his essence.

PROBLEMS OF ISLAMIC MONOTHEISM

ABSOLUTE UNITY

Islamic monotheism is rigid and inflexible. Its view of God's unity is so strong that it allows for no plurality in God at all. Hence, it sees no similarities between monotheism and tritheism, Christianity being placed in the latter category. There are several reasons for this misunderstanding. For one thing, there appears to be a misunderstanding of the biblical text related to God (see discussion in Chapter 12). Muslims also often have a rather grossly anthropomorphic view of what it means for Christ to be a "Son" of God, which often in the Muslim mind implies some kind of sexual generation. But the terms "Father" and "Son" no more necessitate physical generation than the term "Alma Mater" implies that the school

6. See Cragg, 42.
7. Ibid., 42–43.

we graduated from has a physical womb. Paternity can be understood in more than a biological sense.

Deeper still, there is a basic philosophical problem. In the final analysis for many Muslim theologians God has no (knowable) essence or nature from which one can distinguish his three persons (centers of consciousness). This position is known as nominalism. God is absolute Will, and absolute Will must be absolutely one. A plurality of wills (persons) would make it impossible to have any absolute unity. And Muslims believe God is absolutely One (both from revelation and by reason). Reason informed Muhammad that unity is prior to plurality. As Plotinus had put it several centuries earlier, all plurality is made up of unities. Thus, unity is the most ultimate of all. Accepting this Neo-Platonic (i.e., Plotinian) way of thinking leads logically to a denial of the possibility for any plurality of persons in God. Hence, by the very nature of its philosophical commitment to a kind of Plotinianism prevalent throughout the Middle Ages, Islamic thought about God was solidified in an irretractably solitary form of monotheism that allowed no form of trinitarianism.

However, this kind of rigid monotheism is not entirely consistent with some of Islam's own distinctions. As we will see in more detail later (Chapter 11), Muslim scholars, following through consistently on certain teachings in the Qur'an, have made distinctions that would allow for some kind of distinctions within God's unity. For example, they believe the Qur'an is the eternal speech of God, existing in the Mind of God from all eternity (see discussion in Chapter 9). In 85:21–22, we read, "Nay, this is A Glorious Qur'an, (Inscribed) in A Tablet Preserved! [in heaven]." And in 43:3–4, we read, "We have made it A Qur'an in Arabic, That ye may be able To understand (and learn wisdom). And verily, it is In the Mother of the Book, In Our Presence, high (In dignity), full of wisdom" (cf. 13:39). This eternal original is the template of the earthly book we know as the Qur'an.

Muslim scholars insist the Qur'an is uncreated and perfectly expresses the mind of God. Yet they acknowledge that the Qur'an is not identical to the essence of God. Some Muslim scholars even liken the Qur'an to the Divine Logos view of Christ held by orthodox Christians. As Yusuf K. Ibish stated of the Qur'an, "It is not a book in the ordinary sense, nor is it comparable to the Bible, either the Old or New Testaments. It is an expression of Divine Will. If you want to compare it with anything in Christianity, you must compare it with Christ Himself." He adds, "Christ was the expression of the Divine among men, the revelation of the Divine Will. That is what the Qur'an is."[8]

Orthodox Islam describes the relation between God and the Qur'an by noting that "speech is an eternal attribute of God, which as such is with-

---

8. See Waddy, 14.

out beginning or intermission, exactly like His knowledge, His might, and other characteristics of His infinite being."[9] But if speech is an eternal attribute of God that is not identical to God but is somehow distinguishable from him, then does not this allow the very kind of plurality within unity that Christians claim for the Trinity? Thus, it would seem that the Islamic view of God's absolute unity is, by their own distinction, not incompatible with Christian trinitarianism. In other words, the basic Muslim logic of either monotheism or polytheism (which includes tritheism) is invalid. They themselves allow that something can be an eternal expression of God without being numerically identical to him. Thus, to use their own illustration, why can't Christ be the eternal "expression of Divine Will" without being the same person as this Divine Will?

Voluntarism

At the very basis of the classical Islamic view of God is a radical form of voluntarism and nominalism. For traditional Islam, properly speaking, God does not have an essence, at least not a knowable one. Rather, he is Will. True enough, God is said to be just and loving, but he is not essentially just or loving. And he is merciful only because "He hath inscribed For Himself [the rule of] Mercy" (6:12). But it is important to remember that since God is Absolute Will, had he chosen to be otherwise he would not be merciful. There is no nature or essence in God according to which he must act.

There are two basic problems with this radical form of nominalism: a metaphysical one and a moral one.

The orthodox Islamic view of God claims, as we have seen, that God is an absolutely necessary being. He is self-existent, and he cannot not exist. But if God is by nature a necessary kind of being, then it is of his nature to exist. In short, he must have a nature or else he could not be by nature a necessary kind of being. In this same regard, orthodox Islam believes that there are other essential attributes of God, such as self-existence, uncreatedness, and eternality. But if these are all essential characteristics of God, then God must have an essence, otherwise they would not be essential attributes. For this is precisely how essence is defined, namely, as the essential attributes or characteristics of a being.

Furthermore, there is a serious moral problem with Islamic voluntarism. For if God is Will, without any real essence, then he does not do things because they are right; rather, they are right because he does them. In short, God is arbitrary about what is right and wrong. He does not have to do good. For example, God does not have to be merciful; he could be mean if he wanted to be. He does not have to be loving to all; he could

9. Goldziher, 97.

hate, if he chose to do so. Indeed, in the very next verse after it says "God will love you. . . . God is Oft-Forgiving, Most Merciful" (3:31), we read that "God loveth not those Who reject Faith" (v. 32). Further, Allah said in 25:51, "Had it been Our Will, We could have sent A warner to every centre Of Population." But he did not, which smacks of arbitrariness.[10] In other words, love and mercy are not of the essence of God. God could choose not to be loving. This is why Muslim scholars have such difficulty with the question of God's predestination, which we will discuss shortly. But first, a word about Muslim agnosticism.

AGNOSTICISM

Since God has no essence, at least not one that the names (or attributes) of God really describe, the Islamic view of God involves a form of agnosticism. Indeed, the heart of Islam is not to *know* God but to *obey* him. It is not to *meditate* on his essence but to *submit* to his will. As Pfander correctly observed of Muslims, "If they think at all deeply, they find themselves absolutely unable to know God. . . . Thus Islam leads to Agnosticism."[11]

Islamic agnosticism about God is due to the fact that they believe God caused the world by extrinsic causality. Indeed, "the Divine will is an ultimate beyond which neither reason nor revelation go. In the Unity of the single Will, however, these descriptions co-exist with those that relate to mercy, compassion, and glory."[12] God is named from his effects, but he is not to be identified with any of them. The relation between the ultimate cause (God) and his creatures is extrinsic, not intrinsic. That is, God is called good because he causes good, but not because goodness is part of his essence.

Despite all the names of God in the Qur'an, in orthodox Islam we confront a God who is basically unknowable. These names do not tell us anything about what God is like but only how God has willed to act. God's actions do not reflect God's character.

Al-Ghazali, the most prominent theologian in the history of Islam, went so far as to say:

> The end result of the knowledge of the *arifin* [those who know] is their inability to know Him, and their knowledge is, in truth, that they do not know Him and that it is absolutely impossible for them to know Him.[13]

10. Compare by contrast the God of the Bible who loves all (John 3:16), convicts all of sin (John 16:7), and desires that all be saved (2 Pet. 3:9), giving them all the necessary light (Rom. 1:19–20; 2:12–15) and accepting any who come to him (Acts 10:35; Heb. 11:6). See also N. L. Geisler, "Essentialism, Divine" in *Baker Encyclopedia of Christian Apologetics*, 216–18.
11. Pfander, 187.
12. See Cragg, 42–43.
13. Fadlou Shehadi, *Ghazali's Unique Unknowable God* (Leiden: E. J. Brill, 1964), 37.

Fadlou Shehadi, a contemporary scholar of Al-Ghazali, after analyzing Al-Ghazali's arguments about the transcendence of God, concludes,

> If God is a unique kind of being unlike any other being in any respect, more specifically, unlike anything known to man, it would have to follow by Ghazali's own principles that God is utterly unknowable. For, according to Ghazali, things are known by their likeness, and what is utterly unlike what is known to man cannot be known. Furthermore, God would have to be unknowable, completely unknowable, not only to 'the man in the street,' but to prophets and mystics as well. This is a conclusion that Ghazali states very explicitly and not infrequently.[14]

According to Shehadi, "The uncompromising character of Ghazali's agnosticism follows logically from the uncompromising stand on the utter difference of God's nature.[15]

A contemporary scholar of Islam, and one quite well-known in North America for his intellectual and social activism and also involvement in interfaith dialogue, is Isma'il Al-Faruqi. Al-Faruqi expresses the mainstream Islamic thinking on the inability of humans to know God, when he writes:

> He [God] does not reveal Himself to anyone in any way. God reveals only His will. Remember one of the prophets asked God to reveal Himself and God told him, "No, it is not possible for Me to reveal Myself to anyone." . . . This is God's will and that is all we have, and we have it in perfection in the Qur'an. But Islam does not equate the Qur'an with the nature or essence of God. It is the Word of God, the Commandment of God, the Will of God. But God does not reveal Himself to anyone. Christians talk about the revelation of God Himself—by God and of God—but that is the great difference between Christianity and Islam. God is transcendent, and once you talk about self-revelation you have hierophancy and immanence, and then the transcendence of God is compromised. You may not have complete transcendence and self-revelation at the same time.[16]

Shabbir Akhtar, another contemporary Muslim theologian and a graduate of Cambridge University, writes in similar fashion. According to Akhtar,

> The Koran, unlike the Gospel, never comments on the essence of Allah. 'Allah is wise' or 'Allah is loving' may be pieces of revealed information but

14. Ibid., 21–22.
15. Ibid., 48.
16. Al-Faruqi, *Christian Mission and Islamic Da'wah: Proceedings of the Chambesy Dialogue Consultation* (Leicester: The Islamic Foundation, 1982), 47–48.

in contrast to Christianity, Muslims are not enticed to claims that 'Allah is Love' or 'Allah is Wisdom.' Only adjectival descriptions are attributed to the divine being and these merely as they bear on the revelation of God's will for man. The rest remains mysterious.[17]

This is a fundamental point of difference between Islam and the Christian faith (as Al-Faruqi has also pointed out) in regard to their doctrine of God. We must not easily pass over this tension. The logical outcome of Orthodox Islamic theology is agnosticism in regard to the character of God. For Islamic theology, God has willed and has acted in many ways, but these actions in no way reflect the divine character behind them.

Needless to say, there are some significant problems with Islamic agnosticism. We will consider several of them, including a moral, a philosophical, and a religious problem.

As we have seen, according to traditional Islamic teaching, God is not essentially good but only called good because he does good. He is named from his actions. If this is so, then why not also call God evil, since he causes evil? Why not call him faithless, since he causes people not to believe? It would seem consistent to do so, since God is named from his actions. If Muslims reply that there is something in God that is the basis for calling him good but there is nothing in him as the basis for calling him evil, then they have admitted that God's names do tell us something about his essence. In fact, they have admitted an intrinsic relation between the cause (the Creator) and the effect (his creation). This leads to a second problem, a metaphysical one. In short, they would have to give up their view of God.

At the root of medieval views of God is an entrenched Neo-Platonism, springing from the second-century philosopher Plotinus.[18] He believed that the Ultimate (God) was absolutely and indivisibly one, a position that heavily influenced Muslim monotheism. Further, Plotinus held that the One is so utterly transcendent (above and beyond all) that it cannot be known, except by mystical experience. This, too, heavily influenced not only orthodox Muslim agnosticism but Sufi mysticism.[19] The fundamental reason there can be no similarity between the One (God) and what flows from it (the universe) is because God is beyond being, and there is no similarity between being and what is beyond it.[20]

---

17. Shabbir Akhtar, *A Faith for All Seasons* (Chicago: Ivan R. Dee Publisher, 1990), 180–181.

18. See Anderson, *Islam in the Modern World* 68–69.

19. See Appendix 1 for a discussion of Sufi Islam.

20. Plotinus, *The Enneads*, trans. Stephen MacKenna (London: Faber and Faber Limited, 1966), see 3.8.101; 6.9.4; 6.7.29; 5.3.4; 5.5.6.

Here again, the great Christian philosopher and theologian of the late Middle Ages, Thomas Aquinas, provided the definitive answer to Plotinian agnosticism and mysticism, and Muslims who followed after it. Aquinas argued that an effect must resemble its cause since "you cannot give what you have not got." You cannot produce what you do not possess. Hence, if God caused goodness, then he must *be* Goodness. If he caused being, then he must *be* being. Whatever reality we *have* we have from him, and that he *is* by his very nature.[21]

Objections to this view generally confuse either a material or an instrumental cause with an efficient cause. The efficient cause of something is that *by which* it comes to be. The instrumental cause is that *through which* it comes to be. And the material cause is that *out of which* it is made. Now material and instrumental causes do not necessarily resemble their effects but efficient causes do. For example, the painting does not resemble the artist's paint brush, but it does resemble the artist's mind. The reason is because the brush is only the instrumental cause, whereas the artist is the efficient cause. Neither does the computer on which we compare this material resemble the book, but the ideas expressed in this book do resemble those in our minds.

Another mistake is to confuse material and efficient causality.[22] Hot water can cause an egg to get hard. This is because of the material condition of the egg. The same hot water causes wax to get soft. The difference is the material on which the causality is being received. Thus, an infinite God can and does cause a finite world. God is not thereby finite because he caused a finite cosmos. Nor is he contingent because he, as a necessary being, caused a contingent universe. Finiteness and contingency are part of the very material nature of a created being. God is unlike creation in these kinds of ways. On the other hand, everything that exists *has* being, and God *is* Being. Thus, there must be a similarity between Being and being. God is Pure Actuality, with no potentiality whatsoever. Everything else that exists has the potential not to exist. So all created things have actuality, since they actually exist, and potentiality, since they could possibly not exist. God is like creatures in their actuality but unlike them in their potentiality. This is why when we do name God from his effects we must negate whatever implies finitude and limitation or imperfection and attribute to him only the pure attribute or perfection. This is the reason that evil cannot be attributed to God while good can. Evil implies imperfection or privation of some good characteristic. Good, on the other hand, does not in itself imply

21. See N. L. Geisler, *Thomas Aquinas: An Evangelical Appraisal* (Grand Rapids: Baker, 1991), Chap. 10.
22. Ibid.

either limitation or imperfection.[23] So God is good by his very nature, but he cannot be or do evil.

There is also a religious problem with Islamic monotheism. Religious experience within a monotheistic context involves the relation between two persons, the worshiper and God. It is, as Martin Buber correctly observed, an I-Thou relationship.[24] But how can a person worship someone about which he can know nothing? Even in Islam, one is supposed to submit to God. But how can we fall in love with someone whom we know nothing about? As the atheist Ludwig Feuerbach put it, "The truly religious man can't worship a purely negative being. . . . Only when a man loses his taste for religion does the existence of God become one without qualities, an unknowable God."[25]

Some critics have suggested that the extremely transcendent Muslim view of God has led some Muslim sects to deify Muhammad. Since relationship with the transcendent God is seen to be distant, it is only through Muhammad that one even dares to approach the throne of God. In *Qawwalis* (a popular cultural event), Muhammad is praised in verse. This often takes the form of deification: "If *Muhammad* had not been, God himself would not have existed!" This is an allusion to the close relationship Muhammad is supposed to have with God. In the media, Muhammad is often given titles like "Savior of the World" and "Lord of the Universe."[26] The popular deification of Muhammad, who violently opposed any such idolatry, only shows the theological bankruptcy of the Muslim view of God—a God so distant and so unknowable that devotees must make contact with something they can understand, even to the extent of deifying the very prophet who condemned such idolatry.

EXTREME DETERMINISM

Since in Islam the relationship between God and human beings is basically that of Master and slave, God is the sovereign monarch and man must submit to him as an obedient slave. This overpowering picture of God in the Qur'an has created its own tension in Muslim theology regarding God's absolute sovereignty and man's free will. Despite protests to the

23. St. Augustine insightfully observed that what we call good is the positive perfection and evil is a privation of it, since when we take all good from a thing, nothing is left. But when we remove all evil from it, what is left is more perfect. See Augustine's, "Anti-Manichean Writings," in Philip Schaff, ed., *Nicene and Post-Nicene Fathers of the Christian Church*, 1st series, vol. 4 (1886–1888; reprint, Grand Rapids: Eerdmans, 1979).

24. Martin Buber, *I and Thou* (New York, 1970).

25. Ludwig Feuerbach, *The Essence of Christianity*, trans. George Eliot (New York: Harper and Row, 1957), 15.

26. Nazir-Ali, 130–31. Also see our Chapter 8 on Muhammad.

contrary,[27] orthodox Islam teaches the absolute predestination of both good and evil, that all our thoughts, words, and deeds, whether good or evil, were foreseen, foreordained, determined and decreed from all eternity, and that everything that happens takes place according to what has been written for it. This is because God "is the Irresistible" (6:18). Commenting on these kinds of Qur'anic statements, Kenneth Cragg points out that "God" is the *Qadar*, or "determination," of all things, and his *taqdir*, or his "subjection" of everything, covers all humankind and all history. "Nature, whether animate or inanimate, is subject to His command and all that comes into existence—a summer flower or a murderer's deed, a newborn child or a sinner's disbelief—is from Him and of Him." In fact, if "God so willed, there need have been no creation, there need have been no idolatry, there need have been no Hell, there need have been no escape from Hell."[28] Even though Muslim scholar Fazlur Rahman admits to playing down extreme determinism, nonetheless he still admits that "there is no doubt that the Qur'an does make frequent statements to the effect that God leads aright whom He will and leads astray whom He will, or that God has 'sealed up' some people's hearts to truth, etc."[29]

There are four basic problems with this extreme form of predetermination. They are logical, moral, theological, and metaphysical. One involves a contradiction; one eliminates human responsibility; one makes God the author of evil; and one gives rise to pantheism.

The Logical Problem with Islamic Determinism

Even Muslim commentators are forced to acknowledge that God performs contradictory actions. One of the greatest Islamicists, Goldziher, summarizes the situation in this way: "There is probably no other point of doctrine on which equally contradictory teachings can be derived from the Qur'an as on this one."[30] Another scholar notes that "the

----

27. Rahman, for example: "To hold that the Qur'an believes in an absolute determinism of human behavior, denying free choice on man's part, is not only to deny almost the entire content of the Qur'an, but to undercut its very basis: the Qur'an by its own claim is an invitation to man to come to the right path (*hudan li'lnas*)" (Rahman, 20). Haykal too complains that critics of Islamic determinism overlook "the wide scope it leaves open for human freedom of action" (Haykal, 562). But while Muslim apologists would like to "have their cake and eat it too," they overlook clear statements to the contrary in the Qur'an, the hadith, Muslim creeds, and the logical implications of these deterministic affirmations.

28. See Cragg, 44–45.

29. See Rahman, 15.

30. See Goldziher, 78. However, he goes on to propose the solution for this classical theological difficulty: "A large part of those Qur'anic statements commonly used to draw the conclusion that God himself brings about man's sinfulness and leads man astray will be seen in a different light if we understand more precisely the word customarily taken to mean 'to lead astray.'" Thus, "the decisive verb (*adalla*) is not, in this context, to be understood as 'lead astray,' but rather as 'allow to go astray,' that is, not care about someone, not

Quranic doctrine of Predestination is very explicit though not very logical."[31] For example, God is "the One Who leads astray," as well as "the One Who guides." He is "the One Who brings damage," as also does Satan. He is described also by terms like "the Bringer-down," "the Compeller" or "Tyrant," "the Haughty"—all of which, when used of men, have an evil sense.

Many Muslim scholars attempt to reconcile this by pointing out that these contradictions are not in God's nature (which they believe he does not really have), but in the realm of his will. They are not in his essence but in his actions. However, this is an inadequate explanation for two reasons. For one thing, as we have seen, God does have a knowable nature or essence. Hence, Muslim scholars cannot avoid the contradiction that God has logically opposed characteristics by placing them outside his essence within the mystery of his will. Further, actions flow from nature and represent it, so there must be something in the nature that corresponds to the action. Salt water does not flow from a fresh stream.

Others attempt to downplay the harsh extremes of Islamic determinism by creating a distinction, not found in the Qur'an, between what God *does* and what he *allows* his creatures to do by their free choice. This would solve the problem but, as we shall see, only at the expense of rejecting the clear statements of the Qur'an as well as Islamic tradition and creeds.

THE MORAL PROBLEM WITH ISLAMIC DETERMINISM

While many Muslim scholars wish to preserve human responsibility, they can only succeed in doing so by modifying what the Qur'an actually says. Consider the very words of the Qur'an: "Say: 'Nothing will happen to us Except what God has decreed For us'" (9:51); "Whom God doth guide,—He is on the right path: Whom He rejects from His guidance,—Such are the persons who perish. Many are the Jinns and men We have made for Hell" (7:178–79); "The Word is proved true Against the greater part of them: For they do not believe. We have put yokes Round their necks Right up to their chins, So that their heads are Forced up (and they cannot see). And We have put A bar in front of them And a bar behind them, And further, We have Covered them up; so that They cannot see. The same is it to them Whether thou admonish them Or thou do not admonish Them: they will not believe" (36:7–10).

What is more, the Qur'an frankly admits that God could have saved all, but did not desire to do so! "If We had so willed, We could certainly have

---

to show him the way out of his predicament" (pp. 79–80). But a careful look at the context of each of the passages, as well as the traditional Islamic interpretation of them, reveals just the opposite.

31. Stanton, 54–55.

brought Every soul its true guidance: But the Word from Me Will come true, 'I will Fill Hell with *jinn* And men all together'" (32:13). It is extremely difficult to understand how, holding such a view, one can consistently maintain any kind of human responsibility.

THE THEOLOGICAL PROBLEM WITH ISLAMIC DETERMINISM

There is another problem with this severe view of God's sovereign determination of all events: it makes God the author of evil. The hadith portrays God in a similar way. The following tradition is reported by Al-Bukhari:

> Allah's Apostle, the truthful and truly-inspired, said, "Each one of you collected in the womb of his mother for forty days . . . and then Allah sends an angel and orders him to write four things, i.e., his provision, his age, and whether he will be of the wretched or the blessed (in the Hereafter). Then the soul is breathed into him. And by Allah, a person among you (or a man) may do deeds of the people of the Fire till there is only a cubit or an arm-breadth distance between him and the Fire, but then that writing (which Allah has ordered the angel to write) preceeds, and he does the deeds of the people of Paradise and enters it; and a man may do the deeds of the people of Paradise till there is only a cubit or two between him and Paradise, and then that writing preceeds and he does the deeds of the people of the Fire and enters it."[32]

In another hadith we read,

> The Prophet said, "Adam and Moses argued with each other. Moses said to Adam, 'O Adam! You are our father who disappointed us and turned us out of Paradise.' Then Adam said to him, 'O Moses! Allah favoured you with His talk (talked to you directly) and He wrote (the Torah) for you with His own Hand. Do you blame me for action which Allah had written in my fate forty years before my creation?' So Adam confuted Moses, Adam confuted Moses," the Prophet added, repeating the statement three times.[33]

Indeed, one of the most respected Muslim theologians of all time, Al-Ghazali, frankly acknowledges that "He [God] willeth also the unbelief of the unbeliever and the irreligion of the wicked and, without that will, there would neither be unbelief nor irreligion. All we do we do by His will: what He willeth not does not come to pass." And if one should ask why God does not will that men should believe, Al-Ghazali responds, "'We have no right to enquire about what God wills or does. He is perfectly free to will and to do what He pleases.' In creating unbelievers, in willing that

32. Al-Bukhari, vol. 8, 387.
33. Ibid., 399. For similar accounts in Bukhari, see vol. 8, "The Book of Al-Qadr."

they should remain in that state; . . . in willing, in short, all that is evil, God has wise ends in view which it is not necessary that we should know."[34]

THE METAPHYSICAL PROBLEM WITH ISLAMIC DETERMINISM

This extreme form of determinism led some Muslim scholars to the logical conclusion that there is really only one agent in the universe— God. One Muslim theologian wrote, "Not only can He (God) do anything, He actually is the only One Who does anything. When a man writes, it is Allah who has created in his mind the will to write. Allah at the same time gives power to write, then brings about the motion of the hand and the pen and the appearance upon paper. All other things are passive, Allah alone is active."[35] This kind of determinism is at the heart of much of medieval thought and is one of the major reasons the church called upon the great intellect of Thomas Aquinas to respond. Indeed, his famous *Summa contra Gentiles* was occasioned by the need of Christian missionaries dealing with Islam in Spain. History records that he stemmed the influence of this view in the form of Latin Averroism.

This radical predeterminism is expressed in Muslim creedal statements. One reads: "God Most High is the Creator of all actions of His creatures whether of unbelief or belief, of obedience or of rebellion: all of them are by the Will of God and His sentence and His conclusion and His decreeing."[36] Another confesses: "God's one possible quality is His power to create good or evil at any time He wishes, i.e. His decree. . . . Both good things and evil things are the result of God's decree. It is the duty of every Muslim to believe this." Further, "It is He who causes harm and good. Rather the good works of some and the evil of others are signs that God wishes to punish some and to reward others." So, "if God wishes to draw someone close to Himself, then He will give him the grace which will make that person do good works. If He wishes to reject someone and put that person to shame, then He will create sin in him. God creates all things, good and evil. God creates people as well as their actions: He created you as well as what you do" (37:94).[37] In effect the Muslim creed "There is no God but God" is recast to read "There is no one who acts but God."[38] Some Muslim mystics carried this so far that they claimed that "No creature [even] partakes in the confession of God's oneness. God alone confesses the oneness of God."[39]

---

34. Cited by Abdul-Haqq, 152, from Hughe's *Dictionary of Islam*, 147.
35. Nehls, 21.
36. See Cragg, 60–61.
37. Rippin and Knappert, *Textual Sources for the Study of Islam*, 133.
38. Cited by Richard Gramlich, "Mystical Dimensions of Islamic Monotheism," in Schimmel, 141.
39. Ibid., 144.

There is no more vivid example of how Muslim determinism leads to pantheism than in the Islamic mystics who declared that Muslim monotheism is "the annihilation of the traces of what is human, and the isolation of what is divine." Indeed, one Muslim devotee asks God to "blot out my individuality from me, so that You may be my individuality." So, as Gramlich further notes, the Muslim confession of faith rises from "no God but God" beyond "No one acts but God," to "No one has being but God."[40]

CONCLUSION

The attitude of God's absolute control over every aspect of his creation obviously has had a profound impact on Islamic theology and culture. The famous Persian poet, Omar Khayyam, reflects clearly the fatalistic strain of Muslim theology when he writes:

> Tis all a chequer-board of night and days
> Where destiny with men for pieces plays;
> Hither and thither moves and mates and slays,
> And one by one back in the closet lays.

40. Ibid., 142.

8

AN EVALUATION OF MUHAMMAD

We have already set forth the Muslim belief that Muhammad is the last of the prophets, who brought forth the full and final revelation of God to humankind (see Chapter 4). The fact that the Qur'an declares itself to be God's last word, superseding all other revelations and religions—indeed, the claim that Muhammad is a prophet of God, a belief held by one-fifth of the world's population—commands our attention.

MUHAMMAD'S PROPHETIC CLAIM

THE NATURE OF A PROPHET

In order to properly evaluate Muhammad's claim to be a prophet of God, we need to review what is meant by a prophet.[1] In Arabic there are two basic words used of God's messengers. The term *rasul* means "one who is sent" (like the Greek *apostolos*), and the term *nabi* signifies "one who carries information and proclaims news from God" (this is similar to the Hebrew *nabi*).[2]

By nature a prophet must be a mere human being, but one of impeccable (*isma*) character, meaning that he is either sinless or else completely free from all major sins.[3] As to the mission of a prophet, the Qur'an is unequivocal: 16:36 says, "In every community We have raised up a messenger [to proclaim]: 'Worship ye Allah and shun idolatry'" (see also 40:15).

While all prophets have preached the same basic message, that of submission to the divine will, nonetheless Muhammad's message is consid-

1. For further discussion of this point, see Chapter 3.
2. Kateregga and Shenk, 34; and Rauf, 5.
3. Abdalati, 27. Also see Rauf, 5.

151

ered distinctive in that it was the last and final word of God to humankind and it was put in perfect written form and preserved without error. Indeed, Muhammad considered himself "the Seal of the Prophets" (33:40). In a well-known *hadith* Muhammad states his uniqueness this way: "I have been given victory through the inspiring of awe at the distance of a month's journey; I have been given permission to intercede; I have been sent to all mankind; and the prophets have been sealed with me."[4]

Of course, this unique claim to final revelation made it necessary for Muhammad to provide evidence that he superseded Abraham, Moses, Jesus, and others as the prophet of God. Traditionally Islamic apologetics has provided several lines of reasoning for proving the superiority of Muhammad over the previous prophets. The chief of these proofs are:[5] (1) that the Old and New Testaments both contain clear prophecies about him; (2) that the nature of Muhammad's call to be a prophet is miraculous; (3) that the language and the teaching of the Qur'an are without parallel, and thus the Qur'an alone is sufficient proof of the truth of Muhammad's claims; (4) that Muhammad's miracles are a seal set by God Most High on his claims; (5) that his life and character prove him to have been the last and the greatest of prophets.[6]

EVALUATION OF MUSLIM CLAIM FOR BIBLICAL SUPPORT

There is no doubt that Muhammad believed he was called of God. Likewise, his conviction that God gave him revelations through the angel Gabriel seemed unshaken. Of course, as all thinking people know, neither subjective experience nor sincerity of conviction is in itself a proof of the authenticity of that experience. Critics have responded to each one of the evidences offered to support the claim that Muhammad is the unique prophet of God. They have pointed out several things that any thinking Muslim or non-Muslim should take into consideration before coming to a conclusion on the matter.

In a very popular Muslim book, *Muhammad in the Bible*, Abdu 'l-Ahad Dawud argues that the Bible predicts the coming of the prophet Muhammad. He claims that "Muhammad is the real object of the Covenant and in him, and in him alone, are actually and literally fulfilled all the prophecies in the Old Testament."[7] Likewise, of the New Testament he insists that "it is absolutely impossible to get at the truth, the true religion, from these Gospels, unless they are read and examined from an Islamic and

---

4. Annemarie Schimmel, "The Prophet Muhammad as a Centre of Muslim Life and Thought," in Schimmel and Falaturi, 62.

5. Other evidence for the alleged supernatural confirmation of Islam, such as its rapid spread and scientific confirmation, will be considered in Chapter 9.

6. See Pfander, 225–26.

7. Dawud, 11.

Unitarian point of view."[8] He then examines the New Testament, finding Muhammad, not Christ, to be the foretold prophet. Let's examine the texts Dawud and other Muslims use to support these claims.[9]

Deuteronomy 18:15–18. God promised Moses, "I will raise up for them [Israel] a Prophet like you from among their brethren, and will put My words in His mouth, and He shall speak to them all that I command Him" (v. 18). Muslims believe this prophecy is fulfilled in Muhammad, as the Qur'an claims when it refers to "the unlettered Prophet [Muhammad], Whom they find mentioned in their own (Scriptures), in the Law and the Gospels" (7:157).

However, this prophecy could not be a reference to Muhammad for several reasons. First, it is clear that the term "brethren" means fellow Israelites. For the Jewish Levites were told in the same passage that "they shall have no inheritance among their brethren" (v. 2).

Second, since the term "brethren" refers to Israel, not to their Arab antagonists, why would God raise up for Israel a prophet from their enemies?

Third, elsewhere in this book the term "brethren" also means fellow Israelites, not foreigners. God told the Jews to chose a king "from among your brethren," not a "foreigner" (Deut. 17:15). Israel never chose a non-Jewish king.

Fourth, Muhammad came from Ishmael, as even Muslims admit, and heirs to the Jewish throne came from Isaac. According to the Torah, when Abraham prayed, "Oh that Ishmael might live before You!" God answered emphatically, "My covenant I will establish with Isaac" (Gen. 17:21). Later God repeated, "In Isaac your seed shall be called" (Gen. 21:12).

Fifth, the Qur'an itself states that the prophetic line came through Isaac, not Ishmael: "And We bestowed on him Isaac and Jacob, and We established the Prophethood and the Scripture among his seed" (29:27). The Muslim scholar Yusuf Ali adds the word "Abraham" and changes the meaning as follows: "We gave (Abraham) Isaac and Jacob, and ordained Among his progeny Prophethood And Revelation." By adding Abraham, the father of Ishmael, he can include Muhammad, a descendant of Ishmael, in the prophetic line! But Abraham's name is not found in the Arabic text of the Qur'an, which Muslims consider to be perfectly preserved.

Sixth, according to the earliest authentic documents,[10] Jesus, not Muhammad, completely fulfilled this verse, since he was from among his

---

8. Ibid., 156.

9. The discussion on these texts follows that in Norman Geisler and Thomas Howe, *When Critics Ask* (Grand Rapids: Baker, 1992).

10. See Chapter 10 for evidence that the New Testament records are authentic, first-century documents.

Jewish brethren (cf. Gal. 4:4). He also fulfilled Deuteronomy 18:18 perfectly: "He shall speak to them all that I [God] command Him." Jesus said, "I do nothing of Myself; but as My Father taught Me, I speak these things" (John 8:28). And, "I have not spoken on My own authority; but the Father who sent Me gave Me a command, what I should say and what I should speak" (John 12:49). He called himself a "prophet" (Luke 13:33), and the people considered him a prophet (Matt. 21:11; Luke 7:16; 24:19; John 4:19; 6:14; 7:40; 9:17). As the Son of God, Jesus was prophet (speaking to men for God), priest (Heb. 7–10, speaking to God for men), and king (reigning over men for God, Rev. 19-20).

Finally, there are other characteristics of the "Prophet" to come that fit only Jesus, not Muhammad. These include things like speaking with God "face to face" and performing "signs and wonders," which in the Qur'an Muhammad admitted he did not do.

Deuteronomy 33:2. Many Islamic scholars believe that this verse predicts three separate visitations of God: one on "Sinai" to Moses, another to "Seir" through Jesus, and a third in "Paran" (Arabia) through Muhammad who came to Mecca with an army of "ten thousand."

However, this contention can be easily answered by looking at a map of the area. Paran and Seir are near Egypt in the Sinai peninsula (cf. Gen. 14:6; Num. 10:12; 12:16–13:3; Deut. 1:1), not in Palestine where Jesus ministered. Nor was Paran near Mecca, but hundreds of miles away in southern Palestine in the northeastern Sinai.

Furthermore, this verse is speaking of the "Lord" coming, not Muhammad. And the Lord is coming with "ten thousand *saints*," not ten thousand *soldiers*, as Muhammad did. There is no basis in this text for the Muslim contention that it is a prediction of Muhammad.

Finally, this prophecy is said to be one "with which Moses the man of God blessed *the children of Israel* before his death" (Deut. 33:1). If it were a prediction about Islam, which has been a constant enemy of Israel, it could scarcely have been a blessing to Israel. In fact, the chapter goes on to pronounce a blessing on each of the tribes of Israel by God, who "will thrust out the enemy" (v. 27).

Deuteronomy 34:10. This verse claims that "there arose not a prophet since in Israel like unto Moses" (KJV). Muslims argue that this proves that the predicted prophet could not be an Israelite but was Muhammad instead.

In response several things should be noted. First, the "since" means since Moses' death up until the time this last chapter was written, probably by Joshua.[11] Even if Deuteronomy were written much later, as some

---

11. Moses could have written about his own death by supernatural prophecy, for it is entirely within the power of God to reveal the future in minute detail (cf. Dan. 2, 7, 9, 12).

critics believe, it still was composed many centuries before the time of Christ and, therefore, would not eliminate him.

Second, Jesus was the perfect fulfillment of this prediction of the prophet to come, not Muhammad (see comments above on Deut. 18:15–18).

Third, this could not refer to Muhammad, since the prophet to come was like Moses who did "all the signs and wonders which the Lord sent" (Deut. 34:11). Muhammad by his own confession did not perform signs and wonders like Moses and Jesus did (see 2:118; 3:183). Finally, the prophet to come was like Moses who spoke to God "face to face" (Deut. 34:10). Muhammad never even claimed to speak to God directly but got his revelations through an angel (see 25:32; 17:105). Jesus, on the other hand, like Moses, was a direct mediator (1 Tim. 2:5; Heb. 9:15) who communicated directly with God (cf. John 1:18; 12:49; 17). Thus, the prediction could not have referred to Muhammad, as many Muslims claim.

Habakkuk 3:3. The text declares that "God came from Teman, The Holy One from Mount Paran. His glory covered the heavens, And the earth was full of His praise." Some Muslim scholars believe this refers to the prophet Muhammad coming from Paran (Arabia), and use it in connection with a similar text in Deuteronomy 33:2.

As already noted, Paran is not near Mecca where Muhammad came but is hundreds of miles away. Furthermore, the verse is speaking of "God" coming, not Muhammad who denied being God. Finally, the "praise" could not refer to Muhammad (whose name means "the praised one"), since the subject of both "praise" and "glory" is God ("His"), and Muslims would be the first to acknowledge that Muhammad is not God and should not be praised as God.

Psalm 45:3-5. Since this verse speaks of one coming with the "sword" to subdue his enemies, Muslims sometimes cite it as a prediction of their prophet Muhammad, who was known as "the prophet of the sword." They insist it could not refer to Jesus, since he never came with a sword, as he himself admitted (Matt. 26:52).

This contention, however, fails for several reasons. First, the very next verse (v. 6) identifies the person spoken of as "God" whom, according to the New Testament, Jesus claimed to be (John 8:58; 10:30), but Muhammad repeatedly denied being God, saying he was only a human prophet.[12]

Nonetheless, it is not necessary to conclude that he wrote his own obituary here. It is entirely possible that someone, perhaps Joshua, added this final chapter to the books of Moses as a fitting conclusion to the life of this great man of God. It is not at all an uncommon practice for someone to add an obituary to the end of a work by a great man. This is similar to the practice of one author writing a preface to the work of another author.

12. See discussion in Chapter 4.

Further, although Jesus did not come the first time with a sword, the Bible declares that he will at his second coming when the "armies of heaven" will follow him (Rev. 19:11–16); the first time he came to die (Mark 10:45; John 10:10–11). The second time he will come in "flaming fire taking vengeance on those who know not God" (2 Thess. 1:7–8). So there is no warrant in taking this as a prediction of Muhammad. Indeed the New Testament explicitly refers to Christ in this very passage (Heb. 1:8).

Isaiah 21:7. In Isaiah's vision "he saw a chariot with a pair of horsemen, a chariot of donkeys, and a chariot of camels." Some Muslim commentators take the rider on the "donkeys" to be Jesus and the rider on "camels" to be Muhammad, whom they believed superseded Jesus as a prophet. But this is a totally unfounded speculation with no basis in the text or its context.

Even a casual look at the passage reveals that it is speaking about the fall of Babylon. Verse 9 declares: "Babylon is fallen, is fallen!" There is nothing in the text about either Christ or Muhammad. The reference to horses, donkeys, and camels is speaking about the various means by which the news of Babylon's fall had spread. Again, there is absolutely nothing here about the prophet Muhammad.

Matthew 3:11. According to Dawud this prediction of John the Baptist could not refer to Christ and must refer to Muhammad.[13] John said, "He who is coming after me is mightier than I, whose sandals I am not worthy to carry. He will baptize you with the Holy Spirit and fire." Dawud argues that "the very preposition 'after' clearly excludes Jesus from being the foretold Prophet," since "they were both contemporaries and born in one and the same year." Further, "it was not Jesus Christ who could be intended by John, because if such were the case he would have followed Jesus and submitted to him like a disciple and subordinate." What is more, "if Jesus were in reality the person whom the Baptist foretold . . . there would be no necessity nor any sense in his being baptized by his inferior in the river like an ordinary penitent Jew!" Indeed, John "*did not know* the gift of prophecy in Jesus until he heard—*while in prison*—of his miracles." Finally, since the one John proclaimed was to make Jerusalem and its temple more glorious (3:1; Hag. 2:8–9) then it could not have referred to Christ; otherwise this "is to confess the absolute failure of the whole enterprise."[14]

In response, Jesus' ministry did not begin until "after" that of John's, precisely as he had said. John began ministering in Matthew 3:1 and Jesus did not begin until after his baptism (Matt. 3:16–17) and temptation (Matt. 4:1–11). John did defer to Jesus, saying he was unworthy even to

13. See Dawud, 157.
14. Ibid., 158–60, 162.

carry his shoes (Matt. 3:11). In fact, the text says, "John tried to prevent Him [Jesus], saying, 'I have need to be baptized by You, and are You coming to me?' " (Matt. 3:14). Jesus stated his reason for baptism, namely, that it was necessary "to fulfill all righteousness" (Matt. 3:15). Since he came to "fulfill, not destroy, the law" (Matt. 5:17) he had to identify with its demands. Otherwise, he would not have been, as he was, perfectly righteous (Rom. 8:1–5). John clearly knew who Christ was when he baptized him, since he proclaimed him to be "the Lamb of God who takes away the sins of the world" (John 1:29). And he, like the crowd, saw the "Spirit of God" descend on Jesus and the "voice from Heaven" proclaim, "This is My beloved Son, in whom I am well pleased" (Matt. 3:17). While John did express some later questions, these were quickly answered by Christ who assured him by his miracles (Matt. 11:3-5) that he was the Messiah predicted by Isaiah (Isa. 35:5–6; 40:3). Finally, all of the Old Testament prophecies about Messiah (Christ) were not fulfilled at his first coming; some await his coming again. Jesus himself clearly stated that he would not set up his kingdom until the "end of the age," after the "signs of His coming" (Matt. 24:3), when they would "see the Son of Man coming on the clouds of heaven with power and great glory" (Matt. 24:30). Only then "the Son of Man sits on the throne of His glory . . . [and His apostles] on twelve thrones, judging the twelve tribes of Israel" (Matt. 19:28).

Most of the reasons that John's predictions referred to Christ are now obvious. He clearly understood them to refer to Christ, proclaiming him to be "the Lamb of God who takes away the sins of the world" (John 1:29). The Father's voice from heaven when John baptized him confirmed that Jesus was the Messiah, the Son of God of whom John spoke. The respect with which John deferred to Jesus when he reluctantly baptized him (Matt. 3:14) reveals that he considered Jesus his superior. Likewise John's reference to being unworthy even to carry Jesus' shoes indicates his great respect for who Jesus was. Jesus' later reconfirmation of his Messiahship to John in prison by way of miracles reveals that John understood this to validate Jesus' claim to be the Messiah (Matt. 11:2–5). Jesus' eyewitness contemporaries and disciples considered him to be the one predicted in the Old Testament, since that is precisely how they apply the predictions of Malachi (3:1) and Isaiah (40:3) in their writings (Matt. 3:1–3; Mark 1:1–3; Luke 3:4–6). So it is clear without question that Jesus, not Muhammad, is the Messiah predicted by both the Old Testament and by John the Baptist.

John 14:16. Muslim scholars see in Jesus' reference to the coming of the promised "Helper" (Greek *paraclete)* a prediction of Muhammad. They base this on the Qur'anic (61:6) reference to Muhammad as "Ahmad" (*periclytos*), which they take to be the correct rendering of the Greek word *paraclete* here. According to this verse, "Jesus, the Son of

Mary, said: 'O Children of Israel! I am the apostle of God . . . giving glad Tidings of an Apostle to come after me. Whose name shall be Ahmad.'" But again, taken in its context, there is no basis whatsoever for such a conclusion.

Of the over 5,686 Greek manuscripts of the New Testament[15] there is absolutely no manuscript authority for placing the word *periclytos* ("praised one") in the original, as the Muslims claim it should read. Rather, they read *paraclete* ("helper"). In this same passage Jesus clearly identifies the Helper as the Holy Spirit, not Muhammad. Jesus said, "But the Helper, the Holy Spirit, whom the Father will send, will teach you" (John 14:26). The "Helper" was given to Jesus' apostles ("you," v. 16), namely, those who would "bear witness" of him because they "have been with . . . [him] from the beginning" (John 15:27; cf. Acts 1:22; Luke 1:1–2). But Muhammad was not one of Jesus' apostles, as all admit. So he could not have been the one Jesus referred to as the Helper (*paraclete*).

The Helper Jesus promised was to abide with them "forever" (John 16), but Muhammad has been dead for over thirteen centuries! So there is no way he could qualify. And Jesus said to the disciples, "You know Him (the Helper)" (v. 17), but the apostles did not know Muhammad. They could not have, since he was not even born for another six centuries.

Jesus also told his apostles that the Helper will be "in you" (v. 17). Muhammad could not have been "in" Jesus' apostles, since they lived six hundred years before his time and knew nothing about him. Neither was their teaching in accord with Muhammad's. So he could not have been "in" Jesus in some sort of spiritual or doctrinally compatible way.

Jesus affirmed that the Helper would be sent "in My [Jesus'] name" (John 14:26). But no Muslim believes Muhammad was sent by Jesus in Jesus' name. The Helper whom Jesus was about to send would not "speak on His own authority" (John 16:13). But Muhammad constantly testifies to himself in the Qur'an. For example, in 33:40, Muhammad says of himself, "Muhammad is . . . The Apostle of God, And the Seal of the Prophets." The Helper would "glorify" Jesus (John 16:14), but if Islam is right then Muhammad supersedes Jesus, being the last of the prophets and, therefore, "the Seal of the Prophets." As such, he would not be glorifying Jesus who was an earlier and, therefore, in that sense, inferior prophet.

Finally, Jesus asserted that the Helper would come in "not many days" (Acts 1:5), whereas Muhammad did not come for six hundred years. The Helper, however, who was the Holy Spirit (John 14:26), did come in a short time, namely, a few days later on the Day of Pentecost (Acts 1:5;

15. N. L. Geisler and W. E. Nix, *General Introduction to the Bible* (Chicago: Moody Press, 1968), Chapter 22, esp. 387 (latest figure).

2:1f.). So once more the claim that Muhammad is predicted in Scripture is found to be completely groundless.

MUSLIM MISUSE OF SCRIPTURE

A careful observer, looking at these texts in their literary setting, will readily ascertain how they are wrenched out of their context by Muslim apologists, eager to find in Judeo-Christian Scripture something that will show the superiority of Islam over Judaism and Christianity. Islamic scholars complain when Christians try to interpret the Qur'an for them to Christian advantage. But they are guilty of the very thing they charge.

Furthermore, Muslim usage of Scripture is often arbitrary and without textual warrant. Although Islamic scholars are quick to claim that the Scriptures have been corrupted (see Chapter 10), nevertheless, when they come upon a text that they feel can be made to lend credence to their view, they have no problem accepting its authenticity. And this is usually done with total disregard for the textual evidence for the authenticity of the biblical text, which is based on biblical manuscripts that predate the Muslim era. In short, their determination of which biblical texts are authentic is arbitrary and self-serving.

EVALUATION OF MUSLIM CLAIM FOR MUHAMMAD'S DIVINE CALL

For many critics of Islam the Muslim view of Muhammad suffers from an acute case of overclaim. They do not find, for example, support for the claim that he was called to bring the full and final revelation from God in the circumstances that surround Muhammad's call. They point out that during his call he was choked by the angel. Muhammad himself said of the angel, "He choked me with the cloth until I believed that I should die. Then he released me and said: 'Recite!' (*Iqra*)." When he hesitated, he received "twice again the repeated harsh treatment."[16] This seems to many an unusual form of coercion, unlike a gracious and merciful God Muslims claim Allah to be, as well as contrary to the free choice they claim he has granted his creatures.

Muhammad himself questioned the divine origin of the experience. At first he thought he was being deceived by a *jinn* or evil spirit. In fact, Muhammad was at first deathly afraid of the source of his newly found revelation, but he was encouraged by his wife Khadija and her cousin Waraqah to believe that the revelation was the same as that of Moses, and that he, too, would be a prophet of his nation. One of the most widely respected modern Muslim biographers, M. H. Haykal, speaks vividly of Muhammad's plaguing fear that he was demon-possessed:

16. See Andrae, 43-44.

Stricken with panic, Muhammad arose and asked himself, "What did I see? *Did possession of the devil which I feared all along come to pass?*" Muhammad looked to his right and his left but saw nothing. For a while he stood there trembling with fear and stricken with awe. He feared the cave might be haunted and that he might run away still unable to explain what he saw.[17]

Haykal notes that Muhammad had feared demon possession before, but his wife Khadijah talked him out of it. For "as she did on earlier occasions when *Muhammad feared possession by the devil,* so now stood firm by her husband and devoid of the slightest doubt." Thus "respectfully, indeed reverently, she said to him, 'Joy to my cousin! Be firm. By him who dominates Khadijah's soul I pray and hope that you will be the Prophet of this nation. By God, He will not let you down.'"[18] Indeed, Haykal's description of Muhammad's experience of receiving a "revelation" fits that of other mediums. Haykal wrote of the revelation to remove the suspicion of guilt for one of Muhammad's wives:

Silence reigned for a while; nobody could describe it as long or short. Muhammad had not moved from his spot when revelation came to him accompanied by the usual convulsions. He was stretched out in his clothes and a pillow was placed under his head. A'ishah [his wife] later reported, "Thinking that something ominous was about to happen, everyone in the room was frightened except me, for I did not fear a thing, knowing I was innocent. . . ." Muhammad recovered, he sat up and began to wipe his forehead where beads of perspiration had gathered.[19]

Another characteristic often associated with occult "revelations" is contact with the dead (cf. Deut. 18:9–14). Haykal relates an occasion when "the Muslims who overheard him [Muhammad] asked, 'Are you calling the dead?' and the Prophet answered, 'They hear me no less than you do, except that they are unable to answer me.'"[20] According to Haykal, on another occasion Muhammad was found "praying for the dead buried in that cemetery." Haykal even frankly admits that "there is hence no reason to deny the event of the Prophet's visit to the cemetery of Baqi as out of place considering *Muhammad's spiritual and psychic power of communication with the realms of reality and his awareness of spiritual reality that surpasses that of ordinary men.*"[21]

Also clouding the alleged divine origin of his message is the fact that after this there was a long period of silence, which according to some

17. Haykal, 74, emphasis ours.
18. Ibid., 75, emphasis ours.
19. Ibid., 337.
20. Ibid., 231.
21. Ibid., 496, emphasis ours.

accounts lasted about three years, during which time Muhammad fell into the depths of despair, feeling forsaken by God, and even entertaining thoughts of suicide. These circumstances strike many as uncharacteristic of a divine call.

Further, on another occasion Muhammad set forth a revelation he thought was from God but later changed it.[22] God later said to the prophet, "They are but names which ye have named, ye and your fathers, for which Allah hath revealed no warrant" (53:23, Pickthall trans.; cf. 22:51). But unfortunately human deception is always a possibility. Muslims themselves believe that all claimants to revelations opposing the Qur'an involve deception. In view of this it is reasonable to ask: Have Muslims not taken seriously the possibility that Muhammad's first impression was the right one, namely, that he was being deceived by a demon? They acknowledge that Satan is real and that he is a great deceiver. Why then dismiss the possibility that Muhammad himself was being deceived, as he first thought?

Finally, some critics see nothing at all supernatural in the source of Muhammad's ideas, noting that the vast majority of ideas in the Qur'an have known sources, whether Jewish, Christian, pagan, or otherwise (see Chapter 9).

Watt's insightful comments are helpful at this point especially in view of the fact that Watt himself believes in the genuiness of Muhammad's prophetic experience: "The Meccans had numerous contacts with Christians. Their trading caravans took them to the Christian cities of Damascus and Gaza in the Byzantine empire, as well as to Christian Abyssinia and the partly-Christian Yemen. A few Christians also resided in Mecca itself. . . . and it is probable that a few Meccans engaged in religious discussions."

Furthermore, commenting on 16:103, and 25:4f., in which the Meccans charged Muhammad with receiving his ideas from certain foreigners in the city, Watt writes,

> There is no agreement among the Muslim commentators about the identity of the person 'hinted at.' Several names are given, mostly of Christian slaves in Mecca, but of at least one Jew. As is suggested in the second verse quoted, there may well have been more than one person. What is important to notice is that the Qur'an does not deny that Muhammad was receiving information in this way; what it insists on is that any material he received could not have been the Qur'an, since a foreigner could not express himself in clear Arabic. The probability would seem to be that

22. This involves the so-called Satanic Verses that allowed intercession to certain idols (see Chapter 9 for more details). Sometime after this Muhammad received another revelation canceling the lines about praying to idols and substituting what we now find in 53: 21–23. Muhammad's explanation was that Satan had deceived him and inserted the false verses without his knowing it.

Muhammad talked about Biblical matters with people who knew more than the average inhabitant of Mecca, . . . What he was given would be factual knowledge, whereas the meaning and interpretation of the facts would come to him by the usual process of revelation.[23]

Even the noted biographer, Haykal, unwittingly places his finger on a possible source of Muhammad's "revelations." He writes, "The Arab's imagination is by nature strong. Living as he does under the vault of heaven and moving constantly in search of pasture or trade, and being constantly forced into the excesses, exaggerations, and even lies which the life of trade usually entails, the Arab is given to the exercise of his imagination and cultivates it at all times whether for good or for ill, for peace or for war."[24]

Finally, we should mention an incident related in Islamic hadiths that can shed much light on this discussion. One of Muhammad's scribes in Medina was Abdollah b. Abi Sarh. Dashti relates the following story concerning this scribe:

> On a number of occasions he had, with the Prophet's consent, changed the closing words of verses. For example, when the Prophet had said "And God is mighty and wise" (*'aziz, hakim*), 'Abdollah b. Abi Sarh suggested writing down "knowing and wise" (*'alim, hakim*), and the Prophet answered that there was no objection. Having observed a succession of changes of this type, 'Abdollah renounced Islam on the ground that the revelations, if from God, could not be changed at the prompting of a scribe such as himself. After his apostasy he went to Mecca and joined the Qorayshites.[25]

It is also an accepted fact in Sunni tradition that on a few occasions Qur'anic revelations were prompted by the suggestions of Muhammad's loyal follower, Umar b. al-Khattab.[26]

THE QUR'AN AS A TEST FOR TRUTH

When asked to perform miracles to support his claims, Muhammad refused to do as other prophets had (3:181–84). Instead, he claimed that the language and teaching of the Qur'an were proof that his message was divine. Since we will deal with the substance of this claim in Chapter 9, it will suffice here to note briefly the reasons for rejecting that claim. First, even admitting the Qur'an is beautiful in style, it is not perfect or truly unparalleled. Second, there is nothing really unique about the basic con-

23. Watt, *Muhammad's Mecca*, 44–45.
24. Haykal, 319.
25. Dashti, 98.
26. Ibid., 111.

tent of the Qur'an, since even Muhammad insisted that all the prophets before him were given the same message.[27] Third, if literary style is a sign of divine origin, then Muslims would have to conclude that the writings of Homer and Shakespeare were divinely inspired, too. Fourth, offering the Qur'an as a test for his claims is suspect and arbitrary, since it is easy to beg off when confronted with the demand to do something truly supernatural and offer instead one's own homemade "proof" for divine authorization (see 3:183; 17:102; 23:45).[28] Fifth, Muhammad is not the only one to have received revelation from an angel. Judaism, Christianity, and Mormonism all make the same claims, yet Muslims reject them for their false teaching. Why then should we accept the Islamic claim as true (see Chapter 9)?

MUHAMMAD'S MIRACLE CLAIMS

All Muslims hold that miracles confirm Muhammad's claim to be a prophet. But many Muslim apologists claim that his only miracles were the suras of the Qur'an. Indeed, in the Qur'an Muhammad himself never offered any other proof, even when challenged by unbelievers to do so (3:181–84). Nonetheless, miracle stories abound in Muslim tradition. These miracle claims about Muhammad fall into three basic categories: those recorded in the Qur'an; supernatural predictions by Muhammad in the Qur'an; and those found in the *hadith* (Islamic tradition).[29]

Many Muslims use 6:35 to show that Muhammad could do miracles. It reads: "If their spurning is hard On thy mind, yet if Thou wert able to seek A tunnel in the ground Or a ladder to the skies And bring them a Sign,— (What good?)."

However, careful examination of the text reveals that it does not support the claim that Muhammad was able to perform miracles. First of all, it is hypothetical—"*If* Thou were able. . . ." It does not say he was able. Second, the passage even implies that he could not perform miracles. Otherwise, why was he being spurned for not doing so? If he could have done miracles, then he could have easily stopped their spurning that was so "hard On thy [his] mind."

SPLITTING THE MOON

Many Muslims understand 54:1–2 to mean that upon Muhammad's command, before unbelievers, the moon was split in half. It reads: "The

27. See Chapter 3.
28. See also 5:35; 6:37; 7:8–9, 106–8, 116–19; 17:90–93; 20:22–23.
29. For miracles found in the *Hadith,* see Muhammad ibn Isma`il Bukhari, *The Translation of the Meaning of Sahih Al-Bukhari.* Many of the points in this section were suggested by an unpublished paper on Islamic miracles by Mark Foreman (see n. 24 in Chapter 9).

Hour (of Judgment) Is nigh, and the moon Is cleft asunder. But if they see A Sign, they turn away, And say, 'This is (But) transient magic.'"

Here again there are several difficulties with this understanding of the text. First, Muhammad is not mentioned in the passage. Second, the Qur'an does not call this a miracle, though the word sign (*ayah*) is used. Third, if it were a miracle it would contradict other passages that claim Muhammad did not perform feats of nature like this (3:181–84). Fourth, this passage is earlier than the other ones in which unbelievers are calling for a sign. Fifth, a sign like this would have been universally observed throughout the world, but there is no evidence that it was.[30] Sixth, even other Muslim scholars say this is speaking about the resurrection of the last days, not a miracle during Muhammad's day. They maintain that the phrase "the Hour (of judgment)" refers to the end times. The past tense they take as the usual Arabic way of expressing a future prophetic event.

THE MIRACLE OF THE MIRAJ

This story is known as the *Isra* or "night journey." Many Muslims believe that Muhammad, after being transported to Jerusalem, ascended into heaven on the back of a mule. In 17:1, we read: "Glory to (God) Who did take His Servant For a Journey by night From the Sacred Mosque To the Farthest Mosque, Whose precincts We did Bless,—in order that We Might show him some Of Our Signs." Later Muslim traditions expanded on this verse, speaking of Muhammad being escorted by Gabriel through several levels of heaven, being greeted by important people (Adam, John, Jesus, Joseph, Enoch, Aaron, Moses, and Abraham), where he bargains God down in his command to pray fifty times to five times a day.

There is no reason to take this passage as referring to a literal trip to heaven; even many Muslim scholars do not take it so. The noted translator of the Qur'an, Abdullah Yusuf Ali, comments on this passage, noting that "it opens with the mystic Vision of the Ascension of the Holy Prophet; he is transported from the Sacred Mosque (of Mecca) to the Farthest Mosque (of Jerusalem) in a night and shown some of the Signs of God."[31] Even according to one of the earliest Islamic traditions, Muhammad's wife, A'isha, reported that "the apostle's body remained where it was but God removed his spirit by night."[32] Further, even if this were to be understood as a miracle claim, there is no evidence presented to test its authenticity. Since it lacks testability it has no apologetic value.

30. See Pfander, 311–12.
31. Abdullah Yusuf Ali, "Introduction to Sura XVII," in *Meaning of the Glorious Qur'an* (Cairo, Egypt: Dar Al-Kitab Al-Masri, n.d.) 691.
32. Ibn Ishaq, 183.

Finally, by Islam's own definition of a confirming sign, this miracle would have no apologetic value. For according to Muslim scholars themselves, a miracle (*mudjiza*) confirming the authenticity of a prophet: (1) is an act of God that cannot be done by any creature; (2) is contrary to the customary course of things in that class; (3) is aimed at proving the authenticity of that prophet; (4) is preceded by the announcement of a forthcoming miracle; (5) proceeds in the exact manner it was announced; (6) occurs only through the hands of the prophet; (7) in no way disavows Muhammad's prophetic claim; (8) is accompanied by a challenge to reduplicate it; (9) and cannot be followed by a duplication by anyone present.[33] However, there is no evidence in the text that the "miracle of *Miraj*" even comes close to meeting all these criteria (see Chapter 9).

THE MIRACULOUS VICTORY AT BADR

Another miracle claim often attributed to Muhammad is the victory at Badr (see 3:123; 8:17). In 5:12, we read: "O ye who believe! Call in remembrance The favour of God Unto you when Certain men formed the design To stretch out Their hands against you, But (God) held back Their hands from you: So fear God."

According to Islamic tradition, several miracles are said to have occurred here, the most prominent of which was God sending three thousand angels to help in the battle (supposedly identifiable by the turbans they wore) and the miraculous rescue of Muhammad just before a Meccan was going to kill him with a sword. One tradition tells how Muhammad threw a handful of dirt into the Meccan army to blind them and drive them into retreat.

In response to this alleged miracle several things should be observed. First, it is questionable whether all of these passages refer to the same event. Even many Muslim scholars believe sura 8 is speaking of another event and is to be taken figuratively as God casting fear into the heart of Muhammad's enemy, Ubai ibn Khalaf.[34] Sura 5 is taken by some to refer to another event, possibly to the attempted assassination of Muhammad at Usfan.[35]

Second, only sura 3 mentioned Badr and it says nothing about it being a miracle. At best it would reveal God's providential care for Muhammad, not a supernatural event. Certainly it does not speak of a miracle that confirms Muhammad's prophetic credentials, since there is no evidence that it fits the nine critera for such a miracle.

33. See "Mudjiza" in *The Encyclopedia of Islam* (Leiden: E. J. Brill, 1953).
34. See Pfander, 314.
35. See Sale, *A Comprehensive Commentary on the Qur'an* (London: Kegan Paul, Treach, Trubner & Co. Ltd., 1896), vol. 1, 125.

Finally, as many critics have pointed out, if Badr's victory is a sign of divine confirmation, then why was not the subsequent clear defeat at Uhud a sign of divine disapproval? So humiliating was the defeat that they "pulled out two links of chain from Muhammad's wound, and two of his front teeth fell off in the process." In addition, the Muslim dead were mutilated on the battlefield by the enemy. One enemy of Muhammad even "cut off a number of noses and ears [of his troops] in order to make a string and necklace of them."[36] Yet he did not consider this a supernatural sign of divine disfavor.[37]

Muhammad is not the first outnumbered military leader in history to win a big victory. The Israeli six-day war in 1967 was one of the quickest and most decisive battles in the annals of modern warfare. Yet no Muslim would consider it a miraculous sign of the divine approval of Israel over an Arab nation (Egypt).

THE SPLITTING OF MUHAMMAD'S BREAST

According to Islamic tradition, at Muhammad's birth (or just before his ascension), Gabriel is said to have cut open Muhammad's chest. Gabriel removed and cleansed his heart, then filled it with wisdom, and placed it back in the prophet's chest. This is based in part on 94:1–2, 8, which reads: "Have We not Expanded thee thy breast?—And removed from thee Thy burden . . . and to thy Lord Turn (all) thy attention."

However, even most conservative Islamic scholars take this passage as a figure of speech describing the great anxiety Muhammad experienced in his early years at Mecca. The Qur'anic commentator, Yusuf Ali said, "The breast is symbolically the seat of knowledge and of the highest feeling of love and affection."[38]

QUR'ANIC PROPHECIES

Some Muslims offer predictive prophecies in the Qur'an as a proof that Muhammad could perform miracles. But the evidence is not convincing. The suras most often cited are those in which Muhammad promised victory to his troops.

Most of the so-called supernatural predictions are not supernatural at

36. Even Muslim biographer Muhammad Husayn Haykal, acknowledges "the Muslims suffered defeat" here, noting that the enemy was "intoxicated with her victory." See Haykal, 266–67.

37. After the battle of Badr the Qur'an boasts that Muhammad's followers could overcome an army with God's help when outnumbered ten to one (Sura 8:65). Here they were outnumbered only three to one, just as they were in their victory at Badr, and yet they suffered a great defeat.

38. Yusuf Ali, *The Meaning of the Glorious Qur'an*, vol. 2, 1755.

all. What religious military leader is there who might not say to his troops: "God is on our side; we are going to win. Fight on!"? Further, remembering that Muhammad is known as "the prophet of the Sword," with his greatest number of conversions coming after he had forsaken the peaceful but relatively unsuccessful means of spreading his message, it should be no surprise that he would predict victory. And considering the zeal of Muslim forces, who were promised Paradise for their efforts (22:58–59; 3:157–58; 3:170–71), it is no surprise that they were so often victorious. It is little wonder why so many "submitted," considering Muhammad commanded that "the punishment of those Who wage war against God And his Apostle, and strive With might . . . Is: execution, or crucifixion, Or the cutting off of hands And feet from opposite sides, or exile from the land" (5:36).

Further, the only really substantive prediction in the Qur'an was about the Roman victory over the Persian army at Issus (30:2–4), which reads: "The Roman Empire Has been defeated—In a land close by: But they, (even) after (This) defeat of theirs, Will soon be victorious—within a few years." Close scrutiny, however, reveals several things that make this prediction less than spectacular, to say nothing of supernatural.[39] (1) According to Ali "a few years" means three to nine years, but some argue that the real victory did not come until thirteen or fourteen years after the prophecy. The defeat of the Romans by the Persians in the capture of Jerusalem took place about A.D. 614 or 615. The counteroffensive did not begin until A.D. 622, and the victory was not complete until A.D. 625. This would be at least ten or eleven years, not "a few" spoken by Muhammad. (2) Uthman's edition of the Qur'an had no vowel points (they were not added until much later).[40] Hence, in this "prophecy" the word *sayaghlibuna*, "they shall defeat," could have been rendered, with the change of two vowels, *sayughlabuna*, "they shall be defeated."[41] (3) Even if this ambiguity were removed, the prophecy is less than spectacular, since it is neither long-range nor unusual. One would have expected the defeated Romans to bounce back in victory. It took little more than a perceptive reading of the trends of the time to forecast such an event. At best, it could have been a good guess. In any event, there appears to be no sufficient ground for proving it is supernatural.

Finally, the only other alleged prophecy worth mentioning is found in 89:2, where the phrase "By the Nights twice five" is taken by some to be

---

39. For this point and many others made in this section, we are indebted to the excellent work by Joseph Gudel in his master's thesis for Simon Greenleaf School of Law titled, *To Every Muslim an Answer* (1982), 54.

40. H. Spencer, *Islam and the Gospel of God* (Delhi: S.P.C.K., 1956), 21.

41. W. St. Clair Tisdall, *The Source of Islam* (Edinburgh: T & T Clark, n.d.), 137.

a prediction of the ten years of persecution early Muslims experienced.[42] But that this is a far-fetched interpretation is evident from the fact that even the great Islamic scholar and translator of the Qur'an, Abdullah Yusuf Ali, admitted that "by the Ten Nights are usually understood the first ten nights of *Zul-Hajj*, the sacred season of Pilgrimage."[43] In any event, there is certainly no clear prediction of anything that would have been evident to an intelligent observer in advance of the event.[44] Its very use as a predictive prophecy by Muslim scholars shows how desperate they are to find something supernatural in support of the Qur'an.

The evidence that Muhammad possessed a truly supernatural gift of prophecy is lacking. The so-called prophecy is vague and subject to dispute. It is far easier to read this meaning back into it after the event than before it.

If Muhammad possessed the ability to miraculously forecast the future, then surely he would have used it to squelch his opponents. But he never did. Instead, he admitted that he did not do miracles as the prophets before him had and simply offered his own sign (the Qur'an).

Muhammad never offered his alleged prophecy as a proof of his prophethood. Jesus, by contrast, repeatedly offered his ability to do miracles as a proof that he was the Messiah, the Son of God. When about to heal the paralytic he said to the unbelieving Jews, "that you may know that the Son of Man has power on earth to forgive sins"—something the Jews admitted that only God could do.

MIRACLES IN THE *HADITH*

Most miracle claims for Muhammad do not occur in the Qur'an. Indeed, in the Qur'an Muhammad repeatedly refused to perform miracles to confirm his prophetic credentials. Rather, he offered only the Qur'an as his sign (see Chapter 9). The vast majority of alleged miracles occur in the *hadith*, which are considered by Muslims to be second in authority only to the Qur'an. There are hundreds of such miracle stories in the *hadith*. A few will illustrate the point.

SOME MIRACLE STORIES IN THE *HADITH*

Al Bukhari tells the story of Muhammad's miraculous healing of the broken leg of a companion, Addullaha ibn Atig, who was injured while attempting to assassinate one of Muhammad's enemies.

---

42. Hazrat Mirza Bashir-Ud-Din Mahud Ahmad, *Introduction to the Study of the Holy Quran* (London: The London Mosque, 1949), 374f.

43. See Ali, 1731, note 6109.

44. By contrast, there are clear and specific predictive prophecies in the Bible that were given hundreds of years in advance (see Chapter 10).

Several sources relate the story that Muhammad miraculously provided water for ten thousand of his troops at the battle of Hudaibiyah. He allegedly dipped his hand into an empty water bottle and let the water flow through his fingers.

There are numerous stories of miraculous provision of water. There is also one of water being turned into milk.

Several stories exist of trees speaking to Muhammad, saluting him, or moving from him as he passed. Once when Muhammad could not find a private place to relieve himself, two trees are said to have come together to hide him, and then returned when he was finished. Bukhari claims that once Muhammad leaned on a tree and the tree missed his company when he left. There are many stories of wolves and even mountains saluting Muhammad.

Some stories speak of Muhammad miraculously feeding large groups with little food. Anas tells the story of his feeding eighty to ninety men with just a few loaves of barley. Ibn Sa'd relates the story of a woman who invited Muhammad to a meal. He took a thousand men with him and multiplied her small meal to feed them all.

The *hadith* often relates stories of Muhammad's miraculous dealings with his enemies. Once Muhammad cursed one of his enemies whose horse then sank up to its stomach in hard ground. Sa'd said Muhammad once turned a branch of a tree into a steel sword.

An Evaluation of the Alleged Miracles in the *Hadith*

There are many reasons for questioning the authenticity of these stories. Critics have observed the following.

First, none of them are recorded in the Qur'an. In fact, they are in general contrary to the whole spirit of the Muhammad of the Qur'an, who repeatedly refused to do these very kinds of things for unbelievers who challenged him (3:181–84; 4:153; 6:8–9).

Second, these alleged miracles follow the same pattern as the apocryphal miracles of Christ from a century or two after his death. They are a legendary embellishment of people removed from the original events. They do not come from contemporary eyewitnesses of the events.

Third, even among Muslims there is no generally agreed upon list of miracles from the *hadith*. Indeed, the vast majority of stories from the *hadith* are rejected by most Muslim scholars as not being authentic. Different groups accept different collections of them.

Fourth, the collections of the *hadith* that are generally accepted by most Muslims are far removed from the original events by several generations. Indeed, most of those who collected miracle stories lived one hundred to two hundred years after the time of the events—plenty of time for legends to develop. They relied on stories that had been passed on orally for many generations with ample embellishment. Even the stories accepted by Muslims as authentic, as determined by the *isnad* (chain of storytellers), lack credibility. For even these stories are not based on eye-witnesses but rely on many generations of storytellers, often involving hundreds of years. Joseph Horowitz questioned the reliability of the *isnad*:

> The question as to who first circulated these miracle tales would be very easy to answer if we could still look upon the *isnad*, or chain of witnesses, as unquestionably as we are apparently expected to do. It is especially seductive when one and the same report appears in various essentially similar versions. . . . In general the technique of the *isnad* does not make it possible for us to decide where it is a case of taking over oral account and where of coping from the lecture books of teachers.[45]

Fifth, Bukhari, considered to be the most reliable collector, admitted that of the 300,000 *hadith* he collected, he considered only 100,000 might be true. He then narrowed this number down to 7,275, many of which are repetitions so that the total number is in fact near 3,000. That means that even he admitted there were errors in over 295,000 of them!

Sixth, there is no one canon of authenticity for these stories accepted by all Muslims. Most Muslims rank their credibility in descending order as follows: the *Sahih* of Al Bukhari (d. 256 A.H. [after Hijrah]); *Al Sahih* of Muslim (d. 261 A.H.); the *Sunan* of Abu Du'ad (d. 275 A.H.); the *Jami* of Al-Tirmidhi (d. 279 A.H.); the *Suand* of Al Nasa (d. 303 A.H.); and the *Sunan* of Ibn Madja (d. 283 A.H.). Along with these *hadith* there were important biographers who related miracle stories. The most important ones are Ibn Sa'd (d. 123 A.H.), Ibn Ishaq (d. 151 A.H.), and Ibn Hisham (d. 218 A.H.). The above six categories are rejected by the Shia Islam. Yet they, along with other Muslims, accept the Qur'an as it is. Finally, what is of crucial significance here is that none of these miracle stories fit the nine criteria accepted by Muslims for a miracle that can confirm a prophet's claim (*mudjiza*). Hence, by their own standard, none of them have any apologetic value in demonstrating the truth of Islam.

Finally, the origin of the miracle claims of Islam is suspect. It is common knowledge that Islam borrowed many of its beliefs and practices from other religions.[46] This has also been documented by many scholars.[47] It is not surprising that Muslim miracle claims arise, then, as a result of Christian apologists demonstrating the superiority of Jesus to that of Muhammad by way of Jesus' miracles. It was only after two Chris-

45. Joseph Horowitz, "The Growth of the Mohammed Legend," in *The Moslem World*, vol. 10 (1920): 49–58.
46. Dashti, 55.
47. See Shorrosh, and Nehls, 96–102.

tian bishops (Abu Qurra from Edessa and Arethas from Ceasaria) had pointed this out that the Islamic miracle stories began to appear. As Sahas noted, "The implication [of the bishop's challenge] is quite clear: Muhammad's teaching is one that might have merit; but this is not enough to qualify him as a prophet, without supernatural signs. If such signs could be shown one could possibly accept him as a prophet."[48]

Thus, the task for Muslims was clear. If they could invent miracles they could respond to the Christian challenge. It was soon after this that Muhammad's miracle claims began to appear. Sahas notes that "it is quite interesting that several of these (miracle stories) sound as if they are being offered as responses to such Christians as Abu Qurra, and they bear an amazing resemblance to miracles of Jesus found in the Gospels."[49] Likewise, it was during this polemic that Muslims began to interpret certain events in the Qur'an as miracles. All of this points toward one conclusion: the Muhammad miracle stories lack credibility.

THE LACK OF APOLOGETIC VALUE

There are several reasons, however, why these alleged miracles have no apologetic value in proving Muhammad was a prophet of God. First, most of them do not come from the Qur'an (which is claimed to be inspired). Therefore, they lack divine authority for Muslims such as they claim the Qur'an has.

Second, the miracle stories based on Muslim tradition are suspect. They lack eyewitness accounts, contain many contradictions, and, therefore, lack credibility. The absence of these events in the Qur'an, where Muhammad is constantly challenged to support his claims miraculously, is a strong argument that they are not authentic. Surely, if Muhammad could have silenced his critics by proving his supernatural confirmation he would have done so, since he was challenged to do so on many occasions.

Third, nowhere in the Qur'an does Muhammad ever offer the miraculous event in nature as evidence of his divine call. Contemporary Muslim author, Faruqi, claims that "Muslims do not claim any miracles for Muhammad. In their view, what proves Muhammad's prophethood is the sublime beauty and greatness of the revelation itself, the Holy Qur'an, not any inexplicable breaches of natural law which confound human reason."[50] Even though some Muslim scholars dispute this claim, it is true,

48. Daniel J. Sahas, "The Formation of Later Islamic Doctrines as a Response to Byzantine Polemics: The Miracles of Muhammad," in *The Greek Orthodox Theological Review*, vol. 27, nos. 2 and 3 (Summer-Fall 1982), 312.

49. Ibid., 314. For example, Muhammad's ascension into heaven resembles Jesus' ascension (Acts 1). Changing water into milk is like Jesus' transforming water into wine (John 2). And his alleged miraculous feedings resemble Jesus' feeding of the five thousand (John 6).

50. Al-Faruqi, 20.

nonetheless, that Muhammad never performed miraculous feats in nature in support of his claim to be a prophet, even though other prophets did and he was challenged to do likewise (3:183; 4:153; 6:8–9; 17:90–95). Even the great Muslim scholar, Abdullah Yusuf Ali, admitted that Muhammad did not perform any miracle "in the sense of a reversing of Nature." This admission raises serious questions about his prophetic credentials.

Fourth, even Muhammad accepts the fact that God confirmed the prophets before him by miracles. Interestingly, most of the prophets mentioned in the Qur'an are biblical characters. For example, in 6:84–86, after recounting the story of Abraham God declares: "We gave him Isaac and Jacob: all (three) we guided: and before him we guided Noah, and among his progeny, David, Solomon, Job, Joseph, Moses, and Aaron: Thus do we reward those who do good: And Zakariya and John, and Jesus and Elias: All in the ranks of the Righteous: And Ismail and Elisha, and Jonas, and Lot." He refers to God confirming Moses' prophetic credentials by miracles several times (7:106–8; 116–19). He wrote, "Then We [God] sent Moses And his brother Aaron, with Our Signs and Authority manifest" (23:45). The Qur'an also refers to God's miraculous power being manifest through many other prophets (4:63–65). But if Muhammad recognized that God performed miracles through these biblical prophets, then why could he not perform them?

Fifth, Muhammad also accepts the fact that Jesus performed many miracles to prove the divine origin of his message, such as his healings and raising people from the dead. As the Qur'an says, "O Jesus the son of Mary . . . thou healest those Born blind, and lepers, by My leave [permission]. And behold! thou Bringest forth the dead By My leave" (5:113). But if Jesus could perform miraculous feats of nature to confirm his divine commission, and Muhammad refused to do the same, most Christians will find it difficult to believe Muhammad is superior to Christ as a prophet.

Sixth, when Muhammad was challenged to perform miracles to prove his claims he refused to do so. The Qur'an acknowledges that Muhammad's opponents said, "Why is not An angel sent down to him?" to settle the matter (6:8–9). According to Muhammad himself, unbelievers challenged him to prove he was a prophet, saying, "We shall not believe in thee, until thou Cause a spring to gush Forth for us from the earth . . . Or thou cause the sky To fall in pieces, as thou Sayest (will happen), against us; Or thou bring God And the angels before (us) Face to face" (17:90–92). Muhammad's response is illuminating: "Am I aught but a man,—An apostle?" One cannot imagine Moses, Elijah, or Jesus giving such a response. Indeed, Muhammad admitted that when Moses was challenged by Pharaoh he responded with miracles: "(Pharaoh) said: 'If indeed Thou hast come with a Sign, Show it forth,—If thou tellest the truth.' Then (Moses) threw his rod, And behold! it was A serpent, plain (for all to see)! And he drew out his hand, And behold! it was white To all beholders!" (7:106–8). The Qur'an goes on to say, "Thus truth was confirmed" (v. 118). Yet knowing this was God's way to confirm his spokespersons, Muhammad refused to produce similar miracles. Why then should anyone believe he stood in the line of the great prophets of God?

Finally, Muslims offer no good explanation for Muhammad's failure to do miracles. One familiar Islamic argument is that "it is one of the established ways of God that He gives His Prophets that kind of miracles which accord with the genius of the time so that the world may see that it is beyond human power and that the power of God manifests itself in these miracles." Thus, "during the time of Moses the art of sorcery had made the greatest development. Therefore, Moses was given miracles which dumbfounded the sorcerers and at the sight of these miracles the sorcerers accepted the leadership and prophethood of Moses." Similarly, "during the time of the Prophet of Islam, the art of eloquent speech had made great advances. Therefore, the Prophet of Islam was given the miracle of the Qur'an whose eloquence stilled the voices of the greatest poets of his time."[51]

However, there are several serious problems with this reasoning. First of all, there is no evidence that this is "one of the established ways of God." To the contrary, even by the Qur'an's own admission God repeatedly gave miracles of nature through Moses and other prophets, including Jesus. It is God's established way to confirm his prophets through miracles.

Furthermore, it is a whole lot easier to produce a beautiful piece of religious literature than it is to perform miraculous feats of nature, which the Qur'an admits God did through other prophets. In fact, there are many other great pieces of religious literature that teach things contrary to the Qur'an, including the Jewish prophecy of Isaiah, the Christian Sermon on the Mount, and the Hindu Gita. Yet all these teach things contrary to the Qur'an.

In addition, Muhammad's unwillingness (and apparent inability) to perform miraculous feats of nature, when he knew that the prophets before him could and did perform them, will sound like a cop-out to thinking non-Muslims. They will ask, "If God confirmed other prophets by such things, then why did he not do the same for Muhammad and remove all doubt?" In Muhammad's own words (from the Qur'an), "They (will) say: 'Why is not A Sign sent down To him from his Lord?'" since even Muhammad admitted that "God hath certainly Power to send down a Sign" (6:37).

Also, Muhammad gave no such answer to his critics that it was God's established way to confirm his prophets in different ways in different ages according to the genius of the times. Rather, he simply offered his own

51. From Gudel, 38–39.

sign (the Qur'an) and said their reason for rejecting him was unbelief, not his inability to do miracles. He wrote: "Say those without knowledge: 'Why speaketh not God Unto us? Or why cometh not Unto us a Sign?'" Muhammad's answer was clear: "So said the people before them Words of similar import. Their hearts are alike" (2:118; cf. 17:90–93; 3:183).

Finally, even when there are allegedly supernatural events connected to Muhammad's life (though not miracles of nature such as he acknowledges Moses and Jesus did), they can be explained by natural means. For example, Muslims take Muhammad's outstanding victory at the battle of Badr in A.D. 624 as a supernatural indication of divine approval on his behalf. But exactly one year after Badr Muhammad's supporters suffered a humiliating defeat.[52] Yet he did not consider this a supernatural sign of divine disfavor.[53]

MUHAMMAD'S MORAL EXAMPLE

Most students of Islam acknowledge that Muhammad was a generally moral person. But Muslims claim much more. They insist that he was both beyond (major) sin and is the perfect moral example for humankind. They claim that Muhammad "stands in history as the best model for man in piety and perfection. He is a living proof of what man can be and of what he can accomplish in the realm of excellence and virtue."[54] This, they say, is one of "the chief proofs" that Muhammad is the unique prophet from God.[55]

A popular Muslim classic by Kamal ud Din ad Damiri gives us the following description of the beloved prophet.

> Mohammed is the most favored of mankind, the most honored of all apostles, the prophet of mercy. . . . He is the best of prophets, and his nation is the best of nations; . . . He was perfect in intellect, and was of noble origin. He had an absolutely graceful form, complete generosity, perfect bravery, excessive humility, useful knowledge . . . perfect fear of God and sublime piety. He was the most eloquent and the most perfect of mankind in every variety of perfection.[56]

52. So humiliating was the defeat that they "pulled out two links of chain from Muhammad's wound, and two of his front teeth fell off in the process." In addition the Muslim dead were mutilated on the battlefield by the enemy. One enemy even "cut off a number of noses and ears in order to make a string and necklace of them." See Haykal, 266–67.

53. The Qur'an boasts that Muhammad's followers could overcome an army with God's help when outnumbered ten to one (8:65). But here they were outnumbered only three to one, just as they were in their victory at Badr, and yet they suffered a great defeat. This is scarcely a sign of a miraculous victory.

54. Abdalati, 8.

55. See Pfander, 225–26.

56. See Gudel, 72.

There are at least several areas where questions arise about the alleged moral perfection of Muhammad. The first is the matter of polygamy.

The Problem of Polygamy. According to the Qur'an a man may have four wives (4:3). This raises at least two questions. First, is polygamy moral? Second, was Muhammad consistent with his own law? And if not, how can he be considered the flawless moral example for human-kind?

In the Judeo-Christian tradition polygamy is considered morally wrong. Although God *permitted* it along with other human frailties and sins, he never *commanded* it.[57] The Qur'an, however, clearly sanctions polygamy, allowing that a man may have four wives if he is able to provide for them: "Marry women of your choice, Two, or three, or four" (4:3). Without presupposing the truth of the Christian revelation, there are many arguments against polygamy from a general moral point of view common to both Muslims and Christians. First, monogamy should be recognized by *precedent,* since God gave the first man only one wife (Eve). Second, it is implied by *proportion,* since the amount of males and females God brings into the world are about equal. Finally, monogamy is implied by *parity.* If men can marry several wives, why can't a wife have several husbands? It seems only fair.

Even the popular Muslim biographer, Haykal, tacitly acknowledged the superiority of monogamy when he affirmed that "the happiness of the family and that of the community can best be served by the limita-

---

57. That monogamy is God's standard for the human race is clear from the following facts: (1) From the very beginning God set the pattern by creating a monogamous marriage relationship with one man and one woman, Adam and Eve (Gen. 1:27; 2:21–25). (2) This God-established example of one woman for one man, was the general practice of the human race (Gen. 4:1) until interrupted by sin (Gen. 4:23). (3) The Law of Moses clearly commands, "You shall not multiply wives" (Deut. 17:17). (4) The warning against polygamy is repeated in the very passage where it numbers Solomon's many wives (1 Kings 11:2), warning that "you shall not intermarry with them, nor they with you." (5) Our Lord reaffirmed God's original intention by citing this passage (Matt. 19:4) and noting that God created one "male and [one] female" and joined them in marriage. (6) The New Testament stresses that "each man [should] have his own wife, and let each woman have her own husband" (1 Cor. 7:2). (7) Likewise, Paul insisted that a church leader should be "the husband of one wife" (1 Tim. 3:2, 12). (8) Indeed, monogamous marriage is a prefiguration of the relation between Christ and his bride, the Church (Eph. 5:31–32).

In fact, the Bible reveals that God severely punished those who practiced polygamy, as is evidenced by the following: (1) Polygamy is first mentioned in the context of a sinful society in rebellion against God where the murderer "Lamech took for himself two wives" (Gen. 4:19, 23). (2) God repeatedly warned polygamists of the consequences of their actions "lest his heart turn away" from God (Deut. 17:17; cf. 1 Kings 11:2). (3) God never *commanded* polygamy—like divorce, he only *permitted* it because of the hardness of their hearts (Deut. 24:1; Matt. 19:8). (4) Every polygamist in the Bible, including David and Solomon (1 Chron. 14:3), paid dearly for his sins. (5) God hates polygamy, as he hates divorce, since it destroys his ideal for the family (cf. Mal. 2:16). Taken from Geisler and Howe, 183–84.

tions which monogamy imposes."[58] Indeed, Muhammad's relations with his wives is itself an argument against polygamy. Haykal notes, for example, problems stemming from polygamy: "the wives of the Prophet went so far as to plot against their husband." This is understandable in so far as Haykal admits that "he [Muhammad] often ignored some of his wives, and avoided others on many occasions."[59] He adds, "Indeed, favoritism for some of his wives had created such controversy and antagonism among the 'Mothers of the Believers' that Muhammad once thought of divorcing some of them."[60] All of this falls short of an exemplary moral situation both in principle and in practice.

Even laying aside for the moment the question of whether polygamy, as taught in the Qur'an, is morally right there remains another serious problem that many feel flaws the character of Muhammad. Muhammad received a revelation from God that a man should have no more than four wives at one time, yet he had many more. A Muslim defender of Muhammad, writing in *The Prophet of Islam as the Ideal Husband,* admitted that he had fifteen wives! Yet he told others they could have only four wives. How can someone be a perfect moral example for the whole human race and not even live by one of the basic laws he laid down as from God?

The Muslim answer is unconvincing. They claim that the prophet received a "revelation" that God had made an exception for him but not for anyone else. Muhammad quotes God as saying: "Prophet! We have Made lawful to thee Thy wives. . . . And any believing women Who dedicates her soul To the Prophet if the Prophet Wishes to wed her;" but adds quickly, "this Only *for thee,* and not For the Believers (at large)" (33:50, emphasis added)! What is more, Muhammad even received *an alleged divine sanction to marry Zainab, the divorced wife of his adopted son* (33:37). Interestingly, this divorce was caused by the prophet's admiration for Zainab's beauty.

In addition to all this, we are asked to believe that God made a special exception to another divinely revealed law to give each wife her conjugal rights "justly," that is, to observe a fixed rotation among them. Muhammad insists that God told him that he could have whichever wife he wanted when he wanted her: "Thou mayest defer (the turn Of) any of them that thou Pleasest, and thou mayest receive Any thou pleasest" (33:51). Apparently even God had to put the brakes on Muhammad's love for women. For eventually he received a revelation that said, "It is not lawful for thee (To marry more) women After this, nor to change

58. See Haykal, 294.
59. Ibid., 436. The reason given is even more revealing, namely, he avoided them "in order to discourage their abuse of his compassion" [!].
60. Ibid., 437.

Them for (other) wives, Even though their beauty Attract thee" (33:52). A look at Muhammad's inconsistency makes one wonder how anyone with open eyes can consider him to be a perfect moral example and ideal husband.

The Lower Status of Women. The Qur'an and tradition accord a lower status for women than for men. The superior status of men is based directly on commands in the Qur'an. As already noted, men can marry several wives (polygamy) but women cannot marry several husbands (polyandry). The Qur'an (2:228) admits that men have a degree of advantage over women. The Qur'an explicitly affords men the right to divorce their wives but does not accord the equal right to women, claiming, "Men have a degree of advantage over them" (2:228).[61] On one occasion Muhammad sanctioned the beating of a female servant in order to elicit the truth from her. Haykal reports that "the servant was called in and Ali immediately seized her and struck her painfully and repeatedly as he commanded her to tell the truth to the Prophet of God."[62] Finally, according to the Qur'an, men can even beat their wives: "Men are in charge of women because Allah hath made the one to excell the other. ... As for those from whom ye fear rebellion, admonish them and *banish them to beds apart, and scourge them*" (4:34).[63] In addition to this, Muslim women must wear a veil, stand behind their husbands, and kneel behind them in prayer. The law requires that two women must bear witness in civil contracts as opposed to one man.[64]

In a *hadith* found in the *Sahih* of Al-Bukhari we find the following narrative describing the inferior status of women in Islam:

> Narrated [by] Ibn 'Abbas: The Prophet said: "I was shown the Hell-fire and that the majority of its dwellers were women who were ungrateful." It was asked, "Do they disbelieve in Allah?" (or are they ungrateful to Allah?) He replied, "They are ungrateful to their husbands and are ungrateful for the favors and the good (charitable deeds) done to them."[65]

In view of all these statements about women, one finds it incredible to hear Muslim apologists say, "Evidently, Muhammad not only honored woman more than did any other man, but he raised her to the status which truly belongs to her—an accomplishment of which Muhammad

61. See Rippin and Knappert, 113–15.
62. See Haykal, 336.
63. Quran, Pickthall translation, emphasis added. Ali softens this verse by adding the word "lightly" not found in the Arabic, as follows: "(And last) beat them (lightly)."
64. See Abdalati, 189–91.
65. Al-Bukhari, vol. 1, 29.

alone has so far been capable"[!][66] Another Muslim writer states, "Islam has given woman rights and privileges which she has never enjoyed under other religious or constitutional systems."[67] The facts show just the opposite.

Muhammad's Moral Imperfection in General. Muhammad was far from sinless. Even the Qur'an speaks of his need to ask God for forgiveness on many occasions. For example, in 40:55 God told him, "Patiently, then, persevere: For the Promise of God Is true: and *ask God forgiveness For thy fault.*" On another occasion God told Muhammad, "Know, therefore, that There is no god But God, and *ask Forgiveness for thy fault,* and for the men And women who believe" (47:19, emphasis added). This makes it absolutely clear that forgiveness was to be sought for his sins, not just for others (48:2).

In view of the facts about Muhammad recorded in the Qur'an, Muhammad's character was certainly far from flawless. Even one of the most widely accepted modern biographers of Muhammad admits that he sinned. Speaking of one occasion, Haykal said flatly, "Muhammad did in fact err when he frowned in the face of [the blind beggar] ibn Umm Maktum and sent him away."[68] Haykal adds, "in this regard he [Muhammad] was as fallible as anyone."[69] If so, then it is difficult to believe that Muhammad can be so eulogized by Muslims. However much an improvement Muhammad's morals may have been over many others of his day, he certainly seems to fall short of the perfect example for all men of all times that many Muslims claim for him. Unlike the Jesus of the Gospels, he certainly would not want to challenge his foes with the question: "Which of you convicts Me of sin?" (John 8:46).

The Problem of Holy Wars (Jihad). Laying aside the question of whether war is ever justified,[70] Muhammad believed in holy wars (the *jihad*). Muhammad, by divine revelation, commands his followers: "fight in the cause Of God" (2:244). He adds, "fight and slay The Pagans wherever ye find them" (9:5). And "when ye meet The Unbelievers (in fight) Smite at their necks" (47:4). In general, they were to "Fight those who believe not In God nor the Last Day" (9:29). Indeed, Paradise is promised for those who fight for God: "Those who have left their homes . . . Or fought or been slain,—Verily, I will blot out From them their iniquities, And admit them into Gardens With rivers flowing beneath;—A reward

66. See Haykal, 298.
67. See Abdalati, 184. For further critique of Islamic and Qur'anic attitudes toward women, see Dashti, 113–120.
68. See Haykal, 134.
69. Ibid., 134.
70. See N. L. Geisler, *Christian Ethics: Options and Issues* (Grand Rapids: Baker, 1989), Chapter 12.

from the Presence Of God, and from His Presence Is the best of rewards" (3:195; cf. 2:244; 4:95 cf. 8:12). These "holy wars" were carried out "in the cause Of God" (2:244) against "unbelievers." In 5:36–38, we read: "the punishment of those Who wage war against God [i.e., unbelievers] And His Apostle, and strive With might and main For mischief through the land Is: execution, or crucifixion, Or the cutting off of hands And feet from opposite sides, Or exile from the land." Acknowledging that these are appropriate punishments, depending on "the circumstances," Ali offers little consolation when he notes that the more cruel forms of Arabian treatment of enemies, such as, "piercing of eyes and leaving the unfortunate victim exposed to a tropical sun," were abolished![71] Such war on and persecution of enemies on religious grounds—by whatever means—is seen by most critics as a clear example of religious intolerance.[72]

The Problem of Moral Expediency. Muhammad sanctioned his followers' raiding of the commercial Meccan caravans.[73] The prophet himself led three such raids. Doubtless the purpose of these attacks was not only to obtain financial reward, but also to impress the Meccans with the growing power of the Muslim force. Critics of Islam raise serious moral questions about this kind of piracy. At the minimum they feel these actions cast a dark shadow over Muhammad's alleged moral perfection.

Another time Muhammad sanctioned a follower to lie to an enemy named Khalid in order to kill him. This he did. Then, at a safe distance, but in the presence of the man's wives "he fell on him with his sword and killed him. Khalid's women were the only witnesses and they began to cry and mourn for him."[74]

On other occasions Muhammad had no aversion to politically expedient assassinations. When a prominent Jew, Ka'b Ibn Al-Ashraf, had stirred up some discord against Muhammad and composed a satirical poem about him, the prophet asked, "Who will deliver me from Ka'b?" Immediately four persons volunteered and shortly returned to Muhammad with Ka'b's head in their hands.[75] Noted modern Islamic biographer, Husayn Haykal, acknowledges many such assassinations in his book *The Life of Muhammad.* Of one he wrote, "the Prophet ordered the

71. Yusuf Ali, *Holy Qur'an,* note 738, 252.
72. In view of these clear commands to use the sword aggressively to spread Islam and Muslim practice down through the centuries, Muslim claims that "this fight is waged solely for the freedom to call men unto God and unto His religion" have a hollow ring (see Haykal, 212).
73. Ibid., 357f.
74. Ibid., 273.
75. See Gudel, 74.

execution of Uqbah ibn Abu Muayt. When Uqbah pleaded, 'Who will take care of my children, O Muhammad?' Muhammad answered, 'The fire.'"[76]

The Qur'an itself informs us that Muhammad was not indisposed to breaking promises when he found it advantageous. He even got a "revelation" to break a long-standing pledge to avoid killing during a sacred month of Arab: "They ask thee Concerning fighting In the Prohibited Month. Say: 'Fighting therein Is a grave (offense)'; But graver is it In the sight of God To prevent access To the path of God" (2:217). Again, "God has already ordained For you, (O men), The dissolution of your oaths (In some cases)" (66:2). Rather than consistency, Muhammad's moral life was sometimes characterized by expediency.

The Problem of Retaliation. On at least two occasions Muhammad ordered people assassinated for composing poems that mocked him. This extremely oversensitive overreaction to ridicule is defended by some in this unconvincing way: "For a man like Muhammad, whose success depended to a large extent upon the esteem which he could win, a malicious satirical composition could be more dangerous than a lost battle."[77] But as critics point out this is merely a pragmatic, the end-justifies-the-means ethic.

Even though, as Haykal admits, "the Muslims were always opposed to killing any woman or children," nonetheless, "a Jewish woman was executed because she had killed a Muslim by dropping a millstone on his head."[78] Haykal reports that on another occasion "both slave women [who had allegedly spoken against Muhammad in song] were indicted and ordered executed with their master."[79] When it was believed that one woman, Abu 'Afk, had insulted Muhammad (by a poem), one of Muhammad's followers "attacked her during the night while she was surrounded by her children, one of whom she was nursing." And *"after removing the child from his victim, he killed her."*[80] All of this certainly does not seem worthy of one held up to be the great moral example for all humankind.

The zeal with which Muhammad's followers would kill for him was infamous. Haykal records the words of one devotee who would have killed his daughter at Muhammad's command. Umar ibn al Khattab, the second Caliph of Islam, declared fanatically, "By God, if he [Muhammad]

76. See Haykal, 234 (cf. 236–37, 243).
77. See Gudel, 74.
78. See Haykal, 314.
79. Ibid., 410.
80. Ibid., 243, emphasis added.

were to ask me to strike off her head, I would do so without hesitation" [!].[81]

The Problem of Mercilessness. Muhammad attacked the last Jewish tribe of Medina based on the suspicion that they had plotted with the Meccan enemies against Muslims. Unlike the previous two Jewish tribes who had been simply expelled from the city, this time all the men of the tribe were put to death and the women and children were sold into slavery. Even some who try to justify this admit this was an act of "cruelty" and attempt to explain it away by claiming that "one must see Muhammad's cruelty toward the Jews against the background of the fact that their scorn and rejection was the greatest disappointment of his life, and for a time they threatened completely to destroy his prophetic authority." [82] Even if this were so, two wrongs do not make a right. In any case, would this justify killing the men and making slaves of the women and children? [83] And, what is more, does this kind of activity exemplify a person who is supposed to be of flawless moral character, the model for all humankind?

In spite of all this evidence against Muhammad being a perfect moral example, Haykal, a noted defender of Islam, responds with the incredible claim that, even if "their claims were true, we would still refute them with the simple argument that *the great stand above the law*" [!].[84]

SUMMARY

Islam claims that Muhammad is the last of the prophets with the full and final revelation of God (in the Qur'an). Muslims offer several things in support of this claim, such as predictions by Muhammad in the Qur'an, the miraculous nature of the Qur'an, miracles performed by Muhammad, and his perfect moral character. However, as we have seen, the evidence for these falls far short of the claim to be supernatural either because there is no real evidence that the events actually happened or because there was nothing really supernatural about the events themselves.

81. Ibid., 439. As Dashti aptly observes, "Sometimes killings which were really motivated either by desire to make a show of valor or by personal grudge were passed off as service to Islam" (Dashti, ibid., 101).

82. See Andrae, 155–56.

83. Muslim attempts to defend against this charge usually involve the logical fallacy of "diverting the issue" by claiming that Christian civilizations have done the same (see Haykal, 237). Even if so, this does not justify the prophet's retaliatory killing of women. One can scarcely imagine Jesus doing or approving such a reprehensible deed.

84. See Haykal, 298, emphasis ours.

Of course, a Muslim can continue to accept this by faith. But to insist that it is demonstrated by the evidence is another thing altogether. And the non-Muslim who agrees with the Socratic injunction that "the unexamined life is not worth living" (and it may be added, "the unexamined Faith is not worth believing") will no doubt look elsewhere to find a faith founded on fact.

9

An Evaluation of the Qur'an

The Qur'an is at the heart of Islam. If its claims can be substantiated, then Islam is true and all opposing religious claims, including those of Judaism and Christianity, are false. As we saw in Chapter 5, the Qur'an claims to be the verbally inspired Word of God, copied from the original in heaven. Furthermore, other religious claims to the contrary, the Qur'an claims to be the full and final revelation of God through Muhammad, the last and greatest of the prophets who supersedes Moses, Jesus, and all other prophets before him. It is of utmost importance, then, for anyone who rejects Islam to understand what Muslims claim about the Qur'an and to examine the evidence Muslims offer in support of it.

A Review of the Islamic View of the Qur'an

Before evaluating the Qur'an's claims about its own divine and unique authority, it is necessary to review the basic claims about the nature of the Qur'an. These include its inspiration by God, its errorlessness, and its finality.

Inspiration of the Qur'an

The great Sunni authority, Abu Hanifa, expressed the orthodox belief that "the Quran is the word of God, and is His inspired word and revelation. It is a necessary attribute of God. It is not God, but still is inseparable from God." Of course, "It is written in a volume, it is read in a language . . . but God's word is uncreated."[1]

---

1. *Kitab al-Wasiyah*, 77. Taken from Abdul-Haqq, 62. Also see Al-Maturidi's defense of the orthodox position against the Mutazilites in Williams, 182.

Muslim scholar, Yusuf K. Ibish declared: "It is not a book in the ordinary sense, nor is it comparable to the Bible, either the Old or New Testaments. . . . If you want to compare it with anything in Christianity, you must compare it with Christ Himself." He adds, "Christ was the expression of the Divine among men, the revelation of the Divine Will. That is what the Qur'an is."[2] In short, whereas in Christianity the Word became flesh, in Islam the Word became a Book! The Qur'an itself claims (in 39:1–2) "The revelation Of this Book Is from God, The Exalted in Power, Full of Wisdom. Verily it is We Who have Revealed the Book to thee In Truth." In 55:1–2 it says, "(God) Most Gracious! It is He Who has Taught the Qur'an." (See also 3:7; 41:2–3; 12:1–2; 20:113; 25:6; 2:2-4; 43:43–44; 6:19; 39:41.)

ERRORLESS AND ETERNAL

Of course, it would follow that if the Qur'an is the very Word of God, it would be completely without error, since God cannot utter error. Indeed, this is precisely what the Qur'an claims for itself, saying, "Praise be to God, Who hath sent to His Servant The Book, and hath allowed Therein no Crookedness" (18:1). As we shall see, orthodox Muslims believe this extends to everything the Qur'an teaches, even to matters of science.

Muslims also believe that the Qur'an is a copy from its original, the heavenly "Mother of the Book." In 85:21–22, we read, "Nay, this is A Glorious Qur'an, (Inscribed) in A Tablet Preserved!" And in 43:3–4, we read, "We have made it A Qur'an in Arabic, That ye may be able To understand (and learn wisdom). And verily, it is In the Mother of the Book, In Our Presence, high (In dignity), full of wisdom" (cf. 13:39). This eternal original is the template of the earthly book we know as the Qur'an.

FINAL REVELATION TO HUMANKIND

Muslims do not believe the Qur'an is simply one holy book among other existing and uncorrupted divine revelations. The Qur'an is the eternal Word of God that descended (*tanzil*) to Muhammad in order to be the final Light and Guidance for humankind. According to orthodox Islam, the Qur'an by its very nature supersedes all previous revelations.

On many occasions the Qur'an refers to itself as a "Clear Argument" (*al-Burhan*), or "Light" (*an-Nur*), or "The Explanation" (*al-Bayan*).[3] In fact, after its introduction (in sura 1), the Qur'an begins with this claim: "This is the Book: In it is guidance sure, without doubt, To those who fear God" (2:2).

2. Waddy, 14.
3. Ajijola, 104.

Abdul Ahad Dawud says of the finality of the Qur'an, "For after the Revelation of the Will and Word of Allah in the Holy Qur'an there is the end of the prophecy and of revelation."[4] In 10:37, we read: "This Qur'an . . . is A confirmation of (revelations) That went before it, And a fuller explanation Of the Book—wherein There is no doubt—From the Lord of the Worlds." Kateregga concludes, "the Qur'an, as the final revelation, is the perfection and culmination of all the truth contained in the earlier Scriptures (revelation)." Though sent in Arabic "it is the Book for all times and for all mankind. The purpose of the Qur'an is to guard the previous revelations by restoring the eternal truth of Allah."[5] Classical Muslim theologian, Ibn Taymiyya, claimed that "the guidance and true religion which is in the *shari'a* brought by Muhammad is more perfect than what was in the two previous religious laws."[6] In brief, the Qur'an is unique and the final revelation of God. "It is on account of these special features of the Qur'an that all the people of the world have been directed to have faith in it, to give up all other books and to follow it alone, because it contains all that is essential for living in accordance with God's pleasure."[7]

THE QUR'AN IS A DIVINE MIRACLE

The Qur'an is not only the ultimate divine revelation, but for Muslims (including Muhammad himself), it is also the ultimate divine miracle. The "miracle of the Qur'an" is perhaps the most fundamental and popular doctrine about the Qur'an. Indeed, Muhammad claimed that the Qur'an was the only miracle he offered his hearers.

The miraculous nature of the Qur'an is in a sense the foundation of Islam and the most essential evidence for the prophethood of Muhammad. Classical theologian Al-Baqillani, in his book *Ijaz al-Qur'an*, insists that "What makes it necessary to pay quite particular attention to that [branch of Qur'anic] science [known as] *Ijaz al-Qur'an* is that the prophetic office of the Prophet—upon whom be peace—is built upon this miracle."[8]

Muslim apologists have offered many arguments for the miraculous nature of the Qur'an. However, most Islamic scholars place more emphasis on the first few arguments, especially the first one—the unique literary style of the Qur'an.

4. Gudel, 35–36. Also see Dawud.
5. Kateregga and Shenk, 27.
6. Ibn Taymiyya, 350–69.
7. See Ajijola, 96; cf. 94–96.
8. Jeffery, *Islam: Muhammad and His Religion*, 54.

The Argument for the Divine Origin of the Qur'an

Unique Literary Style

For most Muslims, by far the most impressive evidence for the supernatural nature of the Qur'an has been that it "is wonderfully arranged, and marvelously composed, and so exalted in its literary elegance as to be beyond what any mere creature could attain."[9] By revelation Muhammad claimed that "this Qur'an is not such As can be produced By other than God" (10:37). He boasts that "if the whole Of mankind and *jinn* Were to gather together To produce the like Of this Qur'an, they Could not produce The like thereof, even if They backed up each other With help and support" (17:88; cf. 2:118, 151, 253; 3:108; 28:86–87).

Yusuf Ali, the noted translator of the Qur'an, declares that "No human composition could contain the beauty, power, and spiritual insight of the Qur'an."[10] Muslims believe that "the Qur'an is the greatest wonder among the wonders of the world. It repeatedly challenged the people of the world to bring a chapter like it, but they failed and the challenge remains unanswered up to this day." They believe that the Qur'an "is second to none in the world according to the unanimous decision of the learned men in points of diction, style, rhetoric, thoughts and soundness of laws and regulations to shape the destinies of mankind."[11]

The Qur'an itself states the fundamental challenge to unbelievers in 2:23: "And if ye are in doubt As to what We have revealed From time to time to Our servant, Then produce a Sura Like thereunto; And call your witnesses or helpers (If there are any) besides God, If your (doubts) are true" (cf. 10:38).

Concerning Muhammad's challenge to the unbelievers about producing a chapter like the Qur'an, the Muslim apologist, Ajijola, claims that "the diction and style of the Qur'an are magnificent and appropriate to its Divine origin." Above all, "the Qur'an has by virtue of its claim of Divine origin, challenged man to produce, even unitedly, just a few lines comparable to those of the Qur'an." Hence, he adds, "The challenge has remained unanswered to this day. . . . What a challenge the like of which man has never seen and shall never see!"[12]

---

9. See Jeffery, 57.
10. See Gudel, 38. For a detailed explanation of the doctrine of the inimitability of the Qur'an, see the article by Al-Rummani in Rippin and Knappert, *Textual Sources for the Study of Islam*, 49–59.
11. Nehls, 38.
12. Ajijola, 90.

In comparing the miracle of the Qur'an with those of other prophets, one defender of Islam went so far as to say that "the miraculousness in the composition of the Qur'an is more effective in its kind and more eminent than the healing of the born-blind and the leprous and the quickening of the dead and the changing of the rod into a serpent, etc." Why? "Since many may believe that these signs were accomplished by tricks and clever manipulations. But there can be no doubt about the miraculousness of the eloquence of the Qur'an, because eloquence is something natural and not one of the skills which can be acquired."[13]

MUHAMMAD'S ILLITERACY

This argument goes hand-in-hand with the former one. In fact, they form a unit. In any event, the latter gives strength to the former. For Muslims argue that it is a marvel in itself that such a literary wonder as the Qur'an was produced at all. But it is even more marvelous that it was written by someone who was illiterate. How else, they claim, could this be explained except by supernatural revelation? The Qur'an says flatly that Muhammad was an "unlettered Prophet" (7:157). Or, as Pickthall translated it, Muhammad was "one who can neither read nor write."

Hence, Muslims believe that only by divine revelation could someone who was illiterate produce such a literary masterpiece as the Qur'an. To reinforce their claim they insist that even the best trained scholars in the Arabic language cannot to this day equal the eloquence of the Qur'an. Muhammad's challenge still stands to the unbelievers: "Say [to them]: 'Bring then A Sura like unto it'" (10:38).

PERFECT PRESERVATION

Another evidence often given by Muslims for the miraculous nature of the Qur'an is its marvelous preservation. As we read in 15:9, "We have, without doubt, Sent down the Message; And We will assuredly Guard it (from corruption)." Maulana Muhammad Ali claims that "the Qur'an is one, and no copy differing in even a diacritical point is met with in one among the four hundred millions of Muslims." While "there are, and always have been, contending sects, but the same Qur'an is in the possession of one and all. . . . A manuscript with the slightest variation in the text is unknown."[14]

Muslim scholars point out that, in contrast to other holy books, "the Holy Qur'an is the only divinely revealed scripture in the history of mankind which has been preserved to the present time in its exact original

13. Al-Baqillani, *Miracle and Magic*, 16.
14. Maulana Muhammad Ali, *Muhammad and Christ* (Lahore, India: The Ahmadiyya Anjuman-i-Ishaat-i-Islam, 1921), 7.

form." By this is meant that "the Qur'an has been preserved in the Arabic wording in which it was revealed to Prophet Muhammad (peace be on him) and in the exact order in which he himself placed it as commanded by Divine revelation."[15] This unprecedented and unparalleled marvel of perfect preservation is taken by Muslims as a sign of God's supernatural intervention.

PROPHECIES IN THE QUR'AN

Some Muslim defenders make a big point of the fact that the Qur'an contains accurate predictions which, they claim, could only come by the aid of God who knows all things, even the future. The prophecy most often cited is found in 30:2–4. It is claimed to have predicted the victory of the Romans over the Persians "a few years" before it happened. It reads as follows: "The Roman Empire . . . Will soon be victorious—Within a few years." Yusuf Ali claims that "a few years" means a short period of time ranging from three to nine years. And the period of time between when the Romans lost Jerusalem (A.D. 614–15) and their victory over the Persians at Issus (A.D. 622) was seven years. This, many Muslims claim, is proof of the supernatural nature of the Qur'an.

Another "prophecy" offered in defense of the miraculous nature of the Qur'an is in 89:1–5, which some scholars take to refer to the ten years of persecution Islam suffered before the famous *Hijrah* of Muhammad to Medina. Other, less notable "fulfilled prophecies" are also offered by Muslim apologists. Most of these are promises to the Islamic forces that they will be victorious.

> Say to those who reject Faith: "Soon will ye be vanquished And gathered together To Hell,—an evil bed Indeed (to lie on)!" (3:12).
>
> But their Lord inspired (This Message) to them: "Verily We shall cause The wrong-doers to perish! And verily We shall Cause you to abide In the land, and succeed them" (14:13–14).
>
> Soon will We [God] show them Our Signs in the (furthest) Regions (of the earth), and In their own souls, until It becomes manifest to them That this is the Truth (41:53).

In his lengthy work *The Religion of Islam*, the Muslim scholar Muhammad Ali exuberantly claims that "we find prophecy after prophecy announced in the surest and most certain terms to the effect that the great forces of opposition should be brought to naught, that the enemies of Islam should be put to shame and perish . . . that Islam

15. Haneef, 18–19.

should spread to the farthest corners of the earth and that it should ultimately be triumphant over all religions of the world."[16]

THE UNITY OF THE QUR'AN

Muslims sometimes appeal to the self-consistency of the Qur'an as an evidence of its divine origin: "Do they [unbelievers] not consider The Qur'an (with care)? Had it been from other Than God, they would surely Have found therein Much discrepancy" (4:82). Commenting on this verse, Yusuf Ali claimed that "the unity of the Qur'an is admittedly greater than that of any other sacred book. And yet how can we account for it except through the unity of God's purpose and design?" He adds, "From a mere human point of view we should have expected much discrepancy, because (1) the Messenger who promulgated it was not a learned man or philosopher, (2) it was promulgated at various times and in various circumstances, and (3) it is addressed to all grades of mankind." Yet he believes that "it fits together better than a jig-saw puzzle."[17] Susanne Haneef insists that if we look at "its total consistency from beginning to end ... it becomes impossible to ascribe the Qur'an to human authorship."[18]

THE SCIENTIFIC ACCURACY OF THE QUR'AN

Some contemporary defenders of Islam argue from its scientific accuracy to its divine authority. This argument is gaining popularity in recent times, bolstered by a widely circulated book titled *The Bible, The Qur'an and Science*, by a French writer, Maurice Bucaille. The purpose of the book is to show that while the Bible holds numerous internal and scientific contradictions, the Qur'an is free from such complications. Bucaille writes,

> The ideas in this study are to be developed from a purely scientific point of view. They will lead to the conclusion that it is inconceivable for a human being living in the Seventh century A.D. to have expressed assertions in the Qur'an on highly varied subjects that do not belong to his period and for them to be in keeping with what was to be revealed only centuries later. For me, there can be no human explanation of the Qur'an.[19]

In addition to Bucaille's book, there is now a host of such books in Islamic countries (but with much less sophistication), which show

---

16. Muhammad Ali, *The Religion of Islam* (Lahore, Pakistan: The Ahmadiyyah Anjuman Isha'at Islam, 1950), 249.

17. Yusuf Ali, *Holy Qur'an*, 205.

18. See Gudel, 39.

19. Bucaille, 130.

the miraculousness of the Qur'an as supported by the latest scientific discoveries.

THE AMAZING MATHEMATICAL STRUCTURE OF THE QUR'AN

One recently very popular proof for the Qur'an's divine origin is its alleged mathematical miraculousness. For example, the world-renowned Muslim debater, Ahmad Deedat, in his *Miracle of the Qur'an*, claims that the Qur'an is a mathematical miracle based on the number nineteen. This number is chosen because it is the sum of adding up the numerical value of the letters in the word "one," and the message of the Qur'an is that God is one.[20] Rashad Khalifa, the Imam of the mosque of Tucson, Arizona, in his book *The Computer Speaks: God's Message to the World*, summarizes the argument in nineteen points (what else?). Here are the first few:

(1) The opening statement of the Quran consists of nineteen arabic alphabets.
(2) The famous words that constituted the first Quranic revelation were nineteen words.
(3) The last Quranic revelation consisted of nineteen words.
(4) The Quran consists of 114 chapters, that is, 19 x 6.[21]

What does all this prove? According to Khalifa, "The Quranic initials and their mathematical distribution prove two things beyond a shadow of doubt: The Quran is the word of God and the Quran has been perfectly preserved."[22] Many mystical or esoteric sects of Islam also find interrelations among different mathematical numbers as a solid proof for the inspiration of the Qur'an.

CHANGED LIVES

One final proof for the Qur'an sometimes offered is that of the changed lives and cultures that are considered a direct result of the Qur'anic influence. In regard to this point, Ajijola writes,

> The transformation wrought by the Holy Qur'an is unparalleled in the history of the world and thus its claim to being unique stands as unchallenged today as it did thirteen centuries ago. . . . No faith ever imparted such a new life to its votaries on such a wide scale—a life affecting all branches of human activity; a transformation of the individual, of the family, of the

20. The Arabic word for one is *wahid*. In Arabic letters are used for numbers. The four Arabic letters of this word have numerical value that comes to a total of 19.

21. Rashad Khalifa, *The Computer Speaks: God's Message to the World* (Tuscon: Iman, Mosque of Tuscon, Arizona, U.S.A., 1981), 198, 200.

22. Khalifa, *Quran: Visual Presentation of the Miracle*, 200.

society, of the nation, of the country; and awakening material as well as moral, intellectual as well as spiritual. The Qur'an effected a transformation of humanity from the lowest depth of degradation to the highest pinnacle of civilization within an incredibly short time where centuries of reformation work had proved fruitless.[23]

AN EXAMINATION OF THE EVIDENCE

The Islamic claim for the Qur'an is unparalleled by any other major religion. And the evidences offered for this claim are many and varied. They call for careful scrutiny by any thoughtful person interested in the truth. We will treat the responses in the same order in which the evidences were presented above.

UNIQUE LITERARY STYLE

Is the Qur'an a miracle? Muhammad claimed it was, and most Muslims believe that, indeed, it was the only miracle he offered as proof of his claims to be a prophet. Before we evaluate this claim for the divine origin of the Qur'an, it is necessary to understand what is meant by this kind of miracle.

Muslims use various terms for miracles. For Muslims a miracle is always an act of God. It is not really a violation of nature, which is only the way God works customarily and repeatedly. Thus, miracles are seen as *khawarik*, "the breaker of usage." There are many words for miracle in Arabic, but the only one used in the Qur'an is *ayah*, a sign (2:118, 151, 253; 3:108; 28:86–87).[24] The technical term used by Muslim scholars to designate a miracle that confirms prophethood is *mudjiza*. To qualify it needs to be (1) an act of God that cannot be done by any creature; (2) contrary to the customary course of things in that class; (3) aimed at proving the authenticity of that prophet; (4) preceded by the announcement of a forthcoming miracle; (5) carried out in the exact manner it was announced; (6) accomplished only through the hands of the prophet; (7) in no way contrary to his prophetic claim; (8) accompanied by a challenge to reduplicate it; (9) by anyone present. Muslims believe that Moses, Elijah, and Jesus performed miracles that fulfilled these criteria.[25] The question is: Does the eloquence of the Qur'an meet these criteria? The answer is negative whether one considers either the form or

---

23. See Ajijola, ibid., 100–101.
24. The discussion here follows that by Mark W. Foreman in an excellent unpublished paper on "An Evaluation of Islamic Miracle Claims in the Life of Muhammad" (Liberty University, Lynchburg, Va., 1991).
25. See "Mudjiza" in *The Encyclopedia of Islam*.

the content of the Qur'an. First, let's consider its alleged miraculous literary form.

Eloquence is highly questionable as a test for divine inspiration. At best it only proves that Muhammad was extremely gifted. After all Mozart wrote his first symphony at the age of six! In fact Mozart was even more talented, since his entire music corpus was produced before age thirty-five; Muhammad did not begin to produce the suras of the Qur'an until age forty. But what Muslim would say that Mozart's works are miraculous like the Qur'an?[26] If eloquence were the test, then a case could be made for the divine authority of many literary classics. Homer would qualify as a prophet for producing the *Iliad* and the *Odyssey*. Shakespeare is without peer in the English language. But Muslims would scarcely accept the challenge to produce a work like *Romeo and Juliet* or else accept the divine inspiration of the works of Shakespeare.

Furthermore, the Qur'an is not unrivaled, even among works in Arabic. The Islamic scholar, C. G. Pfander, points out that "it is by no means the universal opinion of unprejudiced Arabic scholars that the literary style of the Qur'an is superior to that of all other books in the Arabic language." For example, "some doubt whether in eloquence and poetry it surpasses the Mu'allaqat, or the Magamat or Hariri, though in Muslim lands few people are courageous enough to express such an opinion."[27] The Iranian Shi'ite scholar Ali Dashti contends, however, that the Qur'an possesses numerous grammatical irregularities. He notes that

> The Quran contains sentences which are incomplete and not fully intelligible without the aid of commentaries; foreign words, unfamiliar Arabic words, and words used with other than the normal meaning; adjectives and verbs inflected without observance of the concord of gender and number; illogical and ungrammatically applied pronouns which sometimes have no referent; and predicates which in rhymed passages are often remote from the subjects.

He adds, "these and other such aberrations in the language have given scope to critics who deny the Quran's eloquence."[28] He lists numerous examples (74:1; 4:160; 20:66; 2:172, and so on), one of which is "In verse 9 of *sura* 49 (*ol-Hojorat*), 'If two parties of believers have started to fight each other, make peace between them', the verb meaning 'have started to fight' is in the plural, whereas it ought to be in the dual like its subject 'two parties'." Anis A. Shorrosh lists other literary flaws in the Qur'an. For example, in 2:177 he points out that the word

26. See Foreman, 14.
27. Pfander, 264.
28. Dashti, 48–49.

S*abireen* in Arabic should have been *Sabiroon* because of its position in the sentence. Likewise, *Sabieen* is more correct Arabic than *Sabioon* in 5:69. Also, Shorrosh notes that there is "a gross error in Arabic" in 3:59.[29] Dashti concludes: "to sum up, more than one hundred Quranic aberrations from the normal rules and structure of Arabic have been noted."[30] To say the least, the Arabic of the Qur'an, while often eloquent, is neither perfect nor unparalleled.

What is more, even some early Muslim scholars admitted that the Qur'an was not perfect in its literary form. Dashti notes that "among the Moslem scholars of the early period, before bigotry and hyperbole prevailed, were some such as Ebrahim on-Nassam who openly acknowledged that the arrangement and syntax of the Quran are not miraculous and that works of equal or greater value could be produced by other God-fearing persons." Although some condemned this view (based on their interpretation of 17:90), other "pupils and later admirers of on-Nassam, such as Ebn Hazm and ol Khayyat, wrote in his defense, and several other leading exponents of the Motazelite school shared his opinion."[31]

Even if the Qur'an were the most eloquent book in Arabic, this would hardly prove it has divine authority. For the same could be argued for the most eloquent book in Hebrew or Greek or any other language. As Pfander observed, "even were it proved beyond the possibility of doubt that the Qur'an far surpassed all other books in eloquence, elegance, and poetry, that would no more prove its inspiration than a man's strength would demonstrate his wisdom or a woman's beauty her virtue."[32] In other words, there is no logical connection between literary eloquence and divine authority. The sovereign God (whom Muslims accept) could choose to speak in plain everyday language, if he wished. At best one might attempt to argue (unsuccessfully, I believe)[33] that if God said it, he would say it most eloquently. But even so it would be a logical fallacy to argue that simply because it is eloquent that God must have said it.

---

29. Shorrosh, 199–200.

30. See Dashti, 50. He notes also that Qur'anic scholars, like Mahmud oz-Zamakhshari (A.D. 1075–1144), "have attempted in vain to explain them away but only by begging the question and presuming that the grammatical errors in it must be solved by changing the rules of Arabic grammar" (51).

31. Ibid., 48.

32. Pfander, 267.

33. Even on the Muslim view of God's sovereignty (see Chapter 1), Allah could choose to speak in whatever way he wished. No one can dictate to him the literary manner in which he must express himself.

Other religious leaders have given the beautiful literary style of their work as a sign of its divine origin. Would Muslims accept the inspiration of these works? For example, the Persian founder of the Manichaeans, Mani, "is said to have claimed that men should believe in him as the Paraclete ["Helper" Jesus promised in John 14] because he produced a book called *Artand,* full of beautiful pictures." Further, "he said that the book had been given him by God, that no living man could paint pictures equal in beauty to those contained in it, and that therefore it had evidently come from God Himself."[34] Yet no Muslim will accept this claim. Why then should non-Muslims accept literary beauty as a valid test for divine authority?

Finally, the beauty of the Qur'an is by no means an agreed conclusion of "all learned men." In fact many people in the West sympathize with the judgment of Carlyle who said this of the Qur'an: "It is as toilsome reading as I ever undertook, a wearisome, confused jumble, crude, incondite. Nothing but a sense of duty could carry any European through the Koran." For the readers who are not familiar with the content of the Qur'an we will cite a few suras (rendered by the noted Muslim scholar Yusuf Ali) and let the readers judge for themselves the truth about the alleged unsurpassed beauty of every sura of the Qur'an.

Sura 111:
   Perish the hand Of the Father of Flame! Perish he! No profit to him From all his wealth, And all his gains! Burnt soon will he be In a Fire Of blazing Flame! His wife shall carry The (crackling) wood—As fuel!—A twisted rope Of palm-leaf fibre Round her (own) neck!

Sura 109:
   Say: O ye That reject Faith! I worship not that Which ye worship, Nor will ye worship That which I worship. And I will not worship That which ye have been Wont to worship, Nor will ye worship That which I worship. To you be your Way, And to me mine.

Sura 105:
   Seest thou not How thy Lord dealt With the Companions Of the Elephant? Did He not make Their treacherous plan Go astray? And He sent against them Flights of Birds, Striking them with stones Of baked clay. Then did He make them Like an empty field Of stalks and straw, (Of which the corn) Has been eaten up.

Sura 97:
   We have indeed revealed This (Message) In the Night of Power: And what will explain To thee what the Night Of Power is? The Night of Power is

34. See Pfander, 264.

better than A thousand Months. Therein come down The angels and the Spirit By God's permission, On every errand: Peace! . . . This Until the rise of Morn!

Sura 91:

By the Sun And his (glorious) splendour; By the Moon As she follows him; By the Day as it shows up (the Sun's) glory; By the Night as it Conceals it; By the Firmament And its (wonderful) structure; By the Earth And its (wide) expanse: By the Soul, And the proportion and order Given to it; And its enlightment As to its wrong And its right; Truly he succeeds That purifies it, And he fails That corrupts it! The Thamud (people) Rejected (their prophet) Through their inordinate Wrong-doing. Behold, the most wicked Man among them was Deputed (for impiety). But the apostle of God Said to them: "It is A She-camel of God! And (bar her not From) having her drink!" Then they rejected him (As a false prophet), And they hamstrung her. So their Lord, on account Of their crime, obliterated Their traces and made them Equal (in destruction High and low)! And for Him Is no fear Of its consequences.

Those familiar with Arabic find these texts less than the most elegant expressions in the history of literature and religion.

MUHAMMAD'S ILLITERACY

Many Muslims contend that the content of the Qur'an is a proof of its divine origin. They insist that there is no way a book with this message could have come from an illiterate prophet like Muhammad. Critics, however, offer the following reasons to the contrary.

Some question whether Muhammad was actually illiterate. As one authority notes, the Arabic words *al umni,* translated "the unlettered" prophet in the Qur'an (7:157), "may be [rendered] 'heathen' rather than 'illiterate'." Pfander agrees, affirming that the Arabic phrase does not mean "'the Unlettered Prophet' but 'the Gentile Prophet' . . . and does not imply illiteracy."[35] Indeed, this is how the term is rendered in 62:2. "He it is Who hath sent among gentiles (*al umni*)," as do several other suras (2:73; 3:19, 69; 7:156).

There is some evidence to suggest that Muhammad may not have been completely illiterate. For example, "when the Treaty of Hudaibah was being signed, Muhammad took the pen from Ali, struck out the words in which Ali had designated him 'the apostle of God' and wrote instead with his own hand the words, 'son of Abdu'llah.'" And "tradition tells us too that, when he was dying, Muhammad called for pen and ink,

---

35. Ibid., 254. Also see Watt, *Bell's Introduction to the Qu'ran,* 33–34.

to write a command appointing his successor, but his strength failed him before writing-materials were brought."[36]

Furthermore, W. Montgomery Watt informs us that "it is known that many Meccans were able to read and write, and there is therefore a presumption that an efficient merchant, as Muhammad was, knew something of the arts."[37] Indeed, even Muslim scholars refer to Muhammad as being "perfect in intellect."[38] Furthermore, even if Muhammad lacked formal training in earlier years, there is no reason why an intelligent person such as he could not have caught up on his own later. He would not be the only "self-taught" literary figure in the history of humanity.

Even if it were granted that Muhammad was illiterate, it does not follow logically that the Qur'an was dictated to him by God. There are other possible explanations. Even if he was not formally trained, Muhammad was a bright person possessing great skills. In addition, his scribe could have stylized it. This was not an uncommon practice at that time. Homer was blind, so he probably did not write his epics himself. Finally, some critics argue that it is possible that Muhammad's first impression was right, that he received the information from a superintelligent evil spirit.[39] In this event the Qur'an would not reflect Muhammad's intelligence but that of the spirit. In any event, it is not implausible that even a formally untrained person could have been the source of the Qur'an.

PERFECT PRESERVATION

Does perfect preservation prove divine inspiration? Qur'an critics give a negative answer for several reasons.

First, there is often serious overstatement as to the preservation of the Qur'an. While it is true that the present Qur'an is generally a very good copy of the seventh-century Uthmanic recension, it is not true that this is exactly the way it came from Muhammad.[40] Many lines of evidence can be offered in support of this conclusion.

(1) As was already pointed out (in Chapter 5), the Quran was originally memorized by devout followers, most of whom where killed shortly after Muhammad's death. According to early tradition, Muhammad's scribes wrote on pieces of paper, stones, palm leaves, shoulder blades, ribs, and bits of leather. Muslims believe that during the lifetime of Muhammad the Qur'an was written down. But, according to the testimony of Zayd, a

36. Ibid., 255.
37. W. Montgomery Watt, *Muhammad: Prophet and Statesman* (reprint: London: Oxford University Press, 1967), 40.
38. See Gudel, 72.
39. See Chapter 8 for a further discussion of this point.
40. John Gilchrist, *Jam' al-Qur'an: The Codification of the Qur'an Text* (Benoni, South Africa: Jesus to the Muslims, 1989).

contemporary and follower of Muhammad, he was requested by Abu Bakr to "search out the [various chapters and verses of] the Qur'an and gather it together." He responded, "Accordingly, I sought out the Qur'an: I gather it together from leafless palm-branches and thin white stones and men's breasts."[41] Some time later, during the reign of Uthman, the third Muslim Caliph, it was reported that several Muslim communities were using different versions of the Qur'an. Once again, Zayd was called in to oversee the official revised version of the Qur'an. It is this version that has remained uniform and intact to this day, not any alleged original version that came directly from Muhammad.

(2) Noted European archaeologist Arthur Jeffery wrote a book titled *Materials for the History of the Text of the Qur'an* in which he related the state of the Qur'an text prior to its standardization under Uthman. It reveals, contrary to Muslim claims, that there were several different texts prior to Uthman's revision.

Jeffery concludes that "when we come to the accounts of 'Uthman's recension, it quickly becomes clear that his work was no mere matter of removing dialectical peculiarities in reading [as many Muslims claim], but was a necessary stroke of policy to establish a standard text for the whole empire." Further, he adds, "there were wide divergences between the collections that had been digested into Codicies in the great Metropolitan centres of Madina, Mecca, Basra, Kufa and Damascus." So "'Uthman's solution was to canonize the Madinan Codex and order all others to be destroyed." Therefore, he concludes, "there can be little doubt that the text canonized by 'Uthman was only one among several types of text in existence at the time."[42]

In agreement with this general observation, Watt in discussing the variations between just two codices—that of ibn Mas'ud of Rufa and ibn Ka'b of Syria—writes, "No copies exist of any of the early codices, but the list of variant readings from the two just mentioned is extensive, running to a thousand or more items in both cases."[43]

Recent discoveries confirm the textual corruption of the Qur'an. Jay Smith has documented just how extensive these corruptions have been, thus undermining the traditional Islamic claim of an uncorrupted version of the Qur'an.[44]

(3) Contrary to popular Islamic belief, not all Muslims today accept one and the same version of the Qur'an. The Sunnite Muslims accept the

41. See Pfander, 258–59.
42. See Jeffery, 7–8.
43. Watt, *Bell's Introduction to the Qur'an*, 45.
44. See www.debate.org.uk/topics/history/bib-qur/contents and www.answeringislam.org/quran/text/index.

Sahih tradition of Masud, one of the few people authorized by Muhammad to teach the Qur'an, as authoritative. Yet the Ibn Masud Codex of the Qur'an used by them has multitudinous variations from the Uthmanic recension. In the second sura alone there are nearly 150 variations. It takes Jeffery some ninety-four pages to show the variations between the two. He also demonstrates that the variant readings were not just a matter of dialect, as many Muslims claim. For instance, some of the variations involve a whole clause and others omit complete sentences. Jeffery concludes that "it is quite clear that the text which 'Uthman canonized was only one out of many rival texts . . . [and] there is grave suspicion that 'Uthman may have seriously edited the text he canonized."[45]

(4) Widely accepted Islamic tradition reveals certain things not found in the present Qur'an. One tells us that A'isha, one of Muhammad's wives, said: "Among what was sent down of the Qur'an were ten well known (verses) about—Suckling, which prohibited: then they were annulled by five well known ones. Then the Apostle of God deceased, and they are what is recited of the Qur'an."[46] Another example of something not found in today's Qur'an is what Umar said: "Verily God sent Muhammad with the truth, and He sent down upon him the Book, accordingly the Verse of Stoning was part of what God Most High sent Down: the Apostle of God stoned, and we stoned after him, and in the Book of God stoning is the adulterer's due."[47] This original revelation was apparently changed and one hundred stripes has replaced stoning as the punishment for adultery (24:2).

(5) The so-called Satanic Verses illustrate another change in the original text. According to one version of these verses Muhammad had an early revelation in Mecca, which allowed intercession to certain idols.

> Did you consider al-hat and al-Uzza
> And al-Manat, the third, the other?
> Those are the swans exalted;
> Their intercession is expected;
> Their likes are not neglected.[48]

Some time after this Muhammad received another revelation canceling the last three lines (verses) and substituting what we now find in 53:21–23, which omits the part about interceding to these pagan gods.

45. See Watt, ix–x.
46. See Pfander, 256.
47. Ibid., 256.
48. See Watt, 60.

According to Watt, both versions had been recited publicly. Muhammad's explanation was that Satan had deceived him and inserted the false verses without his knowing it.[49]

(6) Clair-Tisdall, famous worker among Muslims, points out that even in the present Qur'an there are some variations.

> Among various readings may be mentioned: (1) in Surah XXVIII, 48, some read "sahirani" for "sihrani": (2) in Surah XXXII, 6, after "ummahatuhum" one reading adds the words "wa hua abun lahum": (3) in Surah XXXIV, 18, for "rabbana ba'id" some read "rabuna ba'ada": (4) in Surah XXXVIII, 22, for "tis'un" another reading is "tis'atun": (5) in Surah XIX, 35, for "tantaruna" some read "yamtaruna".[50]

(7) Although Shi'ite Muslims are in the minority, they are the second largest Islamic sect in the world, with over one hundred million followers. They claim that Caliph Uthman intentionally eliminated many verses from the Qur'an that spoke of Ali.[51]

L. Bevan Jones summed up the matter well in his book, *The People of the Mosque*, when he said: "while it may be true that no other work has remained for twelve centuries with so pure a text, it is probably equally true that no other has suffered so drastic a purging."[52] The purging took place early and, hence, the Muslim claim that it has been preserved perfectly since is misdirected.

(8) Even if the present Qur'an were a perfect word-for-word copy of the original as given by Muhammad, it would not prove the original was inspired of God. All it would demonstrate is that today's Qur'an is a carbon copy of whatever Muhammad said; it would say or prove nothing about the truth of what he said. The Muslim claim that they have the true religion, because they have the only perfectly copied Holy Book, is as logically fallacious as someone claiming it is better to have a perfect printing of a counterfeit thousand dollar bill than a slightly imperfect printing of a genuine one! The crucial question, which Muslim apologists beg by this argument, is whether the original is God's Word, not whether they possess a perfect copy of it.

---

49. Ibid., 60–61.
50. W. St. Clair Tisdall, *A Manual of the Leading Muhammedan Objections to Christianity* (London: Society for Promoting Christian Knowledge, 1904), 60.
51. Ibid., 59. Also see B. Todd Lawson, "Note for the Study of a 'Shi'i Qur'an,'" in *Journal of Semetic Studies* (Autumn 1991), vol. 36, no. 2, 279–96.
52. L. Bevan Jones, *The People of the Mosque* (London: Student Christian Movement Press, 1932), 62.

PROPHECIES IN THE QUR'AN

Does the Qur'an contain predictive prophecies that prove its divine origin? Few outside the Muslim camp are convinced that there are really any unusual predictions made in the Qur'an, to say nothing of supernatural ones. Consider the following facts that undermine the alleged miraculous nature of Qur'anic predictions.

First of all, most of the so-called supernatural predictions are not supernatural at all. To begin with, what religious military leader is there who might not say to his troops: "God is on our side; we are going to win. Fight on!"? Further, remembering that Muhammad is known as "the prophet of the Sword," with his greatest number of conversions coming after he had forsaken the peaceful but relatively unsuccessful means of spreading his message, it should be no surprise that he would predict victory.

Also, considering the zeal of Muslim forces, who were promised Paradise for their efforts (22:58–59; 3:157–58; 3:170–71), it is no surprise that they were so often victorious. Finally, it is little wonder why so many "submitted," considering Muhammad commanded that "The punishment of those Who wage war against God And His Apostle, and strive With might . . . Is: execution, or crucifixion, Or the cutting off of hands And feet from opposite sides, Or exile from the land" (5:36).

Second, the only really substantive prediction was about the Roman victory over the Persian army at Issus (in 30:2–4), which reads: "The Roman Empire Has been defeated—In a land close by: But they, (even) after (This) defeat of theirs, Will soon be victorious—Within a few years." Close scrutiny, however, reveals several things that make this prediction less than spectacular, to say nothing of supernatural.[53] (1) According to Ali "a few years" means three to nine years, but some argue that the real victory did not come until thirteen or fourteen years after the prophecy. The defeat of the Romans by the Persians in the capture of Jerusalem took place about A.D. 614 or 615. The counter-offensive did not begin until A.D. 622 and the victory was not complete until A.D. 625. This would be at least ten or eleven years, not "a few" spoken by Muhammad. (2) Uthman's edition of the Qur'an had no vowel points (they were not added until much later).[54] Hence, in this "prophecy" the word *sayaghlibuna*, "they shall defeat," could have been rendered, with the change of two vowels, *sayughlabuna*, "they shall be defeated."[55] In fact, it is inter-

---

53. For this point and many others made in this section we are indebted to the excellent work by Joseph Gudel in his master's thesis for Simon Greenleaf School of Law titled, *To Every Muslim an Answer* (April 1982), 54.

54. Spencer, 21.

55. See Tisdall, 137.

esting to note that "a variant text reverses the passive and active verbs, so that the Byzantines are said to have defeated (others) in the past, but are to be defeated in a few years."[56] (3) Even if this ambiguity were removed, the prophecy is less than spectacular, since it is neither long-range nor unusual. One would have expected the defeated Romans to bounce back in victory. It took little more than a perceptive reading of the trends of time to forecast such an event. At best, it could have been a good guess. In any event, there appears to be no sufficient grounds for proving it is supernatural.

Finally, the only other alleged prophecy worth mentioning is found in 89:2, where the phrase "By the Nights twice five" is taken by some to be a prediction of the ten years of persecution early Muslims experienced.[57] But this is a far-fetched interpretation. Even the great Islamic scholar and translator of the Qur'an, Abdullah Yusuf Ali, admitted that "By the Ten Nights are usually understood the first ten nights of Zul-Hajj, the sacred season of Pilgrimage."[58] In any event, there is certainly no clear prediction of anything that would have been evident to an intelligent observer in advance of the event.[59] Its very usage as a predictive prophecy by Muslim scholars shows how desperate they are to find something supernatural in support of the Qur'an.

THE UNITY OF THE QUR'AN

Insisting that the Qur'an must be divine revelation because it is self-consistent and noncontradictory is also not convincing. Some critics raise significant questions about how totally consistent the Qur'an is. For one thing, they point out that the most blatant contradiction in Muhammad's revelations came by way of later revelations expunging former ones—such as the command to stone adulterers being changed to one hundred stripes (24:2), and the so-called Satanic Verses on worshiping pagan gods being replaced with some that omit this (53:21–23).[60]

The whole concept of abrogation (*mansukh*) discussed earlier (in Chapter 5) is one way some previous mistakes were corrected by later verses (called *nasikh*). This is taught in 2:106 which says, "Such of Our revelations as We abrogate or cause to be forgotten, We bring (in place) one better or the like thereof. Knowest thou not that Allah is Able to do

56. Watt, *Muhammad's Mecca*, 14.

57. Ahmad, *Introduction to the Study of the Holy Quran*, 374f.

58. Yusuf Ali, *The Meaning of the Glorious Qur'an*, 1731, note 6109.

59. By contrast, there are clear and specific predictive prophecies in the Bible that were given hundreds of years in advance (see Chapter 10).

60. See comments above, notes 47–48.

all things?" For example, what is called "the sword verse" (9:5) supposedly annuls 124 verses that originally encouraged tolerance (cf. 2:256).[61] The Qur'an says emphatically, "Let there be no compulsion In religions" (2:256), yet in other places it urges Muslims to "Fight those who believe not" (9:29) and "fight and slay The Pagans wherever ye find them" (9:5).

A contradiction can also be found in the fact that the Qur'an claims that "no change there can be in the Words of God" (10:64), which Muslims say the Qur'an is. For "there is none That can alter the Words (and Decrees) of God" (6:34). Yet the Qur'an teaches the doctrine of abrogation by which later revelations annul previous ones. We read of (2:106) "revelations . . . We abrogate or cause to be forgotten." Further, Muhammad admits that "we substitute one revelation For another," admitting in the same verse that his contemporaries called him a "forger" for so doing!

As Nehls keenly observes, "we should like to find out how a divine revelation can be improved. We would have expected it to have been perfect and true right from the start."[62] Of course, some Muslims, like Ali, claim that abrogation is just "progressive revelation," adapting God's message to different people living at different periods of time. Nehls points out, however, that "2:106 [on abrogation] does not speak of culture or progressive revelation with reference to scriptures given prior to Mohammed, but to Quranic verses only!"[63] It makes sense to believe that God progressively revealed himself over 1,500 years of time (as in the Bible). However, Nehls adds, "we find it unacceptable that within a space of 20 years a need for change or correction can become necessary. This surely suggests that either God is not all-knowing or else the recorder made corrections."[64] This seems particularly true in view of the fact that the corrected verses are often near the ones being corrected. What is more, there are verses that the Qur'anic abrogations apparently forgot to redact. In 7:54 (and 32:4) we are told that the world was made in six days. But in 41:9–12 it says it took God a total of eight days to create the world (two plus four plus two). But both cannot be correct.[65]

61. This point is made by Shorrosh, 163.
62. See Nehls, 11.
63. Ibid., 12.
64. Ibid., 14.
65. Even the Muslim commentator Ali admits "this is a difficult passage." He and other commentators attempt to explain the two days (Sura 41:9), four days (v. 10), and the two days (v. 12) = eight days by making the four days overlap with the first two days. However, this is unconvincing for several reasons. First, why spell them out as separate events if they are the same? Further, they describe different acts of creation. The first speaks of the creation of "the earth in two days" (v. 9) and the second of "all things to give them nourishment in due proportion in four days" (v. 10). These are presented as different and successive events.

The Qur'an also claims that humans are responsible for their own choices (18:29), yet it also claims that God has sealed the fate of all in advance. "Every man's fate We have fastened On his own neck: On the Day of Judgment We shall bring out For him a scroll, Which he will see Spread open" (17:13; also see 10:99–100).

Again, even if the Qur'an were consistent, at best unity or self-consistency is only a negative test for truth, not a positive one. Of course, if a book is from God who cannot err, then it won't have any contradictions in it. However, just because a book has no contradictions does not mean God is the author. It is a logical fallacy[66] to assume so. As John W. Montgomery insightfully observes, Euclid's geometry is self-consistent, but this is no ground to call it divinely authoritative.[67]

Self-consistency is the same kind of argument others (like some Christians) use for their Holy Books that oppose the Qur'an on many points. But both cannot be true. Hence, unity in itself does not prove divine authenticity. Both the Jewish Bible and the New Testament, known through existing manuscripts, are at least as equally self-consistent as the Qur'an. But no Muslim would admit they are thereby inspired of God.

SCIENTIFIC ACCURACY

This argument has gained popularity in recent times, primarily due to Bucaille's book *The Bible, The Qur'an and Science*, in which Christianity is attacked for holding back the progress of science and the Qur'an is exalted as promoting science. Indeed, he insists that the Qur'an marvelously foreshadowed modern science in many of its statements, thus miraculously confirming its divine origin. Here again Muslim apologists are misdireced in their overzealous attempt to prove the divine origin of the Qur'an.

The first thing perceptive critics note is that it was Christianity, not Islam, that was the mother of modern science. The great philosopher, Alfred North Whitehead, declared in his famous work *Science and the Modern World* that Christianity is the mother of science. M. B. Foster, writing for the prestigious English philosophy journal *Mind* noted that the Christian doctrine of creation is the origin of modern science.[68] The

---

66. In logic it is called an illicit conversion of an "A" (universal affirmative) proposition. For example, just because "All dogs are four-legged animals" does not mean that "All four-legged animals are dogs."

67. John Warwick Montgomery, *Faith Founded on Fact* (Nashville: Thomas Nelson, 1978), 94.

68. M. B. Foster, "The Christian Doctrine of Creation and the Rise of Modern Science," in *Mind* (1934), vol. 43, 447–68; and Alfred North Whitehead, *Science in the Modern World* (New York: The Free Press, 1925), 13–14. See also Stanley L. Jaki, *The Savior of Science* (Edinburgh: Scottish Academic Press, 1990).

very founders of almost every area of modern science were men working from a Christian worldview. This includes men like Copernicus, Kepler, Kelvin, Newton, Pascall, Boyle, Maxwell, Agassiz, and others.[69]

So while Islamic monotheism made many contributions to modern culture, it is an overstatement for it to claim credit for the origin of modern science. In fact, many Islamic critics point out that Muslim armies destroyed vast resources of knowledge. Pfander, for example, notes that under the Caliph Umar the Muslim soldiers destroyed both the vast libraries at Alexandria and Persia. When the general asked Umar what he should do with the books, he is said to have replied: "Cast them into the rivers. For, if in these books there is guidance, then we have still better guidance in the Book of God. If, on the contrary, there is in them that which will lead astray, then may God protect us from them."[70]

It is a serious mistake to assume that a book is inspired simply because it conforms with modern science. Both Muslim and Christian apologists have made this error. There are many reasons why these claims are invalid. (1) Science changes. Thus, what appears to be "harmony" between them today may vanish tomorrow. (2) Many embarrassing mistakes have been made by defenders attempting to see modern scientific theories in their Holy Book. The Roman Catholic Church's treatment of Galileo is only one example.[71] (3) Even if perfect harmony could be demonstrated between the Qur'an and scientific fact, this would not prove the divine inspiration of the Qur'an. It would simply prove that the Qur'an made no scientific error. Simply because a book is free of scientific error does not make it inspired of God. At best, scientific accuracy is only a negative test for truth. If error were found in the Qur'an, it would prove that it was not the Word of God. But simply because the Qur'an were shown to be scientifically faultless would not prove that it was the Word of God. And, of course, the same applies to the Bible or any other religious book.

Some critics question just how scientifically accurate the Qur'an really is. Take, for example, the Qur'an's highly controversial statement that human beings are formed from a clot of blood: "Then We made the sperm Into a clot of congealed blood; Then of that clot We made A (foetus) lump; then We Made out of that lump Bones and clothed the bones With flesh" (23:14). This is scarcely a scientific description of embyronic

---

69. Norman L. Geisler, *Origin Science: A Proposal for the Creation-Evolution Controversy* (Grand Rapids: Baker, 1987), 37–52.

70. See Pfander, 365.

71. Even in Galileo's case it should be observed that he was a Christian working from a Christian perspective that the world is God's creation and should be so studied. It was the Roman Catholic Church that made the mistake in condemning him, not the Christian worldview that led Galileo to his scientific discoveries.

development. In order to avoid the problem, Bucaille retranslates the verse, rendering the Arabic word *alaq* ("blood clot") as "the thing which clings."[72] However, this is questionable. It is contrary to recognized Islamic authorities who did three major English translations of the Qur'an: Ali, Pickthall, and Arberry. Further, Bucaille himself recognized that "a majority of translations describe ... man's formation from a 'blood clot' or 'adhesion'."[73] This leaves the impression that his own homemade translation was generated to solve the problem, since he recognizes that "a statement of this kind is totally unacceptable to scientists specializing in this field."[74]

Likewise, other critics note that the Qur'an in 18:86 speaks of one traveling west "till, when he reached the setting-place of the sun, he found it setting in a muddy spring." But even in his attempt to explain this problem, Ali admits this has "puzzled Commentators." Nor does he really explain the problem but simply asserts that this cannot be "the extreme west, for there is no such thing."[75] Indeed, there is no extreme west, nor can anyone traveling west eventually come to the place where the sun sets. But this is what the text says, unscientific as it may be.

Others have noted that the so-called scientific foreshadowing of the Qur'an is highly questionable. Kenneth Cragg notes that "it has been frequently claimed by some Muslim exegetes of the Quran that modern inventions and scientific data, even nuclear fission, have been anticipated there and can now be detected in passages not hitherto appreciated for their prescience. Meanings earlier unsuspected disclose themselves as science proceeds." This conclusion, however, "is strongly repudiated by others as the kind of corroboration the Qur'an, as a 'spiritual' Scripture, neither needs nor approves. ... Muhammad Kamil Husain called all such exegesis 'pseudo'. ... Fazlur Rahman ... also deplored it."[76]

Finally, even if the Qur'an were proven to be scientifically accurate, it would not thereby make it divinely authoritative. All it would prove is that the Qur'an made no scientific blunders. This would not be unparalleled. Some Jewish scholars claim the same for the Torah, and many Christians claim exactly the same thing for the Bible, using very similar arguments. But Bucaille would not allow that this thereby demonstrates that the Old and New Testaments are the Word of God.

72. See Bucaille, 204.
73. Ibid., 198.
74. Ibid.
75. Yusuf Ali, *Holy Qur'an*, 754, note 2430.
76. Cragg, "Contemporary Trends in Islam," in Woodberry, 42.

AMAZING MATHEMATICAL STRUCTURE

One popular proof for the Qur'an's divine origin is its alleged mathematical miraculousness based on the number nineteen. Needless to say such an apologetic method does not find a great deal of acceptance in scholarly circles, and this for good reason.

No Muslim would accept a message claimed to be from God if it taught idolatry or immorality. In fact no message containing such claims should be accepted on mathematical grounds alone. So even if the Qur'an were a mathematical "miracle," this would not be sufficient to prove that it was of God.[77]

Even if the odds are astronomic against the Qur'an having all these amazing combinations of the number 19, it proves nothing more than that there is a mathematical order behind the language of the Qur'an. Since language is an expression of the order of human thought, and since this order can often be reduced to mathematical expression, it should be no surprise that a mathematical order can be found behind the language of the Qur'an.

Further, the same kind of argument (only based on the number seven) could be used to prove the inspiration of the Bible. Take the first verse of the Bible "In the beginning God created the heavens and the earth." Nehls points out that:

> The verse consists of 7 Hebrew words and 28 letters (7x4). There are three nouns: "God, heavens, earth". . . . their total numeric value . . . is 777 (7x11). The verb "created" has the value 203 (7x29). The object is contained in the first three words—with 14 letters (7x2). The other four words contain the subject—also with 14 letters (7x2) [and so on].[78]

But no Muslim would allow this as an argument in favor of the divine inspiration of the Bible. At best the argument is esoteric and unconvincing. Even most Muslim scholars avoid using it.

CHANGED LIVES

Many Muslim apologists point to the transformation of lives and culture by the Qur'an as a proof of its divine origin. But critics point out that this is an insufficient test for its alleged heavenly origin.

First of all, this is the kind of thing that should be expected. For when one fervently believes something to be true he lives by it. But this still

77. For a further discussion of this and other arguments critiqing this view, see Nehls, 124–32.

78. Ibid., 127. For a Christian approach to the mathematical structure of the Bible, see Jerry Lucas and Del Washburn, *Theomatics: God's Best Kept Secret Revealed* (New York: Stein & Day Pub., 1977).

leaves open the question as to whether it is the Word of God. Any set of ideas fervently believed and applied will transform believers and their culture. This is true whether the ideas are Buddhist, Christian, Islamic, or Jewish. But this simple fact does not prove that God inspired all their Holy Books. What Muslim would accept the argument that Karl Marx's *Das Capital* is inspired because it has transformed millions of lives and many cultures?

Many critics find it no surprise that so many converted to Islam when it is remembered what the promised reward was for those who did and the threatened punishment for those who fought against Muhammad. Those who "submitted" were promised Paradise with beautiful women (2:25; 4:57). But "the punishment of those Who wage war against God And His Apostle, and strive With might . . . Is: execution, or crucifixion, Or the cutting off of hands And feet from opposite sides, Or exile from the land" (5:36). Islamic tradition reports that Muhammad gave the following exhortation to his followers: "The sword is the key of heaven and of hell; a drop of blood shed in the cause of God, a night spent in arms, is of more avail than two month's fasting and prayer. Whoever falls in battle, his sins are forgiven at the day of judgement."[79] Furthermore, human greed played a part. "Arab warriors were . . . entitled to four-fifths of all the booty they gathered in the form of movable goods and captives."[80] What is more, it was of great advantage for the enemy to submit. Polytheists had two choices: submit or die. Christians and Jews had another alternative: they could pay heavy taxes (9:5, 29). Also Islamic conquests were successful because in some of the conquered lands the people were fed up with the maltreatment of their Roman rulers and willingly accepted Islam due to its emphasis on equality and brotherhood.

Anis Shorrosh summarizes several reasons why Islam spread so quickly among Arabic people. These include the fact that Islam glorified Arabic people, customs, and language; it provided an incentive to conquer and plunder other lands; it utilized their ability to fight in the desert; it provided a heavenly reward for dying, and it adopted many pre-Islamic practices.[81] Even if one points to more positive reasons, such as, moral, political, and cultural improvements, there seems to be no reason to posit anything but natural causes for the spread of Islam.

Finally, if one is going to press the argument from changed lives, defenders of Christianity offer one that would seem to be equally strong,

---

79. Edward Gibbon, *The History of the Decline and Fall of the Roman Empire*, vol. 5, ed. J. B. Bury (London: Methuen & Co., 1898), 360–61.

80. John B. Noss, *Man's Religions* (New York: The Macmillan Co., 1956), 711.

81. See Shorrosh, 180–83.

if not stronger. In his famous *Evidences of Christianity*, William Paley sums it up this way:

> For what are we comparing? A Galilean peasant accompanied by a few fishermen with a conqueror at the head of his army. We compare Jesus, without force, without power, without support, without one external circumstance of attraction or influence, prevailing against the prejudices, the learning, the hierarchy, of his country, against the ancient religious opinions, the pompous religious rites, the philosophy, the wisdom, the authority, of the Roman empire, in the most polished and enlightened period of its existence,—with Mahomet making his way amongst Arabs; collecting followers in the midst of conquests and triumphs, in the darkest ages and countries of the world, and when success in arms not only operated by that command of men's wills and persons which attend prosperous undertakings, but was considered as a sure testimony of Divine approbation. That multitudes, persuaded by this argument, should join the train of a victorious chief; that still greater multitudes should, without any argument, bow down before irresistible power—is a conduct in which we cannot see much to surprise us; in which we can see nothing that resembles the causes by which the establishment of Christianity was effected.[82]

THE RAPID SPREAD OF ISLAM

The last of the major "proofs" offered by Muslim apologists that Muhammad is a prophet of God is the rapid growth of Islam. According to one Muslim apologist, "the rapid spread of Islam shows that God Most High sent it as His final revelation to men."[83]

First, it is a highly disputed test for truth that is not widely accepted or very convincing. Further, it is a double-edged test for truth. According to the earliest records (in the Book of Acts), Christianity also spread very rapidly immediately after Christ. And in spite of a couple centuries of Roman persecution, Christianity took over the remains of the Roman Empire. Third, unlike Christianity, Islam did not spread very quickly at the very beginning (see Chapter 4). Initially, Muhammad attracted very few followers. It was only after Muhammad began to use the sword in defense of Islam that it grew more rapidly—scarcely a convincing proof of its divine origin. Of course, Christian crusaders (twelfth–fourteenth centuries) also engaged in an equally unjustified use of the sword, since

---

82. William Paley, *Evidences of Christianity* (London: 1851), 257. Many Muslim critics argue that the spread of Christianity in many lands was certainly not always due to peaceful propaganda but also through the use of wars. While this may be true of some later periods, such as the Crusades, it certainly was not true of early Christianity (first to third centuries) when it grew from 120 (Acts 1–2) to the dominant spiritual force in the Roman world before Constantine was converted in A.D. 313.

83. See Pfander, 226.

Jesus forbid his disciples to spread his message this way (Matt. 26:52). However, by contrast with Islam, the early and phenomenal growth of Christianity occurred without the use of the sword. Indeed, early Christianity grew the most when the Roman government was using the sword on Christians during the first three centuries.

As the great Yale church historian of the twentieth century, Kenneth Scott Latourette, points out, "It is one of the commonplaces of history that in its first three centuries Christianity met persistent and often severe persecution, persecution which rose to a crescendo early in the fourth century, but that it spread in spite of opposition and was even strengthened by it."[84] Also as Latourette explains, "One of the factors to which is attributed the triumph of Christianity is the endorsement of Constantine. But, as we have suggested, the faith was already so strong by the time when Constantine espoused it that it would probably have won without him. Indeed, one of the motives sometimes ascribed to his support is his supposed desire to enlist the cooperation of what had become the strongest element in the Empire, the Christian community."[85]

Finally, there are perfectly natural incentives for the many converts to Islam. Muslim soldiers were promised Paradise as a reward for dying. And the people who did not submit to Islam were threatened with death, slavery, or taxation. There is no need to appeal to the supernatural to account for the growth of Islam under these conditions.

Islamic scholar Wilfred Cantwell Smith pinpoints the Muslim dilemma well. He incisively points out that if Muslims believe Islam is God-willed and destined to dominate the world, then its failure to do so must be an indication that God's sovereign will is being frustrated. But Muslims deny that God's will can be frustrated. Hence, logically they must conclude that it is not God-willed. Haykal's response that men are free and any defeat or setbacks are to be attributed to them misses the point.[86] For it does not matter how God does it, through freedom or without it, if in fact God has willed the supremacy of Islam, then his sovereign will has been frustrated. For Islam is not and has not been since the time of its inception the enduring dominant religion of the world numerically, spiritually, or culturally. Furthermore, even if Islam should have a sudden burst of success and surpass all other religions this would not prove it is of God. Logically, all that success proves is that it succeeded, not necessarily that it is true. For even after something succeeds we can still ask: Are its beliefs true or false?

84. Kenneth Scott Latourette, *A History of Christianity: Beginning to 1500* (San Francisco: Harper, 1975), 1:81.

85. Ibid., 105.

86. See Haykal, 605.

SUMMARY

The Qur'an claims to be the Word of God, but it does not prove to be the Word of God. It has claims without supporting credentials. None of the arguments offered by its apologists is convincing. Each contains fallacies. Of course one can continue to *believe* in the divine origin of the Qur'an without evidence to support it. But those who seek a reasonable faith will have to look elsewhere. Further, it lacks the very distinguishing characteristic it believes both Judaism and Christianity possess, namely, supernatural confirmation by God.

Part Three

A POSITIVE DEFENSE OF THE CHRISTIAN PERSPECTIVE

In Part One we set forth the basic doctrines of orthodox Islam. Part Two evaluated basic Muslim beliefs, pointing out misunderstandings, inconsistencies, and inaccuracies. In this final section we will offer a positive defense of the Christian point of view over and against Islam. This will be done by way of a rational defense of crucial Christian beliefs, such as the authenticity of the Bible, the deity of Christ, the doctrine of the Trinity, and salvation through Christ's death on the cross for our sins.

10

A DEFENSE OF THE BIBLE

In order to support their claim that the Qur'an is the inspired word of God, superseding all previous revelations, Muslims sustain an attack upon all competing claims. For the most part their efforts are directed against their chief rival, the Bible. Their accusations fall into two basic categories: first, the text of Scripture has been changed or forged; second, doctrinal mistakes have crept into Christian teaching, such as the belief in the incarnation of Christ, the trinity of the Godhead, and the doctrine of original sin.[1]

Strangely, sometimes the Qur'an gives the Judeo-Christian Scriptures such noble titles as: "the Book of God," "the Word of God," "a light and guidance to man," "a decision for all matters," "a guidance and mercy," "the lucid Book," "the illumination (*al-furqan*)," "the gospel with its guidance and light, confirming the preceding Law," and "a guidance and warning to those who fear God."[2] Christians are told to look into their own Scriptures to find God's revelation for them (5:50). And even Muhammad himself at one point is exhorted to test the truthfulness of his own message with the contents of the previous divine revelations to Jews and Christians (10:94).

However, the above praise for the Bible is misleading, since Muslims hasten to claim that the Qur'an supersedes all previous revelations based on their concept of progressive revelation. By this they hope to show that the Qur'an fulfills, and even sets aside the previous, less complete revelations (such as the Bible). One Islamic theologian echoes this conviction by stating that while a Muslim needs to believe in the Torah (Law of

1. Waardenburg, 261–63.
2. Takle, 217.

Moses), the *Zabur* (the Psalms of David), and the *Injil* (Gospel), nevertheless he claims that "according to the most eminent theologians" the
books in their present state "have been tampered with." He goes on to
say, "It is to be believed that the Qur'an is the noblest of the books. . . . It
is the last of the God-given scriptures to come down, it abrogates all the
books which preceded it. . . . It is impossible for it to suffer any change or
alteration."[3] Even though this is the most common view among Islamic
scholars, still many Muslims claim to believe in the sacredness and truthfulness of the present-day Bible. This, however, is largely lip service on
their part, since due to their firm belief in the all-sufficiency of the
Qur'an, very few ever study the Bible.

CHARGES AGAINST THE OLD TESTAMENT

Muslims often show a less favorable view of the previous Scriptures,
mainly due to the distortions imposed on them by the teachers of the
Law. The charges against people of the Book and their tampering with the
Scriptures include: concealing God's Word (2:42; 3:71), verbally distorting the message in their books (3:78; 4:46), not believing in all the parts of
their Scriptures (2:85), and not knowing what their own Scriptures really
teach (2:78). Even though in their historical contexts most of these
charges were directed against the Jews, by implication Muslims have also
included Christians in the above criticisms.

Due to the above ambiguities in the Qur'anic accounts, Muslims hold
various views (that are sometimes in conflict) regarding the Bible. For
instance, the well-known Muslim reformer, Muhammad Abduh writes,
"The Bible, the New Testament and the Qur'an are three concordant
books; religious men study all three and respect them equally. Thus the
divine teaching is completed, and the true religion shines across the centuries."[4] Another Muslim author tries to harmonize the three great world
religions in this way: "Judaism lays stress on Justice and Right: Christianity, on Love and Charity: Islam, on Brotherhood and Peace."[5] However,
the most typical Islamic approach to this subject is characterized by
comments of the Muslim apologist, Ajijola:

> The first five books of the Old Testament do not constitute the original
> Torah, but parts of the Torah have been mingled up with other narratives
> written by human beings and the original guidance of the Lord is lost in
> that quagmire. Similarly the four Gospels of Christ are not the original Gos-
> pels as they came from Prophet Jesus . . . the original and the fictitious, the

3. Jeffery, *Islam, Muhammad and His Religion,* 126–28.
4. Dermenghem, 138.
5. Waddy, 116.

Divine and the human are so intermingled that the grain cannot be separated from the chaff. The fact is that the original Word of God is preserved neither with the Jews nor with the Christians. Qur'an, on the other hand, is fully preserved and not a jot or tittle has been changed or left out in it.[6]

These charges bring us once again to the Islamic doctrine of *tahrif,* or corruption of the Judeo-Christian Scriptures. Based on some of the above Qur'anic verses and, more important, exposure to the actual contents of other scriptures, Muslim theologians have generally formulated two different responses. According to Nazir-Ali, "the early Muslim commentators (e.g., Al-Tabari and Ar-Razi) believed that the alteration is *tahrif bi'al ma'ni,* a corruption of the meaning of the text without tampering with the text itself. Gradually, the dominant view changed to *tahrif bi'al-lafz,* corruption of the text itself."[7] The Spanish theologians Ibn-Hazm, and Al-Biruni, along with most Muslims, uphold this view.

Another Qur'anic scholar claims that "the biblical Torah was apparently not identical with the pure *tawrat* given as a revelation to Moses, but there was considerable variation in opinion on the question to what extent the former scriptures were corrupted." On the one hand, "Ibn-Hazm, who was the first thinker to consider the problem of *tabdil* [change] systematically, contended . . . that the text itself had been changed or forged (*taghyr*), and he drew attention to immoral stories which had found a place within the corpus." On the other hand, "Ibn-Khaldun held that the text itself had not been forged but that Jews and Christians had misinterpreted their scripture, especially those texts which predicted or announced the mission of Muhammad and the coming of Islam."[8]

Whether a Muslim scholar shows more or less respect for the Bible, and whether or how he will quote from it depends on his particular interpretation of *tabdil.* Ibn-Hazm, for instance, rejects nearly the whole Old Testament as a forgery, but cheerfully quotes the *tawrat* when bad reports are given of the faith and behavior of the *Banu Isra'il* as proofs against the Jews and their religion.

CHARGES AGAINST THE NEW TESTAMENT

Noted Muslim commentator Yusuf Ali contends that "the *Injil* spoken of by the Qur'an is not the New Testament. It is not the four Gospels now received as canonical. It is the single Gospel which, Islam teaches, was revealed to Jesus, and which he taught. Fragments of it survive in the

6. Ajijola, 79.
7. Nazir-Ali, 46.
8. Waardenburg, 257.

received canonical Gospels and in some others of which traces survive."[9] Direct allegations against New Testament and Christian teaching are made. These include the charges that there have been a change and forgery of textual divine revelation, and that there have been doctrinal mistakes such as the belief in the incarnation of Christ, the trinity of the Godhead, and the doctrine of original sin.[10]

Another important debate among Muslim theologians on this point is the question of the eternal destiny of people of the Book. Although the average Muslim might consider anyone who has been a "good person" worthy of eternal salvation, accounting for all the Qur'anic evidences on this subject has created much uncertainty.

Among the classical orthodox theologians, Jews and Christians were generally regarded as unbelievers (*kafar*), because of their rejection of Muhammad as a true prophet from God. For example, in the Qur'anic commentary of Tabari, one of the most respected Muslim commentators of all time, we notice that even though the author distinguishes between the people of the book and the polytheists (*mushrikun*), and expresses a higher opinion of the former, he clearly declares that the majority of Jews and Christians are in unbelief and transgression because of their refusal to acknowledge Muhammad's truthfulness.[11]

Added to this is the charge against Christian belief in the divinity of Christ as the Son of God, a belief that amounts to committing the unpardonable sin of *shirk*, and is emphatically condemned throughout the Qur'an. The condemnation of Christians is captured in 5:75: "They do blaspheme who say: 'God is Christ the son of Mary'. . . . Whoever joins other gods with God, God will forbid him the Garden, and the Fire will be his abode."

On the other hand, the contemporary Muslim theologian, Fazlur Rahman, goes against what he admits is "the vast majority of Muslim commentators." He champions the opinion that salvation is not acquired by formally joining the Muslim faith, but as the Qur'an points out, by believing in God and the last day and doing good deeds.[12] The debate continues and each individual Muslim can take a different side of this issue based on his own understanding of the matter.[13]

9. A. Yusuf Ali, *The Holy Qur'an*, 287.

10. See Waardenburg, 261–63.

11. Antes, 104–5. Also see *Islamochristiana*, 1980, vol. 6, 105–48.

12. Rahman, 166–67. Of course, his views are considered unorthodox by traditional Muslims.

13. Regarding the salvation of other groups such as Hindus, Buddhists, and Zoroastrians, Muslim opinion also varies. Some Muslims view these religions as being originally similar to Islam and from God but no longer true to their origin, while others reject them as false religions from the very beginning (see also Chapter 6).

A RESPONSE TO ISLAMIC CHARGES

These Islamic views about the Bible are critically flawed. One evidence is the internal inconsistency within the Muslim view of Scripture itself. Another is that it is contrary to the factual evidence.

There is serious tension in the Islamic rejection of the authenticity of the current New Testament. This tension can be focused by the following teachings from the Qur'an:

- The original New Testament ("Gospel") is a revelation of God (5:46, 67, 69, 71).
- Jesus was a prophet and his words should be believed by Muslims (4:171; 5:78). As the Muslim scholar Mufassir notes, "Muslims believe all prophets to be truthful because they are commissioned in the service of humanity by Almighty God (Allah)."[14]
- Christians were obligated to accept the New Testament of Muhammad's day (seventh century A.D., 10:94).

In this sura Muhammad is told: "If thou wert in doubt As to what We have revealed Unto thee, then ask those Who have been reading The Book [the Bible] from before thee; The truth hath indeed come To thee from thy Lord; So be in no wise Of those who doubt." Abdul Haqq notes that "the learned doctors of Islam are sadly embarrassed by this verse, referring the prophet as it does to the people of the Book who would solve his doubts."[15] One of the strangest interpretations is that the sura is actually addressed to those who question his claim. Others claim that "it was Muhammad himself who is addressed, but, however much they change and turn the compass, it ever points to the same celestial pole—the purity and preservation of the Scriptures." However, Haqq adds, "If again, we take the party addressed to be those who doubted the truth of Islam, this throws open the whole foundation of the prophet's mission; regarding which they are referred to the Jews [or Christians] for an answer to their doubts; which would only strengthen the argument for the authority of the Scripture—a result the Muslim critics would hardly be prepared for."[16]

Christians respond to this verse by making two crucial points. First, Muhammad would not have asked them to accept a corrupted version of the New Testament. Second, the New Testament today is substantially

14. Sulaiman Shahid Mufassir, *Jesus, a Prophet of Islam* (Indianapolis: American Trust Publications, 1980), i.

15. Abdul-Haqq, 23. Taken from W. Muir, *The Beacon of Truth* (London: The Religious Tract Society), 1894.

16. See Abdul-Haqq, 100.

identical to the New Testament of Muhammad's day, since today's New Testament is based on existing manuscripts that go back even centuries before Muhammad's day. Hence, by the logic of this verse Muslims should accept the authenticity of today's Bible. But if they do, then they should accept the doctrines of the deity of Christ and the Trinity (see Chapters 11 and 12) since that is what the New Testament teaches. However, Muslims categorically reject these teachings. Hence, the dilemma within the Islamic view.

There is another inconsistency within the Islamic (Qur'anic) view regarding the Bible. They claim that the Bible is "the Word of God" (2:75). However, Muslims also insist that God's words cannot be altered or changed. But, as Pfander points out, "if both these statements are correct . . . then it follows that the Bible has not been changed and corrupted either before or since Muhammad's time."[17] However, Islamic teaching insists that the Bible has been corrupted. Thus the contradiction.

Furthermore, as Islamic scholar Richard Bell points out, it is unreasonable to suppose that Jews and Christians would conspire together to change the Old Testament. For ". . . their [the Jews] feeling towards the Christians had always been hostile."[18] Why would two hostile parties (Jews and Christians), who shared a common Old Testament, conspire to change it to support the views of a common enemy, the Muslims? It does not make any sense. What is more, at the supposed time of the textual changes Jews and Christians were spread all over the world, making the supposed collaboration to corrupt the text impossible. And the number of copies of the Old Testament in circulation were too numerous to guarantee that the changes would be uniform. Also, there is no mention of any such changes by former Jews or Christians of the time who became Muslims—something that they surely would have reported if it were true.[19]

Furthermore, Muslim rejection of the New Testament is contrary to the overwhelming manuscript evidence. All the Gospels are preserved in the Chester Beatty Papyri, dated about A.D. 250. And the vast majority of the New Testament exists in the Vaticanus Ms. (B) that dates from about A.D. 325–50. In addition there are nearly 5,700 other manuscripts of the New Testament dating from the second century A.D. to the fifteenth century (hundreds of which are from before the time of Muhammad) that confirm the same substantial text of the whole New Testament existing in Muhammad's day.

17. Pfander, 101.
18. Bell, 164–65.
19. For a further elaboration of these points see Josh McDowell and John Gilchrist, *The Islam Debate* (San Bernardino: Here's Life Publishers, 1983), 52–53.

The New Testament text of Muhammad's day is confirmed by these same manuscripts to be the same basic New Testament text of Jesus' day. For these manuscripts provide an unbroken chain of testimony to the very threshold of the first century for the authenticity of the New Testament text we possess today. For example, the earliest fragment of the New Testament, the John Ryland Fragment, is dated about A.D. 117–38. It preserves verses from John 18 just as they are found in later manuscripts and in today's New Testament. Likewise, the Bodmer Papyri from the second century A.D. preserve the whole books of Peter and Jude as we have them today. There is absolutely no evidence to indicate that the New Testament message was destroyed or distorted, as Muslims claim it was.[20]

Finally, Muslims use liberal critics of the New Testament in an attempt to show that the New Testament was corrupted, misplaced, and outdated. However, the late liberal New Testament scholar, Bishop John Robinson, concluded that the Gospel record was written well within the lives of the apostles, somewhere between 40 and 60 A.D. Likewise, former Bultmannian New Testament critic Eta Linnemann has more recently concluded that negative New Testament criticism, which holds that the New Testament as preserved in the manuscripts does not accurately preserve the words and deeds of Jesus, is defunct. This former disciple of Rudolph Bultmann writes: "As time passes, I become more and more convinced that to a considerable degree New Testament criticism as practiced by those committed to historical-critical theology does not deserve to be called science."[21] The author adds, "The Gospels are not works of literature that creatively reshape already finished material after the manner in which Goethe reshaped the popular book about Dr. Faust."[22] Rather, "Every Gospel presents a complete, unique testimony. It owes its existence to direct or indirect eyewitnesses."[23] (Further evidence for the reliability of the New Testament is found in Appendix 4.)

Furthermore, the use of these liberal critics by Muslim apologists is misplaced, since it undermines their own view of the Qur'an. Muslim writers are fond of quoting the conclusions of liberal critics of the Bible without giving serious consideration to their presuppositions. For example, the same antisupernaturalism that led liberal critics of the Bible to deny that Moses wrote the Pentateuch, noting the different words for God used in different passages, would likewise argue that the Qur'an did not come from Muhammad. For the Qur'an also uses different names for

20. For further support of this point, see Geisler and Nix, Chapter 22.
21. Eta Linnemann, *Is There a Synoptic Problem? Rethinking the Literary Dependence of the First Three Gospels* (Grand Rapids: Baker, 1992), 9.
22. Ibid., 104.
23. Ibid., 194.

God in different places. *Allah* is used for God in suras 4, 9, 24, 33, but *Rab* is used in suras 18, 23, and 25.[24] Muslims seem blissfully unaware that the views of these critics are based on an antisupernatural bias that, if applied to the Qur'an and the *hadith*, would destroy basic Muslim beliefs as well. In short, Muslims cannot appeal to criticisms of the New Testament that are based on the belief that miracles do not occur, unless they wish to undermine their own faith.

To summarize, if Christians in Muhammad's day were obligated to accept the New Testament, and if abundant manuscript evidence confirms that the New Testament of today is essentially the same, then it follows that, according to the teachings of the Qur'an itself, Christians are obligated to accept the teachings of the New Testament today. But the New Testament today affirms that Jesus is the Son of God who died on the cross for our sins and rose again three days later (see Chapters 11 and 13). But this is contrary to the Qur'an. Thus, Muslim rejection of the authenticity of the New Testament is inconsistent with their own belief in the inspiration of the Qur'an.

INCONSISTENT USE OF THE BIBLE

Muslims do not reject all of the New Testament. In fact, they often appeal to certain New Testament passages to support their belief that Jesus did not claim to be God. However their selection of "authentic" passages is arbitrary, suited only to fit their doctrinal interests. If select passages seem to support their own doctrines, they will be declared authentic. If, on the other hand, as is the case with the vast majority of texts, they do not support Islamic beliefs, they will arbitrarily be pronounced corrupt.

When Muslims pronounce certain biblical passages authentic, it is not because they recognize there is good manuscript evidence for it as opposed to those they consider unauthentic. As a matter of fact, as we have just seen, these have the same manuscript authority as the so-called unauthentic ones. The whole concept of corruption or *tahrif*, crucial as it is to the Islamic claim, has absolutely no textual support. The Bible has overwhelming manuscript support that predates Muhammad by centuries. Indeed, as we have seen, there is more manuscript evidence for the New Testament than for any book from the ancient world.

Furthermore, even the conclusions drawn from the select passages they pronounce "authentic" are based on a misunderstanding of the passages' meaning. Since many of these involve the deity of Christ and the

24. See R. K. Harrison, *An Introduction to the Old Testament* (Grand Rapids: Eerdmans, 1979), 517.

Trinity, the reader is referred to Chapter 12 for a detailed discussion of these misinterpreted texts. For now, we turn our attention to another Muslim attempt to support the Qur'an: the effort to prove errors in the Bible.

In his popular book, *The Bible, The Qur'an and Science*, Bucaille contends that "quotations from the Gospels themselves show flat contradictions."[25] He believes that "monumental errors are to be found in the Bible."[26] Bucaille's list, however, is neither monumental nor difficult. Since we have compressively answered these kinds of criticisms elsewhere,[27] we will respond only to the ones most often used by Muslim apologists.

Genesis 1:2. According to Bucaille, Genesis 1 is "a masterpiece of inaccuracy from a scientific point of view."[28] He cites the fact that Genesis 1:2 mentions water in an early stage of the earth's history, yet he insists, "to mention the existence of water at this period is however simply pure allegory."[29]

This is a strange charge for several reasons. Bucaille himself admits that "there is every indication that at the initial stage of the formation of the universe a gaseous mass existed."[30] Yet water itself has a gaseous state known as vapor. Further, scientific views change. The theories of today are often discarded tomorrow. So even if there were some theory today holding that there was no water in the initial state of our universe, it may be found to be false tomorrow. Furthermore, there was water in the early stages of earth's history, at least in the form of vapor. This is one of the reasons life as we know it is possible on earth, unlike other planets in our solar system or elsewhere. So in his haste to find errors in the Bible Bucaille has made one of his own. Finally, scientific theory cannot overrule a fact of God's revelation. Bucaille would never allow a scientific view, no matter how widely held, to overthrow his belief that the Qur'an is a miracle. Yet most modern scientists reject miracles.

Genesis 1:3–5. About Genesis 1:3–5 Bucaille affirms, "it is illogical, however, to mention the result (light) on the first day, when the cause of this light [the sun] was created three days later."[31]

But almost anyone with an even elementary knowledge of science and the Bible can answer this objection. For the sun is not the only source of light in the universe. Further, it is not necessary to understand the text as

25. Bucaille, 115.
26. Ibid., 127.
27. See Geisler and Howe.
28. See Bucaille, 40.
29. Ibid., 41.
30. Ibid.
31. Ibid.

saying the sun was created on the fourth day. It may have been only *made to appear* on the fourth day, after the mist of water vapor had cleared away so that its outline became visible.[32] Before this its light may have been shining through, just as it does on a misty day, without observers on earth being able to see the outline of the sun.

Genesis 1:6-8. According to Genesis 1:6–8 God made "a firmament in the midst of the waters." But Bucaille calls this a "myth," insisting that "this image of the division of the waters into two masses is scientifically unacceptable."[33]

It is true that the Hebrew word for the "firmament" (*raqia*) that God created (Gen. 1:6; cf. Job 37:18) originally meant a solid object.[34] However, meaning is not determined by origin (etymology) but by usage. Originally, the English word "board" referred to a wooden plank. But when we speak of a member of a corporate board, it no longer has that meaning. Likewise, when used of the atmosphere above the earth, "firmament" clearly does not mean something solid. The related word *raqa* (beat out, spread out) is correctly rendered "expanse" by many translations. So just as metal spreads out when beaten (Exod. 39:3; Isa. 40:19), the firmament too is a thinned out area. The root meaning "spread out" can be used independently of "beat out," as it is in several passages (Ps. 136:6; Isa. 42:5; 44:24). Isaiah writes: "So says Jehovah God, He who created the heavens and *stretched them out,* spreading out the earth and its offspring" (Isa. 42:5 NKJV, emphasis added). This same verb is used of extending curtains or tents in which to dwell, which would make no sense unless there was no empty space there in which to live. Isaiah, for example, spoke of the Lord "who sits on the circle of the earth, and its people are like grasshoppers; who *stretches out the heavens like a curtain, and spreads them out like a tent to dwell in*" (Isa. 40:22 NKJV, emphasis added). Also, the Bible speaks of rain falling through the sky (Job 36:27–28). But this makes no sense if the sky is a metal dome. It is absurd to suppose that there were little holes in a metal dome through which the drops could fall.[35]

The same creation account in Genesis speaks of birds that "fly above the earth across the face of the firmament" (Gen. 1:20). But this would be impossible if the sky were solid. Thus, it is more appropriate to translate

32. The Hebrew word for made, *asah,* occurs about 1,200 times in the Old Testament. It has a wide range of meanings, including: did, made, show, appear, made to appear, etc.

33. See Bucaille, 41.

34. The discussion here follows that in Geisler and Howe, 229–30.

35. The Bible does speak figuratively of the "windows of heaven" opening for the flood (Gen. 7:11). But this may not be meant any more literally than our English idiom, "It is raining cats and dogs" (meaning it is raining very hard).

raqia by the word "expanse" (as the NASB and NIV do). And in this sense there is no conflict with the concept of space in modern science.

Even taken literally, Job's parallel statement (Job 37:18) does not affirm that the "skies" *are* a "metal mirror" but simply that they are "*as* [like]" a mirror. In other words, it is a comparison that need not be taken literally, any more than God is really a "strong tower" (Prov. 18:10). Further, the point of comparison in Job is not the solidity of the "skies" or a mirror but their durability (cf. "strong" [*chazuq*], v. 18). So when all is considered, there is no evidence that the Bible affirms that the sky of firmament is a metallic dome. And thus there is no conflict here with modern science, as Muslim critics claim.

Genesis 1:19–23. Islamic scholars find two things unacceptable in Genesis 1:19–23: "the fact that continents emerged at the period in earth's history, when it was still covered with water" and "what is totally unacceptable is that a highly organized vegetable kingdom with reproduction by seed could have appeared before the existence of the sun."[36]

In response, we note that the first point is unsubstantiated, and the second one we have already answered above under Genesis 1:3–5. In brief, Bucaille has dogmatized science in the first criticism and is improperly informed. To whom is it "totally unacceptable" that God created seed-bearing plants early in earth's history? To a nontheistic evolutionist, perhaps, who rejects God and his special work of creation. But this certainly should not be unacceptable to a Muslim, like Bucaille, who claims to believe the Qur'an. For the Qur'an teaches that God is "almighty" and can do anything he desires (2:159). Furthermore, the Qur'an affirms that God created the world and all that is in it in a few days. Why should it be thought unacceptable, then, to believe that on one of these days (the third one in the Bible) God created seed-bearing plants? At best, the only contradiction here is between the Bible and a prevalent current scientific *hypothesis.*[37] There is no contradiction between the Bible and scientific *fact.*

Genesis 1:14-19. Muslim critics state that "to place the creation of the Sun and Moon after the creation of the Earth is contrary to the most firmly established ideas on the formation of the elements of the Solar System."[38]

But here again, there are two problems. One is to assume that even the most prevailing scientific ideas are to be taken as absolute fact. Indeed, it

36. See Bucaille, 42.

37. For a critique of current evolutionary thinking, see Michael Denton, *Evolution: A Theory in Crisis* (Bethesda, Md.: Adler & Adler, 1985); and Phillip E. Johnson, *Darwin on Trial* (Washington, D.C.: Regnery Gateway, 1991). Our own treatment is found in Geisler, *Origin Science,* esp. Chapters 5–7.

38. See Bucaille, 42.

is strange that Muslims use this argument, since they too point to the mistake of many theologians in assuming that the almost universally prevailing scientific view of a geocentric (earth-centered) universe was a scientific fact. In like manner, prevailing scientific ideas about the origin of the sun and moon *could* be wrong.

Furthermore, as we have seen above in comments on Genesis 1:3–5, it is not necessary to believe that the sun and moon were created on the fourth day. Rather, for whatever reason (perhaps as the original vapor disappeared), their form may have only been made visible from the face of the earth on the fourth day. At any rate, there is no real contradiction here and certainly no "momentous" one, as Muslims overenthusiastically proclaim.

Of Genesis 1:20–30, Bucaille insists that "this passage contains assertions which are unacceptable," such as, "the animal kingdom began with the appearance of creatures of the sea and winged birds." However, according to modern science, birds did not appear until after reptiles and other land animals. "This order of appearance, beasts of the earth after birds, is not therefore acceptable."[39]

Here again, the mistake is not in the infallible Bible but in Bucaille's fallible interpretation of it, as well as in his flawed understanding of science. First, he has a mistaken interpretation of the Bible. It does not actually say that God created feathered birds before reptiles. It simply refers to winged creatures (Gen. 1:21).[40] And, according to science, there were winged creatures that existed before feathered birds. Winged dinosaurs are an example. Their mention along with the "great sea creatures" (probably including dinosaurs) is further indication that the reference here may be to winged dinosaurs, not to feathered birds.

Furthermore, Bucaille seems to assume an evolutionary basis for his criticism. But, as we have already noted, evolution is not a proven fact but an unsubstantiated hypothesis. To offer as scientific proof that "numerous biological characteristics common to both species makes this deduction possible" is to make a fallacious deduction. For common characteristics do not prove common ancestry; it may be an indication of a common Creator. After all, there is a progressive similarity in automobiles from the first ones to current ones. No one, however, believes that one evolved from another by natural processes. Only intelligent intervention (creation) can account for the origin of the successive models of cars.[41]

39. Ibid., 42–43.
40. This is often translated "birds" (i.e., flying animals) but is never rendered "*feathered* creatures."
41. See Denton or Johnson for a critique of evolution.

Finally, some contemporary scientists are questioning the long-held assumption that all winged creatures appeared after reptiles. Some fossils of flying marine animals have been found in earlier strata that were commonly assigned to the origin of reptiles. In any event, there is no flat contradiction here between scientific fact and Genesis. It is only between various theories of science and some misinterpretations of Genesis.

Genesis 1:24–31. As for Genesis 1:24–31, Bucaille only repeats his charge (just answered) that the "error was to place the appearance of beasts of the earth after that of the birds."[42] Interestingly, he admits that the Bible is right in that "man's appearance is however correctly situated after the other species of living things."[43]

Genesis 2:1–3. Commenting on the biblical teaching that God created in six days (Genesis 2:1–3), Bucaille contends that "today we are perfectly aware that the formation of the Universe and the Earth took place in stages that lasted for very long periods." Aware that these "days" of Genesis could be taken as long periods of time, he simply repeats his unsubstantiated charge that "the succession of episodes it contains is in absolute contradiction with elementary scientific knowledge."[44] But this has already been shown above to be without factual or logical grounds.

Genesis 2:4f. As for Genesis 2:4f, Bucaille adopts the outdated critical view that Genesis 2 contradicts the account given in Genesis 1. The charge here is that Genesis 1 declares that animals were created before humans, while Genesis 2:19 seems to reverse this, saying, "the Lord God formed every beast of the field . . . and brought them to Adam to see what he would call them," implying Adam was created before they were.

The solution to this problem, however, becomes apparent when we take a closer look at the two texts. The differences appear from the fact that Genesis 1 gives the *order* of events; Genesis 2 provides more *content* about them. Genesis 2 does not contradict Chapter 1, since it does not affirm exactly when God created the animals. He simply says he brought the animals (which he had previously created) to Adam in order that he might name them. The focus in Chapter 2 is on the naming of the animals, not on creating them. Thus, Genesis 2:4, stressing the naming (not the creating) of animals, simply says: "The Lord God [who had previously] formed every beast of the field . . . brought them to Adam to see what he would call them."

Genesis 1 provides the outline of events, and Chapter 2 gives details. Taken together, the two chapters provide a harmonious and more com-

42. See Bucaille, 43.
43. Ibid.
44. Ibid., 45.

plete picture of the creation events. The differences, then, can be summarized as follows:

GENESIS 1	GENESIS 2
Chronological order	Topical Order
Outline	Details
Creating Animals	Naming Animals

Once this is understood, there is absolutely no contradiction at all. The two texts are perfectly complementary.

ALLEGED CONTRADICTIONS IN LIFESPANS OF PREDELUVIANS

According to Bucaille, "In Genesis (6:3) God decided just before the Flood to limit man's lifespan to one hundred and twenty years. . . . Further on however, we note in Genesis (11:10-32) that the ten descendants of Noah had lifespans that range from 148 to 600 years. . . . The contradiction between these two passages is quite obvious."[45]

Of course, the contradiction in this text is obvious only to those who overlook the context. First of all, even on the assumption that this text refers to the lifespan of Noah's descendants, it does not say that this shortening of life would take place *immediately.* It may refer only to the eventual lifespan of the postdeluvians. Indeed, Moses, who wrote these words, lived to exactly 120 years (Deut. 34:7).

Furthermore, there is no necessity to take it as a reference to the lifespan of individuals after the flood at all. It may refer, rather, to the length of time humankind then had left before God would send the flood. This fits better with the immediate context that speaks of how long God would exhort humankind to repent before he sent a flood. The text reads: "My Spirit shall not always strive with man forever, for he is indeed flesh; yet his days shall be one hundred and twenty years" (Gen. 6:3). So there is no contradiction here at all, to say nothing of a monumental one.

Genesis 5, 11. According to the years listed in these genealogies, there are only about two thousand years before Abraham, who lived about 2000 B.C. But according to Bucaille, modern science has established that human beings originated "tens of thousands of years," even millions of years before the time of Christ. Thus, the Bible contradicts modern science.[46]

Once more Bucaille errs in both science and Scripture. First, there is not, as he falsely claims, an "obvious incompatibility between what we can derive from the numerical data in Genesis about the date of man's appearance on Earth and the *firmly established facts of modern scientific*

45. Ibid., 39–40.
46. Ibid., 46–48.

knowledge."[47] In fact, the age of humankind on earth in terms of tens of thousands of years is far from a matter of being a "firmly established" fact. As a matter of fact, it is a highly disputed subject, with no indisputable evidence that places man in many tens of thousands of years B.C., to say nothing of millions of years.[48]

Second, Bucaille misinterprets the biblical text, assuming that there are no gaps in its genealogical lists. Matthew 1:8, for example, says "Joram begot Uzziah." However, 1 Chronicles 3:11 lists "Joram [and then] his son, Ahaziah his son, Joash his son, Amaziah his son . . ." before we get to Uzziah (also called "Azariah"). In other words, there is a three-generation gap here in the genealogical list. Ahaziah was apparently the immediate son of Joram, and Uzziah was a distant "son" (descendant). Just as the word "son" in the Bible also means grandson or great-grandson, even so the term "begotten" can be used of a grandson, great-grandson, and so on. In other words, "begot" means "became the ancestor of," and the one "begotten" is the "descendant of." Matthew, therefore, is not giving a complete chronology, but an abbreviated genealogy of Christ's ancestry.

MATTHEW 1:8	1 CHRONICLES 3:11–12
Joram	Joram
	Ahaziah
	Joash
	Amaziah
Uzziah	Uzziah (also called Azariah)

The same is true of Genesis 5 and 11. For example, Genesis 11:12 does not list Cainan between Arphaxad and Salah (Shelah). But in the list given in Luke 3:36 it does. So here too is another time gap in the genealogical lists. Since there are proven gaps in this abbreviated list, it is wrong to assume that one can add up all the numbers and get an accurate figure of the time Adam appeared on earth. Since the Bible does not give a precise time that humans first appeared on earth, there is no contradiction with the claims of modern science. Furthermore, it is not a proven *fact* (but only a widely accepted theory) that humankind has been on earth for tens of thousands of years, as Bucaille claims.

Genesis 6:8. Islamic critics see problems in what they consider to be two contradictory accounts of Noah's flood. Bucaille points out that "rainwater is given as the agent of the Flood in one (Yahvist) passage, but

47. Ibid., 48, emphasis ours.
48. See N. L. Geisler and Peter Bocchino, *Unshakable Foundations* (Minneapolis: Bethany, 2001), Chapter 8.

in another (Sacerdotal), the Flood is given a double cause; rainwater and the waters of the Earth."[49]

That such obviously complementary statements as these should be offered as flat contradictions is in itself reason to have confidence in the Scriptures. There is absolutely no conflict at all here. One passage is simply giving an additional source of water. The first passage did not say that rain would be the *only* source of water. The Muslim critic would have to add this to the text in order to find an error there. But then the error would not be in the Bible but in the Muslim critic who added this to the Bible!

The same can be said about the Islamic charge that the Bible gives different lengths of time that the flood lasted. Each text is speaking about a different period of time. Genesis 7:24 (and 8:3) speaks of the flood waters lasting 150 days. But other verses say it was only 40 days (Gen. 7:4, 12, 17). These numbers refer to different things. Forty days refers to how long it "rained" (7:12), and 150 days speaks of how long the flood "waters prevailed" (cf. 7:24), at the end of which "the waters decreased" (8:3). After this it was not until the fifth month after the rain began that the ark rested on Mount Ararat (8:4). Then about eleven months after the rain began the waters dried up (8:13). And exactly one year and ten days after the flood began Noah and his family emerged on dry ground (8:14).

Bucaille also sees a contradiction in the biblical assertion that only through Noah's three sons was the earth repopulated after the flood, "so that when Abraham was born roughly three centuries later, he found a humanity that was already reformed into separate communities." He asks, "how could this reconstruction have taken place in such short time? This simple observation deprives the narration of all verisimilitude."[50] But again, it is the critic's claim that lacks credibility, not the biblical narrative. Even on the assumption challenged above under Genesis 6:8 that there were only about 4,000 years before Christ, there was plenty of time between Noah and Abraham to populate the earth with tens of thousands of people. Assuming that the average family had only 10 children (Jacob had 12) and that children were not born until their parents reached 50, there would have been over one half million people in 350 years. And assuming only a third of these were still alive in Abraham's time, there would still be over 160,000. And even subtracting for unnatural deaths, there would still be some 100,000, which was more than necessary to form humanity into "separate communities."

Furthermore, as we have seen above, there were gaps in the genealogical tables, and there have been many more generations between Noah

49. Bucaille, 49.
50. Ibid., 50.

and Abraham than the six or seven allotted, assuming a closed genealogy. And with only one more generation the population could have been in the multimillions! Now no doubt the population was much less, say only tens of thousands, but the point is that there is absolutely no factual or logical contradiction here.

Matthew 1:1f. Most Muslim critics of the Bible make a big point out of the seeming contradiction between Matthew and Luke's genealogical list of Christ's ancestors.[51] For example, Jesus has a different grandfather in Luke 3:23 (Heli) than he does in Matthew 1:16 (Jacob). Which one is the right one?

In response, we simply point to the obvious, namely, that two genealogies should be expected, since there are two different lines of ancestors, one traced through his *legal* father Joseph, and the other through his *actual* mother, Mary. Matthew gives the *official* line, emphasizing the Jewish Messiah's credentials. Jews believed that the Messiah would come from the seed of Abraham and the line of David (Matt. 1:1). Luke, with a broader Greek audience in view, presented Jesus as the Perfect Man (which was the quest of Greek thought). Thus, he traces Jesus back to the first man, Adam (Luke 3:38).

That Matthew gives Jesus' paternal genealogy and Luke his maternal genealogy is further supported by several facts. While both lines trace Christ to David, each is through a different son of David. Matthew traces Jesus through Joseph (his legal father)[52] to David's son, Solomon the king, by whom Christ rightfully inherited the throne of David (2 Sam. 7:12f). Luke's purpose, on the other hand, is to show Christ as an actual human. So he traces Christ to David's son, Nathan, through his actual mother, Mary, through whom he can rightfully claim to be fully human, the redeemer of humanity.

Luke does not say that he is giving Jesus' genealogy through Joseph. Rather, he notes that Jesus was "as was supposed" (Luke 3:23) the son of Joseph, while he was actually the son of Mary. That Luke would record Mary's genealogy fits with his interest as a doctor in mothers and birth and with his emphasis on women in his Gospel that has been called "the Gospel for Women."

Finally, the fact that the two genealogies have some names in common (such as Shealtiel and Zerubbabel, Matt. 1:12; Luke 3:27) does not prove they are the same genealogy for two reasons. One, these are not uncom-

---

51. Ibid., 94ff.

52. Since Jesus was born of a virgin, he had no actual (biological) human father. But he did have a legal father, since he was born to a virgin who was legally engaged to Joseph (cf. Matt. 1:18–19). And according to Jewish law, any child born to a man's fiancee was legally his child.

mon names. Second, even the same genealogy (Luke's) has a repeat of the names Joseph and Judah (vv. 26, 30).

The two genealogies can be summarized as follows:

	MATTHEW	LUKE
MATTHEW	LUKE	
David	David	
Solomon	Nathan	
Rehoboam	Mattathah	
Abijah	Menan	
Asa	Melea	
Jehoshaphat	Eliakim	
Jacob	Heli	
Joseph (legal father)	Mary (actual mother)	
Jesus	Jesus	

John 13:1. Bucaille sees a contradiction in the fact that John informs us that Jesus ate the Last Supper "before the feast of the Passover" (John 13:1). However, here the contradiction exists only in the critic's mind, not in the text of Scripture, since he provides absolutely no evidence that any other text of Scripture contradicts this. Perhaps Bucaille hits the height of superficiality when he mentions in this connection the fact that "the Last Supper and the Passion in John's Gospel are both very long, twice as long as in Mark and Luke."[53] Just how this is supposed to prove the Bible is filled with "momentous" contradictions one is hard pressed to discover!

Alleged Contradictions in Resurrection Accounts. Muslim apologists often point to alleged contradictions in the Gospel accounts of Jesus' resurrection and ascension. But when properly understood in context, none of them is real, only imagined.[54] For example, Bucaille's primary argument is that different accounts list different appearances, as though this proved that they could not all be correct. Indeed, in the very same manner, the Qur'an lists a different number of days that it took God to create (cf. 32:4 with 41:9). Yet Muslims do not find it difficult to see how all these harmonize.[55] Since we will speak of the resurrection accounts in more detail in Chapter 11, we will reserve further comment until then. It will suffice to say here that neither Bucaille nor any other Muslim apologists have proven a genuine contradiction in the Bible. Indeed, in their futile quest to find something wrong with the Bible they reveal what is wrong with their own view.

53. See Bucaille, 104.
54. For an excellent discussion of various resurrection accounts see John Wenham, *Easter Enigma, Are the Resurrection Stories in Conflict* (Exeter: Paternoster Press, 1984).
55. See discussion on this point in Chapter 2.

Islamic critics have long contended that there are numerous errors in the Bible. However, they are long on criticism and short on proof. In fact, they have not discovered a single error in the Bible. Rather, the only errors to be found are in their criticisms. Indeed, we have carefully examined every error in the Bible alleged over the past forty years and have not found a single one! Eight hundred of these alleged errors are discussed in our book, *When Critics Ask*.[56] We have found that, while there are biblical difficulties, there are no demonstrable biblical errors. Other scholars have come to the same conclusion.[57]

The Bible has been scrutinized by some of the best legal minds in our history and found to be authentic. The great Harvard legal expert, Simon Greenleaf, examined the New Testament carefully by legal standards and concluded that "copies which had been as universally received and acted upon as the Four Gospels, would have been received in evidence in any court of justice, without the slightest hesitation."[58] Thus the Bible stands solid, even under the stringent cross-examination of great legal minds.

CONCLUSION

One of the evidences Muslims give for the inspiration of the Qur'an is that it presents God speaking in the first person. Thus, it seems to them to carry the mark of authentic words from God. In this regard, it is hard for Muslims to understand how a book like the Bible, with its variety of human literary forms usually spoken from a human perspective, can possibly be the Word of God. What they forget, however, is that the Qur'an itself sometimes speaks from a purely human point of view. The very first sura, for example, is a human prayer in which God is addressed in the second and third persons. After the introductory formula, it begins: "Praise be to God, The Cherisher and Sustainer of the Worlds. . . . Thee do we worship, And Thine aid we seek" (1:2, 5).

Furthermore, the Bible also has many sections where God is speaking in the first person. This is most evident in the prophetic sections of the Old Testament in phrases like, "Thus says the Lord" or "The word of the Lord came to me" (Isa. 1:10, 18; 6:8; Jer. 1:4; Ezek. 1:3, and so on). Yet Muslims are unwilling to accept these sections of the Bible as they are to be the Word of God.

Finally, even though the Bible is written by human beings, nevertheless, these men claimed to be inspired of God. The apostle Paul, for exam-

---

56. See Geisler and Howe.

57. See the noted linguist Gleason Archer's *Encyclopedia of Biblical Difficulties* (Grand Rapids: Zondervan, 1982).

58. Simon Greenleaf, *The Testimony of the Evangelists* (reprint: Grand Rapids: Baker, 1984), 9–10.

ple, claims that his writings are in "words which the Holy Spirit teaches" (1 Cor. 2:13). Indeed, he said of the whole Old Testament that "all Scripture is given by inspiration of God" (2 Tim. 3:16). And Peter declared that "prophecy never came by the will of man, but holy men of God spoke as they were moved by the Holy Spirit" (2 Pet. 1:21). So there is no reason to reject the divine character of the Bible simply because it was produced through the instrumentality of human authors and literary styles. Indeed, as we have seen, all alleged contradictions in the Bible are just that—*alleged* contradictions, not real ones.

11

A Defense of the Deity of Christ

Islam claims Jesus was a mere human being, a prophet of God, superseded by Muhammad who was the last and greatest of the prophets. Christianity insists Jesus is God in human flesh. Whatever other points of commonality there may be between these two forms of monotheism, there is no adjudicating this conflict. Both beliefs are at the heart of their system, and each is diametrically opposed to the other. Since we have already considered the evidence for Muhammad's claim, it remains to examine the Christian claim that Christ is the very Son of God. Since the evidence for these claims is centered around Jesus' death on the cross and resurrection three days later, and since Muslims deny both, these claims will be the focus of this chapter.

MUSLIM MISUNDERSTANDINGS

According to Christian monotheism, God is one in essence (just like in Islamic monotheism), but three in persons. One of these persons is Christ, the Son of God who, like human sons, is of the same nature as his Father but is a different person. Muslim misunderstanding of Christian monotheism begins when they claim, as Ajijola does, that "Jesus claimed only to be a prophet or a messenger of God. The Gospels also accord Jesus a status not a shade higher than that of Prophet and Messenger."[1] Noted Muslim commentator Abdalati declares that "all [the passages about Jesus in the Qur'an] emphasize the fact that Jesus never claimed to be a god or the Son of God, and that he was only the servant and apostle

1. Ajijola, 183.

233

of the Lord in the pattern of those before him."[2] Mufassir adds, "the biblical expression 'Son of God' cannot be said to have ever come, authentically, from the lips of Jesus himself."[3]

At the heart of Christianity is the death and resurrection of Christ. Muslims deny that Jesus died on the cross and rose again from the dead three days later. Christians, on the other hand, not only claim that this is the central truth of Christianity but that it is also the central proof of Christ's claim to be the Son of God in human flesh. Thus, it is necessary to address the Muslim misunderstanding about the death of Christ. Since the significance of Christ's death will be discussed later (in Chapter 13), we will treat only the *fact* of Christ's death here.

Contrary to Islamic thought, there is overwhelming historical and factual evidence that Jesus died on the cross and rose again on the third day. The evidence for Christ's death is greater than for that of almost any event in the ancient world.

Many skeptics and Muslims believe that Jesus did not die on the cross. Some say that he took a drug that put him in a coma-like state and that he later revived in the tomb. But the Bible says repeatedly that Christ died on the cross (Rom. 5:8; 1 Cor. 15:3; 1 Thess. 4:14). But Jesus never fainted or swooned or was drugged on the cross. In fact, he refused the drug customarily offered to the victim before crucifixion to help deaden pain (Matt. 27:34), and accepted only "vinegar" later (v. 48) to quench his thirst.

Contrary to Muslim belief, the evidence that Christ actually died on the cross is overwhelming.[4] Consider the following.

First of all, the Old Testament predicted that Christ would die (Isa. 53:5–10; Ps. 22:16; Dan. 9:26; Zech. 12:10). And Jesus fulfilled the Old Testament prophecies about the Messiah (Matt. 4:14; 5:17–18; 8:17; John 4:25–26; 5:39).

Second, Jesus announced many times during his ministry that he was going to die (John 2:19–21; 10:10–11; Matt. 12:40; Mark 8:31). Typical is Matthew 17:22–23 that says, "The Son of Man is about to be betrayed into the hands of men and they will kill Him, and the third day He will be raised."

Third, all the predictions of his resurrection, both in the Old Testament (Ps. 16:10; Isa. 26:19; Dan. 12:2), and in the New Testament (John 2:19–21; Matt. 12:40; 17:22–23) are based on the fact that he would die. Only a dead body can be resurrected.

---

2. Abdalati, 158.
3. Mufassir, 22.
4. For a response to Ahmed Deedat's arguments that Christ never died on the cross, see McDowell and Gilchnst, 47f.

Fourth, the nature and extent of Jesus' injuries indicate that he must have died. He had no sleep the night before he was crucified. He was beaten several times and whipped. And he collapsed on the way to his crucifixion carrying his cross. This in itself, to say nothing of the crucifixion to follow, was totally exhausting and life-draining.

Fifth, the nature of the crucifixion assures death. Jesus was on the cross from 9 A.M. (Mark 15:25) in the morning until just before sunset. He bled from wounded hands and feet plus from the thorns that pierced his head. There would be a tremendous loss of blood from enduring this for more than six hours. Plus, crucifixion demands that one constantly pull himself up in order to breathe, causing excruciating pain. Doing this all day would kill nearly anyone even if they were previously in good health.

Sixth, the piercing of Jesus' side with the spear, from which came "blood and water" (John 19:34), is proof that he had physically died before the piercing. When this has happened, it is a medical proof that the person has already died.

Seventh, Jesus said he was in the act of dying on the cross when he declared "Father, into Your hands I commend My spirit" (Luke 23:46). And "having said this, He breathed His last" (v. 46). John renders this, "He gave up His spirit" (John 19:30). His death cry was heard by those who stood by (Luke 23:47–49).

Eighth, the Roman soldiers, accustomed to crucifixion and death, pronounced Jesus dead. Although it was a common practice to break the legs of the victim to speed death (so that the person can no longer lift himself and breathe), they did not even break Jesus' legs (John 19:33).

Ninth, Pilate double-checked to make sure Jesus was dead before he gave the corpse to Joseph to be buried. "Summoning the centurion, he asked him if He had been dead for some time. And when he found out from the centurion, he granted the body to Joseph" (Mark 15:44–45).

Tenth, Jesus was wrapped in about seventy-five pounds of cloth and spices and placed in a sealed tomb for three days (John 19:39–40; Matt. 27:60). If he was not dead by then, which he clearly was, he would have died from lack of food, water, and medical treatment.

Eleventh, medical authorities who have examined the circumstances and nature of Christ's death have concluded that he actually died on the cross.[5] An article in the *Journal of the American Medical Association* (March 21, 1986) concludes:

5. A number of noted medical experts have written in confirmation of Christ's death on the cross, including Dr. Pierre Barbet, *A Doctor at Calvary,* and W. Stroud, *Treatise on the Physical Cause of the Death of Christ and Its Relation to the Principles and Practice of Christianity,* 2nd ed. (London: Hamilton & Adams, 1871), 28–156, 489–94.

Clearly, the weight of historical and medical evidence indicates that Jesus was dead before the wound to his side was inflicted and supports the traditional view that the spear, thrust between his right rib, probably perforated not only the right lung but also the pericardium and heart and thereby ensured his death. Accordingly, interpretations based on the assumption that Jesus did not die on the cross appear to be at odds with modern medical knowledge.[6]

Twelveth, non-Christian historians and writers from the first and second centuries recorded the death of Christ. The Jewish historian of the time of Christ, Josephus, believed that Jesus died on the cross. He wrote, "Pilate, at the suggestion of the principal men among us, had *condemned him to the cross.*"[7] Likewise, the Roman historian, Cornelius Tacitus, wrote: "a wise man who was called Jesus. . . . *Pilate condemned Him to be condemned and to die.*" He also noted that Jesus' disciples "reported that He had appeared to them three days after *His crucifixion* and that He was alive."[8] According to Julius Africanus (c. A.D. 221), the first-century historian, Thallus (c. A.D. 52), "when discussing the darkness which fell upon the land *during the crucifixion of Christ,*" spoke of it as an eclipse.[9] The second-century Greek writer, Lucian, speaks of Christ as "*the man who was crucified in Palestine* because he introduced a new cult into the world." He calls him the "*crucified sophist.*"[10] The "letter of Mara Bar-Serapion" (c. A.D. 73), housed in the British Museum, speaks of Christ's death, asking: "What advantage did the Jews gain from *executing their wise King?*"[11] Indeed, even the Jewish Talmud says, "*on the eve of Passover they hanged Yeshu (of Nazareth). . . .* Let everyone knowing aught in his defense come and plead for him. But they found naught in his defense and *hanged him on the eve of Passover.*"[12] Finally, there was the Roman writer, Phlegon, who spoke of Christ's death and resurrection in his *Chronicles,* saying, "Jesus, while alive, was of no assistance to himself, but that *he arose after death, and exhibited the marks of his punishment, and showed how his hands had been pierced by nails.*"[13] Phlegon even men-

6. See *The Journal of the American Medical Association* (March 21, 1986), 1463.

7. Flavius Josephus, "Antiquities of the Jews" 18:3, trans. William Whiston, *Josephus: Complete Works* (Grand Rapids: Kregel, 1963), 379, emphasis ours.

8. Cornelius Tacitus (A.D. 55?—after 117), *Annals,* 15.44.

9. See F. F. Bruce, *The New Testament Documents: Are They Reliable?* (Chicago: Inter-Varsity Press, 1968), 113.

10. Lucian, *On the Death of Peregrine.*

11. See Bruce, 114.

12. *Babylonian Talmud* (Sanhedrin 43a, "Eve of Passover").

13. Phlegon, "Chronicles," as cited by Origen, "Against Celsus" from *The Ante-Nicene Fathers,* trans. Alexander Roberts and James Donaldson (Grand Rapids: Eerdmans, 1976), vol. 4, 455, emphasis ours.

tioned "the eclipse in the time of Tiberius Caesar, in whose reign Jesus appears to have been crucified, and the great earthquakes which then took place."[14]

Thirteenth, the earliest Christian writers after the time of Christ affirmed his death on the cross by crucifixion. Polycarp, a disciple of the apostle John, repeatedly affirmed the death of Christ, speaking, for example, of "our Lord Jesus Christ, who for our sins suffered even unto death."[15] Ignatius (A.D. c. 30–c. 107) was a friend of Polycarp. He clearly affirmed the suffering and death of Christ, saying, "And *He really suffered and died*, and rose again." Otherwise, he adds, all his apostles who suffered for this belief, died in vain. "But, (in truth) none of these sufferings were in vain; for *the Lord was really crucified* by the ungodly."[16] In his *Dialogue With Trypho* the Jew, Justin Martyr notes that Jews of his day believed that "Jesus [was] a Galilean deceiver, whom we crucified."[17]

This unbroken testimony from the Old Testament to the early church fathers, including believers and unbelievers, Jews and Gentiles, is overwhelming evidence that Jesus really suffered and died on the cross. But if it is an established fact that Jesus died, then it is also a fact that he rose from the dead, since the evidence is equally strong that he rose from the dead. Thus, this would miraculously confirm his unique claim to be the Son of God. Let us take a look at the evidence.

PROOF THAT JESUS IS THE SON OF GOD

There are several basic steps in the argument that Jesus is the Son of God. First, are the New Testament documents that record the words of Christ accurate? Second, did the writers of the manuscripts give an accurate account of what Jesus taught? Third, did Jesus actually claim to be the Son of God? Fourth, did Jesus perform unique miracles that confirmed he was the Son of God?

THE RELIABILITY OF NEW TESTAMENT DOCUMENTS

It may come as a surprise to those not familiar with the facts that there is more documentary evidence for the reliability of the New Testament

14. Ibid.

15. Polycarp, "The Epistle of Polycarp to the Philippians," Chapter 1 in "The Apostolic Fathers," ed. A. Cleveland Coxe, in Roberts and Donaldson, 33.

16. Ignatius, *The Epistle of Ignatius to the Tarsians*, Chapter 3 in "The Apostolic Fathers," ed. by A. Cleveland Coxe, in Roberts and Donaldson, *The Ante-Nicene Fathers* 107; emphasis ours.

17. Justin Martyr, *Dialogue with Trypho*.

than for any other book from the ancient world.[18] Nevertheless, as we shall see, it is true for several reasons.

It is not uncommon for some of the great classics from antiquity to survive in only a handful of manuscript copies. According to the great Manchester scholar F. F. Bruce, we have about nine or ten good copies of Caesar's *Gallic War*, twenty copies of Livy's *Roman History*, two copies of Tacitus's *Annals*, and eight manuscripts of Thucydides' *History*.[19] The most documented secular work from the ancient world is Homer's *Iliad*, surviving in some 643 manuscript copies. By contrast, there are now over 5,686 Greek manuscripts of the New Testament. *The New Testament is the most highly documented book from the ancient world!*[20]

One of the marks of a good manuscript is its age. Generally the older the better, since the closer to the time of original composition the less likely it is that the text has been corrupted. Most books from the ancient world survive not only in a handful of manuscripts but in manuscripts that were made about one thousand years after they were originally composed. This is true of the above books. (It is rare to have, as the *Odyssey* does, only one manuscript copied five hundred years after the original). The New Testament, by contrast, survives in complete books from a little over 150 years after the books were composed. And one fragment[21] survives from within about a generation of the time it was composed. No other book from the ancient world has as small a time gap (between composition and earliest manuscript copies) as the New Testament.

Muslims make a strong point of the fact that the Qur'an has been completely preserved. While this is largely true, at least after the Uthmanic revisions, it misses the point, since the Qur'an is only a *medieval* book (seventh century A.D.). But most Muslims are totally unaware that for an *ancient* book (first century A.D.) the New Testament is the most accurately copied book in the world.[22]

There is widespread misunderstanding among Muslims and others about the so-called errors in the biblical manuscripts. Some have estimated there are about 200,000 of them. These are not really "errors" but only *variant* readings, the vast majority of which are strictly gram-

---

18. The Qur'an comes from the medieval world, not the ancient world.
19. See Bruce, 16.
20. Geisler and Nix, Chapter 26.
21. John Rylands papyri (P52), dated A.D. 117–38.
22. We deal only with the New Testament here because it alone is crucial for establishing the claims of Christ. However, the manuscript evidence overwhelmingly supports the accuracy of the Old Testament manuscripts as well. See the discussion in Geisler and Nix, Chapter 21.

matical. These readings are spread throughout more than 5,300 manuscripts, so that a variant spelling of one letter of one word in one verse in 3,000 manuscripts is counted as 3,000 "errors." The famous textual scholars Westcott and Hort estimated that only one-sixtieth of these variants rise above "trivialities." This would leave a text 98.33 percent pure.[23] The great scholar A. T. Robertson said that the real concern is only with a "thousandth part of the entire text."[24] This would make the New Testament 99.9 percent free of significant variants. The noted historian Philip Schaff calculated that, of the 150,000 variants known in his day, only 400 affected the meaning of the passage, only 50 were of real significance, and *not even one* affected "an article of faith or a precept of duty which is not abundantly sustained by other and undoubted passages, or by the whole tenor of Scripture teaching."[25]

The overwhelming evidence for the reliability of the New Testament manuscripts over other books from the ancient world is summarized in the following comparisons:[26]

Author/Book	Date Written	Earliest Copies	Time Gap	No. of Copies	Percent Accuracy
Hindu, *Mahabharata*	13th cent. B.C.				90
Homer, *Iliad*	800 B.C.			643	95
Herodotus, *History*	480–425 B.C.	c. A.D. 900	c. 1,350 yrs.	8	?
Thucydides, *History*	460–400 B.C.	c. A.D. 900	c. 1,300 yrs.	8	?
Plato	400 B.C.	c. A.D. 900	c. 1,300 yrs.	7	?
Demosthenes	300 B.C.	c. A.D. 1100	c. 1,400 yrs.	200	?
Caesar, *Gallic Wars*	100–44 B.C.	c. A.D. 900	c. 1,000 yrs.	10	?
Livy, *History of Rome*	59 B.C.–A.D. 17	4th cent. (partial) mostly 10th cent.	c. 400 yrs. c. 1,000 yrs.	1 partial 19 copies	?
Tacitus, *Annals*	A.D. 100	c. A.D. 1100	c. 1,000 yrs.	20	?

23. See Geisler and Nix, 365.

24. A. T. Robertson, *An Introduction to the Textual Criticism of the New Testament* (Nashville: Broadman, 1925), 22.

25. Philip Schaff, *Companion to the Greek Testament and English Version* (New York: Harper, 1883), 177.

26. See Geisler and Nix, 408.

Author/Book	Date Written	Earliest Copies	Time Gap	No. of Copies	Percent Accuracy
Pliny Secundus, *Natural History*	A.D. 61–113	c. 850	c. 750 yrs.	7	?
New Testament	A.D. 50–100	c. 114 (fragment)	+50 yrs.		
		c. 200 (books)	100 yrs.		
		c. 250 (most of N.T.)	150 yrs.		
		c. 325 (complete N.T.)	225 yrs.	5,686	99+

(From Geisler and Nix, *General Introduction to the Bible*, 408)

Of course, like any ancient book, there are minor transcription errors in the copies. But none of these affect the message of the Bible. To illustrate, note the following telegrams, one that is received one day and the other the next.

1) "Y#U HAVE WON TEN MILLION DOLLARS."
2) "YO# HAVE WON TEN MILLION DOLLARS."

Even if we received only the first telegram we know what the exact message is in spite of the error. And if we received twenty telegrams, each one having a similar mistake in a different place, we would say that the message is beyond all reasonable doubt. Now it is noteworthy that the New Testament manuscripts have a much smaller percentage of significant copyist errors than this telegram.[27] Further, with some 5,700 manuscripts (compared to a few telegrams), the real message of the New Testament is no more affected than is the message of the telegram.

By comparison with the New Testament, most other books from the ancient world are not nearly so well authenticated. The well-known New Testament scholar Bruce Metzger estimated that the *Mahabharata* of Hinduism is copied with only about 90 percent accuracy and Homer's *Iliad* with about 95 percent. By comparison, he estimated the New Testament is about 99.5 percent accurate.[28] So the New Testament text can be

27. For examples and classes of scribal errors, see ibid., 469–73.
28. Bruce Metzger, *Chapters in the History of New Testament Textual Criticism* (Grand Rapids: Eerdmans, 1963).

reconstructed with over 99 percent accuracy. And, what is more, *100* percent of the message of the New Testament has been preserved in its manuscripts!

Islamic scholars recognize the textual scholar Sir Frederic Kenyon as an authority on the subject. Yusuf Ali, the great Muslim scholar and translator of the Qur'an, cites Kenyon several times as a recognized authority on ancient manuscripts. Yet Kenyon concluded that:

> The number of manuscripts of the New Testament, of early translations from it, and of quotations from it in the oldest writers of the Church, is so large that it is practically certain that the true reading of every doubtful passage is preserved in some one or other of these ancient authorities. This can be said of no other ancient book in the world.[29]

THE RELIABILITY OF NEW TESTAMENT WITNESSES

Tracing the manuscripts back to the first century does not prove, of course, that those who wrote them were either honest or accurate. In order to establish the truth of what the manuscripts say, one must examine the evidence relating to the witnesses.

NEW TESTAMENT WRITERS WERE CONTEMPORARIES OF THE EVENTS

Most (if not all) of the New Testament claims to be written by eyewitnesses and contemporaries of the events of Jesus' ministry (c. A.D. 29–33). Matthew is written by a disciple and observer who gives long and direct quotes from Jesus (e.g., 5–7; 13; 23; 24–25). He was accustomed to taking records as a tax collector (Matt. 9:9). Mark was a disciple of Peter (1 Peter 5:13) and an eyewitness of Christ (2 Peter 1:16). Luke was an educated contemporary of Christ who said that "just as those who from the beginning were eyewitnesses and servants of the word" (viz., the apostles), so too "it seemed fitting for me as well, beginning, to write it out for you in consecutive order" (Luke 1:1–3). John the apostle was a direct eyewitness (John 21:24; cf. 1 John 1:1), as was Peter (2 Peter 1:16). Paul was a contemporary of Christ and a witness of his resurrection (1 Cor. 15:8). Paul lists many others who saw the resurrected Christ, together with a group of over five hundred, most of whom were still alive when he wrote (1 Cor. 15:6).

The evidence that these claims should be taken at face value is weighty. First, there is the general rule of historical research expressed by the philosopher Immanuel Kant. This rule says in effect that historical reports are "innocent until proven guilty." That is, what purports to be authentic would be accepted as authentic, until it is shown to be unau-

29. Frederic Kenyon, *Our Bible and the Ancient Manuscripts*, 4th ed. (New York: Harper, 1958), 55.

thentic. As many have pointed out, this is indeed the rule used in the normal discourses of life. Were the opposite used, there would be a breakdown of all everyday communication.

Second, there is what is known in law as the "ancient document rule." According to this rule, "a writing is sufficiently authenticated as an ancient document if the party who offers it satisfies the judge that the writing is thirty years old, that is unsuspicious in appearance, and further proves that the writing is produced from a place of custody natural for such a document." According to the noted American legal authority, McCormick, "Any combination of circumstances sufficient to support a finding of genuineness will be appropriate authentication."[30] Now, using the rule, the New Testament should be considered authentic. It is an ancient document whose transmission can be traced and whose custodianship has been proper. In fact, many great legal minds have been convinced of the truth of Christianity on the basis of the rules of evidence used to try life-and-death cases in the courtroom. Simon Greenleaf, a professor of law at Harvard who wrote the book on legal evidence, was converted to Christianity in just this way.[31] Using the canons of legal evidence he concludes that, "Copies which had been as universally received and acted upon as the Four Gospels, would have been received in evidence in any court of justice, without the slightest hesitation."[32]

Third, the early dating of the New Testament manuscripts supports their truthfulness. The most knowledgeable scholars date the New Testament books within the lifetime of the eyewitnesses and alleged authors. Archaeologist Nelson Glueck wrote, "We can already say emphatically that there is no longer any solid basis for dating any book of the New Testament after about A.D. 80."[33] The renowned paleographer William F. Albright declared that "every book of the New Testament was written by a baptized Jew between the forties and the eighties of the first century A.D. (very probably between about A.D. 50 and 75)."[34]

The tendency of Muslim scholars, like Deedat, to follow the older more liberal Christian scholars who give a late date for the New Testament is ill-fated. Many of these scholars have had to change their position in view of more recent arguments (see Appendix 4). Even the radical death-of-God theologian Bishop John Robinson, famous for writing *Honest to God,*

30. *McCormick's Handbook of the Law of Evidence*, 2d ed. (St. Paul, Minn.: West, 1972), sec. 223.
31. John W. Montgomery, *The Law above the Law* (Minneapolis: Bethany, 1975).
32. Greenleaf, 9–10.
33. Nelson Glueck, *Rivers in the Desert: A History of the Negev* (Philadelphia: Jewish Publication Society, 1969), 136.
34. Interview with William F. Albright, *Christianity Today*, January 18, 1963, 359.

became honest with the facts and declared that the New Testament was written by contemporaries *beginning as early as seven years or so after the events* and were circulated among other eyewitnesses and/or contemporaries of the events.[35] Another Bultmannian scholar has broken ranks with the radical view, arguing that the Gospels were written by eyewitness disciples of Jesus. After exposing the bankruptcy of the critical presuppositions, she forthrightly proclaimed, "That is why I say 'No' to historical-critical theology. I regard everything that I taught and wrote . . . as refuse. I wish to use this opportunity to mention that I have pitched my two books *Gleichnisse Jesu* . . . and *Studien zur Passionsgeschichte* . . . I threw them into the trash with my own hands in 1978."[36] Subsequently, she has produced a scholarly tome on the Gospels, showing that there is no literary dependency on prior sources, as she had once argued as a critic of the Bible.[37]

Indeed, there are many good reasons for holding that the Gospel writers were first-century contemporaries of Christ who gave independent, firsthand accounts of what Jesus said and did.[38] The manuscript evidence (listed above) reveals that the New Testament was a first-century document. The critical arguments against the authenticity of the New Testament documents are not based on factual evidence but on an unjustified antisupernatural bias that even Muslims reject. To put it another way, if this same critical bias accepted by Muslim scholars against the Bible were applied to the Qur'an, they would have to reject the Qur'an as well! The New Testament writings were cited by contemporary first-century documents, such as the *Shepherd of Hermas*, showing that they must have been in existence in the first century. The Gospel of John claims to be written by an eyewitness disciple (John). He signs off his book, saying, "This is the disciple who testifies of these things, and wrote these things: and we know that his testimony is true" (John 21:24).

Luke claims to be a careful contemporary historian of the events he records, saying, "having had perfect understanding of all things from the very first, [I decided] to write to you an orderly account . . . that you may know the certainty of those things in which you were instructed" (Luke 1:3, 4). After spending many years researching the area, the noted expert on the first-century Near East, Sir William Ramsay, concluded that Luke was a first-rate historian. For in reference to thirty-two countries, fifty-

35. John A. T. Robinson, *Honest to God* (Philadelphia: Westminster, 1963), esp. 352–53.

36. Eta Linnemann, *Historical Criticism of the Bible: Methodology or Ideology?* (Grand Rapids: Baker, 1990), 20.

37. Ibid.

38. For a more detailed argument, see Geisler and Nix, 440–47.

four cities, and nine islands he did not make a single mistake![39] The New Testament writers were honest men who willingly died for what they believed. And they were careful to distinguish their words from those of Jesus, revealing that they were not inventing them but reporting them (Acts 20:35; 1 Cor. 7:10, 12, 25; Rev. 1:17–20; 2:1f; 3:1f; 22:16–20). The New Testament is markedly different from Christian folklore, such as is found in the second- and third-century Christian apocryphal books. Noted Oxford expert on literature and myths, C. S. Lewis, insightfully notes about New Testament critics:

> I distrust them as critics. They seem to me to lack literary judgement, to be imperceptive about the very quality of the texts they are reading. . . . If he tells me that something in a Gospel is legend or romance, I want to know how many legends and romances he has read. . . . I have been reading poems, romances, vision-literature, legends, myths all my life. I know what they are like. I know that not one of them is like this [the Gospels].[40]

In short, there is no basis for the Muslim claim that the New Testament is dependent on earlier sources. Rather, it is clearly a firsthand, first-century account by disciples and contemporaries of Christ. And contrary to widely believed liberal myths, each account is independent. Everyone acknowledges the differences between and independence of John and Luke, which is all that is necessary to manifest their authenticity. And, even though it is unnecessary for the overall argument in defense of the authenticity of the basic life and words of Christ, a good case can be made for the independence of the Synoptic Gospels (Matthew, Mark, and Luke) as well.[41]

Fourth, the science of archaeology has confirmed the historical accuracy of the Gospel records. This can be dramatically illustrated through the writings of Sir William Ramsay, whose conversion from a skeptical view of the New Testament was supported by a lifetime of research in the Near Eastern world. Ramsay speaks for himself:

> I began with a mind unfavorable to it [Acts], for the ingenuity and apparent completeness of the Tubingen theory had at one time quite convinced me. It did not lie then in my line of life to investigate the subject minutely; but more recently I found myself often brought in contact with the book of Acts as an authority for the topography, antiquities, and society of Asia Minor. It

39. Sir William Ramsay, *St. Paul the Traveller and the Roman Citizen* (New York: G. Putnam's Sons, 1896), esp. 8.

40. C. S. Lewis, *Christian Reflections* (Grand Rapids: Eerdmans, 1967), 154–55.

41. For a strong argument by a former biblical critic that the Gospels are not literally dependent on one another, see Linnemann, ibid.

was gradually borne in upon me that in various details the narrative showed marvelous truth.[42]

As already noted, Ramsay discovered that Luke was a first-rate historian, not making a single error in the numerous details he was able to check. Noted Roman historian Colin Hemer has demonstrated the historicity and authenticity of the New Testament in an incredible way.[43] His work shows: 1) that the Books of Acts was written no later than A.D. 62; 2) that it is minutely accurate history written by an eyewitness and contemporary of the events of Jesus' life; 3) that the same highly accurate contemporary historian, Dr. Luke, also wrote a Gospel (cf. Acts 1:1 and Luke 1:1) which tells the same basic story as the other Gospels, namely, that Jesus claimed to be and proved to be the Son of God by numerous and incredible miracles, and that he died on the Cross and rose from the grave three days later. This is of course a strong confirmation of the central Christian message and a refutation of the central message of Islam that God has no Son and that Jesus did not die on the Cross and rise from the dead three days later. So Luke's narration of the life and miracles of Christ must likewise be accepted as authentic. And since Luke's narration of Christ's life and miracles in it accord with that of the other Gospels, we have here an archaeological confirmation of the Gospels that record the miracles and resurrection of Christ. In brief, from a strictly historical point of view, we could not have better evidence for the authenticity of events than we possess for the events in the life of Christ recorded in the New Testament.

HUME'S CRITERIA FOR CREDIBILITY

David Hume, perhaps the greatest skeptic of modern times, outlines the basic criteria that he believes necessary for testing the credibility of witnesses: "We entertain suspicion concerning any matter of fact when the witnesses contradict each other, when they are but few or of a doubtful character, when they have an interest in what they affirm, when they deliver their testimony with hesitation, or with too violent asseverations [declarations]."[44] Basically, these can be translated into four questions: Do the witnesses contradict each other? Are there a sufficient number of witnesses? Were the witnesses truthful? Were they nonprejudicial? Let us apply Hume's tests to the New Testament witnesses for the resurrection of Christ.

42. See Ramsay, 8.
43. See Colin Hemer, *Acts in the Setting of Hellenic History* (Winona Lake, IN: Eisenbrauns, 1990).
44. Hume, 120.

The evidence is that the testimony of the witnesses is not contradictory.[45] Each New Testament writer tells a crucial and overlapping part of the whole story. Christ was crucified (around A.D. 30) under Pontius Pilate in Jerusalem. He claimed to be the Son of God and offered miracles in support of his claim. He was crucified, confirmed to be dead and buried, and yet three days later the tomb was empty. Further, to many groups of people on many occasions over the next month or so, Jesus physically appeared in the same nail-scarred body that had died. He proved his physical reality to them so convincingly that these skeptical men boldly preached the resurrection a little over a month later in the same city, whereupon thousands of Jews were converted to Christianity.

To be sure, there are minor discrepancies in the Gospel accounts. One account (Matt. 28:5) says there was one angel at the tomb; John says there were two angels (John 20:12). But two things should be noted about these kinds of discrepancies. First, they are conflicts but not contradictions. That is, they are not irreconcilable. Matthew does not say there was *only* one angel there, that would be a contradiction. The simple rule of harmony is this: "Where there are two, there is one."[46] Second, conflict of testimony is just what one would expect from authentic, independent witnesses. Any perceptive judge who heard several witnesses give identical testimony would discount their testimony, assuming they were in collusion.

There are twenty-seven books in the New Testament. As already noted, they were written by some nine different persons, all of whom were eyewitnesses or contemporaries of the events they recorded. Of these books, six are crucial to the topic of New Testament miracles (Matthew, Mark, Luke, John, Acts, and 1 Corinthians). All of these books bear witness to the miracle of the resurrection. Further, even critical scholars now acknowledge that these books are first-century documents most of which were written before A.D. 70, while contemporaries of Christ were still alive. Virtually all scholars acknowledge that 1 Corinthians was written by the apostle Paul around A.D. 55 or 56, only about two decades after the death of Christ. This is a powerful witness to the reality of the miracle of the resurrection for several reasons. It is a very early document, written a little more than two decades after the event occurred. It is written by an eyewitness of the resurrected Christ (1 Cor. 15:8; cf. Acts 9). It provides a list referring to over five hundred eyewitnesses of the resurrection (1 Cor. 15:6). It contains a reference to the fact that most of these witnesses were still alive and could check out the reliability of the evidence for the resurrection.

45. For further support of this point, see Geisler and Howe, Chapter 10.
46. For a further discussion on all the rules of harmonization, see Geisler and Howe, Chapter 1.

Few challenge the fact that the New Testament provides one of the greatest standards of morality known to man in Jesus' emphasis on love (Matt. 22:36–37) and in the Sermon on the Mount (Matt. 5–7). His apostles repeated this same teaching in their writings (cf. Rom. 13; 1 Cor. 13; Gal. 5). Furthermore, their lives exemplified their moral teaching. Most of them even died for what they taught about Christ (2 Tim. 4:6–8; 2 Peter 1:14), an unmistakable sign of their sincerity.

In addition to teaching that truth is a divine imperative (Rom. 12:9), it is evident that the New Testament writers were scrupulous about expressing it in their writings. Peter declared: "We did not follow cunningly devised fables" (2 Peter 1:16). The apostle Paul insisted, "Do not lie one to another" (Col. 3:9). The New Testament writers were honest men, most of whom sealed the truth of their testimony with their own willingness to die for the truth of what they had written. Where the New Testament writers' statements overlap with the discovery of historians and archaeologists, they have proven to be accurate. Noted archaeologist Nelson Glueck concludes, "It may be stated categorically that no archaeological discovery has ever controverted a Biblical reference. Scores of archaeological findings have been made which confirm in clear outline or exact detail historical statements in the Bible."[47] Millar Burrows notes that "more than one archaeologist has found his respect for the Bible increased by the experience of excavation in Palestine."[48] Clifford A. Wilson has added still more support to the historical reliability of the Bible.[49] In fact, there is no proof that the New Testament writers ever lied in their writings or deliberately falsified the facts of the case. If they were asked in court "to swear to tell the truth, the whole truth, and nothing but the truth" their testimony would be accepted as valid by any unbiased jury in the world. In brief, as the great Harvard legal expert concluded, their testimony is devoid of any sign of perjury.[50]

EVIDENCE FOR THE RESURRECTION

There is every reason to believe that New Testament witnesses of the miracles of Christ, particularly of his resurrection, were not predisposed to believe the events to which they gave testimony.

First, the apostles themselves did not believe the testimony of others that Christ had risen from the dead. When the women reported it, "their words seemed to them like idle tales, and they did not believe them"

47. Glueck, 31.
48. Millar Burrows, *What Mean These Stones?* (New Haven: American Schools of Oriental Research, 1941), 1.
49. Clifford A. Wilson, *Rocks, Relics, and Biblical Reliability* (Grand Rapids: Zondervan, 1977).
50. Cited in note 31.

(Luke 24:11). Even when some of the disciples saw Christ themselves they were "slow of heart to believe" (Luke 24:25). Indeed, when Jesus appeared to ten apostles and showed them his crucifixion scars, "they still did not believe for joy, and marveled" (Luke 24:41). And even after they were convinced by Jesus' eating of food, their absent colleague Thomas protested that he would not believe unless he could put his finger in the scars in Jesus' hand (John 20:25).

Second, Jesus not only appeared to believers; he also appeared to unbelievers. He appeared to his unbelieving half-brother James (John 7:5; 1 Cor. 15:7). Indeed, he appeared to the greatest unbeliever of the day—a Jewish Pharisee named Saul of Tarsus (Acts 9). If Jesus had only appeared to those who were either believers or with the propensity to believe, then there might be some legitimacy to the charge that the witnesses were prejudiced. But just the opposite is the case.

Third, the witnesses to the resurrection had nothing to gain personally for their witness to the resurrection. They were persecuted and threatened with death for their stand (Acts 4, 5, 8). As a matter of fact, most of the apostles were martyred for their belief. Certainly, it would have been much more profitable personally for them to deny the resurrection. Rather, they proclaimed and defended it in the face of death.

Fourth, to discount their testimonies because they believed in the resurrected Christ is like discounting an eyewitness of a murder because he actually saw it occur! The prejudice in this case is not with the witnesses but with those who reject their testimony.

Evidence That Jesus Claimed to Be the Son of God

Since Muslims believe that Jesus performed miracles to confirm his claims to be speaking for God, we need not spend much time on this point. The Qur'an affirms Jesus' virgin birth (19:16–21; 3:37–47), and his many miraculous acts recorded in the New Testament (and even the New Testament Apocrypha), such as his healings and raising people from the dead (see 19:29–31; 5:110). The Qur'an even affirms that God "raised him up" to heaven (4:158),[51] though Muslims do not believe this refers to Jesus' resurrection three days after his crucifixion, as recorded in the Gospels.[52] But the fact that Jesus performed miracles, even resurrections, to prove his message was of God, is clearly affirmed by the Qur'an. So Muslims believe in the supernatural birth, life, and end of the life of Christ on earth (viz., the ascension). He is in fact the only prophet who possessed all three of these. This makes him, even according to the

---

51. For an excellent work on all the Qur'anic references to Jesus, see Parrinder.
52. Rather, they believe this sura is a reference to Jesus' ascension.

Muslims' own teaching, the most unique supernatural person ever to live.

Christians, of course, believe more. Unlike Muslims, they believe that Jesus is also the unique Son of God. But since Muslims believe that whatever Jesus taught was true, it remains to provide evidence for Christ's claim to be the Son of God.

Like the Qur'an, the Bible also lays down miracles as the test for the authenticity of a prophet (Exod. 4; 1 Kings 18; John 3:2; Heb. 2:3–4). What remains, then, is to examine the evidence to see if indeed the words of the Jewish Rabbi Nicodemus were correct, when he said to Jesus, "We know that you are a teacher come from God; for no one can do these signs that You do unless God is with him" (John 3:2).

Since we have already shown that the New Testament documents and witnesses are reliable, it remains only to see what they tell us about the claims of Christ. In brief, they inform us that Jesus of Nazareth, born of the virgin Mary, claimed to be the unique Son of God, deity incarnated in human flesh. There are a number of ways in which Jesus claimed to be the Son of God. In an attempt to find support for this conclusion, Muslim scholars often misconstrue biblical claims about Christ. These will be considered later (in Chapter 12).

MUSLIM MISUNDERSTANDING OF "SON OF GOD"

Before discussing Jesus' specific claims to be the Son of God, it is necessary to respond briefly to the Muslim misunderstanding of this claim. Many Muslims understand the phrase "Son of God" to imply that Jesus was the offspring of physical relations. Indeed, appeal is often made to 19:35 which declares: "It is not befitting To (the majesty of) God That He should beget A son." Indeed, many Muslims grossly conceive of Jesus as the offspring of sexual relations between God and the virgin Mary. This, of course, is a straw man and is easily refuted by reference to what the Bible actually says about the miraculous conception of Jesus without any sexual relations (Matt. 1:18–24; Luke 1:26–35). There is, however, another problem in the Muslim mind with the phrase "Son of God." There are two Arabic words for "son" that must be distinguished. The word *walad* denotes a son born of sexual relations. Jesus is definitely not a son in this sense. However, there is another Arabic word for son, *ibn*, that can be used in a wider figurative or metaphorical sense. A traveler, for example, is spoken of as a "son of the road" (*ibnussabil*). It is in this wider sense that it makes sense to speak of Jesus as the "Son (*ibn*) of God."

JESUS' CLAIM TO BE GOD

Jehovah or Yahweh (YHWH) is the special name given by God for himself in the Old Testament. It is the name revealed to Moses in Exodus 3:14, when God said, "I AM THAT I AM." While other titles for God may be used of men (*Adonai* [Lord] in Gen. 18:12) or false gods (*elohim* [gods] in Deut. 6:14), Jehovah is only used to refer to the one true God. No other person or thing was to be worshiped or served (Exod. 20:5), and his name and glory were not to be given to another. Isaiah wrote, "Thus saith Jehovah . . . I am the first, and I am the last; and besides me there is no God" (Isa. 44:6 ASV)[53] and, "I am Jehovah, that is my name; and my glory I will not give to another, neither my praise unto graven images" (42:8).

Yet Jesus claimed to be Jehovah on many occasions. Jesus prayed, "Father, glorify thou me in thy own presence with the glory which I had with thee before the world was made" (John 17:5). But Jehovah of the Old Testament says, "My glory I will not give to another" (Isa. 42:8). Jesus also declares, "I am the first and the last" (Rev. 1:17)—precisely the words Jehovah uses in Isaiah 42:8. Jesus says, "I am the good shepherd," (John 10:11), but the Old Testament says, "Jehovah is my shepherd" (Ps. 23:1). Further, Jesus claims to be the judge of all men (John 5:27f.; Matt. 25:31f.), but Joel quotes Jehovah as saying, "for there I will sit to judge all the nations round about" (Joel 3:12). Likewise, Jesus spoke of himself as the "bridegroom" (Matt. 25:1) while the Old Testament identifies Jehovah in this way (Isa. 62:5; Hos. 2:16). While the Psalmist declares, "Jehovah is our light" (Ps. 27:1), Jesus says, "I am the light of the world" (John 8:12).

Perhaps the strongest claim Jesus made to be Jehovah is in John 8:58, where he says, "Before Abraham was, I am." This statement claims not only existence before Abraham, but equality with the "I AM" of Exodus 3:14. The Jews around him clearly understood his meaning and picked up stones to kill him for blaspheming (cf. John 8:58; 10:31–33). The same claim is made in Mark 14:62 and John 18:5–6.

Jesus claimed to be equal with God in other ways. One was by claiming for himself the prerogatives of God. He said to a paralytic, "My son, your sins are forgiven" (Mark 2:5f.). The scribes correctly responded, "Who can forgive sins but God alone?" So, to prove that his claim was not an empty boast he healed the man, offering direct proof that what he had said about forgiving sins was true also.

Another prerogative that Jesus claimed was the power to raise and judge the dead: "Truly, truly I say to you, the hour is coming and now is, when the dead will hear the voice of the Son of God, and those who hear will live . . . and come forth, those who have done good, to the resurrection of life, and those who have done evil, to the resurrection of judgment" (John 5:29). He removed all doubt about his meaning when he

---

53. Bible references in this section are taken from the American Standard Version since they translate the sacred name for God (Yahweh) as Jehovah.

added, "For as the Father raised the dead and gives them life, so also the Son gives life to whom He will" (v. 21). But the Old Testament clearly teaches that only God is the giver of life (1 Sam. 2:6; Deut. 32:39) and the one to raise the dead (Ps. 2:7) and the only judge (Joel 3:12; Deut. 32:35). Jesus boldly assumed for himself powers that only God has.

Jesus also claimed that he should be honored as God. He said that all men should, "Honor the Son, even as they honor the Father. He who does not honor the Son does not honor the father." The Jews listening knew that no one should claim to be equal with God in this way and again they reached for stones (John 5:18).

Even the Qur'an recognizes that Jesus is the Messiah (5:14, 75). But the Old Testament teaches that the coming Messiah would be God himself. So when Jesus claimed to be that Messiah, he was also claiming to be God. For example, the prophet Isaiah (9:6) calls the Messiah, "Mighty God." The psalmist wrote of the Messiah, "Thy throne, O God, is for ever and ever" (Ps. 45:6; cf. Heb. 1:8). Psalm 110:1 records a conversation between the Father and the Son: "Jehovah said to my Lord (*Adoni*), sit thou at my right hand." Jesus applied this passage to himself in Matthew 22:43–44. In the great messianic prophecy of Daniel 7, the Son of Man is called the "ancient of days" (v. 22), a phrase used twice in the same passage of God the Father (vv. 9, 13). Jesus also said he was the Messiah at his trial before the high priest. When asked, "Are you the Christ [Greek for Messiah], the Son of the Blessed?" Jesus responded, "I am; and you will see the Son of Man sitting at the right hand of Power, and coming with the clouds of heaven." At this, the high priest tore his robe and said, "Why do we still need witnesses? You have heard this blasphemy!" (Mark 14:61–64). There was no doubt that in claiming to be Messiah (see also Luke 24:27; Matt. 26:54), Jesus also claimed to be God.

The Old Testament forbids worshiping anyone other than God (Exod. 20:1–4; Deut. 5:6–9). The New Testament agrees, showing that men refused worship (Acts 14:15) as did angels (Rev. 22:8–9). But Jesus accepted worship on numerous occasions, showing his claim to be God. A healed leper worshiped him (Matt. 8:2), and a ruler knelt before him with a request (Matt. 9:18). After he stilled the storm, "those in the boat worshiped Him saying, 'Truly you are the Son of God'" (Matt. 14:33). A group of Canaanite women (Matt. 15:25), the mother of James and John (Matt. 20:20), the Gerasene demoniac (Mark 5:6), all worshiped Jesus without one word of rebuke. But Christ also elicited worship in some cases, as when Thomas saw the risen Christ and cried out, "My Lord and my God" (John 20:28). This could only be done by a person who seriously considered himself to be God.

Jesus also put his words on a par with God's. "You have heard that it was said to men of old . . . But I say unto you" (Matt. 5:21–22) is repeated over and over again. "All authority in heaven and on earth has been given to me. Go therefore and make disciples of all nations" (Matt. 28:18-19). God had given the Ten Commandments to Moses, but Jesus said, "A new commandment I give to you, that you love one another" (John 13:34). Jesus said, "Till heaven and earth pass away, not an iota, not a dot will pass from the Law" (Matt. 5:18), but later Jesus said of his own words, "Heaven and earth will pass away, but my words will not pass away" (Matt. 24:35). Speaking of those who reject him, Jesus said, "The word that I have spoken will be his judge on the last day" (John 12:48). There is no question that Jesus expected his words to have equal authority with God's declarations in the Old Testament.

Jesus not only asked men to believe in him and obey his commandments, but he also asked them to pray in his name. "Whatever you ask in my name, I will do it. . . . If you ask anything in my name, I will do it" (John 14:13–14). "If you abide in me and my words abide in you, ask whatever you will, and it will be done for you" (John 15:7). Jesus even insisted, "no man comes to the Father, but by me" (John 14:6). In response to this the disciples not only prayed in Jesus' name (1 Cor. 5:4), but prayed to Christ (Acts 7:59). Jesus certainly intended that his name be invoked both before God and as God in prayer.

In view of these many clear ways in which Jesus claimed to be God, any unbiased observer aware of the Gospels should recognize, whether he accepts the claim or not, that Jesus of Nazareth did indeed claim to be God in human flesh. That is, he claimed to be identical to the Jehovah of the Old Testament.

In addition to Jesus' claim about himself, his disciples also acknowledged his claim to deity. This they manifested in many ways.

In agreement with their Master, Jesus' Apostles called him "the first and the last" (Rev. 1:17; 2:8; 22:13), "the true light" (John 1:9), their "rock" or "stone" (1 Cor. 10:4; 1 Pet. 2:6–8; cf. Ps. 18:2; 95:1), the "bridegroom" (Eph. 5:28–33; Rev. 21:2), "the chief Shepherd" (1 Pet. 5:4), and "the great Shepherd" (Heb. 13:20). The Old Testament role of "redeemer" (Hos. 13:14; Ps. 130:7) is given to Jesus in the New Testament (Tit. 2:13; Rev. 5:9). He is seen as the forgiver of sins (Acts 5:31; Col. 3:13; cf. Jer. 31:34; Ps. 130:4) and savior of the world (John 4:42; cf. Isa. 43:3). The apostles also taught that, "Jesus Christ . . . is to judge the living and the dead" (2 Tim. 4:1). All of these titles are given to Jehovah in the Old Testament but to Jesus in the New.

The New Testament opens with a passage concluding that Jesus is Immanuel (God with us), which refers to the messianic prediction of Isaiah 7:14. The very title "Christ" carries the same meaning as the Hebrew appellation "Messiah" (Anointed). In Zechariah 12:10, Jehovah says, "They will look on me whom they have pierced." But the New Testament writers apply this passage to Jesus twice (John 19:37; Rev. 1:7) as referring to his crucifixion. Paul interprets Isaiah's message, "For I am God, and there is no other. . . . To me every knee shall bow and every tongue swear," (Isa. 45:22-23) as applying to his Lord, "at the name of Jesus every knee shall bow . . . and every tongue confess that Jesus Christ is Lord to the glory of God the Father" (Phil. 2:10). The implications of this are strong, because Paul says that all created beings will call Jesus both Messiah (Christ) and Jehovah (Lord).

Some things only God can do, but these very things are attributed to Jesus by his disciples. He is said to be able to raise the dead (John 5, 11) and forgive sins (Acts 5:31; 13:38). Moreover, he is said to have been the primary agent in creating the universe (John 1:2; Col. 1:16) and in sustaining its existence (Col. 1:17). Surely only God can be said to be the Creator of all things, but the disciples claim this power for Jesus.

The disciples' use of Jesus' name as the agent and recipient of prayer has been noted (1 Cor. 5:4; Acts 7:59). Often in prayers or benedictions, Jesus' name is used alongside God's, as in, "grace to you and peace from God the Father and our Lord Jesus Christ" (Gal. 1:3; Eph. 1:2). The name of Jesus appears with equal status to God's in the so-called trinitarian formulas. For example, the command to go and baptize "in *the name* [singular] of the Father, and of the Son, and of the Holy Spirit" (Matt. 28:19, emphasis added). Again this association is made at the end of 2 Corinthians, "The grace of the Lord Jesus Christ and the love of God and the fellowship of the Holy Spirit be with you all" (13:14). If there is only one God, then these three persons must by nature be equated.

Thomas saw his wounds and cried, "My Lord and my God!" (John 20:28). Paul calls Jesus, "the one in whom the fullness of deity dwells bodily" (Col. 2:9). In Titus, Jesus is called, "our great God and savior" (2:13), and the writer to the Hebrews says of him, "Thy throne, O God, is forever" (1:8). Paul says that before Christ existed in the "form of man," which clearly refers to being really human, he existed in the "form of God" (Phil. 2:5–8). The parallel phrases suggest that if Jesus was fully human, then he was also fully God. A similar phrase, "the image of God," is used in Colossians 1:15 to mean the manifestation of God himself. This description is strengthened in Hebrews where it says, "He reflects the glory of God and bears the very stamp of His nature, upholding the universe by the power of His word" (Heb. 1:3). The prologue to John's Gospel also minces no words, stating, "In the beginning was the Word, and the Word was with God, and *the Word [Jesus] was God*" (John 1:1, emphasis ours).

The disciples did not simply believe that Christ was more than a man, they believed him to be greater than any created being including angels. Paul says Jesus is "far above all rule and authority and power and dominion, and above every name that is named, not only in this age but also in that which is to come" (Eph. 1:21). The demons submitted to his command (Matt. 8:32) and even angels that refused to be worshiped are seen worshiping him (Rev. 22:8–9). The author of Hebrews presents a complete argument for Christ's superiority over angels saying, "For to what angel did God ever say, 'Thou art my Son, today I have begotten Thee?' . . . And when He again brings the first-born into the world, He says, 'Let all God's angels worship Him'" (Heb. 1:5–6). There could be no clearer teaching that Christ was not an angel, but God whom the angels were to worship.

In summary, there is manifold testimony from Jesus himself and from those who knew him best that Jesus claimed to be God and that his followers believed that to be the case. They claimed for the carpenter of Nazareth unique titles, powers, prerogatives and activities that apply only to God. Whether or not this was the case, there is no doubt that this is what they believed and what Jesus thought of himself. As C. S. Lewis insightfully observed, when confronted with the boldness of Christ's claims, we are faced with distinct alternatives.

> I am trying here to prevent anyone saying the really foolish things that people often say about Him: "I'm ready to accept Jesus as a great moral teacher, but I don't accept His claim to be God." That is the one thing we must not say. A man who was merely a man and said the sort of thing Jesus said would not be a great moral teacher. He would rather be a lunatic—on a level with the man who says he is a poached egg—Or else he would be the Devil of Hell.[54]

JESUS' MIRACULOUS PROPHETIC CONFIRMATION TO BE GOD

To say that Jesus and his disciples made claims that he was God in human flesh does not in itself prove that he is God. The real question is whether or not there is any good reason to believe that the claims are true. What kind of evidence did Jesus offer to support his claims to deity? The answer is: he offered unique and repeated supernatural confirmations of his claims, the very thing Muhammad recognized as the mark of a true prophet in biblical times (see 2:92, 210, 248). The logic of this argument goes like this:

1. A miracle is an act of God that confirms the truth claim associated with it.
2. Jesus offered unique and multiple lines of miraculous evidence to confirm his claim to be God:

54. C. S. Lewis, *Mere Christianity* (New York: The Macmillan Co., 1943), 55–56.

a) His fulfillment of prophecy,
b) His sinless life and miraculous deeds, and
c) His resurrection from the dead.
3. Therefore, Jesus' unique miracles confirm that he is God.

There were dozens of predictive prophecies in the Old Testament regarding the Messiah. Consider the following predictions made centuries in advance that Jesus would be:

1) born of a woman (Gen. 3:15; cf. Gal. 4:4);
2) born of a virgin (Isa. 7:14; cf. Matt. 1:21f.);
3) "cut off" (die) 483 years after the declaration to reconstruct the city of Jerusalem in 444 B.C. (Dan. 9:24f.);[55]
4) of the seed of Abraham (Gen. 12:1–3 and 22:18; cf. Matt. 1:1 and Gal. 3:16);
5) of the tribe of Judah (Gen. 49:10; cf. Luke 3:23, 33 and Heb. 7:14);
6) of the house of David (2 Sam. 7:12f.; cf. Matt. 1:1);
7) born in Bethlehem (Mic. 5:2; cf. Matt. 2:1 and Luke 2:4–7);
8) anointed by the Holy Spirit (Isa. 11:2; cf. Matt. 3:16–17);
9) heralded by the messenger of the Lord (Isa. 40:3 and Mal. 3:1; cf. Matt. 3:1–2);
10) that Jesus would perform miracles (Isa. 35:5–6; cf. Matt. 9:35);
11) would cleanse the temple (Mal. 3:1; cf. Matt. 21:12f.);
12) would be rejected by Jews (Ps. 118:22; cf. 1 Pet. 2:7);
13) die a humiliating death (Ps. 22 and Isa. 53; cf. Matt. 9:35) involving:
    a) rejection by his own people (Isa. 53:3; cf. John 1:10–11; 7:5, 48);
    b) silence before his accusers (Isa. 53:7; cf. Matt. 27:12–19);
    c) mockery (Ps. 22:7–8; cf. Matt. 27:31);
    d) piercing of his hands and feet (Ps. 22:16; cf. Luke 23:33);
    e) death along with thieves (Isa. 53:12; cf. Matt. 27:44);
    f) prayer for his persecutors (Isa. 53:12; cf. Luke 23:43);
    g) piercing of his side (Zech. 12:10; cf. John 19:34);
    h) burial in a rich man's tomb (Isa. 53:9; cf. Matt. 27:57–60);
    i) casting lots for his garments (Ps. 22:18; cf. John 19:23–24);
14) that he would rise from the dead (Ps. 2:7 and 16:10; cf. Acts 2:31 and Mark 16:6);
15) ascend into heaven (Ps. 68:8; cf. Acts 1:9);
16) and sit at the right hand of God (Ps. 110:1; cf. Heb. 1:3).

---

55. Professor Harold W. Hoehner shows that this was fulfilled to the year when Jesus was crucified in 33 A.D. See his *Chronological Aspects of the Life of Christ* (Grand Rapids: Zondervan, 1976), 115–38.

It is important to understand that these prophecies were written hundreds of years before Christ was born. No one could have been reading the trends of the times or just making intelligent guesses, like the "prophecies" we see in the checkout line at the supermarket. They could not be done by natural powers reading the trends of the times.

Furthermore, unlike the alleged prophecies of Muhammad in the Qur'an (see Chapter 9), notice the specific nature of biblical predictions, pointing to the very time, tribe (Judah), lineage (Davidic), city of birth (Bethlehem) of Christ. What is more, even the most liberal critics admit that the prophetic books were completed at least four hundred years before Christ and the Book of Daniel by about 165 B.C. Though there is good evidence to date most of these books much earlier (some of the Psalms and earlier prophets were in the eighth and ninth centuries B.C.), it would make little difference. It is humanly impossible to make clear, repeated, and accurate predictions two hundred years in the future. But God knows all things and can predict the future with no difficulty. So even using the late date for the Old Testament given by critics, the fulfillment of these prophecies in a theistic universe is miraculous and points to a divine confirmation of Jesus as the Messiah.

Some have suggested that there is a natural explanation for what only seem to be supernatural predictions here. One explanation is that the prophecies were accidentally fulfilled in Jesus. In other words, he happened to be in the right place at the right time. But what are we to say about the prophecies involving miracles? He just happened to make the blind man see? He just happened to be resurrected from the dead? These hardly seem like chance events. If there is a God who is in control of the universe, as we have said, then chance is ruled out. Furthermore, it is unlikely that all these events would have converged in the life of one man. Mathematicians[56] have calculated the probability of 16 predictions being fulfilled in one man at 1 in 10^{45}. If we go to forty-eight predictions, the probability is 1 in 10^{157}. It is almost impossible for us to conceive of a number that big.

But it is not just a logical improbability that rules out this theory; it is the moral implausibility of an all-powerful and all-knowing God letting things get out of control so that all his plans for prophetic fulfillment are ruined by someone who just happened to be in the right place at the right time. God cannot lie, nor can he break a promise (Heb. 6:18). So we must conclude that he did not allow his prophetic promises to be thwarted by chance. All the evidence points to Jesus as the divinely appointed fulfillment of the Messianic prophecies. He was God's man confirmed by God's signs. In brief, if God made the predictions to be ful-

---

56.   Peter W. Stoner, *Science Speaks* (Wheaton: Van Kampen Press, 1952), 108.

filled in the life of Christ, then he would not allow them to be fulfilled in the life of any other. The God of truth would not allow a lie to be confirmed as true.

EVIDENCE OF JESUS' MIRACULOUS AND SINLESS LIFE

The very nature of Christ's life demonstrates his claim to deity. To live a truly sinless life would be a momentous accomplishment for any human being in itself, but to claim to be God and offer a sinless life as evidence is another matter. Muhammad never did.[57] Some of Jesus' enemies brought false accusations against him, but the verdict of Pilate at his trial has been the verdict of history: "I find no crime in this man" (Luke 23:4). A soldier at the cross agreed saying, "Certainly this man was innocent" (Luke 23:47), and the thief on the cross next to Jesus said, "This man has done nothing wrong" (Luke 23:41). But the real test is what those who were closest to Jesus said of his character. His disciples had lived and worked with him for several years at close range, yet their opinions of him are not diminished at all. Peter called Christ, "a lamb without spot or blemish" (1 Pet. 1:19) and added "no guile was found on his lips" (2:22). John called him "Jesus Christ the righteous" (1 John 2:1; cf. 3:7). Paul expressed the unanimous belief of the early church that Christ "knew no sin" (2 Cor. 5:21), and the writer of Hebrews says that Jesus was tempted as a man "yet without sinning" (4:15). Jesus himself once challenged his accusers, "Which of you convicts me of sin?" (John 8:46), but no one was able to find him guilty of anything. He forbid retaliation on one's enemies (Matt. 5:38–42) and, unlike Muhammad, he never used the sword to spread his message (Matt. 26:52). This being the case, the impeccable character of Christ gives a double testimony to the truth of his claim. It provides supporting evidence as he suggested, but it also assures us that he was not lying when he said that he was God.

Beyond the moral aspects of his life, we are confronted with the miraculous nature of Jesus' ministry, which even Muslims acknowledge is a divine confirmation of a prophet's claim. Jesus, however, did perform an unprecedented display of miracles. He turned water to wine (John 2:7f.), walked on water (Matt. 14:25), multiplied bread (John 6:11f.), opened the eyes of the blind (John 9:7f.), made the lame to walk (Mark 2:3f.), cast out demons (Mark 3:11f.), healed the multitudes of all kinds of sickness (Matt. 9:35), including leprosy (Mark 1:40-42), and even raised the dead to life on several occasions (John 11:43–44; Luke 7:11–15; Mark 5:35f.). When asked if he was the Messiah, Jesus used his miracles as evidence to

---

57. Muslims believe in the basic sinlessness of Muhammad and all prophets, at least after becoming a prophet. However, Muhammad fell far short of this claim.

support the claim saying, "Go and tell John what you hear and see: the blind receive their sight and the lame walk, lepers are cleansed and the deaf hear, and the dead are raised up" (Matt. 11:4–5). This special outpouring of miracles was a special sign that the Messiah had come (see Isa. 35:5–6). The Jewish leader Nicodemus even said, "Rabbi, we know that you are a teacher come from God; for no one can do these signs that you do unless God is with Him" (John 3:2). To a first-century Jew, miracles such as Christ performed were clear indications of God's approval of the performer's message. But in Jesus' case, part of that message was that he was God in human flesh. Thus, his miracles verify his claim to be true deity.

JESUS' MIRACULOUS RESURRECTION

The third line of evidence supporting Jesus' claim to be God is the greatest of them all. Nothing like it is claimed by any other religion and no miracle has as much historical evidence to confirm it. Jesus Christ rose from the dead on the third day in the same physical body, now transformed, in which he died. In this resurrected physical body he appeared to more than five hundred of his disciples on twelve different occasions over a forty-day period and conversed with them. Consider the overwhelming evidence summarized in this chart:

THE ORDER OF THE TWELVE APPEARANCES OF CHRIST

PERSONS	SAW	HEARD	TOUCHED	OTHER EVIDENCE
1. Mary (John 20:10–18)	X	X	X	Empty tomb
2. Mary & Women (Matt. 28:1–10)	X	X	X	Empty tomb
3. Peter (1 Cor. 15:5)	X	X*		Empty tomb, Clothes
4. Two Disciples (Luke 24:13–35)	X	X		Ate with him
5. Ten Apostles (Luke 24:36–49; John 20:19–23)	X	X	X**	Saw wounds, Ate food
6. Eleven Apostles (John 20:24–31)	X	X	X**	Saw wounds
7. Seven Apostles (John 21)	X	X		Ate food
8. All Apostles (Matt. 28:16–20; Mark 16:14–18)	X	X		

PERSONS	SAW	HEARD	TOUCHED	OTHER EVIDENCE
9. 500 Brethren (1 Cor. 15:6)	X	X*		
10. James (1 Cor. 15:7)	X	X*		
11. All Apostles (Acts 1:4–8)	X	X		Ate with him
12. Paul (Acts 9:1–9; 1 Cor. 15:8)	X	X		

*Implied   **Offered himself to be touched

The nature, extent, and times of these appearances remove any doubt that Jesus indeed rose from the dead in the numerically same body of flesh and bones in which he died. Notice he appeared to over five hundred people on twelve different occasions scattered over a forty-day period of time (Acts 1:3). During each appearance he was seen and heard with the natural senses of the observer. On four occasions he was either touched or offered himself to be touched. Twice he definitely was touched with physical hands. Four times Jesus ate physical food with his disciples. Four times they saw his empty tomb, and twice he showed them his crucifixion scars. He literally exhausted the ways it is possible to prove that he rose bodily from the grave. No event in the ancient world has more eyewitness verification than does the resurrection of Jesus.

What is even more amazing about the resurrection of Christ is the fact that both the Old Testament and Jesus himself predicted that he would rise from the dead. This highlights the evidential value of the resurrection of Christ in a unique way.

Jewish prophets predicted the resurrection both in specific statements and by logical deduction. First, there are specific passages that the apostles cited from the Old Testament as applying to the resurrection of Christ. Peter says that since we know that David died and was buried, he must have been speaking of the Christ when he said, "Thou wilt not abandon my soul to Hades, nor allow Thy Holy One to undergo decay" (Ps. 16:8–11 quoted in Acts 2:25–31). No doubt it was passages like this that Paul used in the Jewish synagogues when "he argued with them from the scriptures, explaining and proving that it was necessary for the Christ to suffer and to rise from the dead" (Acts 17:2–3).

Also, the Old Testament teaches the resurrection by logical deduction. There is clear teaching that the Messiah was to die (Isa. 53; Ps. 22) and equally evident teaching that he is to have an enduring political reign from Jerusalem (Isa. 9:6; Dan. 2:44; Zech. 13:1). There is no viable way to reconcile these two teachings unless the Messiah who dies is raised from the dead to reign forever.[58] Jesus died before he could begin a reign. Only by his resurrection could the prophecies of a Messianic kingdom be fulfilled.

On several occasions Jesus also predicted his resurrection from the dead. Even in the earliest part of his ministry, he said, "Destroy this temple [of my body] and in three days I will raise it up again" (John 2:19, 21). In Matthew 12:40, later he said, "As Jonah was three days and nights in the belly of the whale, so will the Son of Man be three days and nights in the heart of the earth." To those who had seen his miracles and still stubbornly would not believe, he often said, "An evil and adulterous generation seeks for a sign; and a sign will not be given it, except the sign of Jonah" (Matt. 12:39; 16:4). After Peter's confession, "He began to teach them that the son of man must suffer many things . . . and be killed, and after three days rise again" (Mark 8:31), and this became a central part of his teaching from that point until his death (Mark 14:58; Matt. 27:63). Further, Jesus taught that he would raise himself from the dead, saying of his life, "I have the power to lay it down and I have the power to take it up again" (John 10:18).[59]

In brief, Jesus claimed to be God and proved to be God. He proved it by a convergence of three unprecedented sets of miracles: fulfilled prophecy, a miraculous life, and his resurrection from the dead. This unique convergence of supernatural events not only confirms his claim to be God in human flesh, but it also demonstrates Jesus' claim to be the only way to God. He said, "I am the way, the truth, and the life. No one comes to the Father except by Me" (John 14:6; cf. 10:1, 9–10). Jesus' apostles added, "Nor is there salvation in any other, for there is no other name under heaven given among men by which we must be saved" (Acts 4:12; cf. 1 Tim. 2:5).

ONE LAST OBJECTION

Earlier we showed how David Hume's argument about the self-canceling nature of miracle claims undermined the Muslim claim about Muhammad

58. There is no indication in the Old Testament, as some Jewish scholars have suggested, that there were to be two Messiahs, one suffering and one reigning. References to the Messiah are always in the singular (cf. Dan. 9:26; Isa. 9:6; 53:1f.), and no second Messiah is ever designated.

59. Famous philosopher of science, Karl Popper, argued that whenever a "risky prediction" is fulfilled, it counts as confirmation of the theory that comes with it. If so, then the fulfillment of Jesus' prediction of his own resurrection is confirmation of his claim to be God. For what could be riskier than predicting your own resurrection? If a person will not accept that as evidence of a truth claim, then he has a bias that will not accept anything as evidence.

(see Chapter 4). And we have just shown how this very same argument proves that Christ's claims are miraculously confirmed. It remains now to show that this divine confirmation is unique to Christianity and no other religion.

Hume argues that "every miracle, therefore, pretended to have been wrought in any of these religions (and all of them abound in miracles) . . . so has it the same force, though more indirectly, to overthrow every other system: and in destroying a rival system, it likewise destroys the credit of those miracles on which that system was established." In short, since a miracle's "direct scope is to establish the particular system to which it is attributed, so has it the same force . . . to overthrow every other system."[60] In other words, miracles, being all of the same kind, are self-canceling as witnesses to the truth of a religious system.

Rather than being a disproof of New Testament miracles, Hume's argument unwittingly supports the authenticity of Jesus' miracles. For while this is a sound argument against all non-Christian miracle claims, such as those of Islam, it is not an argument against the unique miracles performed by Christ. We may restate the argument this way.

1. All non-Christian religions (which claim miracles) are supported by similar "miracles" claims.[61]
2. But such "miracles" have no evidential value (since they are self-canceling and based on poor testimony).
3. Therefore, no non-Christian religion is supported by miracles.

If this is so, then one can argue, in addition, that only Christianity is divinely confirmed as true.

1. Only Christianity has unique miracle claims confirmed by sufficient testimony.
2. What has unique miraculous confirmation of its claims is true (as opposed to contrary views).
3. Therefore, Christianity is true (as opposed to contrary views, such as Islam).

SUMMARY

No other world religious leader has been confirmed by a convergence of unique miracles as Jesus has. Indeed, as we have seen (in Chapter 8), Muhammad refused to perform miracles like Jesus did to support his

60. Ibid., 129–30.
61. For a discussion of so-called Satanic miracles and other alleged miracles, see N. L. Geisler, *Signs and Wonders* (Wheaton: Tyndale House, 1988), esp. Chapters 4 through 8.

claim (see 3:181–84). In fact, no other world religious leader claimed to be God, including Muhammad. And, regardless of what they claimed for themselves, no other world religious leader ever proved his claims by fulfilling numerous prophecies made hundreds of years in advance, living a miraculous and sinless life, and predicting and accomplishing his own resurrection from the dead. Thus, Jesus alone deserves to be recognized as the Son of God, God incarnated in human flesh.

12

A DEFENSE OF THE TRINITY

As Christian doctrine, the deity of Christ and the Trinity are inseparable. If one accepts the biblical teaching about the deity of Christ, then he
has already acknowledged that there is more than one person in the Godhead. Conversely, if the doctrine of the Trinity is received, then the deity
of Christ is already part of it. This is precisely why Muslims reject both,
since to accept either is to them a denial of the absolute unity of God.

MUSLIM MISUNDERSTANDING OF BIBLICAL DATA ON THE TRINITY

There are several obstacles in the Muslim mind that hinder accepting
the Christian doctrine of the triunity of God. Some are philosophical and
others are biblical. We have already discussed how Islamic scholars
engage in an arbitrary and selective use of the biblical texts as it suits their
purposes (see Chapter 10). However, even the texts they pronounce
"authentic" are twisted or misinterpreted to support their teachings. An
examination of several of the more important ones will illustrate our
point.

Perhaps no concept in all of Christian terminology receives such a violent reaction from Muslims as Jesus is the "only begotten" son of God.
This raises red flags immediately in the Islamic mind. Indeed, as we shall
see, they understand it in a grossly anthropomorphic manner. Clearing
away this misunderstanding is necessary to open the Muslim mind to the
concept of the Trinity.

The Bible refers to Christ as the "only begotten" Son of God (John
1:18; cf. 3:16). However, Muslim scholars often misconstrue this in a
fleshly, carnal sense of someone literally begetting children. For them, to

beget implies a physical act. This they believe is absurd, since God is a Spirit with no body. As the noted Muslim apologist Deedat contends, "He [God] does not beget because begetting is an animal act. It belongs to the lower animal act of sex. We do not attribute such an act to God."[1] For the Islamic mind begetting is creating and "God cannot create another God. . . . He cannot create another uncreated."[2] The foregoing statements reveal the degree to which the biblical concept of Christ's sonship is misunderstood by Muslim scholars. For no orthodox Christian scholar believes that "begat" is to be equated with "made" or "create." No wonder Dawud concludes that from a "Muslim point of belief the Christian dogma concerning the eternal birth or generation of the Son is blasphemy."[3]

However, this extreme reaction to Christ's eternal Sonship is both unnecessary and unfounded. The phrase "only begotten" does not refer to *physical generation* but to a *special relationship* with the Father. Like the biblical phrase "Firstborn" (Col. 1:15), it means priority in *rank,* not in *time* (cf. vs. 16–17). It could be translated, as the New International Version does, God's "One and Only" Son. It does not imply creation by the Father but unique relation to him. Just as an earthly father and son have a special filial relationship, even so the eternal Father and his eternal Son are uniquely related. It does not refer to any physical generation but to an eternal procession from the Father. Just as for Muslims the Word of God (Qur'an) is not identical to God but eternally proceeds from him, even so for Christians, Christ, God's "Word" (4:171) eternally proceeds from him. Words like "generation" and "procession" are used by Christians of Christ in a filial and relational sense, not in a carnal and physical sense.

Misunderstanding of Christ's sonship reaches an apex when some Muslim scholars confuse it with his virgin Birth. Nazir-Ali notes that "in the Muslim mind the generation of the Son often means his birth of the Virgin Mary."[4] As Shorrosh notes, many Muslims believe Christians have "made Mary a goddess, Jesus her son, and God almighty her husband."[5] With such a carnal misrepresentation of a spiritual reality, little wonder Muslims reject the Christian concept of eternal Father and Son.

Islamic misunderstanding of the Trinity is encouraged by the words of Muhammad who said, "O Jesus, son of Mary! didst thou say unto mankind: Take me and my mother for two gods beside Allah?" (5:119).

1. Ahmed Deedat in a debate with Anis A. Shorrosh cited in Shorrosh, 254.
2. Ibid., 259.
3. Dawud, 205.
4. Nazir-Ali, 29.
5. See Shorrosh, 114.

Even Christians living hundreds of years before Muhammad condemned such a gross misunderstanding of the sonship of Christ. The Christian writer Lactantius, writing about A.D. 306, said, "He who hears the words 'Son of God' spoken must not conceive in his mind such great wickedness as to fancy that God procreated through marriage and union with any female,—a thing which is not done except by an animal possessed of a body and subject to death." Furthermore, "since God is alone, with whom could He unite? or [sic], since He was of such great might as to be able to accomplish whatever He wished, He certainly had no need for the comradeship of another for the purpose of creating."[6] In summation, the Muslim rejection of the eternal sonship of Christ is based on a serious misunderstanding of the Christian concept of what it means for Christ to be God's Son. "Son" should be understood in a figurative sense (like the Arabic word, *ibn*), not in a physical sense (as in the Arabic word, *walad*).

Another text often distorted by Muslim scholars is this great passage proclaiming Christ's deity: "In the beginning was the Word, and the Word was with God, and the Word was God" (John 1:1). Without any textual support in the thousands of Greek manuscripts, they render the last phrase: "and the Word was God's." Muslim scholar Dawud declares, without any warrant whatsoever, "the Greek form of the genitive case 'Theou,' i.e., 'God's' was corrupted into 'Theos'; that is, 'God,' in the nominative form of the name!"[7]

This mistranslation is arbitrary and without any basis in fact, since in the nearly 5,700 manuscripts there is no authority for it whatsoever. Furthermore, it is contrary to the rest of the message of John's Gospel where the claims that Christ is God are repeated over and over (John 8:58; 10:30; 12:41; 20:28).

When Jesus challenged Thomas to believe, after Thomas saw him in his physical resurrection body, Thomas confessed Jesus' deity, declaring, "My Lord and My God" (John 20:28). Many Muslim writers diminish this proclamation of Christ's deity by reducing it to a mere exclamation, "my God!" Deedat declares, "What? He was calling Jesus his Lord and his God? No. This is an exclamation people call out." He adds, "If I said to Anis, 'my God,' would I mean Anis is my God? No. This is a particular expression."[8]

However, there are several clear indications that this is a misunderstanding of Thomas's proclamation. First, in an obvious reference to the content of Thomas's confession of Jesus as "my Lord and my God," Jesus

6. Pfander, 164.
7. See Dawud, 16–17.
8. See Shorrosh, 278.

blessed him for what he had correctly "seen" and "believed" (John 20:29). Second, Thomas's confession of Christ's deity comes at the climax of the Gospel where Jesus' disciples are said to gain increasing belief in Christ based on his miraculous signs (John 2:11; 12:37). Third, Thomas's confession of Christ's deity fits with the stated theme of the Gospel of John "that you may believe that Jesus is the Christ, the Son of God, and that believing you may have life in His Name" (John 20:31).

No doubt there was an exclamatory note in Thomas's pronouncement of Christ's deity, but to reduce it to a meaningless emotional ejaculation both misses the point of the passage and borders on claiming that Jesus blessed Thomas for profanity (i.e., using God's Name in vain).

In Matthew 22:43, citing Psalm 110, Jesus says, "How then does David in the Spirit call Him [the Messiah] 'Lord?'" According to the Muslim scholar Dawud, "By his expression that the 'Lord,' or the 'Adon,' could not be a son of David, Jesus excludes himself from that title."[9]

However, a careful look at the context of this passage reveals just the opposite. Jesus stumped his skeptical Jewish questioners by putting them in a dilemma. How could David call the Messiah "Lord" (as he did in Psalm 110:1), when the Scriptures also say the Messiah would be the "Son of David" (which they do in 2 Sam. 7:12f.)? The only answer to this is that the Messiah must be both man to be David's son (offspring) *and* God to be David's Lord. In other words, in affirming these two truths from Scripture, Jesus is claiming to be both God and man. The Islamic mind should have no more difficulty understanding how Jesus can unite in one person both divine and human natures than their own belief that human beings combine both spirit and flesh, the enduring and the transient in one person (89:27-30; cf. 3:185). For even according to Muslim belief, whatever Almighty God, the Creator and Ruler of all things, wills in his infinite Wisdom he is also able to accomplish for "He is the irresistable" (6:61).[10]

Many Islamic scholars claim that Jesus denied being God when he rebuked the rich young ruler, saying, "Why do you call Me good? No one is good except God alone" (Mark 10:18). However, a careful look at this text in its context reveals that Jesus never denied his deity here. He simply rebuked this wealthy young man for making this careless appellation without thinking through its implication. Nowhere did Jesus say, "I am not God, as you claim." Nor did he say, "I am not good." Indeed, both the Bible and Qur'an teach that Jesus is sinless (John 8:46; Heb. 4:15). Rather, Jesus challenged him to examine what he was really saying when he called Jesus "Good Master." In essence, Jesus was saying, "Do you realize

---

9. See Dawud, 89.

10. Others translate this "He [God] is Omnipotent over His slaves" (Pickthall translation).

what you are saying when you call Me 'Good Master'? Only God is good. Are you calling me God?" The fact that the young ruler refused to do what Jesus said, proves that he did not really consider Jesus his master. But nowhere did Jesus deny that he was either the Master or God of the rich young ruler. Indeed, elsewhere Jesus freely claimed to be both Lord and Master of all (Matt. 7:21–27; 28:18; John 12:40).

Jesus' assertion that "My Father is greater than I" (John 14:28) is also misunderstood by Muslims. It is taken out of its actual context to mean that the Father is greater in *nature*, but Jesus meant only that the Father is greater in *office*. This is evident from the fact that in this same Gospel of John Jesus claims to be the "I Am" or Yahweh of the Old Testament (Exod. 3:14). He also claimed to be "equal with God" (John 10:30, 33). In addition, he received worship on numerous occasions (John 9:38; cf. Matt. 2:11; 8:2; 9:18; 14:33; 15:25; 28:9, 17; Luke 24:52). He also said, "He who does not honor the Son does not honor the Father who sent Him" (John 5:23).

Further, when Jesus spoke of the Father being "greater" it was in the context of his "going to the Father" (John 14:28). Only a few chapters later Jesus speaks to the Father, saying, "I have finished the work which You have given me to do" (John 17:4). But this functional difference of his role as Son in the very next verse reveals that it was not to be used to diminish the fact that Jesus was equal to the Father in nature and glory. For Jesus said, "O, Father, glorify Me together with Yourself, with the glory which I had with You before the world was" (John 17:5).

Another verse misunderstood by Muslim critics is John 17:21, where Jesus said of his disciples, "That they all may be one, as You, Father, are in Me, and I in You; that they also may be one in Us." H. M. Baagil argues on the basis of this that if Jesus is God because he is in God, why are the disciples not God, as they are like Jesus also in God?[11] The misunderstanding here is simple but basic: Jesus is speaking *relationally* not *essentially*. That is, we can have an intimate *relationship* with God as Jesus did. But we cannot be of the same *essence* of God as Jesus was, for he shared God's eternal glory "before the world was" (v. 3). Jesus is in God because he is God. However, we are not in God because we are God, but only because we have a relationship with him.

This survey of some key biblical passages misinterpreted by Muslims illustrates an important point made by an Islamic scholar. He correctly noted that "Christian missionaries, or certain Orientalists who are either themselves theologians, or who are well disposed to Christian theology . . . overestimate the role of Jesus in the Koran. They are misled by the way of understanding Jesus which they retain from their Christian Tradition.

11. *Christian Muslim Dialogue* (Kingdom of Saudi Arabia: Maramer, 1984), 17.

It is no surprise that, under such circumstances, they arrive at false conclusions and evaluations."[12] But this sword cuts both ways. For many Muslim scholars do the same with the Bible, reading their own misunderstanding into the text rather than seeking to understand what the text actually teaches. This is particularly true when it comes to understanding what the Bible claims about God and Christ as the Son of God. So just as Christians should allow Muslims to interpret their own Book (the Qur'an) on these matters, even so Muslims should allow Christians to interpret their own Book (the Bible). For example, just as it is wrong-headed for Christians to twist verses in the Qur'an to teach the deity of Christ, likewise it is misdirected for Muslims to distort verses of the Bible to deny the deity of Christ. For someone to read the New Testament and not see the deity of Christ is like a person looking up on a bright and cloudless day claiming that he cannot see the sun!

MUSLIM MISUNDERSTANDING OF PHILOSOPHICAL CONCEPTS

In addition to misunderstanding the biblical data, Islamic scholars also offer philosophical objections to the doctrine of the Trinity. These too must be cleared away before they will be able to understand the biblical teaching about a plurality of persons within the unity of God.

The emphasis on the oneness of God is fundamental to Islam. One Muslim scholar said, "In fact, Islam, like other religions before it in their original clarity and purity, is nothing other than the declaration of the Unity of God, and its message is a call to testify to this Unity."[13] Another author adds, "The Unity of Allah is the distinguishing characteristic of Islam. This is the purest form of monotheism, i.e., the worship of Allah Who was neither begotten nor beget nor had any associates with Him in His Godhead. Islam teaches this in the most unequivocal terms."[14]

Because of this uncompromising emphasis on God's absolute unity, in Islam the greatest of all sins is the sin of *shirk*, or assigning partners to God. The Qur'an sternly declares "God forgiveth not (The sin of) joining other gods With Him; but He forgiveth Whom He pleaseth other sins Than this: one who joins Other gods with God, Hath strayed far, far away (From the Right)" (4:116). However, as we will see, this is a misunderstanding of the unity of God.

12. Smail Balic, "The Image of Jesus in Contemporary Islamic Theology," in Schimmel and Falaturi, 3.

13. Mahmud, 20.

14. Ajijola, 55.

Both Islam and Christianity proclaim that God is one in essence. What is in dispute is whether there can be any plurality of persons in this unity of nature. The inadequacies in the Muslim view of God arise in part out of their misunderstanding of Christian monotheism. Many Muslims misconstrue the Christian view of God as tritheism rather than as monotheism. This arises because of a misunderstanding of the very nature of trinitarianism. Christians do not confess three gods; they believe in only one God. This is evident from both the biblical base and the theological expression of the doctrine. The Bible declares emphatically: "The Lord our God, the Lord is one!" (Deut. 6:4). Both Jesus (Mark 12:29) and the apostles repeat this formula in the New Testament (1 Cor. 8:4, 6). And early Christian creeds speak of Christ being one in "substance" or "essence" with God. The Athenasian Creed, for example, reads: "We worship one God in Trinity, and Trinity in Unity; Neither confounding the Persons; nor dividing the Substance (Essence)." So Christianity is a form of monotheism in that it believes in one and only one God, not three gods.

Many Muslims complain that the Christian concept of the Trinity is too complex. They forget, however, that truth is not always simple. As C. S. Lewis aptly puts it, "If Christianity was something we were making up, of course we could make it easier. But it is not. We cannot compete, in simplicity, with people who are inventing religions. How could we? We are dealing with Fact. Of course anyone can be simple if he has no facts to bother about."[15]

The fact confronting Christians that led them to formulate this complex truth was, of course, the claim of Jesus of Nazareth to be God (see Chapter 11). This led them of necessity to posit a plurality within deity and thus the doctrine of the Trinity, since this Jesus was not the same as the one whom he addressed as Father. So Christians believe and Muslims deny that there are three persons in this one God. At this point the problem gets philosophical. One aspect of the problem can be expressed in mathematical terms.

Muslim scholars make a big point of computing the mathematical impossibility of the Trinity. After all, does not $1+1+1=3$? It certainly does if you *add* them, but Christians insist that this is the wrong way to understand the Trinity. The triunity of God is more like $1 \times 1 \times 1 = 1$. In other words, we *multiply*, not add, the one God in three persons. That is, God is triune, not triplex. His one essence has multiple personalities. Thus, there is no more mathematical problem in conceiving the Trinity than there is in understanding 1 to the third power (1^3).

---

15. Lewis, *Mere Christianity*, 145.

At the heart of the Muslim inability to understand the Trinity is the Neo-Platonic concept of oneness. The second-century A.D. philosopher, Plotinus, who heavily influenced the thinking of the Middle Ages, viewed God (the Ultimate) as the One, an absolute unity in which is no multiplicity at all. This One was so absolutely simple that it could not even know itself, since self-knowledge implies a distinction between knower and known. It was not until it emanated one level down (in the *Nous*, or Mind) that it could reflect back on itself and therefore know itself. For Plotinus, the One itself was beyond knowing, beyond consciousness, and even beyond being. It was so undividedly simple that in itself it had no mind, thoughts, personality, or consciousness. In brief, it was void of everything, even being. Thus, it could not be known, except by its effects that, however, did not resemble itself.[16]

It is not difficult to see strong similarities between the Plotinian and Muslim views of God (see Chapters 1 and 7). Nor is it hard to see the difficulty with this view. It preserves a rigid unity in God but only at the expense of real personality. It clings to a rigid simplicity but only by sacrificing his relatability. In short, it leaves us with an empty and barren concept of deity. By reducing God to a bare unity we are left with a barren unity. As Joseph Ratzinger insightfully notes,

> The unrelated, unrelatable, absolutely one could not be a person. There is no such thing as a person in the categorical singular. This is already apparent in the words in which the concept of person grew up; the Greek word *"prosopon"* means literally "(a) look towards"; with the prefix *"pros"* (toward) it includes the notion of relatedness as an integral part of itself. . . . To this extent the overstepping of the singular is implicit in the concept of person.[17]

For Muslims God not only has unity but he has singularity. But these are not the same. It is possible to have unity without singularity. For there could be plurality within the unity. Indeed, this is precisely what the Trinity is, namely, a plurality of persons within the unity of one essence. Human analogies help to illustrate the point. My mind, my thoughts, and my words have a unity, but they are not a singularity, since they are all different. Likewise, Christ can be an expression of the same nature as God without being the same person as the Father.

In this connection, Muslim monotheism sacrifices plurality in an attempt to avoid duality. In avoiding the one extreme of admitting any

16. Plotinus, *The Enneads*, trans. Stephen MacKenna (London: Faber and Faber Ltd., 1966), I, 6; III, 8–9; V, 1, 8; VI, 8, 18.

17. Joseph Ratzinger, *Introduction to Christianity*, trans. J. R. Foster (New York: The Seabury Press, 1979), 128–29.

partners to God, Islam goes to the other extreme and denies any personal plurality in God. But, as Joseph Ratzinger observes, "the belief in the Trinity, which recognizes the plurality in the unity of God, is the only way to the final elimination of dualism as a means of expanding plurality alongside unity; only through this belief is the positive validation of plurality given a definite base. God stands above singular and plural. He bursts both categories."[18]

A DEFENSE OF THE BIBLICAL CONCEPT OF THE TRINITY

Since both Muslims and Christians agree that there is at least one person in God, the person Christians call Father, and since we have already given a defense of the Christian belief that Jesus Christ is God the Son (see Chapter 11), it remains only to say a word about the Holy Spirit of God.

The same revelation from God that declares Christ to be the Son of God also mentions another member of the triunity of God called the Spirit of God, or Holy Spirit. He too is equally God with the Father and the Son, and he too is a distinct person. The deity of the Holy Spirit is revealed in several ways. First, he is called "God" (Acts 5:3–4). Second, he possesses the attributes of deity such as omnipresence (cf. Ps. 139:7–12) and omniscience (1 Cor. 2:10–11). Third, he is associated with God the Father in the act of creation (Gen. 1:2). Fourth, he is involved with the other members of the Godhead in the work of redemption (John 3:5–6; Rom. 8:9f.; Titus 3:5–7). Fifth, he is associated with the other members of the Trinity under the one "name" of God (Matt. 28:18–20). Finally, the Holy Spirit appears along with the Father and Son in Christian benedictions (2 Cor. 13:14).

Not only does the Holy Spirit possess deity but he also has his own personality. He is one with God in essence but different in person. That he is a distinct person is clear from several basic facts. The Holy Spirit is addressed with the personal pronoun "he" (John 14:26; 16:13). He does things only persons can do, such as teach (John 14:26; 1 John 2:27), convict of sin (John 16:7–7), and be grieved by our sin (Eph. 4:30). Finally, the Holy Spirit has all the characteristics of personality, namely, intellect (1 Cor. 2:10–11), will (1 Cor. 12:11), and feeling (Eph. 4:30).

That the three members of the Trinity are distinct persons, and not one and the same person is clear from the fact that each person is mentioned in distinction from the other. For one thing, the Father and Son carried on conversations with each other. The Son prayed to the Father (John 17). The Father spoke from heaven about the Son at his baptism

18. Ibid.

(Matt. 3:15–17). Indeed, the Holy Spirit was present at the same time, revealing that they are three distinct persons, coexisting simultaneously. Further, the fact that they have separate titles (Father, Son, and Spirit) indicate they are not one person. Also, each member of the Trinity has special functions that help us to identify them. For example, the Father planned salvation (John 3:16; Eph. 1:4); the Son accomplished it by the Cross (John 17:4; 19:30; Heb. 1:1–2) and resurrection (Rom. 4:25; 1 Cor. 15:1–6), and the Holy Spirit applies it to the lives of the believers (John 3:5; Eph. 4:30; Titus 3:5–7). The Son submits to the Father (1 Cor. 11:3; 15:28), and the Holy Spirit glorifies the Son (John 16:14).

The doctrine of the Trinity cannot be proven by human reason; it is only known because it is revealed by special revelation (in the Bible). However, just because it is beyond reason does not mean that it goes against reason. It is not irrational or contradictory, as Muslim scholars believe.

The philosophical law of noncontradiction informs us that something cannot be both true and false at the same time and in the same sense. This is the fundamental law of all rational thought, and the doctrine of the Trinity does not violate it. This can be shown by stating first of all what the Trinity is not. The Trinity is not the belief that God is three persons and only one person at the same time and in the same sense. That would be a contradiction. Rather, it is the belief that there are three persons in one *nature*. This may be a mystery, but it is not a contradiction. That is, it may go beyond reason's ability to comprehend completely, but it does not go against reason's ability to apprehend consistently.

Further, the Trinity is not the belief that there are three natures in one nature or three essences in one essence. That would be a contradiction. Rather, Christians affirm that there are three *persons* in one *essence*. This is not contradictory because it makes a distinction between person and essence. Or, to put it in terms of the law of noncontradiction, while God is one and many at the same time, he is not one and many in the *same sense*. He is one in the sense of his essence but many in the sense of his persons. So there is no violation of the law of noncontradiction in the doctrine of the Trinity.

Perhaps a model of the Trinity will help to grasp its intelligibility. When we say God has one essence and three persons we mean he has one What and three Whos. Consider the following diagram:

Notice that the three Whos (persons) each share the same What (essence). So

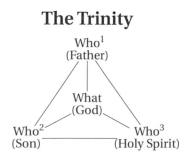

The Trinity

Who[1]
(Father)

What
(God)

Who[2]   Who[3]
(Son)   (Holy Spirit)

God is a unity of essence with a plurality of persons. Each person is different, yet they share a common nature.

God is one in his substance but three in his relationships. The unity is in his essence (what God is), and the plurality is in God's persons (how he relates). This plurality of relationships is both internal and external. Within the Trinity each member relates to the other in a certain way. For example, the Father is related to the Son as Father, and the Son is related to the Father as Son. That is their external and internal relationship by the very makeup of the Trinity. Also, the Father sends the Spirit, and the Spirit testifies of the Son (John 14:26). These are their functions by their very participation in the unity of the Godhead. Each having a different relationship to the other, but all sharing the same essence.

No analogy of the Trinity is perfect, but some are better than others. First, some bad illustrations should be repudiated. The Trinity is *not* like a chain with three links. For these are three separate and separable parts, but God is neither separated or separable. Neither is God like the same actor playing three different parts in a play. For God is simulateously three persons, not one person playing three sucessive roles. Nor is God like the three states of water: solid, liquid, and gaseous. For normally water is not in all three of these states at the same time, but God is always three persons at the same time. Unlike other bad analogies, at least this one does not imply tritheism. However, it does reflect another heresy known as modalism.

Most erroneous illustrations of the Trinity tend to support the charge that trinitarianism is really tritheism, since they contain separable parts. The more helpful analogies retain unity while they show a simultaneous plurality. There are several that fit this description.

A Mathematical Illustration of the Trinity. As noted above, God is like 1^3 (1x1x1). Notice there are three ones but they equal only one, not three. This is precisely what there is in God, namely, three persons who are only one God. Of course, no illustration of the Trinity is perfect, but this does show how there can be both three and one at the same time in an indivisible reationship. Viewed in this way it is a good illustration of the Trinity.

A Geometric Illustration of the Trinity. Perhaps the most widely used illustration of the Trinity is the triangle. It is usually put in this form.

Notice that there is only one triangle, yet there are three corners. Observe also that, if there is to be a triangle, these corners must be inseparable and simultaneous. In this sense it is a good illustra-

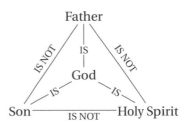

tion of the Trinity. Of course, the triangle is finite and God is infinite, so it is not a perfect illustration. But for the point it is trying to make it serves its purpose well. Also, by adding a circle touching (but not overlapping) with the lower left corner of the triangle, some of the mystery can be taken from the way the two natures of Christ relate to his one person.

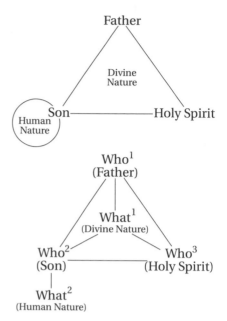

We must point out that Christ is one person (the lower left point of the triangle), yet he has two natures. His divine nature is the triangle and his human nature is the circle touching it. They unite at that point. That is, his two natures are cojoined in one person. Or, in terms of the above model, in Christ there are two Whats and one Who, whereas, in God there are three Whos and one What.

It should be pointed out in this connection that there are two ways *not* to diagram the relation between the two natures of Christ. Each is considered a heresy by orthodox Christians.

Monophysite Error   Nestorian Error

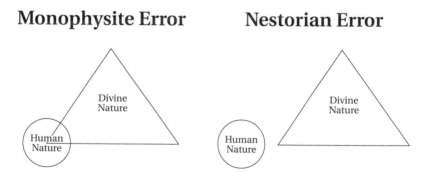

In the first diagram where the circle overlaps with the triangle we have the monophysite heresy that confuses the two natures of Christ. This is not only heresy but is also an absurdity, since the divine nature of Christ is infinite and the human nature is finite. And it is impossible to have an infinite finite, an unlimited limited.

The second diagram where the circle and triangle do not even touch is the Nestorian heresy, which posits two persons as well as two natures in

Christ. If this were so, then when Christ sacrificed his life on the cross, it was not the person who is also divine, the Son of God, who died for us. In this case, the atoning sacrifice of Christ would have no divine value and could not be efficacious for our sins. Only if one and the same person, who is both God and man, dies on the cross for our sin can we be saved. For unless Jesus is both God and man he cannot reconcile God and man. But the Bible says clearly, "there is one God, and one mediator between God and man, the man Christ Jesus" (1 Tim. 2:5).

Since Christ is one Who (person) with two Whats (natures), whenever one question is asked about him it must be separated into two questions, one applying to each nature. For example, did he get tired? Answer: as God, no; as man, yes. Did Christ get hungry? In his divine nature, no; in his human nature, yes. Did Christ die? In his human nature, he did die. But in his divine nature he did not die. The person who died was the God-man, but his Godness did not die.

When this same logic is applied to other theological questions raised by Muslims it yields the same kind of answer. Did Jesus know everything? As God he did, since God is omniscient. But as man Jesus said he did not know the time of his second coming (Matt. 24:36), and as a child he didn't know everything, since "he increased in wisdom" (Luke 2:52).

Another often asked question is: Could Jesus sin? The answer is the same: as God he could not have sinned; as man he could have sinned (but he didn't). God cannot sin. For example, the Bible says "it is impossible for God to lie" (Heb. 6:18; cf. Titus 1:2). Yet Jesus was "in all points tempted as we are, yet without sin" (Heb. 4:15). That is to say, while he never sinned (2 Cor. 5:21; 1 Pet. 1:19; 1 John 3:3), he was really tempted and therefore it was possible for him to sin. Otherwise, his temptation would have been a charade. Jesus possessed the power of free choice, which means that whatever moral choice he made, he could have done otherwise. This means that when he chose not to sin (which was always), he could have sinned (but did not) as man.

Dividing every question of Christ into two and referring them to each nature unlocks a lot of theological puzzles that otherwise remain shrouded in mystery. And it makes it possible to avoid alleged logical contradictions that are urged upon Christians by Muslims and by other nonbelievers.

A Moral Illustration of the Trinity. One illustration, suggested by St. Augustine, has value in illuminating the Trinity. The Bible informs us that "God is love" (1 John 4:16). But love is triune, since it involves a lover, the loved one (beloved), and a spirit of love between them. To apply this to the Trinity, the Father is the Lover; the Son is the Beloved (i.e., the One loved), and the Holy Spirit is the Spirit of love. Yet love is one—three in one. This illustration has the advantage of being personal, since it involves love, a characteristic that flows only from persons.

An Anthropological Illustration. Since man is made in the image of God (Gen. 1:27), it should be no surprise that he bears some kind of similarity to the Trinity in human beings. First, we wish to disown trichotomy (that man is body, soul, and spirit) as an appropriate illustration of the Trinity. For even if true (and many Christians reject it for a dichotomy of just body and soul), it would be a bad illustration. Body and soul can be and are separated at death (2 Cor. 5:8; Phil. 1:23; Rev. 6:9), but the nature and persons of the Trinity cannot be separated.

A better illustration based in human nature would be, as suggested earlier, the relation between our mind, its ideas, and the expression of these ideas in words. There is obviously a unity among all three of these without there being an identity. In this sense, they illustrate the Trinity.

Islamic Illustrations of Plurality in Unity. Perhaps the best illustration of a plurality in deity for the Muslim mind is, as we mentioned earlier (in Chapter 11), the relation between the Qur'an and God. As one Islamic scholar stated it, the Qur'an "is an expression of Divine Will. If you want to compare it with anything in Christianity, you must compare it with Christ Himself. Christ was the expression of the Divine among men, the revelation of the Divine Will. That is what the Qur'an is."[19] Orthodox Muslims believe the Qur'an is eternal and uncreated, yet it is not the same as God but is an expression of God's mind as imperishable as God himself. Surely, there is here a plurality within unity, something that is other than God but is nonetheless one with God. Indeed, the very fact that Muslim scholars see an analogy with the Christian doctrine of the deity of Christ reveals the value of this illustration. For Muslims hold that there are two eternal and uncreated things but only one God. And Christians hold to three uncreated and eternal persons but only one God.

Further, some have pointed to the fact that Muhammad was simultaneously a prophet, a husband, and a leader. Why then should a Muslim reject the idea of a plurality of functions (persons) in God. Within the Islamic system is the very proof that plurality within unity, as it relates to God, is not unintelligible. By the same token, then, there is no reason Muslims should reject the doctrine of the Trinity as nonsensical.

SUMMARY

At the heart of the difference between Islam and Christianity stands the Christian doctrine of the Trinity. Muslims protest that it is neither biblical nor intelligible. Yet we have seen that in order to maintain the

19. Yusuf K. Ibish in an article entitled, "The Muslim Lives by the Qur'an," cited by Waddy, 14.

former they have twisted scriptural texts out of context. And to hold the latter, to be consistent, they must reject not only clear logical distinctions but their own view of the relation of the Qur'an to God. In brief, there is no good reason to reject the doctrine of the Trinity. Furthermore, we provided evidence (in Chapter 11) that Christ is indeed the Son of God. Thus, Christian trinitarianism, with all its richness of interpersonal relations within the Godhead and with God's creatures, is to be preferred over a barren and rigid Muslim monotheism.

13

A DEFENSE OF SALVATION BY THE CROSS

As we have already seen (in Chapter 6), Islamic theology is violently opposed to salvation by grace through faith, based on the crucified and risen Christ. There are many reasons Muslims reject the orthodox Christian view of salvation, but several stand out.

First, it implies that humans are inherently sinful and in need of salvation, but Islam flatly rejects the Christian doctrine of depravity. Second, it rejects the Christian claim that Jesus is the Son of God who, by his death as the God-man, brought reconciliation between humankind and God. Third, the idea of God allowing a prophet of his to suffer an ignominious death like crucifixion is contrary to the Islamic concept of God's providential care for his special servants.

Cragg writes,

> The immediate impression on the general reader from what the Qur'an has to tell him about Jesus is that of its brevity. . . . It is further surprising that within the limits of some ninety verses in all no less than sixty-four belong to the extended, and partly duplicate, nativity stories. . . . This leaves a bare twenty-six or so verses to present the rest and some reiteration here reduces the total still further. It has often been observed that the New Testament Gospels are really passion narratives with extended introduction. It could well be said that the Jesus cycle in the Qur'an is nativity narratives with attenuated sequel.[1]

1. Cragg, *Jesus and the Muslim*, 25–26.

Cragg adds that "Jesus had a specific—some would say a limited—mission to Jewry is stressed in the Qur'an. Only Muhammad as the 'seal of the prophets' belongs to all times and places." Thus, "the 'universality' which Christianity is alleged to have 'read into' Jesus, violating this more explicitly Jewish vocation, is seen as part of that de-Semiticisation of Jesus' Gospel, which is attributed to the early Gentile Church."[2]

Many Western scholars find Muhammad's reason for dismissing the Christian doctrine of salvation through the cross in the fact the major prophets in history have always been victorious against their enemies. If the Christ of God were killed on the cross by his adversaries, then what would have become of the constant Qur'anic theme that those who did not obey God's prophet did not triumph? Was not the admission of the cross an acknowledgment that the unrighteous had ultimately triumphed over the righteous?[3]

We will discuss the Islamic understanding of salvation by the sacrificial death and resurrection of Christ. Then we will evaluate their view, offering criticisms from a Christian perspective.

MUSLIM MISUNDERSTANDINGS OF CHRISTIAN SALVATION

While Muslims believe, as Christians do, in the virgin birth, as well as the death, resurrection, ascension, and second coming of Christ, it is easy to overstate these misleading similarities. At the very heart of Christianity (1 Cor. 15:1–6) is the belief that Jesus died on the cross for humankind's sins and rose again three days later. But Islam categorically rejects this teaching. Most Muslims do not believe Jesus died on the cross, and none believe he paid the penalty for the sins of the world there. Further, while Islam teaches the resurrection of Christ, it is usually only viewed as part of the general resurrection on the last day. Thus while they hold that Jesus ascended into heaven after his time on earth, most do not believe that he was resurrected before his ascension. And none believe he was resurrected three days after his crucifixion. In fact, almost no Muslim scholars believe that Christ was crucified at all and those that do have been condemned as heretical.

Further, for Muslims, Christ's second coming is not, as Christians believe, to set up a kingdom on earth but to tell Christians to follow Muhammad. According to one Muslim tradition, "Jesus, son of Mary, will descend to the earth, will marry, have children, and live 45 years, after which he will die and be buried along with me [Mohammad] in my grave.

2. Ibid., 27.
3. Bell, 154.

Then Jesus, son of Mary, and I shall arise from the grave between Abu Bakr and Umar."[4]

Muslim Scholar Shaikh Ahmed Zaki Yamani declared that "in the great debate between Christians and Muslims . . . there are areas of fundamental principles where no amount of logical discourse can bring the two sides nearer to each other and where therefore the existence of an impasse must be recognized." Thus "issues like the Trinity, the Divinity of Christ and the Crucifixion, so central to Christian beliefs, have no place in the Islamic faith, having been categorically refuted by the Quran."[5] Muslims are so vehemently opposed to belief in the crucifixion of Christ that some label it demonic. Ibn Taymiyya declared that "the first goal of the demon is to lead people astray by delivering to them false information, as did the one who informed the apostles that he was Christ who was crucified."[6]

MUSLIM MISUNDERSTANDING ABOUT CHRIST'S DEATH

Muslim misunderstanding of the crucifixion is represented in the statement of Ibn Taymiyya, that "not a single one of the Christians was a witness with them [the Jews]. Rather the apostles kept a distance through fear, and not one of them witnessed the crucifixion."[7] This, of course, is both false and misleading. It is false because the Gospel record states that the apostle John was standing right there by the cross during the crucifixion (John 19:26; cf. 20:20–25). And Peter may have been there at a distance (see Mark 14:54). Furthermore, in addition there were other followers of Christ at the cross, including Mary the mother of Jesus (John 20:25–26) and other women (Luke 23:27; John 19:25). It is misleading because it implies that one cannot be sure that Jesus died on the cross unless his apostles were there. The Roman soldiers charged under the penalty of death to faithfully execute their duty were sufficient witnesses to the death of Christ. They were professional executioners and were accustomed to putting people to death. Furthermore, there were other people present, including the two thieves on adjacent crosses (Matt. 27:38), the crowd (Matt. 27:39) called "a great multitude" (Luke 23:27), and the Jew-

---

4. A. R. I. Doi, "The Status of Prophet Jesus in Islam-II," in *Muslim World League Journal* (June 1982), 23. According to the Islamic tradition (*sound hadith*) Muhammad said, "It is impending that the son of Mary will descend among you as a just judge, a righteous *imam*; he will break the cross, kill the pig, and impose the *jizya* [a special tax on unbelievers paid to Muslim rulers for their protection]." Ibn Taymiyya, 306.

5. Ahmed Zaki Yamani, in Watt, *Islam and Christianity Today*, ix–x.

6. Ibn Taymiyya, 110.

7. Ibid., 305.

ish leaders (Matt. 27:41), who because of their hatred of him had every motivation to assure that Jesus was put to death there. Even if none of Jesus' followers were there—and several were—the many other witnesses of the crucifixion would have been more than enough to establish the fact of his death.

The evidence that Jesus actually died physically on the cross is overwhelming. For one, the Old Testament predicted it (Isa. 53:5–10; Ps. 22:16; Dan. 9:26; Zech. 12:10), and Jesus fulfilled the Old Testament prophecies about the Messiah (Matt. 4:14; 5:17–18; 8:17; John 4:25–26; 5:39). Furthermore, Jesus announced it in advance over and over again (Matt. 12:40; 17:22–23; 20:18; Mark 10:45; John 2:19–20; John 10:10–11). Also, all the predictions of his resurrection (Ps. 16:10; Isa. 26:19; Dan. 12:2; John 2:19–21; Matt. 12:40; 17:22–23) are based on the fact that he would die. Only a dead body can be resurrected. What is more, the nature and extent of Jesus' injuries indicate that he must have died, the very process of crucifixion assuring his death. Likewise, the piercing of Jesus' side with the spear, from which came "blood and water" (John 19:34), is medical proof that he had physically died. Also, Jesus declared his own death at its very moment, saying, "Father, into Your hands I commend My spirit" (Luke 23:46; cf. John 19:30). And Jesus' death cry was heard by those who stood by (John 19:47–49). Furthermore, the Roman soldiers, accustomed to crucifixion and death, pronounced Jesus dead (John 19:33). On top of all this, Pilate double-checked to make sure Jesus was dead before he gave the corpse to Joseph to be buried (Mark 15:44–45). In addition, Jesus was wrapped in about seventy-five pounds of cloth and spices and placed in a sealed tomb for three days (John 19:39–40; Matt. 27:60). If he was not dead by then, which he clearly was, he would have died from lack of food, water, and medical treatment. Finally, medical authorities who have carefully examined the evidence have concluded that he actually died on the cross, insisting that "the weight of historical and medical evidence indicates that Jesus was dead before the wound to his side was inflicted.... Accordingly, interpretations based on the assumption that Jesus did not die on the cross appear to be at odds with modern medical knowledge."[8]

Muslim ambiguity about the death of Christ has led to a rather confusing state of affairs that can be clarified as follows:

1) All Muslims agree that Jesus did not die on the cross for our sins.

8. See the article on Christ's death in the *Journal of the American Medical Association* (March 21, 1986), 1463.

2) Almost all Muslims believe that Jesus did not die on the cross at all but that someone else was crucified in his place, such as Judas (see Appenix 2) or Simon who carried Jesus' cross.
3) Almost all Muslims hold that Jesus did not die at all before he ascended into heaven but that he will die after his second coming and will be raised later with others in the general resurrection of the last days.

Mufassir summarized the heart of the Islamic view well when he said, "Muslims believe that Jesus was not crucified. It was the intention of his enemies to put him to death on the cross, but God saved him from their plot."[9] Several passages in the Qur'an are the basis for Muslim agreement that Jesus was not crucified on the cross for our sins; 4:157–58 is a key text. At face value it seems to say that Jesus did not die at all. It certainly denies that he died by crucifixion. It reads:

> That they said (in boast), "We killed Christ Jesus the son of Mary, the Apostle of God";—But they killed him not, Nor crucified him, But so it was made to appear to them, And those who differ therein are full of doubts, With no (certain) knowledge, But only conjecture to follow, for of a surety they killed him not:—Nay, God raised him up Unto Himself; and God Is exalted in power, wise.

The reason for Islamic disbelief in the crucifixion of Jesus centers on two theological concepts: sovereignty and depravity. More precisely, it is based on the unique Islamic concept of sovereignty of God and their rejection of the Christian belief in the depravity of man.

The Muslim view of God's sovereignty as the reason for rejection of the crucifixion of Christ is reflected in the following text:

> Say, Who then can do aught against Allah, if He had willed to destroy the Messiah son of Mary, and his mother and everyone on earth? Allah's is the Sovereignty of the heavens and the earth and all that is between them. He createth what He will: And Allah is Able to do all things (5:17).

A sovereign God has control over all things. And he would not allow his servant to suffer such an ignominious death at the hands of his enemies as a crucifixion. Rather, a sovereign God, such as Allah, would deliver his servant from his enemies. Abdalati, in a typical Muslim fashion, asks, "Is it consistent with God's Mercy and Wisdom to believe that Jesus was humiliated and murdered the way he is said to have been?"[10] As the

---

9. Mufassir, 5.
10. Abdalati, 160.

Qur'an states, "When Allah said: O Jesus! Lo! I am gathering thee and causing thee to ascend unto Me, and am cleansing thee of those who disbelieve and am setting those who follow thee above those who disbelieve until the Day of Resurrection" (3:55).

This argument, however, is highly debatable for many reasons. For one thing, this is a humanly devised idea of what God would or would not do. But it is utterly presumptuous for mortal man to tell a sovereign God (as Muslims believe him to be) how he should or should not act. As the prophet Isaiah informs us, God said, "My thoughts are not your thoughts, Nor are your ways My ways" (Isa. 55:8). Indeed, even Muslims believe that God is omnipotent and can do anything he pleases to do (Sura 30:5).

Further, the very concept of sovereignty held by Muslims is that God can do anything. Why then could God have not permitted Jesus to be crucified, if he had wished?

For another thing, the prophet Isaiah instructs us that God did indeed approve of the ignominious death of his Servant, declaring: "He has no form of comeliness; And when we see Him, There is no beauty that we should desire Him. He is despised, and rejected by men, A Man of sorrows and acquainted with grief. And we hid as it were our faces from Him; . . . Yet we esteemed Him stricken, Smitten by God, and afflicted." "But," he continues, "He was wounded for our transgressions, He was bruised for our iniquities; the chastisement of our peace was upon Him, And by His stripes we are healed" (Isa. 53:2–5). So Jesus' crucifixion was not only approved by God, it was predicted (cf. Zech. 12:10; Ps. 22:16). It should be no surprise to a reader of the New Testament that the message of the crucifixion is offensive to unbelievers. Indeed, Paul even referred to the "offense of the cross" but added that "it pleased God through the foolishness of the message preached to save those who believe" (1 Cor. 1:21). For "the foolishness of God is wiser than men" (v. 25).

Indeed, even the Qur'an gives a beautiful example of a substitutionary atonement in Abraham's sacrifice of his son on Mount Moriah:

> He said: "O my son! I see in vision that I offer thee in *sacrifice.* . . . "So when they had both Submitted their wills (to God), And he laid him Prostrate on his forehead (For *sacrifice*), We [God] called out to him, "O Abraham! . . . And We *ransomed* him With a momentous *sacrifice*" (37:102–7, emphasis ours).

The use of the words "sacrifice" and "ransom" are precisely what Christians mean by Christ's death on the cross. In fact, Jesus used such words of his own death (Mark 10:45). So the sacrificial death of Christ is not un-Qur'anic.

Then, too, the whole idea of God allowing insulting experiences to happen to his servant is not un-Muslim. Muhammad's biographer,

Haykal, tells of insulting experiences suffered by Muhammad. He notes, for example, that "the tribe of Thaqif, however, not only repudiated Muhammad's call but sent their servants to insult him and throw him out of their city. He ran away from them and took shelter near a wall. . . . There he sat under a vine pondering his defeat with the sight of the sons of Rabi'ah."[11]

What is more, even if Muslims assume that God will deliver his prophets from their enemies, it is wrong to conclude that he did not deliver Christ from his enemies. Indeed, this is precisely what the resurrection is. For "God raised [Christ] up, having loosed the pains of death, because it was not possible that He should be held by it" (Acts 2:24). According to the Scriptures, God raised Christ up because, as he said: "You are My son, Today I have begotten You [from the dead]" (Acts 13:33). Further, the Scriptures declare that God kept his promise to his people (in Ps. 16:10) and saw to it that "His [Christ's] soul was not left in Hades, nor did His flesh see corruption" (Acts 2:31). Thus, "He was exalted to the right hand of God" (v. 33). Indeed, it was by Christ's death and resurrection that "death is swallowed up in victory" (1 Cor. 15:54), and we can say, "O Death, where is your sting? O Hades, where is your victory?" (1 Cor. 15:55).

Finally, the death and resurrection of Christ did, contrary to Islamic teaching, manifest God's mercy. Indeed, without it there would have been no mercy for a sinful world. Paul wrote: "For when we were still without strength, in due time Christ died for the ungodly." Thus "God demonstrated His own love toward us, in that while we were still sinners, Christ died for us" (Rom. 5:6, 8). He adds elsewhere that it is "not by works of righteousness which we have done, but according to His [God's] mercy He saved us" (Titus 3:5). As Jesus himself said, "Greater love has no one than this, than to lay down one's life for his friends" (John 15:13). Yet he died for us when "we were [His] enemies" (Rom. 5:10).

The other Muslim reason given for rejecting the crucifixion is the concomitant doctrine of depravity. Islamic scholars are quick to point out the connection between the Christian claim that Jesus died on the cross for our sins and the doctrine of depravity. Doi notes that "connected with the Christian belief in crucifixion of Isa [Jesus] is the irreconcilable concept of original sin."[12] He adds categorically that "Islam does not believe in the doctrine of the original sin (see Chapter 2). It is not Adam's sin that a child inherits and manifests at birth. Every child is born sinless and the sins of the fathers are not visited upon the children." Further, "Islam denies emphatically the concept of original sin and hereditary depravity.

---

11. Haykal, 137.
12. See Doi, 23.

Every child is born pure and true; every departure in after-life from the path of truth and rectitude is due to imperfect education." Citing the prophet Muhammad, Doi affirms that "Every child is born in a religious mold; it is his parents who make him afterward a Jew, a Christian, or a Sabaean. . . . In other words, good and evil is not created in man at birth. Infants have no positive moral character." Rather, "every human being . . . has two inclinations—one prompting him to do good and impelling him thereto, and the other prompting him to do evil and thereto impelling him; but the assistance of God is nigh."[13]

But here again the rejection of total depravity is without foundation for many reasons. Even Muslims have to acknowledge that human beings are sinful. Otherwise, why do they need God's mercy? Indeed, why do they believe that so many (including all Christians) have committed the greatest of all sins, attributing partners to God (4:116)? Further, why did God need to send prophets to warn them of their sin, if they are not constant sinners? Also, why are the unbelievers sent to hell to suffer? This seems to imply great sinfulness to deserve such a severe penalty as suffering in hell. Finally, it is both unrealistic and un-Qur'anic to deny the inherent sinfulness of humankind. Indeed, "some Muslim theologians have held to a doctrine of Hereditary Sin. . . . Also, there is a famous tradition that the Prophet of Islam said, 'No child is born but the devil hath touched it, except Mary and her son Jesus.'"[14] Further, "Other passages refer to humankind as sinful (or unjust—*zulum*—14:34/37; 33:72), foolish (33:72), ungrateful (14:34/37), weak (4:28/32), despairing or boastful (11:9/12–10/13), quarrel-some (16:4), and rebellious (96:6)."[15] The Qur'an even declares that "if God were to punish Men for their wrong-doing, He would not leave, on the (earth), A single living creature" (16:61). Ayatollah Khomeini even went so far as to say "that man's calamity is his carnal desires, and this exists in everybody, and is rooted in the nature of man."[16] In view of these admissions there is no reason to reject the Christian doctrine of the depravity of humankind.

A DEFENSE OF THE CHRISTIAN VIEW OF SALVATION

We will divide our comments into two broad categories. First, we will offer a response to the Islamic misunderstanding of salvation by the cru-

13. Ibid., 20.
14. Nazir-Ali, 165.
15. For an excellent discussion on this subject see Woodberry, 155.
16. From an article in an Iranian newspaper as cited by Woodberry, 159.

cifixion/death and resurrection of Christ. Then, we will give a rationale for the Christian position on salvation, in hope of rendering the credible intelligible to the Muslim mind.

Totally apart from the nature of the Islamic rejection of human depravity, it is not a sufficient basis for rejecting a historical fact such as the crucifixion of Christ. The factual evidence for Christ's death on the cross "under Pontius Pilate" is more than ample (see discussion above), and it stands on its own apart from any theological beliefs.

INADEQUATE BASIS FOR REJECTING THE DEATH OF CHRIST

Indeed, even granting what Muslims admit about Christ's crucifixion and death, there is no reason to reject the biblical account. For example, Muslims teach that:

1) Jesus would die (3:55; cf. 19:33).[17]
2) Jesus would one day rise from the dead (19:33).[18]
3) Jesus' disciples who witnessed the event believed that it was Jesus, not someone else in his place, who was crucified on the cross.
4) The Roman soldiers and the Jews believed that it was Jesus of Nazareth whom they had crucified.
5) Jesus could and did perform miracles, including raising people from the dead.

If 1) and 2) are accepted by Muslims, then there is no reason they should reject the fact that Jesus died on the Cross and raised himself from the dead.

Implausible Muslim speculation, such as Judas or Simon died in Jesus' place or that he only swooned on the cross, does not help their already flimsy hypothesis (see Appendix 2). Al-Tabari, well-known Muslim historian and commentator on the Qur'an, reports that Wahab B. Munabih, who lived around A.D. 700 propagated the lore that someone was substituted for Jesus on the Cross. His version is reported as follows:

> They brought him the gibbet on which they intended to crucify him, but God raised him up to Himself and a simulacrum was crucified in his place. He remained there for seven hours, and then his mother and another woman whom He had cured of madness came to weep for him. But Jesus

17. However, most Muslims believe that Jesus did not die while on earth the first time but will only die after he returns to earth at his second coming.

18. Muslims believe that Jesus will only rise from the dead in the general resurrection after he returns to earth and dies.

came to them and said, "God has raised me up to Himself, and this is a mere simulacrum."[19]

Another example of the growth of this legendary tradition of Islam is found in the view of Thalabi, who lived some three hundred years after Munabih. "The shape of Jesus was put on Judas who has pointed him out, and they crucified him instead, supposing that he was Jesus. After three hours God took Jesus to Himself and raised him up to heaven."[20]

More recently, Doi offers the hypothesis that when the Roman soldiers came with Judas to arrest Jesus "the two Jews got mixed up in the dark, and the soldiers mistakenly arrested Judas instead of Jesus. Jesus was thus saved and raised up."[21] In support of this view Muslims often cite the spurious *Gospel of Barnabas* (see Appendix 3).

Substitution legends are not unique to Islam. Some early opponents of Christianity offered similar speculations. According to the second-century church father Frenacus, Basilides the gnostic taught that "at the Crucifixion He [Jesus] changed form with Simon of Cyrene who had carried the cross. The Jews mistaking Simon for Jesus nailed him to the cross. Jesus stood by deriding their error before ascending to heaven."[22] In the third century A.D. Mani of Persia taught that the son of the widow of Nain whom Jesus raised from the dead was put to death in his place. According to another Manichaean tradition, the devil, who was trying to crucify Jesus, himself fell victim to the crucifixion. In the tenth century A.D. Photius wrote about the apocryphal book, *The Travels of Paul,* in which it was said that another was crucified in Jesus' place.[23]

INADEQUATE BASIS FOR MUSLIM SUBSTITUTION LEGENDS

There are many reasons why the substitution legends are not historically credible. First, they are contrary to the extant record of eyewitness testimony that it was "Jesus of Nazareth" who was crucified (Matt. 27; Mark 14; Luke 23; John 19).

Second, these substitution legends are contrary to the earliest extra-biblical Jewish, Roman, and Samaritan testimony about the death of Christ.[24] Tacitus's *Annals* speak of "Christ, who was executed under Pon-

---

19. Abdul-Haqq, 135–36. Taken from F. F. Bruce, *Jesus and Christian Origins Outside the New Testament* (Grand Rapids: Eerdmans, 1974), 178.
20. Ibid., 179.
21. Doi, 21.
22. J. B. Lightfoot, *The Apostolic Fathers,* 156f. Cited by Haqq, 136.
23. Ibid., 136.
24. Gary Habermas, *Ancient Evidence for the Life of Jesus* (Nashville: Thomas Nelson, 1984), 87–118.

tius Pilate in the reign of Tiberius."[25] In the second century Justin Martyr referred to the "Acts of Pontius Pilate" under whom "nails were fixed in Jesus' hands and feet on the cross; and after he was crucified, his executioners cast lots for his garments."[26] Josephus, the first-century Jewish historian, wrote that "there was a wise man who was called Jesus. . . . Pilate condemned him to be crucified and to die."[27] The Jewish Talmud, speaking of Jesus' "execution," declares that "on the eve of Passover Yeshua [Jesus] was hanged."[28] The earliest reference to Christ outside the New Testament is in Thallus, a Palestinian historian writing about A.D. 52, who spoke of the "darkness which accompanied the crucifixion of Christ."[29] There is also a Syriac manuscript in the British Museum (from some time after A.D. 73) by Mara bar Serapion that asks: "What advantage did the Jews gain from executing their king? It was just after that their kingdom was abolished."[30] In spite of the fact that all of these writers were opponents of Christianity, they are in agreement that Jesus of Nazareth was crucified under Pontius Pilate.

Third, there is not a shred of first-century testimony to the contrary by friend or foe of Christianity. The earliest substitution legends are not from the first century, and were heavily influenced by Gnosticism (A.D. 150f.). And none of them is based on any documented evidence of eyewitnesses or contemporaries of the events.

Fourth, these legends are implausible, since they demand total ignorance on the part of those closest to Jesus, his disciples, his own mother who was present, and on the part of the Romans who crucified him. They suppose that Jesus told his mother and another woman that someone who looked like him was crucified and that they never informed the disciples nor corrected them as they promptly went out to preach under the threat of death that Jesus had died and risen from the dead!

Finally, the Muslim denial of Christ's death by crucifixion is based on a theological misunderstanding. Abdalati, for example, lists the following among his reasons for rejecting the crucifixion of Christ: "Is it just on God's part, or anybody's part for that matter, to make someone repent

---

25. Tacitus, *Annals*, 15.44. Cited by Bruce, 22.

26. Justin, *First Apology*, 35, in *The Ante-Nicene Fathers*, vol. 1, 175.

27. Josephus, *Antiquities*, 18:3, from the Arabic text which is more likely the original, since Josephus merely claims that Jesus' disciples "*reported* that He had appeared to them three days after his crucifixion." This is something more likely for a non-Christian Jewish historian to say than Whiston's version that declares: "he [Jesus] appeared to them alive again the third day." See Josephus, *Josephus: Complete Works*, 379.

28. Michael L. Rodkinson, *The Babylonian Talmud*, "Sanhedrin," 43a (Talmud Society, 1918).

29. See Bruce, 30.

30. Ibid., 31.

for the sins or wrongs of others, the sins to which the repenter is no party?"[31]

This, of course, is based on a complete misunderstanding of what Christians believe about the atonement of Christ. Nowhere in the Bible does it say that Christ repented for our sins. It simply says that he "died for our sins" (1 Cor. 15:3). *Judicially*, he was "made to be sin for us" (2 Cor. 5:21). But at no time did he confess anyone's sins. He taught his disciples to pray, "Our Father . . . forgive us our sins" (Matt. 6:12). However, Jesus never confessed any sin for himself or anyone else. This is a total misunderstanding of the concept of substitutionary atonement. What the Bible teaches is that Jesus took our place. He paid the penalty of death for us. He took our sentence so that we could go free (Mark 10:45; Rom. 4:25; 1 Pet. 2:22; 3:18). This concept of life for life is not foreign to Islam. It is the same principle behind their belief in capital punishment; when a murderer takes another's life, he must forfeit his own as a penalty.

Furthermore, Islam teaches that God is just (see Chapter 1). But absolute justice must be satisfied. God cannot simply *overlook* sin. A penalty must be paid for it, either by the persons themselves or by someone else for them, which enables them to go to heaven. In a letter to a friend explaining why he became a Christian, Daud Rahbar "argues that the *Qur'anic* doctrine of God's justice demands that such a God be himself involved in suffering and be seen as involved in suffering. Only then can he be a just judge of suffering humanity." For "a God that is preserved from suffering will be an arbitrary and capricious judge."[32] In brief, Islam has several doctrines, God's justice and God's forgiveness, heaven and hell, which make no real sense apart from subtitutionary atonement.

Another misconception behind the Islamic rejection of the crucifixion is that a merciful God can forgive sin without justly condemning it. This is reflected in Abdalati's question, "Was God the Most Merciful, the Most Forgiving and the Most High unable to forgive men's sins except by inflicting this cruel and most humiliating alleged crucifixion on one who was not only innocent but also dedicated to His service and cause in a most remarkable way?"[33]

Actually there are two basic mistakes here. It is implied that what Jesus did was not voluntary but inflicted. In actual fact the Gospels declare that Jesus gave his life voluntarily and freely. Jesus said, "I lay down My life that I may take it again. No one takes it from Me, but I lay it down Myself. I have power to lay it down, and I have power to take it again" (John

31. See Abdalati, 160.
32. See Nazir-Ali, 28.
33. See Abdalati, 162.

10:17–18). Indeed, when Jesus died the Bible says "He [freely] gave up His spirit" (John 19:30).

Further, Muslims seem not to appreciate the basis on which the just and holy God they confess can forgive sins. While God is sovereign, he is not arbitrary about right and wrong.[34] Indeed, Muslims, like Christians, believe that God will punish forever those who do not repent of their sins (14:17; 25:11–14). But if God's holy justice demands that those who do not accept him be eternally punished for their sins, then it would seem to follow that God cannot just arbitrarily forgive anyone for anything without there being a just basis for this forgiveness. However, in Muslim theology—with its rejection of the cross—there is forgiveness but no real basis for this forgiveness. For Muslims reject Christ's sacrificial payment for sin to a just God by which he can then justly justify the unjust who accept Christ's payment on their behalf (cf. Rom. 3:21–26). After all, a truly just God cannot simply close his eyes to sin; he cannot overlook evil. So unless someone capable of paying the debt of sin owed to God does so, God is obligated to express his wrath, not his mercy, upon them. Lacking the crucifixion, the Muslim system has no way to explain how Allah can be merciful when he is also just.[35]

The theological blindspot in the Muslim system created by a rejection of Christ's atoning sacrifice leads to other unfounded statements, such as Abdalati's rhetorical question: "Does the [Christian] belief of crucifixion and blood sacrifice appear in any religion apart from pagan creeds or the early Greeks, Romans, Indians, Persians, and the like?"[36] The answer is a clear "Yes." It is the very heart of historic Judaism, as even a casual acquaintance with the Old Testament reveals. Moses told Israel: "The life of the flesh is in the blood, and I have given it to you upon the altar to make atonement for your souls; for it is the blood that makes atonement for the soul" (Lev. 17:11). This is why the children of Israel had to sacrifice the Passover lamb, commemorating their deliverance from bondage (Exod. 12:1f.). This is why the New Testament speaks of Christ as "the Lamb of God who takes away the sin of the world" (John 1:29). And the apostle Paul called "Christ, our passover, [who] was sacrificed for us" (1 Cor. 5:7). The writer of Hebrews adds, "and without the shedding of blood there is no remission" (Heb. 9:22).

Of course, Muslim scholars argue that the original Old Testament was distorted too. However, like the New Testament, the ancient Dead Sea manuscripts of the Old Testament reveal that the Old Testament today is

34. See comments on Islamic voluntarism in Chapter 7.
35. For a classical discussion of this issue in Christian theology, see St. Anselm, *Why God Became Man (Cur Deus Homo)*.
36. See Abdalati, 160.

substantially the same as the one in the time of Christ, over six hundred years before Muhammad.[37] Therefore, since the Qur'an urges the Jews in Muhammad's day to accept God's revelation in the Law (10:94), and since the Jewish Old Testament is substantially the same today as it was in Muhammad's day, then Muslims should accept that blood sacrifices for sins were commanded by God.

Since most Muslims reject the fact of Christ's crucifixion and death on the cross they understandably have great difficulty explaining the resurrection, appearances, and ascension of Christ. Since they believe Christ was merely a human being, they accept the fact of Christ's mortality. Believing in Jesus' eventual resurrection with all other humans in the general resurrection but rejecting his death on the cross, they are forced to find some other place for Christ's death. This dilemma has given rise to ingenious speculation. Many Muslim scholars believe that Jesus Christ was taken up to heaven alive without experiencing death. They suppose that his death will happen sometime when he returns to the earth before the last day. This they take from a literal understanding of 4:157–58 that says, "They killed him not, Nor crucified him, But so it was made to appear to them. . . . Nay, God raised him up to Himself." Others hypothesize that Jesus died a natural death at some unknown time after the crucifixion and remained dead for three hours, or according to another tradition, seven hours—after which he was resurrected and taken to heaven.[38] But, as we have seen, there is absolutely no historical testimony to support such speculation. Further, why an ascension without a resurrection? An ascension is a miraculous acceptance of Christ by God which implies a resurrection first.

A few Islamic writers, like Ahmad Khan of India, believe that Jesus was crucified, but did not die on the cross. Rather, he merely swooned and was taken down after three hours.[39] Other Muslims in north India added the legend that Jesus visited Tibet. Abdul-Haqq notes that Ghulam Ahmad "home brew[ed] a theory that Jesus Christ took His journey to Kasmir . . . after His crucifixion. To further support his theory he conveniently found a grave in Sirinagar, Kashmir, which he declared to be the grave of Jesus." However, the Ahmadiyyas sect's "speculations have been condemned as heretical by the Muslim orthodoxy."[40]

Abdalati notes that "whether he [Jesus] was raised alive in soul and body or in soul only after he died a natural death had not much bearing on the Islamic belief." Why? Because "it is no Article of Faith, because what is important and binding to a Muslim is what God reveals; and God

37. Geisler and Nix, Chapter 21.
38. See Abdul-Haqq, 131.
39. See Abdul-Haqq, 132.
40. Ibid., 133.

revealed that Jesus was not crucified but was raised to Him."[41] He cites in support 4:157, which says, "and those who differ Therein are full of doubts, With no (certain) knowledge, But only conjecture to follow, For of a surety They killed him not:—Nay, God raised him up unto Himself; and God Is Exalted in Power, Wise."

Most Muslims, however, believe that Jesus will be physically resurrected from the dead in the general resurrection of the last day. Anything else appears to be intramural speculation not essential to the Muslim faith. Therefore, rejecting Jesus' death by crucifixion leads to a rejection of his resurrection three days later and leaves the enigma of the ascension before any death or resurrection.

In place of the historic resurrection three days after Jesus' death by crucifixion, most Muslims feel obliged to place the resurrection of Jesus in the general resurrection of all humans in the last days. In support they appeal to 19:33, in which Jesus is alleged to say, "Peace is on me The day I was born, and The day that I die, And the day that I Shall be raised up to life (again)!" This they note is the same phrase used of John the Baptist in 19:15. In another passage God is presented as saying, "O Jesus! Lo! I am gathering thee and causing thee to ascend unto Me" (3:55).

On the surface it would seem that salvation by grace through faith in the death and resurrection of Christ is totally incomprehensible to the Muslim mind. This, we believe, is not the case. While the unbeliever does not *receive* (Greek *dekomai*) God's truth (1 Cor. 2:14), nevertheless, he can *perceive* it. Indeed, according to Romans 1:18–20, unbelievers are "without excuse" for not perceiving God's revelation in nature. And the very fact that unbelievers are called upon to believe the gospel implies that they can understand it (cf. Acts 16:31; 17:30–31). Jesus rebuked unbelievers for not understanding what he was talking about, declaring, "If you were blind, you would have no sin: but now you say, 'We see.' Therefore your sin remains" (John 9:41).

There is nothing contradictory or incredible about salvation by substitution. The Muslim mind should not have any more difficulty with this concept than any other mind. This concept is in accord with a virtually universal human practice. It is considered commendable for people to die in defense of the innocent. Warriors are hailed for dying for their tribe. Soliders are honored for dying for their country. Parents are called compassionate when they die for their children. This is precisely what Jesus did. As the apostle Paul put it, "scarcely for a righteous man will one die; yet perhaps for a good man someone would even dare to die. But . . . while we were still sinners, Christ died for us" (Rom. 5:7–8).

41. See Abdalati, 159.

Further, even in the Islamic understanding sacrificial death occurred. The Muslim practice of *id ghorban* (feat of sacrifice) features the sacrifice of a sheep in memory of Abraham's sacrifice of his son. For some this is associated with the forgiveness of sins. Furthermore, Muslim soldiers who sacrificed their lives for the cause of Islam were awarded Paradise (3:157–58; 22:58–59). If Allah could call upon his servants to die for Islam, why think it so strange that God could call upon his Son to die for salvation of Muslims, indeed of the world?

CONCLUSION

Muslim confusion about the resurrection of Christ stems from their rejection of his death by crucifixion, which we have already discussed. Much of the Islamic rejection of Christ is based on a misunderstanding of the facts about him. Since they believe in the divine inspiration of the original Old and New Testaments, Jesus' virgin birth, sinless life, divinely authoritative teaching, death, eventual resurrection, ascension, and second coming, it is a tragedy that the rejection of his claims to be the Son of God and Savior of the world are lost in the midst of all they do accept.[42] All of this, of course, is based on their unfortunate rejection of the authenticity of the Bible. Perhaps a better understanding of the factual basis for the authenticity of the Bible (see Chapter 10) could pave the way for their taking more seriously the Qur'an when it urges doubters to go to the Scriptures:

> If thou wert in doubt As to what We have revealed Unto thee, then ask those Who have been reading The Book [the Bible] from before thee: The Truth hath indeed come To thee from thy Lord: So be in no wise Of those in doubt (10:94).

42. With a penetrating insight, Stanton comments, "It remains one of the outstanding anomalies of history that the religious genius of Arabia, who staked the truth of his message on the witness of previous Scriptures, should have utterly neglected to verify their contents and should have sucessfully inspired his followers through the ages to a like neglect" (Stanton, 42).

Appendix 1

MUSLIM SECTS AND MOVEMENTS

TWO MAJOR SECTS: SUNNI AND SHI'ITE

Islam is divided into two basic sects, Sunni and Shi'ite. The Sunnis are by far and away the largest group, comprising about 80 percent of all Muslims. These sects arose originally over the political dispute as to who should be the first Caliph or successor to Muhammad. Having failed to appoint one before he died, the Sunnis contended that Muhammad's successor should be elected. The Shi'ites (the party of Ali), on the other hand, insisted that he should come from the bloodline of Muhammad. This would have meant that Ali, Muhammad's cousin and son-in-law, was the only legitimate successor to the Prophet. Therefore, the Shi'ites reject the legitimacy of the first three Caliphs of Islam and view them as people who deliberately deprived Ali of his divine rights.

Many of the factors involved in the historical development of Shi'ite Islam have been political in nature. As Fazlur Rahman points out, "Thus, we see that Shi'ism became, in the early history of Islam, a cover for different forces of social and political discontent. The southern Arabs used it as a facade to assert their pride and independence against the Arabs of the North. In the Iraqi mixed population, it claimed the services of the discontented Persians and contributed to the rise . . . of an extreme Persian cultural, nationalistic movement."[1]

The central motif of Shi'ite thought is derived from the violent and bloody martyrdom of Husayn, Ali's son and Muhammad's grandson, at the battle of Karbala by the troops of the corrupt Islamic government.

1. Rahman, *Islam*, 171.

Rippin and Knappert explain the significance of Husayn's martyrdom in Islamic culture:

> The tales of the battles and Husayn's eventual death are told throughout the Shi'ite world and cannot fail to produce tears in those who listen and participate. . . . Every year, millions of faithful followers in Iraq, Iran, Pakistan, India, and East Africa commemorate the sad events with rituals of mourning. A replica of the mausoleum at Karbala is carried around and the mourners sing hymns and recite prayers during the procession and the night-long mosque service that follows it. Scenes of self-flagellation are common occurrences during the procession.
>
> The 'sacrifice' of Husayn is compared to Abraham's readiness to sacrifice his son in obedience to God and that sacrifice is celebrated on the same day of Ashura with the slaughter of a sheep. This underlies the parallelism with the passion of Jesus in Christianity who is also compared to the lamb slaughtered by Abraham.[2]

In addition to the above political differences, there are also fundamental theological differences between the Sunnis and the Shi'ites. Based on the creed of Hasan ibn Yusuf (d. A.D. 1326), an eminent Shi'ite theologian, Williams explains some of the theological differences in the following summary account:

> Theologically, they [Shi'ites] are Mu'tazili rationalists, believing that the Qur'an is created, and that since God is *essentially* good, He *cannot* do evil. He has created man with free will. . . . It follows that He would not leave man without guidance; thus the books of the prophets have been sent down. Even so, as the sects of Islam attest, confusion arises, so it follows that God has given man in addition to the Prophet an infallible guide in religious matters. This guide is the *Imam.* It is also clear then that the selection of the *Imams* is a matter which could not be left to human error; they were Divinely appointed from birth. The true *Imams* are the direct line of Ali through al-Husayn. . . . [Shi'ites] believe in the doctrines of occultation (ghayba) and return (*raj'a*). The twelfth of the line of *Imams* did not die, as his enemies assert, but like the Qur'anic Jesus, he was taken by God from human sight, and is in occultation. He will return to earth as the *Mahdi*, the awaited messianic figure who . . . will bring the triumph of religion and herald the last judgment.[3]

2. Rippin and Knappert, *Textual Sources for the Study of Islam,* 21–22.

3. Williams, 224–25. For a brief but scholarly treatment of various aspects of Shi'ite Islam, see Goldziher, 167. For two recent sympathetic works on Shi'ite Islam, written by Shi'ite scholars, see Moojan Momen, *An Introduction to Shi'ite Islam: The History and Doctrines of Twelver Shi'ism* (New Haven: Yale University Press, 1985); and Abdulaziz Sachedina, *Islamic Messianism: The Idea of Mahdi in Twelver Shi'ism* (Albany, N.Y.: State University of New York Press, 1981).

SUFISM

The Sufis are the mystical wing of Islam. Sufism is the popular branch of Islamic belief and practice in which Muslims seek after a direct personal experience of God and his divine love. The roots of this movement are traced to very early times in the history of Islam. Abdul-Haqq writes,

> Many early Muslims felt their hearts to be so rusty that they resorted to asceticism and self-renunciation as a measure of relief. The first century of Islam found Muslims possessors of a vast empire in Persia, Mesopotamia, Syria, Egypt, and North Africa. . . . Theirs was a life of luxury, with concubines and slaves, such as was unknown to their ancestors. This new affluent life-style was supported by taxation of the conquered lands and booty from on-going military campaigns. There were people in the community who disliked the increasing worldliness that was affecting the people in general. . . . They began to protest against the secularization of Islam. To highlight their concern they took to clothing themselves in coarse cloth in the manner of Syrian Christian monks, cloth made of coarse wool called "suf." On that account they came to be called "Sufis" in course of time.[4]

In agreement with Abdul-Haqq's judgment, the European Islamicist, Dermenghem, also writes, "Sufism represents a protest, at one and the same time against juridical formalism and against the worldliness resulting from the conquests. It gives primacy to the religion of the heart, to the love of God and to the values of contemplation and asceticism." [5]

Historically, Sufism has played a significant role in the spread of Islam. As one noted scholar of Islam points out, "It is thanks to its mysticism that Islam is an international and universal religion."[6]

In addition to its religious appeal and missionary accomplishment, Sufism has also produced some of the greatest philosophical and literary geniuses in the history of Islam, such as Al-Ghazali, Ibn Rushd (Averroes), Ibn Sina (Avicenna), al-Kindi, and al-Farabi.[7]

It is also important to point out that despite the recent rise of Islamic fundamentalism in the Muslim world, Sufism is not only not declining but in fact it has found a new momentum.[8] Phil Parshall, a longtime mission-

---

4. Abdul-Haqq, 168–69.
5. Dermenghem, 72.
6. See Williams, 137. Also see Phil Parshall, *Bridges to Islam* (Grand Rapids: Baker, 1983), 31–37.
7. See Dermenghem, 74; and Williams, 155–68.
8. See the comments of Professor Yusuf Ibish, an authority on Sufism as well as a political scientist, in Waddy, 151–52.

ary in Pakistan, even goes so far as to say, "It has been calculated that 70 percent of all Muslims are acquainted with the Sufi orders within Islam."[9]

THE DOCTRINES OF SUFISM

We must acknowledge the fact that "Sufism does not present a homogeneous, closed system either in its theories or in its practices. There is no precise agreement even on the definition of general aims."[10] Our treatment of this important branch of Islam will only be confined to a brief discussion of some of Sufism's most basic and commonly accepted concepts and practices.

It is a perplexing but well-established fact that much of Sufi teaching directly contradicts some of the most fundamental doctrines of orthodox Islam. Whereas in orthodox Islam there is a firm belief in the absolute transcendence and the majesty of God, in Sufism, "God is in all things and all things are in Him. All visible and invisible beings are an emanation from Him, and are not really distinct from Him."[11] This Sufi understanding of God leads to another heretical belief that man can attain divinehood by being absorbed into the being of God.

This Neo-Platonic and pantheistic doctrine of Sufism that describes man's ultimate goal as the absorption of human personality into the being of God is called *fanna* (annihilation). One Sufi explains this idea in the following way: "When the temporal associates with the eternal, it has no existence left. You hear and see nothing but Allah when you have reached the conviction that nothing besides Allah exists; when you recognize that you yourself are He, that you are identical with Him; there is nothing that exists except Him."[12]

Such Sufi ideas are especially prevalent in much of Islamic poetry. Jalal al-Din Rumi (d. A.D. 1273), the most celebrated Sufi poet, writes, "In the beginning my soul and yours were but one; my manifestation and yours, my vanishing and yours. . . . It would be false to speak of mine and *yours*; I and *you* have ceased to exist between us."[13] Similarly the Sufi claim that the individual is identified with God abounds in the literature of Muslim mystics.[14]

---

9. See Parshall, 37.
10. See Goldziher, 146.
11. Parshall, 53.
12. See Goldziher, 144.
13. See Goldziher, 135. For other brief examples of Sufi poetry, see Williams, 155–68.
14. For an excellent treatment of this discussion see Richard Gramlich, "Mystical Dimensions of Islamic Monotheism," in Schimmel and Falaturi, 136–48. The classic example of such a claim is found in the tenth-century mystic, Al-Hallaj, who was executed by Muslim authorities due to his declaration that "I am the Truth."

In order to achieve *fanna* the Sufi has to endure a lifelong journey through several stages of spiritual development. This spiritual journey must take place under the guidance of a *pir* (the leader of a Sufi order who himself has "arrived" at the ultimate final stage of *fanna*), and the one who follows a *pir* is called a *murid* (follower).

In popular Islam, the *pirs* are viewed as mediators between God and man and are often believed to possess tremendous supernatural and miraculous powers. As a result of the Sufi's dependence on the *pir* of a particular order (*tariqa*), the Sufis in general ignore a legalistic obedience to the Qur'an or the traditions of Muhammad. For the Sufis what counts is "a personal relationship with God and that is the really important thing in life."[15]

OTHER MINOR SECTS

In addition to the major Muslim sects, there are several minor ones. The Wahhabis, who are primarily in Saudi Arabia, a strong legalistic group who are a radical wing of the Sunnis. Osama bin Laden was a Wahhabi. The Druze sect is located primarily in Lebanon, Syria, and northern Palestine. The Alawite sect is mostly in Syria. The Ahmadiyas are a heretical Muslim group from Pakistan whose founder, Mirza Ghulam Ahmad, claimed to be the promised Mahdi and Messiah. They also believe that Jesus, after escaping crucifixion, went to Kashmir and died in Srinagar. They also deny the virgin birth and sinless nature of Christ, discrediting any superiority of Christ over Muhammad. They are the most active Muslim missionary group in the West.

Beyond these major and minor sects Islam has spawned two other religions: Sikhism in India and an eclectic religion called Baha'i that boasts a prophet, Baha'u'llah, who supersedes Muhammad and has temples scattered around the world.

The Nation of Islam led by Louis Farrakhan is considered a heresy by orthodox Islam, since it claims there is a prophet after Muhammad, namely, the Honorable Elijah Muhammad (see Appendix 6).

15. See Parshall, 68. Parshall's treatment of Sufism and folk Islam is an excellent evangelical analysis of this topic.

Appendix 2

MUSLIM RELIGIOUS PRACTICES

The term "Islam" means submission to the will of God. The person who submits is called a "Muslim," or submitted one. This submission involves both beliefs (*iman*) and practices (*deen*). The basic Muslim believes in one God, the prophets (including his last prophet Muhammad), angels, the Qur'an as the Word of God, and the final day of judgment (with heaven and hell following). These have already been discussed in some detail (in Chapters 1–6).

Here we will briefly outline basic Muslim religious obligations or practices:

- To recite the *shahadah*. This means to "bear witness," which is done by reciting the creed: "There is no god but Allah, and Muhammad is His messenger." Saying this sincerely is all that is necessary to become a Muslim.
- To pray (*salat*). Muslims are required to say seventeen complete prayers each day. They may pray individually or collectively. On Friday at noon Muslims are required to gather at the mosque to pray. Following the prescription in the Qur'an, Muslims are called to prayer five times a day. This is practiced more widely in Muslim countries.
- To fast (*sawm*). Followers of Muhammad commemorate his receiving of the Qur'an by fasting in the ninth lunar month of *Ramadan*. They are expected to refrain from eating food during the daylight hours for this entire month. However, they are allowed to eat and drink from sunset to sunrise during this time.

- To give alms (*zakat*). Muslims are obligated to contribute one-fortieth (2.5 percent) of their income. This is given primarily to the poor and needy.
- To make the Pilgrimage (*hajj*). It is the duty of every Muslim to make a trip to Mecca (in Arabia) at least once in his lifetime, provided he or she is physically and financially able. Each pilgrim must wear a white garment called *ihram*, which is to eliminate all distinctions of class or status during the *hajj*. The trip usually takes a week or more, sometimes even a month, since it involves visiting several sacred sites. After the pilgrimage, a person is entitled to be called a *hajji*.

Appendix 3

THE GOSPEL OF BARNABAS

Muslims often cite *The Gospel of Barnabas* in defense of Islamic teaching. In fact, it is a best seller in Muslim countries. Yusuf Ali refers to it in his commentary on the Qur'an.[1] Suzanne Haneef, in her annotated bibliography on Islam, highly recommends it, saying, "Within it one finds the living Jesus portrayed far more vividly and in character with the mission with which he was entrusted than any other of the four New Testament Gospels has been able to portray him." It is called "essential reading for any seeker of the truth."[2] Typical of Muslim claims is that of Muhammad Ata ur-Rahim, who insisted that "The Gospel of Barnabas is the only known surviving Gospel written by a disciple of Jesus.... [It] was accepted as a Canonical Gospel in the churches of Alexandria up until 325 A.D."[3] Another Muslim author, M. A. Yusseff, argues confidently that "in antiquity and authenticity, no other gospel can come close to *The Gospel of Barnabas*."[4]

These are strange statements in view of the fact that reputable scholars have carefully examined *The Gospel of Barnabas* and find absolutely no basis for its authenticity. After reviewing the evidence in an article in *Islamochristiana*, J. Slomp concluded: "in my opinion scholarly research has proved absolutely that this 'gospel' is a fake. This opinion is also held by a number of Muslim scholars."[5] In their introduction to the Oxford

---

1. Yusuf Ali, *The Meaning of the Glorious Qur'an*, 230.

2. Haneef, 186.

3. Muhammad Ata ur-Rahim, *Jesus, A Prophet of Islam* (Karrachi, Pakistan: Begum Aisha Bawany Waqf, 1981), 41.

4. M. A. Yusseff, *The Dead Sea Scrolls, The Gospel of Barnabas, and the New Testament* (Indianapolis: American Trust Publications, 1985), 5.

5. J. Slomp, "The Gospel in Dispute," in *Islamochristiana* (Rome: Pontificio Instituto di Saudi Arabi, 1978), vol. 4, 68.

edition of *The Gospel of Barnabas*, Longsdale and Ragg conclude that "the true date lies . . . nearer to the sixteenth century than to the first."[6] Likewise, in his classic work "Jomier proved his point by showing beyond any doubt that the G. B. V. [Gospel of Barnabas Vienna ms.] contains an islamicised late medieval gospel forgery."[7]

A central idea in this work is in accord with a basic Muslim claim, namely, that Jesus did not die on the cross. Instead, this book contends that Judas Iscariot was substituted for Jesus (sect. 217). This view has been adopted by many Muslims, since the vast majority of them believe that someone else was substituted on the cross for Jesus.

EVIDENCE FOR AUTHENTICITY LACKING

Our concern here is about the authenticity of this alleged gospel. That is, is it a first-century gospel, written by a disciple of Christ? The evidence is overwhelmingly negative.

First of all, the earliest reference to it comes from a fifth-century work, *Decretum Gelasianum* (Gelasian Decree, by Pope Gelasius, A.D. 492-95). But even this reference is in doubt.[8] However there is no original language manuscript evidence for its existence! Slomp says flatly, "There is no text tradition whatsoever of the G. B. V."[9] By contrast, the New Testament books are verified by nearly 5,700 Greek manuscripts that begin in the second and third centuries A.D. (see Chapter 10).

Second, L. Bevan Jones notes that "the earliest form of it known to us is in an Italian manuscript. This has been closely analyzed by scholars and is judged to belong to the fifteenth or sixteenth century, i.e., 1400 years after the time of Barnabas."[10] Even Muslim defenders of it, like Muhammad Ata ur-Rahim, admit that they have no manuscripts of it before the 1500s.

Third, this gospel is widely used by Muslim apologists today, yet there

6. Longsdale and Luara Ragg, *The Gospel of Barnabas* (Oxford: Clarendon Press, 1907), xxxvii.

7. J. Jomier, Egypte: *Reflexions sur la Recontre al-Azhar* (Vatican au Caire, avil 1978), cited by Slomp, 104.

8. Slomp notes several facts that place this reference to *The Gospel of Barnabas* in doubt. First, only its *name* is mentioned; there are no contents or manuscripts of it from this period. Second, it is mentioned as a spurious book rejected by the church. Third, the "Gelasian Decrees were published immediately after the invention of the printing press and therefore available in many libraries." Hence, "A forger, Jomier believes, could easily have had access to these Decrees and taken hold of the title in order to give his own book some air of truth and respectability" (cited by Slomp, 74).

9. Ibid.

10. L. Bevan Jones, *Christianity Explained to Muslims*, rev. ed. (Calcutta: Baptist Mission Press, 1964), 79.

is no reference to it by any Muslim writer before the fifteenth or sixteenth century. But surely they would have used it if it had been in existence. As Ragg observes, "Against the supposition that the Gospel of Barnabas ever existed in Arabic we must set the argument from the total silence about such a Gospel in the polemical literature of the Moslems. This has been admirably catalogued by Steinschneider in his monograph on the subject."[11]

Ragg goes on to note the many Muslim writers who wrote books who would no doubt have referred to such a work—had it been in existence—such as Ibn Hasm (d. 456 A.H.), Ibn Taimiyyah (d. 728 A.H.), Abu'l-Fadl al-Su'udi (wrote 942 A.H.), and Hajji Khalifah (d. 1067 A.H.). But not one of them, or anyone else, ever refers to it between the seventh and fifteenth centuries when Muslims and Christians were in heated debate.

Fourth, no father or teacher of the Christian church ever quoted it from the first to the fifteenth century. If *The Gospel of Barnabas* had been considered authentic, it more surely would have been cited many times by some Christian teacher during this long period of time, as were all the other canonical books of Scripture. What is more, had this gospel even been in existence, authentic or not, certainly it would have been cited by someone. But no father cited it during its supposed existence for over 1,500 years!

Fifth, sometimes it is confused with the first-century *Epistle of [Pseudo] Barnabas* (c. A.D. 70–90), which is an entirely different book.[12] In this way Muslim scholars falsely allege there is support for an early date. Muhammad Ata ur-Rahim confuses the two books, thus wrongly claiming that it was in circulation in the second and third centuries A.D. This is a strange error since he admits that they are listed as different books in the "Sixty Books" as "Serial No. 18 Epistle of Barnabas. . . . Serial No. 24. Gospel of Barnabas."[13] In one place Rahim even cites by name the "Epistle of Barnabas" as evidence of the existence of the *Gospel of Barnabas!*[14]

Some have mistakenly assumed that the reference to a gospel used by Barnabas referred to in the apocryphal *Acts of Barnabas* (before c. A.D. 478) was *The Gospel of Barnabas.* However, this is clearly false, as the quotation reveals: "Barnabas, having unrolled the Gospel, *which we have received from Matthew his fellow-labourer,* began to teach the Jews."[15] By

---

11. Longsdale and Ragg, xlviii. Steinschneider's monograph is listed as *Abhandlungen für die Kunde des Morgenlandes*, 1877.
12. See Slomp, 37–38.
13. See Ata ur-Rahim, 42–43.
14. Ibid., 42.
15. See Slomp, 110, emphasis ours.

deliberately omitting this emphasized phrase, the impression is given that there is a *Gospel of Barnabas!*

Sixth, the message of the apocryphal *Gospel of Barnabas* is completely refuted by eyewitness first-century documents that possess over five thousand manuscripts to support their authenticity, namely, the New Testament. For example, its teaching that Jesus did not claim to be the Messiah and that he did not die on the cross are thoroughly refuted by eyewitness, first-century documents (see our Chapters 10 and 11).

Seventh, no Muslim should accept the authenticity of *The Gospel of Barnabas* since it clearly contradicts the Qur'an's claim that Jesus was the Messiah. It claims, "Jesus confessed, and said the truth; 'I am not the Messiah. . . . I am indeed sent to the house of Israel as a prophet of salvation; but after me shall come the Messiah" (sects. 42, 48). This is flatly contradictory to the Qur'an, which repeatedly calls Jesus the "Messiah" [the "Christ"] (cf. 5:19, 75).

Eighth, even Muslim scholars like Suzanne Haneef, who highly recommends it, have to admit that "the authenticity of this book has not been unquestionably established" and that "it is believed to be an apocryphal account of the life of Jesus."[16] Other Muslim scholars doubt its authenticity too.[17] For the book contains anachronisms and descriptions of medieval life in western Europe that reveal that it was not written before the fourteenth century. For example, it refers to the year of Jubilee coming every one hundred years, instead of fifty as it was practiced before this time (*The Gospel of Barnabas*, 82). The papal declaration to change it to every one hundred years was made by the church in A.D. 1343. John Gilchrist, in his work titled *Origins and Sources of the Gospel of Barnabas*, concludes that "only one solution can account for this remarkable coincidence. The author of the Gospel of Barnabas only quoted Jesus as speaking of the jubilee year as coming 'every hundred years' because he knew of the decree of Pope Boniface." He added, "but how could he know of this decree unless he lived at the same time as the Pope or sometime afterwards? This is a clear anachronism that compels us to conclude that the Gospel of Barnabas could not have been written earlier than the fourteenth century after Christ."[18] One significant anachronism is the fact that *The Gospel of Barnabas* uses the text from the Roman Catholic Latin Vulgate translation of the Bible (fourth century A.D.), even though Barnabas supposedly wrote it in the first century A.D. Other examples of anach-

16. Haneef claims it was "lost to the world for centuries due to its suppression as a heretical document," but there is not a shred of documented evidence for this. In fact, it was not even mentioned by anyone before it first appeared in the sixth century.

17. See Slomp, 68.

18. John Gilchrist, *Origins and Sources of the Gospel of Barnabas* (Durban, Republic of South Africa: Jesus to the Muslims, 1980), 16–17.

ronisms include a vassal who owes a share of his crop to his lord (*The Gospel of Barnabas*, 122), an illustration of medieval feudalism; a reference to wooden wine casks (ibid., 152), rather than wine skins as were used in Palestine; and a medieval court procedure (ibid., 121).

Ninth, Jomier provides a list of many mistakes and exaggerations in *The Gospel of Barnabas*. There are historical mistakes, such as, "Jesus was born when Pilate was governor, though he did not become governor until 26 or 27 A.D."[19] There are also geographical mistakes. For example, Chapter 20 "stated that Jesus sailed to Nazareth," even though it is not on the seashore.[20] Likewise, *The Gospel of Barnabas* contains exaggerations, such as Chapter 17's mention of 144,000 prophets and 10,000 prophets being slain by Jizebel (in Chapter 18).[21]

Tenth, according to Slomp, "Jomier's study showed many Islamic elements throughout the text that prove beyond any doubt that a Muslim author, probably a convert, worked on the book." Fourteen such influences are noted. For example, Jomier notes that the word "pinnacle" of the temple, where Jesus is said to have preached—hardly a good place!—was translated into arabic by *dikka*, a platform used in mosques.[22] Also, Jesus is represented as coming only for Israel but Muhammad "for the salvation of the whole world" (Chapter 11). Finally, the denial of Jesus to be the Son of God is Qur'anic, as is the fact that Jesus' sermon is modeled after a Muslim *hutba* that begins with praising God and his holy Prophet (Chapter 12).[23]

In summation, the Muslim use of *The Gospel of Barnabas* to support their teaching is devoid of evidence to support it. Indeed, its teachings even contradict the Qur'an. This work, far from being an authentic first-century account of the facts about Jesus, is actually a late medieval fabrication. The only authentic first-century records we have of the life of Christ are found in the New Testament, and it categorically contradicts the teaching of the *Gospel of Barnabas*. For a further critique of this "gospel" the reader should consult David Sox's excellent book titled, *The Gospel of Barnabas*.[24]

19. See Slomp, 9.
20. Ibid.
21. Ibid.
22. Ibid., 7.
23. Ibid.
24. Sox.

Appendix 4

POPULAR MUSLIM ACCUSATIONS AGAINST THE NEW TESTAMENT

This appendix is a brief discussion of the three most popular Muslim charges against Christianity and especially the New Testament that one often encounters in Islamic books or debates. The three areas of debate are: the textual corruption of the New Testament, the historical unreliability of the Gospels, and the evidence of pagan influence on the message of the New Testament.

Since we have already responded to the first charge (in Chapter 10) we will not respond to it at this point. However, we will discuss lack of understanding that lies behind such accusations by quoting from the late Muslim critic of Christianity Ahmed Deedat.

THE CHARGE OF TEXTUAL CORRUPTION

In his booklet entitled, *Is the Bible God's Word?*[1] Deedat attempts to show the textual corruption of the Bible by the fact that there are many English versions that have tried to improve on the King James Version![2] He then lists what he believes are four "great errors" of the Bible—out of what he says are a possible fifty thousand! The first error that Deedat points to in his comparison between the Revised Standard Version of the Bible and the KJV is the fact that the word "virgin" in Isaiah 7:14 has been changed to the phrase "a young woman." The second error is that in John 3:16, the phrase "begotten son" has been changed to "only son." Deedat shows no awareness of the fact that in both of the above instances the

1. Ahmed Deedat, *Is the Bible God's Word?*, 6th print, Dec. 1987.
2. Ibid., 7–11.

original Hebrew and Greek terms have remained identical in all our manuscripts and that only the English phrases have been changed due to the judgment of the translators. So it is not a question of *inspiration* of the Bible by God in the text of its original languages (which is without any error) but of its *translations* by men into different languages (which may contain some nonsubstantive errors).

The last two supposed errors concern the omission of 1 John 5:7 and the shorter ending of Mark in the later translations of the Bible.[3] Once again the invalidity of the charges is obvious to anyone who is even slightly familiar with the science of textual criticism.[4] Christians do not claim that every manuscript of the Bible has been copied without error. In fact, most Christian scholars believe that this verse (1 John 5:7) on the Trinity was not in the original text that God inspired, since it scarcely appears in any manuscript before the fifteenth century. It was probably a gloss (scribal comment in the margin) that was later taken as part of the text by a subsequent translator.[5] Nor does the omission of this verse from many modern translations of the Bible affect the Christian doctrine of the Trinity in the least, since there are many other verses that clearly teach there are three persons in the one and only God (see Chapter 12).

Another example of Deedat's unsubstantiated charges against the Bible is his statement that "out of over four thousand differing manuscripts the Christians boast about, the Church fathers just selected four which tallied with their prejudices and called them [the] Gospels of Matthew, Mark, Luke and John."[6] It is amazing that Deedat does not seem to understand that these thousands of manuscripts are simply copies of the twenty-seven New Testament books and not thousands of separate books or gospels![7]

Further, while many Muslims charge the Bible with textual corruption, they remain blissfully ignorant of the fact that the Qur'an itself has suffered from a multitude of textual variations (see Chapter 9).[8] If the divine authenticity of a book were to be based on the unanimous agreement among all the human-made copies of the original documents, then the

3. Ibid., 12–21. We should also note that Deedat is very fond of quoting Jehovah's Witnesses for support of his charges against the integrity of the biblical text!

4. For two excellent and standard treatments of the subject of New Testament textual criticism, the reader is encouraged to refer to Bruce Metzger, *The Text of the New Testament: Its Transmission, Corruption, and Restoration* (New York: Oxford University Press, 1968, 2d ed.); and Kurt and Barbara Aland, *The Text of the New Testament,* rev. ed. (Grand Rapids: Eerdmans, 1989).

5. See N. L. Geisler and Nix, 483–84.

6. See Deedat, 24.

7. For a complete response to Deedat's charges, see John Gilchrist, *The Textual History of the Qur'an and the Bible* (Villach, Austria: Light of Life, 1988, reprint).

8. See ibid., 27.

Qur'an itself will undoubtedly fail the test! Contrary to the opinion of many Muslims, we do not have the original copy of the Qur'an or even the original official Uthmanic codex. As Gilchrist points out, "the oldest text of the Qur'an still extant dates from the second century after the Hijrah and is compiled on vellum in the early *al-mail* Arabic script. Other early Qur'ans are in *Kufic* script and date from the same time as well."[9]

Sir Norman Anderson's comment in this context is also well-taken. "So, although it is true that today the Kufan text of Hafs is accepted almost everywhere in the Muslim world, the claim commonly made by Muslims that they have the *ipsissima verba* [exact words] of what Muhammad actually said, without any variant readings, rests upon an ignorance of the facts of history."[10]

What many Muslim scholars forget is this parallel with their own Scriptures. Guillaume notes that:

> The truth is that *the textual history of the Qur'an is very similar to that of the Bible* [emphasis ours]. Both books have been preserved remarkably well. Each is, in its basic structure and content, a very fair record of what was originally there. But neither book has been preserved totally without error or textual defect. Both have suffered here and there from variant readings in the early codices known to us but neither has in any way been corrupted. Sincere Christians and Muslims will honestly acknowledge these facts.

He adds that

> The only difference between the Qur'an and the Bible today is that the Christian Church in the interest of truth, carefully preserved the variant readings . . . whereas the Muslims at the time of Uthman deemed it expedient to destroy as far as possible all the evidences of different readings of the Qur'an in the cause of standardizing one text for the whole of the Muslim. . . . These facts must also always be considered against the background of further evidence in the Hadith that the Qur'an today is still not complete.[11]

THE CHARGE OF HISTORICAL UNRELIABILITY

Another often encountered Muslim charge is simply a rehash of the conclusions of the so-called higher-critical scholarship. It seems that Muslim authors never bother to assess the validity of these scholars' presuppositions, methodologies, and arguments, but are just happy to report their skeptical conclusions.

9. See Gilchrist, 27.
10. Anderson, 47.
11. Ibid., 20–21.

Typical of this approach is Muhammad Ata ur-Rahim's *Jesus, A Prophet of Islam.* The author writes:

> More and more people are now aware that the Christianity they know has little to do with the original teaching of Jesus. During the last two centuries the research of the historians has left little room for faith in the Christian "mysteries", but the proven fact that the Christ of the established Church has almost nothing to do with the Jesus of history does not in itself help Christians toward the Truth.[12]

The author goes on to refer to the works of David Strauss, who "almost destroyed the historic credibility not only of the fourth but also of the first three Gospels as well."[13] After such a quick dismissal of the biblical testimony to Jesus, in the chapter ironically entitled "An Historical Account of Jesus," Rahim presumes (without any arguments) the historicity of the "Gospel of Barnabas," gives us a portrayal of Christ based on the writings of some medieval Muslim poets, and concludes that Jesus was the leader of a band of revolutionary Essences![14]

In a similar fashion Rahim dismisses the most well-established fact of Christianity, the crucifixion. He writes, "The 'arrest', the 'trial', and the 'crucifixion' are hedged around with so many contradictions and misstatements, that it is extremely difficult to untangle and penetrate through them in order to arrive at what actually happened."[15] Instead of accepting the Gospel accounts of the events surrounding Jesus' death, the author proposes a typical Islamic version of the situation in which it was Judas who was mistakenly arrested and crucified.[16] The most astonishing proposal of Rahim concerns the role of Pilate. He writes, "Finally, there is another significant fact. In the calendars of the Saints of the Coptic Church, both in Egypt and in Ethiopia, Pilate and his wife appear as 'saints'. This could be possible only if we accept that Pilate, knowing full well that his soldiers had made a wrong arrest, knowingly condemned Judas in place of Jesus, and allowed the latter to escape."[17]

12. Ata ur-Rahim, 13.
13. Ibid., 14.
14. Ibid., 17–38.
15. Ibid., 35.
16. Ibid., 36. It is interesting that Deedat, the most well-known Muslim apologist, departs from the traditional Islamic denial of Jesus' crucifixion, and instead opts for the swoon theory as a way to deny the reality of Jesus' death on the cross. It is noteworthy that Deedat himself has been condemned on this point by orthodox Muslim authorities of South Africa! See John Gilchrist, *The Crucifixion of Christ: A Fact, not Fiction* (Villach, Austria: Light of Life).
17. Ibid., 37.

One wonders how such fanciful accounts without a shred of reliable historical evidence can claim to give us a true picture of the historical Jesus. On what basis should we reject the authenticity of the Gospels in favor of the baseless Muslim speculations or dogmatic Qur'anic assertions? It must seem to the unbiased reader that on this most crucial point concerning Jesus' crucifixion that it is the Qur'an and not the Bible that is mistaken.

It is outside the scope of this appendix to respond fully to the charges against the historical reliability of the Gospels. Much can be said in defense of the Gospels and the rest of the New Testament by way of archaeological discoveries, non-Christian and extrabiblical historical records, and the early date of the composition of the majority of New Testament books.

As one example we cite the conclusion of the classical Roman historian, A. N. Sherwin-White, concerning the historical reliability of the Book of Acts (it is agreed by almost all biblical scholars that the author of Acts was the same as that of the Gospel of Luke): "For the New Testament book of Acts, the confirmation of historicity is overwhelming. . . . Any attempt to reject its basic historicity, even in matters of detail must now appear absurd. Roman historians have long taken it for granted."[18] However, the author admits that due to biased and critical presuppositions "it is astonishing that while Graeco-Roman historians have been growing in confidence, the twentieth-century study of the Gospel narratives, *starting from no less promising material,* has taken so gloomy a turn."[19] But we agree with Craig Blomberg, an evangelical New Testament scholar, that "such gloom should be replaced by a radiant endorsement of the historical reliability of the four gospels, and there are some encouraging signs that in places that is in fact beginning to occur."[20]

18. A. N. Sherwin-White, *Roman Society and Roman Law in the New Testament* (Oxford: Clarendon Press, 1963), 189.

19. Ibid., 187.

20. Craig Blomberg, *The Historical Reliability of the Gospels* (Downers Grove: InterVarsity, 1987), 254. Blomberg's book is an excellent introduction to this field. For a much more detailed and highly technical discussion of these issues, see R. T. France and David Wenham, eds., *Gospel Perspectives* (Sheffield: JSOT Press, 1980–86, 6 vols). Also a brief but classical study of the New Testament's historical reliability is F. F. Bruce, *The New Testament Documents: Are They Reliable?* Another important scholarly discussion concerning a study of the historical Jesus is I. Howard Marshall, *I Believe in the Historical Jesus* (Grand Rapids: Eerdmans, 1977), and *The Origins of New Testament Christology* (Downers Grove: InterVarsity, 1990, updated edition). Two other very helpful books concerning the historical evidence for Christ are Gary Habermas, *The Verdict of History: Conclusive Evidence for the Life of Jesus* (Nashville: Thomas Nelson, Inc., 1988), and R. T. France, *The Evidence for Jesus* (Downers Grove: InterVarsity, 1986). Concerning the early dates for the composition of the New Testament books and their general reliability the reader could consult with John A. T. Robinson's, *Redating the New Testament* (1976) and *Can We Trust the New Testament*

THE CHARGE OF PAGAN INFLUENCE

The last charge that we would briefly address at this point is once again a rehash of outdated negative critical scholarship mixed with a misinformed and misleading Muslim "version" of church history.[21] According to this charge the apostle Paul and some of the later church fathers corrupted much of the purity of Jesus' teachings by mixing the paganism of their day with the original message of Christ. For example, Yousuf Saleem Chisti in his book *What Is Christianity: Being a Critical Examination of Fundamental Doctrines of the Christian Faith,* attributes such doctrines as the deity of Christ and the atonement to the pagan teachings of the apostle Paul, and the doctrine of the Trinity to the pagan formulations of church fathers.[22]

Chisti also attempts to demonstrate the vast influence of mystery religions on Christianity by stating:

> The Christian doctrine of atonement was greatly coloured by the influence of the mystery religions, especially Mithraism, which had its own son of God and virgin Mother, and crucifixion and resurrection after expiating for the sins of mankind and finally his ascension to the 7th heaven.
>
> If you study the teachings of Mithraism side by side with that of Christianity, you are sure to be amazed at the close affinity which is visible between them, so much so that many critics are constrained to conclude that Christianity is the facsimile or the second edition of Mithraism.[23]

The author goes on to list some of these similarities by noting that Mithra was also considered the son of God and savior, was born of a virgin, had twelve disciples, was crucified, rose from the grave the third day, atoned for the sins of humankind, and finally returned to his father in heaven.[24]

By way of a brief response we need to point out that an honest reading of all the New Testament data will clearly demonstrate that Paul did not teach a new religion. Paul, similar to Jesus, taught that Christianity was a

---

(Grand Rapids: Eerdmans, 1977). Robinson's "conservative" conclusions are quite significant in view of the fact that the author himself is a highly critical scholar of the New Testament! Finally, for a consideration of the latest and the most up to date issues in gospel scholarship one can refer to the *Dictionary of Jesus and the Gospels,* ed. Joel Green, Scot McKnight, and Howard Marshall, (Downers Grove: InterVarsity, 1992).

21. See Yusseff, 1985).

22. Yousuf Saleem Chisti, *What Is Christianity: Being A Critical Examination of Fundamental Doctrines of the Christian Faith* (Karachi, Pakistan: World Federation of Islamic Missions, 1970).

23. Ibid., 87.

24. Ibid., 87–88.

fulfillment of Judaism (Rom. 10:4, 9–11; Col. 2:16–17; Matt. 5:18; Luke 16:16–17). Both taught that men are sinners (Mark 3:38; Rom. 3:23) and that Jesus died, with his shed blood providing atonement for sin (Matt. 26:28; Mark 10:45; Eph. 1:7; Rom. 5:8). The death and burial of Jesus were completed by his resurrection (Luke 24:46–47; John 20:25–29; Rom. 10:9). Yet man cannot save himself, but needs God's grace and leading (Matt. 19:25–26; John 4:44; Eph. 2:8–9), which is imparted through faith and surrender to Christ (Mark 1:15; John 6:47; Rom. 10:9–11). The result is a changed life and commitment (Luke 14:25–35; John 15:1–11; 2 Cor. 5:17). Finally, we should remember that Paul's message of the gospel was both checked and approved by the original apostles (Gal. 1–2), demonstrating official recognition that his message was not opposed to that of Jesus.[25]

As we have already pointed out in Chapter 12, even though the Trinity—either the term itself or its specific formulation—does not appear in the Bible, nevertheless, it is a faithful expression dealing with all the biblical data. Also, an accurate understanding of the historical and theological development of this doctrine would amply illustrate that it was exactly because of the dangers of paganism that the Council of Nicea formulated the orthodox doctrine of the Trinity.[26]

In response to the specific charges of the influence of Mithraism on Christianity, Chisti's descriptions of this religion are baseless (it is interesting that the author gives no reference for such alleged similarities). Ronald Nash, the author of *The Gospel and the Greeks*, describes Mithraism in the following way:

> We do know that Mithraism, like its mystery competitors, had a basic myth. Mithra was supposedly born when he emerged from a rock; he was carrying a knife and torch and wearing a Phrygian cap. He battled first with the sun and then with a primeval bull, thought to be the first act of creation. Mithra slew the bull, which then became the ground of life for the human race.[27]

Nash continues,

> Allegations of an early Christian dependence on Mithraism have been rejected on many grounds. Mithraism had no concept of the death and res-

25. See Habermas, 67–72. For further response to the charge that Paul corrupted Jesus' original message, the reader should refer to J. Gresham Machen's classic *The Origin of Paul's Religion* (Grand Rapids: Eerdmans, 1925), F. F. Bruce, *Paul and Jesus* (Grand Rapids: Baker, 1974) and Herman Ridderbos, *Paul and Jesus* (Grand Rapids: Baker, 1957).

26. For a brief treatment of the history of this doctrine, see E. Calvin Beisner, *God in Three Persons* (Wheaton: Tyndale House). Two of the classics in this field are G. L. Prestige, *God in Patristic Thought* (London: S.P.C.K., 1952) and J. N. D. Kelly, *Early Christian Doctrines* (London: Adam and Charles Black, 1958).

27. Ronald Nash, *The Gospel and the Greeks* (Dallas: Word, 1992), 144.

316   Appendix 4

urrection of its god and no place for any concept of rebirth—at least during its early stages. . . . During the early stages of the cult, the notion of rebirth would have been foreign to its basic outlook. . . . Moreover, Mithraism was basically a military cult. Therefore, one must be skeptical about suggestions that it appealed to nonmilitary people like the early Christians.

Perhaps the most important argument against an early Christian dependence on Mithraism is the fact that the timing is all wrong. The flowering of Mithraism occurred after the close of the New Testament canon, too late for it to have influenced the development of first-century Christianity.[28]

In fact, all the allegations of Christian dependence on various mystery religions or Gnostic movements have been rejected by scholars in the fields of biblical and classical studies.[29] The reasons for such a rejection are mainly due to the historical character of Christianity and the early date of the New Testament documents that would not have allowed enough time for mythological developments on one hand, and on the other hand, the complete lack of any early historical evidence in support of the mystery religions. As the British scholar Sir Norman Anderson explains,

The basic difference between Christianity and the mysteries is the historic basis of the one and the mythological character of the others. The deities of the mysteries were no more than "nebulous figures of an imaginary past," while the Christ whom the apostolic *kerygma* proclaimed had lived and died only a few years before the first New Testament documents were written. Even when the apostle Paul wrote his first letter to the Corinthians the majority of some five hundred witnesses to the resurrection were still alive.[30]

Concerning the Qur'an, we would like to point out that, based on the findings of reputable scholars of Islam, much of the content of the Qur'an can be traced to either Jewish or Christian works (often from Jewish or Christian apocrypha) or pagan sources.

Arthur Jeffery, in his technical and scholarly volume *The Foreign Vocabulary of the Qur'an,* ably proves that "not only the greater part of the religious vocabulary, but also most of the cultural vocabulary of the Qur'an is of non-Arabic origin."[31] Some of the vocabulary sources include Abyssinian, Persian, Greek, Syriac, Hebrew, and Coptic.[32]

28. Ibid., 147.
29. Ibid., 119.
30. Sir Norman Anderson, *Christianity and World Religions* (Downers Grove: InterVarsity, 1984), 52–53.
31. Arthur Jeffery, *The Foreign Vocabulary of the Qur'an* (Lahore, Pakistan: Al-Biruni, 1977), 2.
32. Ibid., 12–32.

W. St. Clair-Tisdall, in his classic *The Sources of Islam,* also demonstrates the direct dependence of certain Qur'anic stories of the Old Testament on the Jewish Talmud. The influence of the Jewish apocrypha can be seen on the Qur'anic stories of Cain and Abel, Abraham and the idols, and the Queen of Sheba.[33] The direct influence of Christian apocrypha can be seen in the story of seven sleepers and the childhood miracles of Jesus. For the existence of Zoroastrian doctrines in the Qur'an we can cite the Qur'anic descriptions of the houries (virgins) in Paradise and the *sirat* (the bridge between hell and Paradise).[34] In addition to these, important Muslim practices such as visiting the shrine of Ka'aba, and the many details of the ceremony of *hajj,* including visits to the hills of Safa and Marwa, and also the throwing of stones against a stone pillar symbolizing Satan, were all pre-Islamic practices of pagan Arabia.[35]

It spite of the above evidences, it is interesting that Muslim authors have been most unwilling to address the issue of the human origins of the Qur'an, but have simply repeated their dogmatic assertions about its divine origin. In fact, in our research of Muslim authors we have not even come across an acknowledgment of such problems in the Qur'an, to say nothing of solutions.

In conclusion, it is our sincere hope that the readers will consider the evidences set forth in this book, pursue their specific areas of interest even further, and make their decision concerning the integrity and the reliability of the New Testament based on historical FACTS!

33. Tisdall, *The Sources of Islam,* 11–30. For a host of other similarities, see pp. 39–45.
34. Ibid., 46–59, 74–91.
35. See Dashti, 55, 93–94, 164.

Appendix 5

ISLAM AND VIOLENCE

After the events of September 11, the issue of violence and religion has once again come into intense discussions and debate. It is our conviction that although various political, socioeconomic and cultural factors have significantly contributed to the rise of violence and terrorism in contemporary fundamentalist Islam, we cannot ignore the religious dimension of this violence that goes back to the very heart and origin of Islam.

The point that we'd like to make is quite simple. While many Muslims are peace-loving, nonetheless, those who commit acts of violence and terror in the name of God can find ample justification for their actions, based on the teachings of the Qur'an and the sayings and examples from prophet Muhammad himself! We have often heard in the media that the relationship between Muslim terrorists and Islam is like that of KKK and Christianity. This analogy is clearly false. Christians who have engaged in violence are betraying the explicit teachings and examples of Jesus Christ. On the other hand, Muslims who take upon themselves to destroy their alleged enemies in the name of God can rightly claim to be following the commands of God in the Qur'an and imitating their prophet as their role model.

Our point, of course, should not be taken to imply that all faithful and devout Muslims must become violent in order to be true to the teachings of Islam. No doubt the majority of the Muslim world condemns acts of terror and violence. There are many schools of thought in Islam with various and often conflicting interpretations of the Qur'an. However, the important distinction that we are making is this: The minority groups in Islam who resort to violence are not an aberration to Islam but in fact can legitimately claim to be working within the basic parameters of Islamic *Jihad*. We will now turn to the evidence in support of our claim.

Support for Violence in the Qur'an

The following are only some of the verses in the Qur'an that can and have been used in the history of Islam in support of violence in the name of God and the glories of martyrdom in a holy war.

2:190–193 "Fight in the cause of God those who fight you . . . And slay them wherever ye catch them . . . And fight them on until there is no more tumult or oppression and there prevail justice and faith in God . . ."

2:216 "Fighting is prescribed for you and ye dislike it. But it is possible that ye dislike a thing which is good for you, and that ye love a thing which is bad for you. But God knoweth and ye know not."

2:224 "Then fight in the cause of God and know that God heareth and knoweth all things."

3:157–158 "And if ye are slain or die in the way of God, forgiveness and mercy from God are far better than all they could amass. And if ye die, or are slain, Lo! It is unto God that ye are brought together."

3:169 "Think not of those who are slain in God's way as dead. Nay, they live finding their sustenance in the presence of their Lord."

3:195 ". . . Those who have . . . fought or been slain, verily I will blot out from them their iniquities and admit them into Gardens with rivers flowing beneath; a reward from the presence of God . . ."

4:101 ". . . For the Unbelievers are unto you open enemies."

4:74, 75 "Let those fight in the cause of God who sell the life of this world for the Hereafter. To him who fighteth in the cause of God whether he is slain or gets victory, soon shall we give him a reward of great (value). Those who believe fight in the cause of God and those who reject faith fight in the cause of evil, so fight ye against the friends of Satan, feeble indeed is the cunning of Satan."

4:89 "They but wish that ye should reject faith as they do, and thus be on the same footing as they. But take not friends from their ranks until they flee in the way of God. But if they turn renegades, seize them and slay them wherever ye find them . . ."

4:95 "Not equal are those believers who sit (at home) and receive no hurt and those who strive and fight in the cause of God with their goods and their persons. God hath granted a grade higher to those who strive and fight with their goods and persons than those who sit (at home)."

5:36 "The punishment of those who wage war against God and His apostle and strive with might and main for mischief through the land is: execution, or crucifixion, or the cutting off of hands and feet from opposite sides, or exile from the land. That is their disgrace in this world and a heavy punishment is theirs in the Hereafter."

5:54 "O ye who believe. Take not the Jews and the Christians for your friends and protectors. They are but friends and protectors to each other. And he amongst you that turns to them (for friendship) is of them. Verily God guideth not a people unjust."

8:12–17 "Remember thy Lord inspired the angels (with the message): 'I am with you. Give firmness to the believers. I will instill terror into the hearts of the unbelievers. Smite ye above their necks and smite all their finger tips off them. This because they contend against God and his apostle. If any contend against God and his apostle, God is strict in punishment . . . O ye who believe. When ye meet the unbelievers in hostile array, never turn your backs to them. If any do turn his back to them on such a day, unless it be a stratagem of war . . . he draws on himself the wrath of God and his abode is Hell, an evil refuge (indeed).'"

8:59–60 "Let not the unbelievers think that they can get the better (of the godly). They will never frustrate (them). Against them make ready your strength to the utmost of your power, including steeds of war, to strike terror into (the hearts of) the enemies of God and your enemies and others besides, whom ye may not know, but whom God doth know . . ."

8:65 "O apostle! Rouse the believers to the fight. If there are twenty amongst you, patient and persevering, they will vanquish two hundred. If a hundred they will vanquish a thousand of the unbelievers, for these are a people without understanding."

9:5 ". . . fight and slay the pagans wherever ye find them, and seize them, beleaguer them, and lie in wait for them in every stratagem (of war) . . ."

9:14 "Fight them, and God will punish them by your hands, cover them with shame. . . ."

9:29 "Fight those who believe not in God nor the Last Day nor hold that forbidden which hath been forbidden by God and his apostle nor acknowledge the Religion of Truth (even if they are) of the people of the Book, until they pay the *Jizya* [religious tax] with willing submission, and feel themselves subdued."

47:4 "Therefore, when ye meet the unbelievers, smite at their necks, at length when ye have thoroughly subdued them, bind a bond firmly (on them). . . . but if it had been God's will, he could certainly have exacted retribution from them (himself), but (he lets you fight) in order to test you, some with others. But those who are slain in the way of God, he will never let their deeds be lost."

61:4 "Truly God loves those who fight in His cause in battle array, as if they were a solid cemented structure."

A simple reading of such Qur'anic passages makes it obvious how easy it is for many Muslims to feel hatred and enmity against Jews, Christians, and other non-Muslims. Although many Muslims are very fond of quoting some of the more "open-minded" and "inclusive" verses of the Qur'an, one cannot ignore the weight and impact of the above passages on a devout Muslim who wants to find and obey the will of God as found in the Qur'an. Before we go on to other examples from prophet Muhammad himself, we need to respond to two issues that some Muslims bring up at this point.

ANSWERING SOME OBJECTIONS

Many have claimed that Qur'anic verses in support of fighting were for a special historical situation concerning the beginning of Islam. They argue that since prophet Muhammad was persecuted in Mecca for the first thirteen years of his ministry, he was justified in his military actions in the last ten years of his life in Medina and for the support of the budding Islamic movement. The problem with this reasoning is that nowhere in the Qur'an itself are the above commands to fight restricted to a special time period or against a special people group. Unlike the divine commands found in the Book of Joshua in the Old Testament, that were specific to a time, place, and people group, orthodox Muslims believe that the Qur'anic commands are universal and thus applicable for all times and places.

A second objection that one hears is that Islam is a religion of peace, and war in Islam is only for self-defense. Jamal Badawi, a popular Muslim apologist, claims, "Actual armed *jihad* is permissible under two conditions alone: one is for self-defense, and the other is for fighting against oppression."[1] Although, Badawi is quite accurate in describing the conditions of armed *jihad* in Islam, what he fails to say is that the definitions of "self-defense" and "fighting against oppression" are much broader than usually understood. Many orthodox Muslims believe that if a nation's leaders do not acknowledge the rule of Islam, then those rulers are "oppressors" and thus a legitimate target for war.[2] Many Muslims argue that America is a cultural aggressor by exporting its Hollywood values all over the world, and thus any fight against Americans is done in

1. Cited in Diana Eck, *A New Religious America* (San Francisco: Harper, 2001), 238.
2. See John Kelsay, *Islam and War* (Louisville: Westminster/John Knox Press, 1993), 35.

self-defense.[3] Therefore, there is no end to how a Muslim group can define "self-defense" and "oppression" and thus find an Islamic justification for violence.

SUPPORT FOR VIOLENCE IN THE LIFE OF PROPHET MUHAMMAD

We now turn our attention to just a few examples of some of the actions and sayings of prophet Muhammad to see if Muslims can find any legitimacy for the use of violence as witnessed in the contemporary world. We remind the reader that we will only use the most ancient, authoritative, and original Islamic writings in support of our thesis. The earliest biography of prophet Muhammad was written by Ibn Ishaq in the second century of the Islamic era and was later edited by Ibn Hisham in the third century. This work was translated into English under the title *The Life of Muhammad* by A. Guillaume and published by Oxford University Press in 1955. The following accounts are some of the sayings and actions of prophet Muhammad and his close companions found in this biography.

EXAMPLES FROM THE EARLIEST BIOGRAPHY OF MUHAMMAD

In the constitution of Medina, which the prophet wrote when he and his followers migrated from Mecca in the year 622, we read, "A believer shall not slay a believer for the sake of an unbeliever, nor shall he aid an unbeliever against a believer. . . . Believers are friends one to the other to the exclusion of outsiders. . . . The believers must avenge the blood of one another shed in the way of God."[4]

The first in the series of assassinations that the prophet ordered was an old Jewish man named Ibnu'l-Ashraf. His crime was writing poetry against Muslims. "The apostle said, 'Who will rid me of Ibnu'l-Ashraf?'" One of his followers volunteered and said, "I will deal with him for you, O apostle of God, I will kill him." And the prophet responded by saying, "Do so if you can." The prophet also explicitly gave his assassins permission to lie and use trickery in order to accomplish their mission. The report goes on to describe how the prophet's followers deceived the old man out of his house in the middle of the night and jumped on him with swords and daggers and brutally murdered him. After completing their mission,

---

3. See Mark Galli, "Now What? A Christian response to religious terrorism," *Christianity Today*, October 22, 2001.
4. Ibn Ishaq, 232.

the followers reported back to the prophet that they "had killed God's enemy." The author concludes this incident by writing, "Our attack upon God's enemy cast terror among the Jews, and there was no Jew in Medina who did not fear for his life."[5]

In the very next incident in this biography of prophet Muhammad we read, "The apostle said, 'Kill any Jew that falls into your power.'" The author then recounts the story of two brothers, the younger one of which was a Muslim. Upon hearing this command, the younger Muslim brother kills a Jewish merchant. The older brother became very critical of the action of his younger sibling. In response the younger brother says, "Had the one who ordered me to kill him ordered me to kill you I would have cut your head off." The older brother exclaimed, "'By God, a religion which can bring you to this is marvelous!' and he became a Muslim."[6]

In one of the battles, after one of prophet Muhammad's uncles was savagely killed, Muhammad became so angry that he said, "If God gives me victory over Quraysh in the future I will mutilate 30 of their men." Seeing the grief of their prophet, Muhammad's followers claimed, "By God, if God give us victory over them in the future we will mutilate them as no Arab has ever mutilated anyone." Thankfully, the prophet had a change of mind and later decided to forbid mutilation.[7]

In another famous incident with Jewish people, after having already expelled two Jewish tribes from the city of Medina, the prophet orchestrated the execution of all the adult males of the last Jewish tribe of the city and the taking of all the property and the women and children. The Muslim sources put the number of the Jewish men who were beheaded in one day anywhere between 600 to 900.[8]

On another occasion, the prophet and his companions were looking for the hidden treasure of a conquered tribe. An individual was brought to Muhammad who was supposed to know where the hidden treasure was located. The prophet threatened to kill the individual if he did not tell the Muslims where the treasure was. Upon refusal to cooperate, "The apostle gave orders to al-Zubayr b. al-Awwam, 'Torture him until you extract what he has,' so he kindled a fire with flint and steel on his chest until he was nearly dead. Then the apostle delivered him to Muhammad b. Maslama and he struck off his head."[9]

Upon conquering Mecca, a number of individuals were ordered to be killed by the prophet without any immunity. The crimes committed by

5. Ibid., 367–68.
6. Ibid., 369.
7. Ibid., 387.
8. Ibid., 464.
9. Ibid., 515.

the majority of these people were making "satirical songs" against Muhammad or having insulted him during his ministry in Mecca.[10] One person who was fortunate enough to be pardoned was Abdullah b. Sa'd. "The reason he [Muhammad] ordered him to be killed was that he had been a Muslim and used to write down revelation; then he apostatized and returned to Quraysh." Since Abdullah was a foster brother of a close companion of Muhammad, he was able to receive a hearing from the prophet and ask for immunity. The prophet unwillingly granted the immunity. After the pardoned person left, Muhammad said to his companions, "'I kept silent so that one of you might get up and strike off his head!' One of the Ansar said, 'Then why didn't you give me a sign, O apostle of God?' He answered that a prophet does not kill by pointing."[11]

To one of his commanders whom the prophet was sending on an "expedition," he gave this advice, "Fight everyone in the way of God and kill those who disbelieve in God. Do not be deceitful with the spoil; do not be treacherous, nor mutilate, nor kill children. This is God's ordinance and the practice of his prophet among you."[12]

Another assassination ordered by the prophet was regarding his uncle Abu Sufyan, the leader of the pagan opposition in Mecca. Muslim volunteers traveled to Mecca to carry out this mission. The assassination attempt failed, however. On the way back to Medina, one of the followers of the prophet encountered a one-eyed shepherd who confidently claimed that he would never accept Islam. We pick up the account from the Muslim assassin himself. As soon as the man was "asleep and snoring I got up and killed him in a more horrible way than any man has been killed. I put the end of my bow in his sound eye, then I bore down on it until I forced it out at the back of his neck. . . . When I got to Medina . . . the apostle asked my news and when I told him what had happened he blessed me."[13]

The biography of the prophet follows this account with two more reports of successful assassinations ordered by the prophet. Abu Afak had "showed his disaffection with the apostle" by composing a poem. "The apostle said, 'Who will deal with this rascal for me?' whereupon Salim b. Umayr . . . went forth and killed him."[14] After this assassination, a woman by the name of Asma b. Marwan "displayed disaffection" and also composed a poem against the prophet. "When the apostle heard what she had said he said, 'Who will rid me of Marwan's daughter?'

10. Ibid., 551.
11. Ibid., 550.
12. Ibid., 672.
13. Ibid., 674–75.
14. Ibid., 675.

Umayr . . . who was with him heard him, and that very night he went to her house and killed her. In the morning he came to the apostle and told him what he had done and he [Muhammad] said, 'You have helped God and His apostle, O Umayr.'"[15]

Once again, we think the above sample (which by no means is an exhaustive list of the violence found in the earliest biography of the prophet) is enough to provide more than an adequate justification for the killing and destruction of anyone who opposes the ideology of Islam and its demand for total submission. However, what is even more important for the shaping of Muslim attitude and behavior is not the reports of such a biography but the collections of Muhammad's sayings and actions in the *hadith* literature.

SAYINGS FROM THE *HADITH*

We will now look at a few examples from the *hadith*. The following are a few examples in the *hadith* collection of Bukhari, the most authoritative book in Sunni Islam, second only to the Qur'an (*Sahih Al-Bukhari*, 9 vols. translated by Dr. Muhammad Muhsin Khan, Al Nabawiya: Dar Ahya Us-Sunnah, n.d.).

> Allah's Apostle said, "Know that Paradise is under the shades of swords."[16]

> Allah's Apostle said, "I have been ordered to fight with the people till they say, 'None has the right to be worshipped but Allah,' and whoever says, 'None has the right to be worshipped but Allah,' his life and property will be saved by me . . ."[17]

> It is not fitting for a prophet that he should have prisoners of war (and free them with ransom) until he has made a great slaughter (among his enemies) in the land . . .[18]

> Whoever changed his Islamic religion, then kill him.[19]

> An infidel spy came to the Prophet while he was on a journey. The spy sat with the companions of the Prophet and started talking and then went away. The Prophet said (to his companions), "Chase and kill him." So, I killed him. The Prophet then gave him the belongings of the killed spy.[20]

15. Ibid., 675–76.
16. Al-Bukhari, vol. 4, 55.
17. Ibid., vol. 4, 124.
18. Ibid., vol. 4, 161.
19. Ibid., vol. 9, 45.
20. Ibid., vol. 4, 181–82.

Some people from the tribe of Ukl came to the Prophet and embraced Islam. The climate of Medina did not suit them, so the Prophet ordered them to go to the (herd of milk) camels of charity and to drink their milk and urine (as a medicine). They did so, and after they had recovered from their ailment (became healthy) they turned renegades (reverted from Islam) and killed the shepherd of the camels and took the camels away. The Prophet sent (some people) in their pursuit and so they were (caught and) brought, and the Prophet ordered that their hands and legs should be cut off and that their eyes should be branded with heated pieces of iron, and that their cut hands and legs should not be cauterized, till they die.[21]

The Prophet passed by me at a place called Al-Abwa or Waddan, and was asked whether it was permissible to attack the pagan warriors at night with the probability of exposing their women and children to danger. The Prophet replied, "They (i.e. women and children) are from them (i.e. pagans)."[22]

The above tradition, like many others, is also repeated in other collections of prophet Muhammad's sayings. In the second most authoritative *hadith* collection, *The Sahih of Muslim*, the chapter that discusses this particular saying is entitled, "Permissibility of killing women and children in the night raids, provided it is not deliberate." The author then goes on to write, "It is reported on the authority of Sa'b b. Jaththama that the Prophet of Allah (may peace be upon him), when asked about the women and children of the polytheists being killed during the night raid, said: They are from them"[23]

We will end this discussion with two more traditions from another collection, *Sunan Abu Dawud*. Under a chapter entitled, "Excellence of killing an infidel" we read the following saying. "Abu Harairah reported the Apostle of Allah (may peace be upon him) as saying: An infidel and the one who killed him will never be brought together in Hell." The Muslim translator of this work adds the following footnote to this tradition, "This means that a person who kills an infidel while fighting in Allah's path (i.e. *jihad*) will have his sins remitted and forgiven, and will, therefore, go to Paradise. The infidel will inevitably go to Hell. Thus the man who killed an infidel will not be brought together in Hell with him."[24]

Another chapter in this collection is entitled, "Punishment of a man who abuses the Prophet (may peace be upon him)." The author recounts the story of a Muslim man who killed his slave and concubine by whom

21. Ibid., vol. 8, 519–20.
22. Ibid., vol. 4, 158–59.
23. Abduhl Amid Siddiqi, trans. *The Sahih of Muslim*, vol 3, 946–47.
24. Ahmad Hasan, trans. *Sunan Abu Dawud* (New Delhi: Kitab Bhavan, 1990), vol. 2, 690.

he had two children. Since she "disparaged" the Prophet, the slave owner, "took the dagger, put it on her belly and pressed it till [he] killed her." Upon hearing the reason for this murder, the prophet said, "Oh, be witness, no retaliation is payable for her blood."[25] The next incident in the above chapter is reported by Ali. "A Jewess used to abuse the Prophet (may peace be upon him) and disparage him. A man strangled her till she died. The Apostle of Allah (may peace be upon him) declared that no recompense was payable for her blood."[26] Once again, the translator provides us with the following explanatory notes: "It is unanimously agreed that if a Muslim abuses or insults the Prophet (may peace be upon him) he should be killed. . . . even if a Jew or any non-Muslim abuses the Prophet (may peace be upon him) he will be killed. . . . The punishment for abusing or opposing the Prophet (may peace be upon him) was death."[27]

CONCLUSION

Violence in Islam, whether in the form of terrorism, or the persecution of Christians and other minorities in the Muslim world, or capital punishment for an individual who turns away from Islam, or death threats on Salman Rushdie for allegedly insulting prophet Muhammad, are not simply some isolated incidents or aberrations from the true and peaceful religion of Islam. Such violence in fact goes to the very roots of Islam as found in the Qur'an and the actions and teachings of the prophet of Islam himself. Osama bin Laden quoted some of the very same Qur'anic and *hadith* passages that we have documented here in order to provide religious justification of his actions.[28]

We would like to conclude this section by referring to a program produced by Frontline and shown on PBS around the country entitled, "The Saudi Time Bomb." At one point in this program we were told about the state sponsored religious education in Saudi Arabia. According to Frontline, "approximately 35% of school studies is devoted to compulsory Saudi religious education." One of these textbooks published in 2000 was a collection of prophet Muhammad's sayings, which was used by middle school students in Saudi Arabia. One lesson is entitled, "The Victory of Muslims Over Jews." According to a tradition from prophet Muhammad, "The last hour won't come before the Muslims would fight the Jews and the Muslims will kill them so Jews would hide behind rocks and trees. Then the rocks and trees would call: oh, Muslim, oh, servant of God!

25. Ibid., vol. 3, 1214–15.
26. Ibid., 1215.
27. Ibid., 1215.
28. See the transcript of his video tape in the *New York Times*, 14 December 2001, B4.

There is a Jew, behind me, come and kill him." Like a good textbook, the teachings of this saying are summarized in several propositional statements such as:

- It's fate decided by Allah that the Muslims and Jews will fight till the end of the world.
- This Hadith predicts for the Muslims God's victory over the Jews.
- Jews and Christians are the enemies of believers. They will never approve of the Muslims, beware of them (www.pbs.org/wgbh/pages/frontline/shows/saudi/etc/textbooks.html).

Ideas have consequences. It has also become very clear for our world once again that violent ideas have violent consequences. We are not engaging in old Christian-Muslim polemics when we point out the prevalence of violence throughout the foundations and thus subsequent history of Islam. We are only exposing the teachings in the most original and authoritative sources of Islam. We believe that it is essential for people of goodwill around the world to know that underneath all the political, social, and cultural causes for the rise of violence among Muslims, there is a religious foundation for violence deeply embedded within the very worldview of Islam. The world needs to take the challenge of Islam more seriously than at any other time in the past.

Appendix 6

BLACK ISLAM

WITH STACEY JACOBS

Islam is gaining its largest percentage of converts from the African-American community. One of the dominate sects within Black Islam is called The Nation of Islam, whose current leader is Louis Farrakhan. A brief background of The Nation of Islam will be helpful in understanding its beliefs. It should be noted up front, however, that this group is not considered to be a form of genuine Islam by orthodox Muslims since The Nation of Islam affirms the existence of a prophet after Muhammad. Furthermore, as the following discussion will indicate, they deviate from orthodox Islam in a number of other ways, including their view of God.

I. BACKGROUND

LOUIS FARRAKHAN

When Muhammad died in 1975, his son, Wallace Deen, who sought unification between the Black Muslims and orthodox Islam, succeeded him. Although he initially supported Deen's leadership of the group, this proposed trend was unacceptable to Louis Farrakhan. Farrakhan was the leader of the Harlem Mosque at the time and was essentially second in command in the Nation at that time. Farrakhan preferred the teachings of Elijah Muhammad, and in 1977 broke from the Black Muslims, returning to his mentor's teaching. He started the faction that bears the name "Nation of Islam" (a name also used by Elijah Muhammad). Consequently, the Black Muslims of Wallace Deen joined orthodox Islam and are now known as the American Muslim Mission (or American Muslim Society), where they have laid aside much of the racial hatred perpetrated by Elijah Muhammad, allowing whites to join the group as well.

An example in microcosm of current Nation of Islam rhetoric is well summarized by Sidney Ahlstrom in *A Religious History of the American People:*

> [Their] eschatology teaches that God has come; there is no life after this life; heaven and hell are only two contrasting earthly conditions; the hereafter (which will begin to appear about A.D. 2000) is but the end of the present "spook" civilization of the Caucasian usurpers, including the Christian religion. It will be followed by the redemption of the Black Nation and their glorious rule over all the earth (1972, p. 1068).

Ostensibly, the message of the Nation of Islam (as presented by Farrakhan at the Million-Man March) is one of social atonement and reconciliation; it is a call for the black community to strive for moral and ethical superiority. Farrakhan called the audience to give up drugs, prostitution, and violence, and to commit to improving themselves "spiritually, morally, mentally, socially, politically, and economically" (1995). These are laudable concerns that should transcend race. If lower crime rates, higher economic productivity, and an over-all improvement in the quality of life for African-Americans result from the efforts of Farrakhan, then all people will have reason to rejoice.

In his Million-Man March speech, Farrakhan argued that the United States is rotten at its very foundation because it has been characterized from the beginning by white supremacy. For example, he said:

> The Seal and the Constitution [of the United States—BTB] reflect the thinking of the founding fathers, that this was to be a nation by White people and for White people. Native Americans, Blacks, and all other non-White people were to be the burden bearers for the real citizens of this nation (1995).

Given this, the official beliefs of the Nation of Islam can be examined in order to more clearly see what is presently the basis of its fundamental doctrine.

II. WHAT BLACK MUSLIMS BELIEVE

(Taken from "The Muslim Program" section of *The Final Call* online edition)

1. WE BELIEVE in the One God Whose proper Name is Allah.

2. WE BELIEVE in the Holy Qur'an and in the Scriptures of all the Prophets of God.
3. WE BELIEVE in the truth of the Bible, but we believe that it has been *tampered with and* must be reinterpreted so that mankind will not be snared by the falsehoods that have been added to it.
4. WE BELIEVE in Allah's Prophets and the Scriptures they brought to the people.
5. WE BELIEVE in the resurrection of the dead—not in physical resurrection—but in mental resurrection. We believe that the so-called Negroes are most in need of mental resurrection; therefore they will be resurrected first.

   Furthermore, we believe we are the people of God's choice, as it has been written, that God would choose the rejected and the despised. We can find no other persons fitting this description in these last days more that the so-called Negroes in America. We believe in the resurrection of the righteous.
6. WE BELIEVE in the judgment; we believe this first judgment will take place as God revealed, in America.
7. WE BELIEVE this is the time in history for the separation of the so-called Negroes and the so-called white Americans. We believe the Black man should be freed in name as well as in fact. By this we mean that he should be freed from the names imposed upon him by his former slave masters. Names which identified him as being the slave master's slave. We believe that if we are free indeed, we should go in our own people's names—the black people of the Earth.
8. WE BELIEVE in justice for all, whether in God or not; we believe as others, that we are due equal justice as human beings. We believe in equality—as a nation—of equals. We do not believe that we are equal with our slave masters in the status of "freed slaves." We recognize and respect American citizens as independent peoples and we respect their laws which govern this nation.
9. WE BELIEVE that the offer of integration is hypocritical and is made by those who are trying to deceive the Black peoples into believing that their 400-year-old open enemies of freedom, justice and equality are, all of a sudden, their "friends." Furthermore, we believe that such deception is intended to prevent Black people from realizing that the time in history has arrived for the separation from the whites of this nation.

   If the white people are truthful about their professed friendship toward the so-called Negro, they can prove it by dividing up America with their slaves. We do not believe that America will ever be able to furnish enough jobs for her own millions of unemployed, in addition to jobs for the 20,000,000 black people as well.

10. WE BELIEVE that we who declare ourselves to be righteous Muslims, should not participate in wars which take the lives of humans. We do not believe this nation should force us to take part in such wars, for we have nothing to gain from it unless America agrees to give us the necessary territory wherein we may have something to fight for.

11. WE BELIEVE our women should be respected and protected as the women of other nationalities are respected and protected.

12. WE BELIEVE that Allah (God) appeared in the Person of Master W. Fard Muhammad, July, 1930; the long-awaited "Messiah" of the Christians and the "Mahdi" of the Muslims.

13. WE BELIEVE further and lastly that Allah is God and besides HIM there is no God and He will bring about a universal government of peace wherein we all can live in peace together.

III. VIEW OF GOD

FARRAKHAN'S VIEW OF GOD

Although the wording is monotheistic, "One God," the language used to describe God and his prophets can be interpreted variously as pantheistic, dualistic, and polytheistic, and even panentheist (process theology). Black apologists, Dr. Jerry Buckner claims: "The Nation of Islam is a polytheistic religion. Several references in their literature point to a belief in many gods, and there is a council of 23 scientists-gods who write history." One of them, Yakub, ". . . rebelled against Allah and the council, causing havoc. He created the white race of devils to strike back at the black race."[1]

Louis Farrakhan speaks of God (Allah) as being self-created out of eternal darkness. He wrote: "The Hon. Elijah Muhammad taught us God is self created. The Holy Qur'an says He is not begotten. If God is not begotten, then God is the Originator of Himself. In the process of God's self creation, He had to overcome many things." For one, "He has to overcome frustration with the pace of His own evolution, and the disappointment of that pace gave rise to patience."[2]

Like human beings, God was formed out of darkness. "The darkness out of which God created Himself has no equal, except in the triple dark-

1. See Buckner, "Witnessing to the Nation of Islam," *Christian Research Journal* 20, no. 3 (Jan–Mar 1998), 40–41.

2. Farrakhan, "The Name of the True Religion?" *The Final Call,* February 17, 1998, 20–21.

ness of the womb of the female. God made her womb a replication of the womb out of which He came." Hence, "If light is in the essence of the cell, energy is there, intelligence is there. God formed Himself in the darkness. He had to overcome the darkness." So, "When He (God) comes into existence, He comes into existence a light of Himself, coming up out of the darkness; this is the way we come into existence, bearing witness to His origination." He continues, "He was a light of Himself in darkness. So here we have a duality. His light coming up out of darkness. He was life in the midst of death. Death, in this sense, is described as inanimate matter having no purpose or function."[3]

Farrakhan also speaks of human beings as having a "divine essence," a gold that needs purifying. "When we are purified, we will become the eternal transmitters of God's divine spirit and wisdom, thus making us ... the true house of God." He falls short, however, of absolute pantheism, claiming we are an "image" of God. "When we use the term image, it means that we are like God in form, appearance and semblance. We are a counterpart, a copy, a type, an embodiment. ... It means to mirror or reflect."[4]

If God's self creation is taken literally, then one is left with the logical absurdity that God created himself out of nothing. Giving the benefit of the doubt that God's "self creation" is an eternal process, the best twist one can give to Farrakhan's view is a form of process theology (panentheism).

Likewise, if the "council of the gods" is taken as finite creatures of the one eternal and unbegotten God, then a semblance of monotheism may be retained. If, however, the supreme God (Allah) is just one superior God among the other finite gods, then Farrakhan's view reduces to henotheism, a form of polytheism such as the Greeks had in Zeus. Lacking a systematic theology or metaphysic, Farrakhan does not provide the means to frame a coherent view of God in terms of the traditional categories.

3. Ibid.
4. Ibid.

GLOSSARY

Allah: Muslim name for God.

Abu Bakr: A rich and respected merchant of Mecca, one of the first converts to Islam, and a close friend and companion of Muhammad. According to the Sunnis he was the first Muslim Caliph.

A.H. (After *Hijrah*), abbreviation for the years in Muslim calendar after the flight of Muhammad (in 622 A.D.); used to divide time, as A.D. is for Christians.

Adhan: Daily call to prayer by the *muessin* from the mosque.

Ahad: The oneness of God; the negation of any other number. The denial that God has any partner or companion associated with him.

Ali: The son of Abu Talib, the first cousin of Muhammad, who married Fatimah, the youngest daughter of the Prophet. He is recognized by Shi'ite Muslims as the true successor of Muhammad, from whom come the succession of *Imams.* He is the fourth Caliph according to the Sunnis.

Alms: (See *Sadaga.*)

Aqida: A statement of religious belief, a creedal affirmation.

Ayat: A verse of the Qur'an.

'Ayisha: The third wife of Muhammad and daughter of Abu Bakr.

Bahira: A Nestorian monk who lived in Basrah on the caravan routes and was a strong influence on Muhammad.

Baraka: A blessing.

Bismillah: An Arabic phrase meaning "In the Name of Allah."

Caliph (Khaliph): Title of the spiritual and political leader who took over after Muhammad's death.

Deen: Muslim religious practice, such as, reciting the creed, praying, fasting, and giving alms, as distinct from a belief (*iman*).

Dajjal: Name for anti-Christ who will appear at end of time.

Fatima: The daughter of Muhammad by his first wife.

Fatwa: A religious/legal judgment.

Five Pillars: The chief religious duties of Muslims, namely, to recite the creed (*shahadah*); to pray (*salat*); to fast (*sawm*); to give alms (*zakat*); to make the pilgrimage (*hajj*) to Mecca at least once in their lifetime.

Fatwa: An expert legal opinion of Qur'anic law.

Hadith: Literally, a story; an oral tradition later written down of what the prophet supposedly said (*sunna*), did, or approved of—something said or done in his presence.

Hafiz: One who memorizes the Qur'an, a professional reciter.

Hajj: Pilgrimage to Mecca; one of the Five Pillars of Islam.

Hijrah: Muhammad's flight from Mecca to Medina in A.D. 622, thus the date used by Muslims to divide time before and after, as Christians use B.C. and A.D.

Hanif: An original monotheist, such as Abraham, who holds a prominent position among the prophets.

Huri (pl. *hur'in*): A damsel or maiden in Paradise.

Ibidat: Devotional worship involving performing one's primary duties and good deeds.

Iblis (from *diabolos*): A Qur'anic name for Satan.

Ijma: Consensus of Muslim legal scholars introduced in the eighth century to standardize legal theory and practice, as opposed to *ijtihad* ("to endeavor" or "exert effort"), the individual thought of the earlier period.

Ijtihad: Private opinion, as opposed to *ijma*, or consensus held by Muslim scholars.

Imam: A leader; a person considered by Sunni Muslims to be an authority in Islamic law and theology. A kind of Muslim pope in Shi'ite Islam. Shi'ites accept the succession of Imams. After the twelfth century the *imam* went into hiding when the source of authority was transferred to the *ulama*, who were considered collectively to be the representatives of the hidden Imam.

Iman: A Muslim belief, such as, in God, angels, prophets, Scriptures, and final judgment, as distinguished from Muslim practices (*deen*).

Ijaz: Miraculousness (see *mujiza*).

Injil: The New Testament Gospels as originally revealed by God, but not, as many Muslims believe, the subsequently corrupted text known as the New Testament by Christians.

Isa: Arabic word for Jesus.

Islam: The religion revealed to Muhammad, meaning "submission" (to the will of Allah).

Ishmael: The first son of Abraham by his wife's handmaid, Hagar. Muslims believe Ishmael, not Isaac, was the son of God's promise to Abraham.

Isma: Preservation, in particular, the preservation of the prophets from all sin or at least from all major sins; their impeccability.

Isnad: A chain of authorities through whom a tradition has been handed down from the days of Muhammad.

Jihad: Sacred struggle with word or sword in the cause of Allah; a holy war.

Jinn: Spirits created by God, some good and others evil.

Jizyah: Tax paid by Jews and Christians to Muslim rulers, as opposed to pagans who were forced either to accept Islam or die.

Ka'ba: A cubical stone building in the court of the mosque at Mecca that is called the "House of God," toward which Muslims turn in prayer. This building contains the black stone supposedly given by Adam to Gabriel and used by Abraham who allegedly built the Ka'ba with his son Ishmael. This black stone has been kissed by Muhammad and Muslims since his time.

Khadija: Muhammad's first wife and first to believe that his message was from God.

Khalifa: God's trustee on earth (i.e., man).

Kafir: An unbeliever; the opposite of a believer, *mumin.*

Kufr: Infidelity or apostasy.

Kalam: Speech. It is used of the Word of God, and later of scholastic theology that discussed theology rationally.

Koran: (See Qur'an.)

Mahdi: "The guided one," or coming world leader of righteousness. Sunnis wait for the first one to appear and Shi'ites believe the last Imma, who disappeared in A.D. 874, will someday reappear as the Mahdi.

Mansukh: The abrogation of an earlier revelation (see Nasikh).

Mecca: The birthplace of Muhammad located in Saudi Arabia, considered the most holy city by Islam. It must be visited at least once in a lifetime by all Muslims who are physically and financially able.

Medina: The second most holy city of Islam (after Mecca), previously named Yathrib, where Muhammad fled in A.D. 622 (see *Hijrah*).

Minaret: Tower at a mosque from which the call to prayer is made.

Miraj: Ladder or way of ascent; the Ascension of Muhammad into heaven

Mosque: Building in which Muslims meet regularly for prayer on Friday and at other times.

Muhammad: The founder of Islam, born around A.D. 570 and died A.D. 632. He is considered by the Muslims to be the last and final prophet of God through whom God gave the revelations in the Qur'an.

Mujahidin: Muslims who fight in holy wars (see *Jihad*).

Mujiza: A special miracle granted to a prophet in confirmation of his mission.

Mumin: A believer in contrast to an unbeliever (see *kafir*).

Muslim: Literally, "one who submits" (to God), a follower of Muhammad.

Muessin: Person who does the call to prayer five times daily from the mosque.

Nabi: A prophet sent by God with his message.

Namaz: Prayers. A word commonly used in India for the daily *salat.*

Nasikh: That which abrogates, as *mansukh* is that which is abrogated.

Omar (Umar): According to Sunni teaching, the second Caliph and principal advisor to the first Caliph, Abu Bakr.

Pbuh: Literally, "peace be upon him." A phrase of blessing used by Muslims whenever they refer to a prophet.

Qadar: The determination of all things by God, his decree of good and evil.

Qibla: The point Muslims face in prayer, toward Mecca.

Qur'an (Koran): Believed by Muslims to be the full and final revelation of God to mankind, conveyed to Muhammad by the angel Gabriel over a twenty-three-year period and corresponding perfectly to the eternal original in heaven.

Ramadan: The ninth month of the Muslim lunar year now devoted to fasting, when the Qur'an was supposedly brought down to the first heaven.

Rasul: An apostle, one who brings a message or revelation from God. Muslim tradition lists 124,000 prophets. But the most prominent prophets are five (or six): Muhammad (the Apostle of God), Noah (the Preacher of God), Abraham (the Friend of God), Moses (the Speaker with God), and Jesus (the Word of God). Some also include Adam (the Chosen of God) as the sixth person in the list. Muhammad is believed to be the last and final prophet with the full and final revelation of God in the Qur'an, the "seal of all the prophets."

Sadaqa: Charity, almsgiving to the poor and needy. Muslims are obligated to give one fortieth (2.5 percent) of their income in alms.

Salam: Peace; a greeting of peace.

Salat: Prescribed five daily prayers, one of the *Five Pillars* of Islamic faith. Muslims are required to say 17 complete prayers each day. They may pray individually or collectively. On Friday at noon Muslims are required to gather at the Mosque to pray.

Shahadah: Literally, "to bear witness," which is done by reciting the creed, "There is no God but Allah, and Muhammad is His messenger." Saying this sincerely is all that is necessary to become a Muslim.

Shahid: A witness, and then a martyr who has born witness by his death.

Shirk: Association, in particular the association of any other with God, so as to impugn his absolute uniqueness.

Shi'ites: The major Islamic sect that believes, in contrast to Sunnis, that Muhammad's son-in-law, Ali, was the true successor to Muhammad in the leadership of the Islamic community.

Sirat [or *Seerat*]: Literally, the bridge over hell. Metaphorically, the narrow path to heaven.

Suffis: The mystical wing of Islam that renounces worldly attachments, sees God in all things, and strive for union of their beings with God's. In contrast to orthodox Islamic monotheism (God created all), they tend toward pantheism (God is all). Some have virtually deified Muhammad, something considered anathema by orthodox Muslims.

Sunna: Written Islamic tradition about Muhammad's conduct, considered authoritative by Sunni Muslims.

Sunnis: The main body of Islam that comprizes about 80 percent of all Muslims who, in contrast to the Shi'ites, believe that the true line of succession from Muhammad is found in the four Caliphs: Abu Bakr, Omar, Uthman, and Ali.

Sura (Surah, Surat): A chapter in the Qur'an of which there are a total of 114.

Tabdil: Literally "change," used especially of a textual change or corruption in the Bible.

Tafsir: A commentary on the Qur'an.

Taghyr: Literally "changed or forged," sometimes used of a corruption of the biblical text (see also *tabdil*).

Tahrif: The Islamic doctrine that the original text of the Bible has been corrupted.

Takbir: Praising God by saying "God is great" (*Allahu akbar*).

Taqdir: God's subjection of all mankind and all history.

Taqwa: A pious or virtuous character.

Tawhid: Unity, used especially with regard to God's absolute oneness.

Tawrat: Jewish Torah or Law of Moses.

Ulama: The principles that Muslim scholars arrived at by consensus, considered authoritative by Sunnis; those learned in religious matters (scholars).

Umar: An early convert to Islam and a devoted follower of Muhammad. The second Muslim Caliph.

Uthman: Another early convert to Islam and the third Muslim Caliph.

Wahid: The One, Same God for all. Sometimes used interchangeably with *Ahad*.

Zabur: Original Psalms of David preserved in corrupted form in the Old Testament Book of Psalms.

Zakat: A religious offering of a devout Muslim that is supposed to total one fortieth of his income (2.5 percent), given primarily to the poor and needy.

BIBLIOGRAPHY

Abdalati, Hammudah. *Islam in Focus*. Indianapolis: American Trust Publications, 1975.

Abdul-Haqq, Abdiyah Akbar. *Sharing Your Faith with a Muslim*. Minneapolis: Bethany Fellowship, Inc., 1980.

Ajijola, Alhaj A. D. *The Essence of Faith in Islam*. Lahore, Pakistan: Islamic Publications, Ltd., 1978.

Akhtar, Shabbir. *A Faith for All Seasons*. Chicago: Ivan R. Dee Publisher, 1990.

Al-Faruqi. *Christian Mission and Islamic Da'wah: Proceedings of the Chambesy Dialogue Consultation*. Leicester: The Islamic Foundation, 1982.

Al-Faruqi, Isma'il R. *Islam*. Niles, Ill.: Argus Communications, 1984.

Ali, A. Yusuf. *The Holy Qur'an: Translation and Commentary*. Damascus: Ouloom AlQur'an, 1934.

Ali, Maulana Muhammad. *Muhammad and Christ*. Lahore: The Ahmadiyya Anjuman-i-Ishaat-i-Islam, 1921.

Anderson, Norman. *The World's Religions*. Grand Rapids: Eerdmans, 1987.

———. *Christianity and World Religions*. Downers Grove: InterVarsity, 1984.

———. *Islam in the Modern World*. Leicester: Apollos, 1990.

Andrae, Tor. *Mohammed: The Man and His Faith*. rev. ed. New York: Harper & Row, 1955.

Archer, John Clark. *Mystical Elements in Mohammed*. New Haven: Yale University Press, 1924.

Ata ur-Rahim, Muhammad. *Jesus, A Prophet of Islam*. New York: Diwan Press, n.d.

Al-Baqillani, *Miracle and Magic*. Edited by Richard J. McCarthy. Place de l'Etoile: Librairie Orientale, n.d.

Bell, Richard. *The Origin of Islam in Its Christian Environment*. London: Frank Cass & Co., Ltd., 1968.

Bhatia, H. S. *Studies in Islamic Law, Religion and Society*. New Delhi: Deep & Deep Publications, 1989.

Bucaille, Maurice. *The Bible, the Qur'an and Science*. Delhi: Taj Company, 1988 edition.

Buckner, Jerry. "Witnessing to the Nation of Islam." *Christian Research Journal* 20, no. 3 (Jan.–Mar. 1998), 40–41.

Budd, Jack. *Studies on Islam: A Simple Outline of the Islamic Faith.* Red Sea Mission Team, n.d.

Bukhari. *The Translation of the Meanings of Sahih Al-Bukhari.* Translated by Muhammad Muhsin Khan. Al-Medina: Islamic University. 10 vols.

Chishti, Yousuf Saleem. *What is Christianity: Being a Critical Examination of Fundamental Doctrines of the Christian Faith.* Karachi, Pakistan: World Federation of Islamic Missions, 1970.

Cragg, Kenneth. *The Call of the Minaret.* New York: Oxford University Press, 1964.

———. *Jesus and the Muslim: An Exploration.* London: George Allen & Unwin, 1985.

———. *Muhammad and the Christian.* London: Darton, Longman and Todd, 1984.

Dashti, Ali. *Twenty Three Years: A Study of the Prophetic Career of Mohammad.* London: George Allen & Unwin, 1985.

Dawud, Abdu'l-Ahad. *Muhammad in the Bible.* 2d ed. Kuala Lumpur: Pustaka Antara, 1979.

Deedat, Ahmed. *Is the Bible God's Word?* South Africa, 6th printing, 1987.

Dermenghem, Emile. *Muhammad and the Islamic Tradition.* Westport, CT: Greenwood Press, Publishers, 1974.

Doi, A. R. I. "The Status of Prophet Jesus in Islam." Muslim (Magazine) World League (June 1982).

Farrakhan, Louis. "The Name of the True Religion?" *The Final Call,* February 17, 1998, 20–21.

Gibb, H. A. R. *Mohammedanism: An Historical Survey.* London: Oxford University Press, 1949.

Gibb, H. A. R., and J. H. Kramers. *Shorter Encyclopedia of Islam.* Ithaca: Cornell University Press, 1953.

Gilchrist, John. *The Textual History of the Qur'an and the Bible.* Villach, Austria: Light of Life, 1988.

———. *Jam' al-Qur'an: The Codification of the Qur'an Text.* Benoni: South Africa: Jesus to the Muslims, 1989.

———. *The Crucifixion of Christ: A Fact not Fiction.* Villach, Austria: Light of Life, n.d.

Goldziher, Ignaz. *Introduction to Islamic Theology and Law.* Translated by Andras and Ruth Hamori. Princeton, N.J.: Princeton University Press, 1981.

Gudel, Joseph P. *To Every Muslim An Answer.* Unpublished thesis at Simon Greenleaf School of Law, 1982.

Habermas, Gary. *Ancient Evidence for the Life of Jesus.* Nashville: Thomas Nelson, 1984.

Hameedullah, Muhammad. *Introduction to Islam*. Paris: Centre Culturel Islamique, 1969.

Haneef, Suzanne. *What Everyone Should Know About Islam and Muslims*. Chicago: Kazi Publications, 1979.

Haykal, Muhammad Husayn. *The Life of Muhammad*. Indianapolis: North American Trust Publications, 1976.

Hemer, Colin. *Acts in the Setting of Hellenic History*. Winona Lake, IN: Eisenbrauns, 1990.

Ibn Ishaq. *Sirat Rasul Allah, (The Life of Muhammad)*. Translated by A. Guillaume. New York: Oxford University Press, 1980.

Ibn Taymiyya. *A Muslim Theologian's Response to Christianity*. Edited and translated by Thomas F. Michel. Delmar, N.Y.: Caravan Books, 1984.

Jeffery, Arthur. *Islam: Muhammad and His Religion*. Indianapolis and New York: The Bobbs-Merrill Company, Inc., 1958.

———. *The Foreign Vocabulary of the Qur'an*. Lahore: Al-Biruni, 1977.

———. *Materials For the History of the Text of the Qur'an*. New York: AMS Press, Inc., 1975.

Kateregga, Badru D., and David W. Shenk. *Islam and Christianity: A Muslim and a Christian in Dialogue*. Grand Rapids: Eerdmans, 1981.

Kenyon, Frederic. *Our Bible and the Ancient Manuscripts*. 4th ed. New York: Harper, 1958.

Khalifa, Rashad. *Quran: Visual Presentation of the Miracle*. Karachi: Haider Ali Muljee "Taha," 1987.

Khalifa, Rashad. *The Computor Speaks: God's Message to the World*. Tuscon: Mosque of Tuscon, 1981.

Khouj, Abdullah Muhammad. *The End of the Journey*. Washington, D.C.: The Islamic Center, 1988.

Kochler, Hans. *The Concept of Monotheism in Islam and Christianity*. Wien: Wilhelm Braumuller, 1982.

Latourette, Kenneth Scott. *A History of Christianity: Beginning to 1500*. San Francisco: Harper, 1975.

Linnemann, Eta. *Historical Criticism of the Bible: Methodology or Ideology?* Translated by Robert Yarbrough. Grand Rapids: Baker, 1990.

———. *Is There a Synoptic Problem? Rethinking the Literary Dependence of the First Three Gospels*. Translated by Robert Yarbrough. Grand Rapids: Baker, 1992.

Mahmud, Abdel Haleem. *The Creed of Islam*. World of Islam Festival Trust, 1978.

McDowell, Josh, and John Gilchrist. *The Islam Debate*. San Bernardino, CA: Here's Life Publishers, Inc., 1983.

Mufassir, Sulaiman Shahid. *Jesus, A Prophet of Islam*. Indianapolis: American Trust Publications, 1980.

Nash, Ronald. *The Gospel and the Greeks*. Dallas: Word Publishing, 1992.

Nasr, Seyyed Hossein. *Ideals and Realities of Islam.* London: George Allen & Unwin, Ltd., 1975.

Nazir-Ali, Michael. *Frontiers in Muslim-Christian Encounter.* Oxford: Regnum Books, 1987.

Nehls, Gerhard. *Christians Ask Muslims.* SIM International Life Challenge, 1987.

New Encyclopaedia Britannica. Vol. 22. Encyclopaedia Britannica, Inc., 1985.

Niazi, Kausar. *Creation of Man.* Karachi: Ferozsons, Ltd., 1975.

Paley, William. *Evidences of Christianity.* London: 1851.

Parrinder, Geoffrey. *Jesus in the Qur'an.* New York: Oxford University Press, 1977.

Parshall, Phil. *Beyond the Mosque.* Grand Rapids: Baker, 1985.

———. *Bridges to Islam.* Grand Rapids: Baker, 1983.

Pfander, C. G. *The Mizanu'l Haqq.* Austria: Light of Life, 1986.

Quasem, Muhammad Abul. *Salvation of the Soul and Islamic Devotions.* London: Kegan Paul International, 1983.

Ratzinger, Joseph. *Introduction to Christianity.* Translated by J. R. Foster. New York: The Seabury Press, 1979.

Rahman, Fazlur. *Major Themes of the Qur'an.* Bibliotheca Islamica, 1980.

———. *Islam.* Chicago: University of Chicago Press, 1979.

Rauf, Muhammad Abdul. *Islam: Creed and Worship.* Washington, D.C.: The Islamic Center, 1974.

Rippin, Andrew, and Jan Knappert. *Textual Sources for the Study of Islam.* Manchester: University Press, 1986.

Schimmel, Annemarie. *And Muhammad Is His Messenger.* Chapel Hill and London: The University of North Carolina Press, 1985.

Schimmel, Annemarie, and Abdoldjavad Falaturi. *We Believe In One God.* New York: Seabury Press, 1979.

Sell, Rev. Edward. *The Faith of Islam.* London: Society for Promoting Christian Knowledge, n.d.

Shehadi, Fadlou. *Ghazali's Unique Unknowable God.* Leiden: E. J. Brill, 1964.

Sherwin-White, A. N. *Roman Society and Roman Law in the New Testament.* Oxford: Clarendon Press, 1963.

Shorrosh, Dr. Anis A. *Islam Revealed: A Christian Arab's View of Islam.* Nashville: Thomas Nelson, 1988.

Slomp, J. "The Gospel in Dispute," *Islamochristiana.* Rome: Pontificio Instituto de Saudi Arabia, 1978, vol. 4.

Smith, Jane I., and Yvonne Yazbeck Haddad. *The Islamic Understanding of Death and Resurrection.* Albany: State University of New York Press, 1981.

Sox, David. *The Gospel of Barnabas.* London: George Allen & Unwin, 1984.

Stanton, H. U. Weitbrecht. *The Teaching of the Qur'an.* New York: Biblo and Tannen, 1969.

Tisdall, W. St. Clair. *The Source of Islam.* Edinburgh: T. & T. Clark, n.d.

Torrey, Charles Cutter. *The Jewish Foundation of Islam.* New York: KTAV Publishing House, Inc., 1967.

Understanding Islam and the Muslims: The Embassy of Saudi Arabia, Washington, D.C., n.d.

Waddy, Charis. *The Muslim Mind.* London and New York: Longman, 1976.

Watt, W. Montgomery. *Muhammad at Medina.* Oxford: Clarendon Press, 1956.

————. *Islam and Christianity Today: A Contribution to Dialogue.* London: Routledge & Kegan Paul, 1983.

————. *Muhammad's Mecca.* Edinburgh: Edinburgh University Press, 1988.

————. *Bell's Introduction to the Qur'an.* Edinburgh: Edinburgh University Press, 1970.

Welch, Alford T., and Pierre Cachia. *Islam: Past Influence and Present Challenge.* State University of New York Press, 1979.

Williams, John Alden. *Islam.* New York: George Braziller, 1962.

Woodberry, J. Dudley, ed. *Muslims and Christians on the Emmaus Road.* Monrovia, Calif.: MARC Publications, 1989.

Yusseff, M. A. *The Dead Sea Scrolls, The Gospel of Barnabas and the New Testament.* Indianapolis: American Trust Publications, 1985.

Zwemer, Samuel M. *The Moslem Doctrine of God.* American Tract Society, 1905.

————. *The Muslim Christ.* Edinburgh and London: Oliphant, Anderson and Ferrier, 1912.

SUGGESTED READING

Abdul-Haqq, Abdiyah Akbar. *Sharing Your Faith with a Muslim*. Minneapolis: Bethany Fellowship, 1980.

Anderson, Norman. *Islam in the Modern World*. Leicester: Apollos, 1990.

Cragg, Kenneth. *The Call of the Minaret*. New York: Oxford University Press, 1964.

———. *Jesus and the Muslim: An Exploration*. London: George Allen & Unwin, 1985.

Dashti, Ali. *Twenty Three Years: A Study of the Prophetic Career of Mohammad*. London: George Allen & Unwin, 1985.

Kateregga, Badru D. *Islam and Christianity: A Muslim and a Christian in Dialogue*. Grand Rapids: Eerdmans, 1981.

McDowell, Josh, and John Gilchrist. *The Islam Debate*. San Bernardino, Calif.: Here's Life, 1983.

Morey, Robert. *An Analysis of the Hadith*. Austin, Tex.: Research Education Foundation, 1992.

Nazir-Ali, Michael. *Frontiers in Muslim-Christian Encouter*. Oxford: Regnum, 1987.

Nehls, Gerhard. *Christians Ask Muslims*. SIM International Life Challenge, 1987.

Parrinder, Geoffrey. *Jesus in the Qu'ran*. New York: Oxford University Press, 1977.

Parshall, Phil. *Beyond the Mosque*. Grand Rapids: Baker, 1985.

———. *Bridges to Islam*. Grand Rapids: Baker, 1983.

Pfander, C. G. *The Mizanu'l Haqq*. Austria: Light of Life, 1986.

Shorrosh, Anis A. *Islam Revealed: A Christian Arab's View of Islam*. Nashville: Thomas Nelson, 1988.

Sox, David. *The Gospel of Barnabas*. London: George Allen & Unwin, 1984.

Tisdall, W. St. Clair. *The Source of Islam*. Edinburgh: T. & T. Clark, n.d.

Woodberry, J. Dudley, ed. *Muslims and Christians on the Emmaus Road*. Monrovia, Calif.: MARC Publications, 1989.

Zwemer, Samuel M. *The Moslem Doctrine of God*. American Tract Society, 1905.

———. *The Muslim Christ*. Edinburgh and London: Oliphant, Anderson and Ferrier, 1912.

INDEX OF QUR'ANIC SURAS

INDEX OF PERSONS

INDEX OF SUBJECTS

Norman L. Geisler, Ph.D., is president of Southern Evangelical Seminary. He has published countless articles in academic journals and has authored over fifty books, including *Baker Encyclopedia of Christian Apologetics.*

Abdul Saleeb is a former Muslim who has intensively studied differences between the two religions.